YOUNG JESUS

RESTORING THE "LOST YEARS" OF A SOCIAL ACTIVIST AND RELIGIOUS DISSIDENT

Jean-Pierre Isbouts

STERLING

New York / London
www.sterlingpublishing.com

For my mother and father

STERLING and the distinctive Sterling logo are
registered trademarks of Sterling Publishing Co., Inc.

Library of Congress Cataloging-in-Publication Data Available

2 4 6 8 10 9 7 5 3 1

Published by Sterling Publishing Co., Inc.
387 Park Avenue South, New York, NY 10016
© 2008 by Jean-Pierre Isbouts
Distributed in Canada by Sterling Publishing
c/o Canadian Manda Group, 165 Dufferin Street
Toronto, Ontario, Canada M6K 3H6
Distributed in the United Kingdom by GMC Distribution Services
Castle Place, 166 High Street, Lewes, East Sussex, England BN7 1XU
Distributed in Australia by Capricorn Link (Australia) Pty. Ltd.
P.O. Box 704, Windsor, NSW 2756, Australia

Sterling ISBN-13: 978-1-4027-5713-6
ISBN-10: 1-4027-5713-1

For information about custom editions, special sales, premium and
corporate purchases, please contact Sterling Special Sales
Department at 800-805-5489 or specialsales@sterlingpublishing.com.

CONTENTS

FOREWORD

Why another book about Jesus? Haven't we heard everything there is to know about this charismatic figure from first-century Palestine? The answer is: not really. Most writings invariably focus on the period of Jesus' ministry and his Passion, which altogether comprise no more than the last two or three years of his life. Few books written for a general audience have tackled one of the last remaining mysteries about Jesus, which is the question of what really happened during the "lost years" of his youth and adolescence. To truly understand a man's motives and actions, modern psychology tells us, we must first understand what happened during his formative years. In fact, the inquiry is particularly revealing in the case of Jesus. As this book will attempt to show, the principal impetus for Jesus' work as a social activist and religious dissident was his experience of growing up in Galilee at a time of an intense social and economic crisis.

This book would not have been possible, however, if the last two decades had not seen an explosion of exciting discoveries about the historical Jesus, especially in the fields of historical, anthropological, archaeological, psychological, socioeconomic, and literary research. Unfortunately, most of these discoveries were published in scholarly journals not readily available to the general public. What's more, many scholars tend to operate within the confines of their particular expertise. For example, experts engaged in biblical exegesis (interpretation of biblical texts) tend to focus on this subject area without necessarily involving consonant information from the realms of, say, forensic paleoanthropology or socioeconomic reconstruction. Similarly, authors approaching the Jesus material from a purely archeological perspective may not always include insights from modern source and form criticism that have been so useful in "excavating" the underlying strata of the gospels and other texts from antiquity.

My goal with this book, then, is to use the most dramatic insights from all these diverse fields of expertise as building blocks to reconstruct the youth, adolescence and early adulthood of Jesus. In doing so, I have also availed myself of models not previously used in the study of the historical Jesus, namely recent investigations into the psychological effects of peasant displacement in modern rural societies that bear a close resemblance to the conditions of first-century Galilee.

The result is a reconstruction of a Jesus who, I hope, is bound to fascinate modern readers—particularly young people who, like Jesus, look upon the world with that curious blend of compassionate idealism and revolutionary fervor that is the prerogative of youth. That is why I wanted to tell this story. Though this portrait of Jesus is not intended to replace the traditional image of Jesus as the Christ, it will forcefully remind us of the very roots of Jesus' activism and the desperate social conditions that fired his career as a charismatic healer and religious reformer. *Young Jesus* is, quite simply, the story of a young man who found himself caught up in the maelstrom of intense political and economic crisis, and responded with a unique and highly individual program of reform.

Any attempt to reconstruct the life of the historical Jesus is bound to resort to speculation, and this book is no exception. Though we know the biographical details of many other figures in antiquity, we have no inconvertible proof of who Jesus was, when he lived, or where he spent much of his time, much as we would like to believe otherwise. In some ways, we know more about prophets who lived many centuries before Jesus, such as Jeremiah, than we do about Jesus himself. The reason is that Jesus was a Galilean peasant. He was neither a powerful king, inevitably the subject of history writers, nor affluent enough to afford a personal scribe, as Jeremiah was. The oldest written texts about Jesus, set down by Paul, date to the mid-fifties C.E., more than twenty years after his death on the cross, and they contain very little biographical data. We therefore have to rely on the gospels as well as on circumstantial evidence, both literary and forensic, to reconstruct the life of the man from Nazareth, and we have to use our best judgment to decipher that data. Naturally, interpreting ancient circumstantial evidence is by no means an exact science. No author can ever claim to know for certain whether his or her interpretation is correct. But, of course, that is precisely what makes the effort so exciting.

✣ ✣ ✣

This book is written from a nondenominational, secular perspective for anyone interested in the early years of the historical Jesus. As such, the book may resonate with thinking Christians who wish to deepen their understanding of the role of Jesus in their lives. By the same token, I hope Jewish readers will experience a kinship with their own "roots" from the first-century Second Temple period and with a man who, but for tragic historical incident, might have been a great rabbinic sage of Judaism. Muslim readers too, I trust, may find sympathy with these new insights into *Isa* or Jesus—a man who, after Muhammad and *Musa* (Moses), is one of the most important figures in the Qur'an. Jesus was above all a man of mercy and compassion, the foremost attribute of both Yahweh and Allah, just as the word for mercy—*Rachman*—is the same in Hebrew and Arabic. At the same time, I hope that nonreligious readers may gain a better understanding of the foundations of the Christian ethics that continue to influence the progress of Western civilization.

With all these readers in mind, the book will use terms and indicators recognizable to all denominations. For example, we will refer to the Bible—what Christians call the Old Testament—as the Hebrew Scriptures, and often distinguish between the three principal divisions of the Hebrew Bible, that is, the *Torah* or "Law" (also referred to as the Covenant Law); the *Nevi'im* or "Prophets"; and the *Ketuvim* or "Writings." The first two divisions, the *Law* and the *Prophets*, were groupings that Jesus was undoubtedly familiar with, as many of his statements show. Though the third division, that of the *Writings*, was still being formed in the first-century C.E., we do assume that Jesus knew some of the books, specifically the Psalms. Similarly, we will use both the Christian term "God" as well as the Jewish appellation "YHWH" (the tetragrammaton denoting *Yahweh*).

The Hebrew Scriptures have come down to us in Hebrew (with certain segments in Aramaic) or, in the case of the Septuagint, in a translation in Greek (which in turn was used for the English translation of the Old Testament). The New Testament is also written in Greek, though in a common patois known as *koinè*. For the purpose of this book, all biblical quotations in English have been taken from the 1989 New Revised

Standard Version (NRSV) translation of the Old and New Testaments in the 1989 publication by HarperCollins. Similarly, for excerpts from the Mishnah, I have used the landmark translation by Jacob Neusner, published in 1988 by Yale University Press.

Finally, this book adheres to the now-common practice of using the temporal indicators of B.C.E. ("Before the Common Era") instead of the traditional B.C. ("Before Christ"), and likewise C.E. ("Common Era") rather than A.D. (*Anno Domini,* or "Year of the Lord"), to identify key dates in history.

Young Jesus would have been unthinkable without the contribution of many scholars and experts with whom I had the privilege of sharing my views on the historical Jesus over the years. They include Professor Peter Awn, Dean of General Studies at Columbia University; Dr. Frank Peters, Professor of Middle Eastern Studies at New York University; Dr. Elaine Pagels, Harrington Spear Paine Professor of Religion at Princeton University and the author of the best-seller *Beyond Belief: The Secret Gospel of Thomas;* Professor Khaled Abou El Fadl, Professor of Islamic Law at UCLA; Professor Jean-Pierre M. Ruiz of St. John's University; Dr. Thomas K. Tewell of the Fifth Avenue Presbyterian Church in New York City; Dr. Bernard J. Luskin, Director of the Media Psychology program at Fielding Graduate University in Santa Barbara; Dr. Rick Levy and Dr. Lisa Tatum of the Levy Center in Gaithersburg, Maryland; Dr. Jacob Neusner, Research Professor of Religion and Theology at Bard College in Annandale-on-Hudson, New York; and last but certainly not least, my dear friend Bruce Chilton, Bernard Iddings Bell Professor of Religion at Bard College and author of, among others, the best-seller *Rabbi Jesus.*

In addition, I have profited from the research of many other scholars, notably the recent published work of Marcus Borg, Mark Chancey, John Dominic Crossan, David Fiensy, K. C. Hanson, Zvi Gal, Peter Garnsey, Martin Goodman, John P. Meier, Douglas Oakman, Fabian Udoh, and particularly Richard Horsley. It goes without saying that any errors in the narrative are mine and mine alone.

I must also thank my doctoral students whose research made such an important contribution to this book, including Inger Eberhart, Tracy

Fuchs, Ivone Umar Ghazaleh, James Hirsen, Elise Levy, Brenda Layne Osuna, and Lynn Temenski. A special word of thanks to Ph.D. candidate Janet de Merode, a former director of the World Bank, for her invaluable material related to displaced peasantry in Burma.

I am deeply indebted to my editor, Anne Barthel, for her staunch support, enthusiasm, and insightful suggestions during the editorial process, as well as to Philip Turner and his literary and artistic staff at Sterling Publishing. Many thanks also to the librarians of the Charles E. Young Research Library at UCLA for allowing me to pilfer their stacks for many months on end. A warm word of gratitude to my agent, Peter Miller, and his wonderful staff at PMA Literary and Film Management in New York, who sustained me during the journey to see this book to print. And finally, words cannot begin to express my gratitude to my wife, Cathie, who has been my faithful companion and indefatigable muse throughout our many journeys through Israel and Palestine in search of the historical Jesus.

JEAN-PIERRE ISBOUTS
Santa Monica, California

CHRONOLOGY

166 B.C.E. ——— Judea, a province of the Seleucid Empire, rises in revolt against the anti-Jewish legislation of King Antiochus IV Epiphanes (175–163 B.C.E.).

The rebellion is led by brothers of the Maccabeus family (hence the term "Maccabean Revolt"), which will ultimately establish the Hasmonean dynasty.

152 ——— Antiochus's successor, Demetrius I, appoints Jonathan Maccabeus as governor of Judea in a first step to Judean independence.

150 ——— The next Seleucid king, Alexander Balas, also raises Jonathan to the position of high priest, a title of great religious and political significance. Many pious Jews (*Hasidim*) are dismayed by the Hasmonean usurpation of this position, which is traditionally reserved for descendants of Solomon's priest Zadok. One group, led by a "Righteous Priest" (possibly a Zadokite high priest contender), will break away in protest and establish the Essene movement.

HASMONEAN ERA

142 ——— Jonathan is killed. His brother Simeon succeeds him as king and high priest and secures Judean independence. Control over the Sanhedrin (the Jewish Great Council with considerable legislative and judicial power) is contested by two parties: the conservative, priestly aristocratic Sadducees and the more liberal brotherhood known as the Pharisees.

135 ——— Simeon's successor, John Hyrcanus I (135-104 B.C.E.), expands the territory of Judea to the borders of the Davidic kingdom, incorporating Idumaea and Samaria. Forceful conversion of villages in Idumaea to Judaism.

103 ——— Under the Hasmonean king Alexander Jannaeus (103-76 B.C.E.), Palestine is increasingly Hellenized (shaped by the cultural influence of Ancient Greece). Alexander also expands his kingdom by incorporating Galilee and parts of the Transjordan and coastal regions. A falling-out with Pharisees leads to the destruction of the Pharisaic party as a political force. The Sadducees take control of the Sanhedrin.

76	Alexander is succeeded by his wife, Queen Salome Alexandra (76–67 B.C.E.), who restores many Pharisees in key positions.
67	The death of Queen Alexandra plunges the Hasmonean kingdom into civil war, with Alexander's sons, Hyrcanus II and Aristobulus II, vying for the throne.

ROMAN ERA

63	The Roman general Pompey, who has arrived in the Near East to end the third Mithradatic War, intervenes in the Judean civil war and establishes Palestine as a vassal state of Rome, led by Hyrcanus II as puppet king. Some time later, an Idumaean nobleman called Antipater is appointed governor (*epitropos*) of Judea, serving under Hyrcanus.
47	Antipater's son Herod is appointed governor (*strategos*) of Galilee. With Roman auxiliary forces, Herod is able to suppress a rebellion led by a Galilean named Hezekiah. Herod also ravages the Galilean countryside to raise funds on behalf of Cassius, one of the assassins of Julius Caesar.
40	Parthians invade Judea, ostensibly in support of Antigonus, the son of Aristobulus II, and oust Hyrcanus and Antipater. Herod flees to Rome, where he persuades the Senate to declare him king of all Palestine.
39	Herod lands in Palestine backed by Roman forces, conquers the country, and besieges Jerusalem. In 37, Jerusalem is captured and Antigonus is killed. The reign of King Herod the Great (37-4 B.C.E.) begins.

HERODIAN RULE

30	Octavian, known as Augustus since 27 B.C.E., is confirmed as Roman emperor. Herod begins the construction of a vast harbor in Caesarea and builds a new city near the ancient site of Samaria, known as Sebaste, dedicated to Augustus (*Sebastos* in Greek).

22	In an attempt to curry favor with his Jewish subjects, Herod begins a vast expansion of the Second Temple in Jerusalem, which is not completed until 62 C.E. To finance this and other large construction projects, Herod lays a heavy tax yoke on the peasantry of Judea and Galilee. The Sanhedrin is shorn of political power and reduced to a mostly judicial body. Members of the Sanhedrin who opposed Herod are executed. Herod then imports priestly families from Persia to create a line of high priests whose loyalty to the Herodian dynasty is unquestioned.
7–4	Putative date of birth of Jesus, son of Joseph.
4	Herod dies. His will proposes a division of his kingdom among his sons. Herod's son Archilaus, who is granted the largest share of Judea and Samaria, faces increasing protests over the heavy tax burden. Archilaus responds with a brutal military suppression, then leaves for Rome.
4	During Archilaus's absence, new revolts spread throughout Judea and Galilee, prompted by rumors that Sabinus, a Roman legate, is planning a Roman takeover. A son of the defeated rebel leader Hezekiah, named Judas, leads a new rebellion in Galilee. All resistance is brutally repressed by Roman legions dispatched from Antioch, capital of Roman Syria. Galilee is ravaged. The Galilean city of Sepphoris is burned to the ground.
4	Roman emperor Augustus accepts Herod's will and confirms Archilaus as *Ethnarch* of Judea and Samaria and Herod's son Antipas as Tetrarch of Galilee and Perea.
6 C.E.	Archilaus is removed from office because of his misrule and is banished to Vienne in Roman Gaul. Augustus decides not to grant his territory to either Antipas or another son of Herod and instead turns Judea into a Roman province, to be led by a prefect reporting to the Roman governor in Antioch, Syria. That governor, Quirinius, initiates a census in Judea to determine the tax value of the new province.
6	The Roman census leads to a widespread civil disobedience campaign in Palestine led by "Judas the Galilean." The census is nevertheless enforced.

6–10	Antipas (now known as Herod Antipas) begins the rebuilding of Sepphoris using a Greco-Roman city plan.
14	Emperor Augustus dies and is succeeded by Tiberius (14-37 C.E.).
17–20	Herod Antipas suspends the construction of Sepphoris and decides to build a new, Hellenistic city on the Sea of Galilee, called Tiberias (dedicated to Emperor Tiberius).
26	Pontius Pilatus (known as Pilate) arrives in Caesarea to begin his term as prefect of the Roman province of Judea. He provokes popular outrage by placing army insignia carrying the portrait of the emperor near the Temple precinct in Jerusalem, violating the Jewish law against "graven images."
28	The Aqueduct Affair leads to massive protests against Pilate. Hundreds of demonstrators in Jerusalem are brutally cut down by Roman soldiers hidden among the crowd.
28 (?)	Jesus joins the movement of John the Baptist in the Jordan wilderness. At some later date, John is arrested by Antipas for fear that he, too, may be preparing a revolt.
28 (?)	After John's arrest, Jesus and a small group of other Galilean followers of John flee north, possibly to Bathsaida.
28–29	Beginning of the ministry of Jesus in Galilee.
30 (?)	Jesus and his followers go to Jerusalem to visit the Temple during the Passover festival. Jesus stages a disturbance in the Temple. He is arrested, indicted by a group of Sadducees led by the high priest Caiaphas, and transferred into the custody of the Roman governor for execution. Jesus is crucified on the charge of having plotted sedition against the Roman occupation.

EARLY CHRISTIAN ERA

34–35	Jewish followers of Jesus, now led by Jesus' brother James, are increasingly marginalized in Palestine. One follower, Stephen, is stoned to death by a mob on the instigation of Saul of Tarsus.

35–40 (?)	Saul (now known as Paul) halts his persecution of Jewish Christians and joins the movement.
36	Pilate is removed from office because of his excessive cruelty. At the same time, Caiaphas is removed from his post as high priest.
37	Agrippa I, a grandson of Herod the Great, is appointed king of Judea.
39	Herod Antipas, ruler of Galilee, is removed from office by the Roman emperor Gaius ("Caligula") and exiled to Lugdunum (Lyon) in Roman Gaul.
44	King Herod Agrippa dies; Judea reverts to being a Roman province (now known as Palaestina).
45–46 (?)	The "Jerusalem Conference" leads to a split between James and Paul. The church of James continues to focus its activity on observant Jews in Palestine, while Paul concentrates on converting Gentiles (as well as Jews) in Asia Minor and Greece.
45–50	Possible timing for the text of Jesus' sayings known as "Q" (*Quelle*, or "source").
53–57	Paul writes his principal *oeuvre* of letters (including epistles to the Galatians, Corinthians, and Romans).
62	James is condemned by members of the Sanhedrin under the auspices of the high priest Ananus ben Ananus and stoned to death. The execution leads to protests among observant (i.e., non-Christian) Jews. Ananus is removed from office and replaced as high priest by Jesus, son of Damneus.
64	Putative date for the death of Peter and Paul in Rome, following the Great Fire in that city and Nero's decision to blame it on Rome's Christian community.

66 —————— Growing resentment of corrupt Roman prefects and frequent assassinations precipitate the outbreak of a nationwide Jewish rebellion against Roman rule.

67 —————— The Roman general Vespasian lands in Syria to take command of the war against the Jewish rebellion.

69 —————— Vespasian is declared emperor by his troops. The prosecution of the war against the remnants of the Jewish rebellion is taken over by his son Titus.

70 —————— Titus captures Jerusalem, effectively ending the Jewish War (though pockets of resistance in the Dead Sea area are not defeated until 73-74). The Second Temple is destroyed, marking the end of Second Temple Judaism.

70 —————— "Mark" writes his gospel, possibly in Rome.

75 —————— Josephus completes his book *The Jewish War* in Rome.

75–80 —————— Putative date of the "Gospel of Thomas."

80–85 —————— "Matthew" writes his gospel, possibly in Damascus.

85–90 —————— "Luke" writes his gospel, possibly in Alexandria.

93 —————— Josephus completes his book *Antiquities of the Jews* in Rome.

95–100 —————— "John" writes his gospel, possibly in Ephesus.

INTRODUCTION

Visitors who stroll into Room 14 of London's Tate Gallery, also known as the Pre-Raphaelite Room, often pause in front of a painting by the nineteenth-century British artist John Everett Millais. Both arresting and familiar, the work depicts the workshop of Joseph in Nazareth. Joseph, in Millais's hands, is a tall, ascetic-looking carpenter whose hands betray many years of manual labor. Though he appears to be at work carving a door, his attention is drawn to the center of the painting. There, his pretty young wife, dressed in a long blue gown, kneels down to console her red-haired son. The child's hand, it seems, has been accidentally cut by a nail. Both parents are concerned, but not unduly so—after all, it is merely a scratch. Only the old woman toward the rear of the painting, her brow furrowed, seems to understand the true significance of the moment. For the child is Jesus, and the cut in his palm is an omen of the torment and death that await him.

Pre-Raphaelite artists loved to indulge in such symbolism, presented with medieval-like realism, and this canvas is no exception. In the vision of Millais, the carpenter and his family are simple folk who walk around barefoot amidst the shavings and woodchips that lie strewn about the floor. Through an open door, we can spot a merry group of sheep and the sundrenched fields of Galilee beyond, with tall husks of wheat patiently waiting for harvest time. It is what we think of when picturing Jesus' childhood: the comforting image of a young child raised in the peace of rural Galilee. It is an idyll that, for the time being at least, is still far removed from the horror of the cross to come.

What is so astonishing about this picture, and countless engravings and prints like it throughout the Christian world, is that although it is instantly recognizable, it is not based on any description in the New Testament, the scripture of Christianity. It is, rather, the product of our collective imagination, the result of generations' yearning to fill in the "lost years" of Jesus' youth and adolescence. It is what we would *wish* Jesus' childhood to be, despite the fact that neither the Gospels, nor the letters of Paul, nor any

1

other texts in the Christian canon give us any clue about what Jesus' youth was like at all.

Seen from the vantage point of the biblical tradition, this is nothing short of amazing. In the Hebrew Scriptures, which Christians call the Old Testament, we are often presented with detailed stories about the early years of Israel's patriarchs, such as Isaac, Jacob, or Joseph, or prophets such as Samuel and Jeremiah. But in the Gospels of the New Testament, we will search in vain for historical information about Jesus' childhood and adolescence. For the most part, it is left to our imagination to figure out what life must have been like for Jesus as a young boy in Galilee. All we can glean from the Bible is that Galilee was a rural and largely agricultural region and that Joseph, reportedly, made his living as a "carpenter"—the traditional translation of the Greek word *tektoon* in the Gospel of Mark. And so we comfort ourselves with imagery such as the canvas by John Everett Millais—the iconography of a quiet, secure upbringing in the loving home of a simple craftsman and his wife, surrounded by the bounty of the land.

Unfortunately, the reality was starkly different. Based on the growing evidence that has come to light only in the last decades, Jesus' childhood in Galilee wasn't anything like the traditional image of happy years in the village of Nazareth. On the contrary: by the time Jesus would have been old enough for his *bar mitzvah,* he and his parents had witnessed not one, but two violent revolts in Palestine. These wars were instigated not by a usurper, a pretender to the throne, or any other elite, but by *farmers,* crushed by the triple yoke of taxes, tithes, and tribute. Neither revolt accomplished much, other than to invite years of brutal military repression and economic exploitation. As it happened, this period fully coincided with the childhood of Jesus.

It is unthinkable that the turmoil of early first-century Galilee would have left Jesus and his family untouched. In fact, this book will argue that bearing witness to the escalating socioeconomic crisis of the Galilean peasantry was probably the most defining experience of Jesus' life. It was an experience, moreover, that not only stirred in him the seeds of social activism, but also inspired him to become a religious dissident, wholly devoted to reform Judaism from within.

✛ ✛ ✛

The inevitable question, of course, is why this crucial period is completely ignored in the four canonical Gospels—the four documents that around the third century B.C.E. were selected from other Christian texts to be included in the official canon of Christian Scripture. If, we may ask, these traumatic events in Galilee had such an impact on the young Jesus, why did none of the evangelists remark on it? To answer this question, we must briefly describe the nature of the Gospels and their relationship to other Christian and non-Christian sources that will play such an important role in our story.

THE BIBLE AS HISTORY

Many Jews and Christians today consider the Bible the revealed will of God from start to finish. For them, every word of its text is inviolable and infallible. Specifically, many conservative Jews (as well as Christians) believe that the first five books of the Hebrew Bible, together known as the *Torah,* were revealed verbatim by God to Moses on Mount Sinai. This is why these books—Genesis, Exodus, Leviticus, Numbers, and Deuteronomy—are often referred to as the *Pentateuch,* a Greek word meaning the "Five Rolls" (also known as the "Five Books of Moses"). Many evangelical Christians, moreover, adhere to a *literal* interpretation of the Bible. They believe that every word of the Old and New Testament is true and based on fact, using the criteria of our modern rationalistic world. For them, the Bible is as "real" as if it had rolled off the newspaper presses yesterday.

There is nothing intrinsically wrong with that approach. Every person is entitled to interpret the Bible in his or her own way and to use it as a moral compass in our complex world. However, to take it literally is to fundamentally misunderstand the nature of the Bible. As scholars have found since the days of the European Enlightenment, the Bible did *not* roll off the presses overnight. Rather, it emerged over many generations as an aggregate of oral and written traditions that expressed the hopes and aspirations of a people trying to build a nation in covenant with one God. These include stories that stretch back well into the Middle Bronze Age (2000–1550 B.C.E.), long before the composition of, for example, the *Iliad* and *Odyssey* by Homer. Eventually, as the concept of an Israelite nationhood coalesced (beginning, as some scholars believe, at the time of King David in the early tenth century B.C.E., or perhaps much later during the reign of King Josiah in the seventh century B.C.E.), an effort was begun to organize and harmonize these different oral traditions into a cohesive narrative.[1] This marked the beginning of a long editorial process that ultimately produced the Bible as we know it.

The discovery of these many different underlying traditions in the Old and New Testaments should not detract from the moral and ethical power of the Bible. Nor should we assume that investigating the historical underpinnings of the Bible negates the idea that its narrative has a source in divine inspiration. What such research has demonstrated, however, is that the Hebrew Scriptures are very much the product of the cultural milieu of the Late Bronze and Iron Ages, just as the Gospels bear the mark of the urgent concerns of their own time—in this case, the *latter* part of the first century C.E. Therefore, a better understanding of this historical context will help us to penetrate the meaning of the Gospels and truly grasp the symbolic vocabulary of their language.[2]

THE POWER OF SYMBOLISM

Symbolism is a loaded word in our modern society. We can admire its role in the art, theater, or dance of other cultures; but when it comes to understanding what's happening in our own modern world, we'd rather get it "straight." Too often, we've seen news represented with an inherent bias, liberal or conservative, religious or secular, fundamentalist or reformative. We prefer to get the facts—or, better still, see it live on television with our own eyes.

Of course, things were very different in first-century Palestine. It is no exaggeration to say that perhaps the greatest challenge for anyone wishing to penetrate the Bible is to understand in what kind of a cultural and historical context these texts came about. We are so saturated with media information—through television, radio, the Internet, cell phones, BlackBerrys, billboards, and print media—that it sometimes takes a superhuman effort to imagine what it was like to live in a world where none of these things existed at all. In the New Testament era, and particularly in rural Galilee, the only way in which information was communicated was through the spoken word, or—in the case of the educated elites—in the form of written text. It may sound strange, but in many ways the age of Mozart—the eighteenth century—was closer to the age of Jesus than to our own modern times. Until then, the vast majority of men and women made a living from agriculture, were illiterate or barely literate, did not have proper schooling, and did not know any language other than that spoken by their parents. They lived and died within the confines of their condition, and whatever knowledge they picked up along the way was communicated by oral means to their children and to the children who came after them.

This doesn't mean that people in first-century Galilee lacked imagination. It simply means that in order to appeal to a reader's imagination and impart the full significance of his story, the author in antiquity did not have any medium at his disposal other than the power of his words. And yet for the evangelists it was vitally important that their audience grasp the full significance of the story of Jesus beyond a mere recitation of biographical details. Consequently, they did what authors in antiquity had done for centuries—they availed themselves of another type of illumination, namely, the language of symbolism. By leavening his text with symbolic imagery, the evangelist could illustrate his narrative with the didactic depth and moral gravitas so prized in the ancient world.

To some of us, this may sound suspect. We expect modern historians to tell their story objectively, without any additions that may distort or "fictionalize" the story. But things were quite different for the author in ancient times. The evangelist, like any other learned scribe in antiquity, was expected not only to recount what had happened, but also to convey the *meaning* of what had happened.

In the centuries since, the Enlightenment, the Industrial Revolution, and the pervasive influence of science have all but eliminated our intuitive understanding of symbolic language. It was left to scholars like Carl Jung to recognize that symbolic expression is neither fantasy nor fiction, but a key catalyst in helping our minds to retain, absorb, and interpret pieces of information. This was readily understood by the author of antiquity, and his audience expected no less. Our modern concept of history—as an objective, chronological arrangement of facts—would have struck the reader in the Greco-Roman world as absurd. For him, a story had no purpose unless it imparted a moral or ethical message, and symbolic imagery was one device by which such meaning could be conveyed.

Naturally, a symbolic vocabulary was pointless unless it was readily recognized and understood by the vast majority of people for whom the ancient author wrote. He couldn't just go and invent things—he had to borrow motifs from traditions that were widely known and understood. For much of the Hellenistic world, for example, Greek and Roman mythology was the preferred repository from which a myriad of ideas and motifs could be borrowed. In ancient Palestine, however, few Jews knew or cared about the exploits of pagan gods. They spoke the symbolic language of the Hebrew Scriptures. And so it was to the Old Testament that the evangelists turned, time and again, to find motifs to illustrate their Gospel story and thus endow it with meaning. When, for example, Matthew wants to emphasize the role of Jesus as a new Moses, as the agent of a new covenant with God, he has Mary and Joseph travel to Egypt after the birth in Bethlehem, and then later come back. While the story is not plausible as a historical event (for reasons we shall examine), its symbolic meaning is no less potent. It reminded Matthew's audience of the Exodus, and how the Israelites, too, left Egypt in search of their ultimate destiny. Similarly, Mark has Jesus tarry in the desert for forty days before beginning his ministry. Few Jewish listeners in Mark's time would have failed to see the link to the forty years spent in the desert before the Israelites were ready to enter the Promised Land.

Some authors have adopted the term "Bible Code" to describe such symbolic illuminations in the Gospel text. Others use the Greek term *theologoumenon,* meaning a theological argument couched in the form of a historical statement. Whatever we call it, we must accept that scriptural symbolism (as distinct from historical data) is a vital part of the Gospel stories, and to fail to recognize its intrinsic meaning is to fundamentally miss the point of what the evangelists were trying to say.[3]

WHO WERE THE FOUR EVANGELISTS?

In the foreword to his best-selling book *The Day Christ Died,* author Jim Bishop wrote that the research for his work was done "a long time ago by four fine journalists: Matthew, Mark, Luke and John." It is certainly appealing to imagine our evangelists as four hard-working correspondents tasked with "covering" the lead story of Passover, 30 C.E. Alas, there were no news reporters in first-century Palestine. The reality is that the Gospels are much like any other text in the Bible—or any other document from the Roman era, for that matter. They have a complex history; they used a variety of sources; and they aimed for a very specific purpose.

6

As far as we know, Jesus never produced a written record of his *halakah,* his teaching, in his lifetime. As best we can determine, neither did his apostles. The New Testament book called Acts of the Apostles tells us that the disciples were "uneducated and ordinary men."[4] We must therefore assume that the immediate followers of Jesus were illiterate. It is possible (though not certain) that Jesus could read, since knowledge of the Scriptures was often taught by rote, but nowhere do we find any evidence that Jesus could also write.

Why no one in Jesus' greater circle chose to "publish" Jesus' teachings during his lifetime is understandable. Jesus was relatively young and in the full vigor of life, as were many of his disciples; he was too absorbed by the demands of itinerant preaching to worry about a "testament" of his words and deeds. Most prophets in the Hebrew Scriptures were active for many decades, with plenty of time for their words to eventually be written down. Some, like Jeremiah, could even afford a personal scribe (such as Baruch) to document their oracles and prophecies. But Jesus had neither the time nor the means to commit his thoughts to a scroll. What's more, Jesus' life was violently cut short when his campaign had only just begun: most scholars reckon the period of his ministry at no more than eighteen months.

During the first years after Jesus' crucifixion, word about the great rabbi's wisdom and teachings would have circulated by word of mouth. Inevitably, over the course of a half century, these stories became embroidered and embellished, with individual strands stressing different aspects of Jesus' life. Some of these stories may have been written down by congregations inside or outside of Palestine and produced the "sayings documents" that we'll see later on.

As far as we know, the first attempt to edit these different oral and literary traditions into a comprehensive theological "story" is the Gospel of Mark. Probably written sometime shortly after 70 C.E., it is therefore the oldest Gospel text in the New Testament. Significantly, Mark's Gospel does not provide any information about Jesus' youth and adolescence. Instead, his story begins when Jesus joins the group around John the Baptist in the Jordan—that is, when he was already between thirty and thirty-five years of age. So does the Gospel of John, commonly believed to be the *last* of the four Gospels (written between 80 and 100 C.E.). Only the Gospels of Matthew and Luke (written between 80 and 90 C.E.) offer an insight into the peculiar circumstances of Jesus' paternity and birth, but their accounts are strikingly different—so different, in fact, that scholars suspect that their individual Nativity accounts owe more to Old Testament symbolism than to actual biographical data, as we shall see.

In fact, the problem of using the Gospels as the source for Jesus' childhood is compounded by two facts: one, that the evangelists wrote at least forty years *after* the crucifixion; and two, that they themselves did not live in Palestine at all. Each of the four evangelists operated elsewhere in the Roman Empire. We must thus assume that the Gospel authors were *not* eyewitnesses, but rather composed their books based on secondary data (oral or written transmissions), well after the fact.

This, of course, directly contradicts the Christian tradition that the evangelists moved in the intimate circle of Jesus' disciples, had access to first-generation data, and therefore spoke with evident authority. For example, the author of the oldest Gospel, that of Mark, is traditionally identified with (John) Mark, the friend of Paul and later of the apostle Peter, who visited the community at Colossae[5] and is also mentioned in the closing greetings of Peter's letter from Rome.[6] Bishop Irenaeus wrote around 185 C.E. that Mark was the "disciple and interpreter" of Peter, which suggests that this Mark may have spoken both Latin and Greek (since all of the four Gospels were written in a Greek patois known as *koinê*), both languages that were current in first-century Rome. But the actual text of the Gospel of Mark does not mention a Mark, nor does it identify its author. In fact, the attribution to "Mark" was probably not made until the early second century C.E.

Similarly, the author of the "Gospel of Luke" is traditionally associated with the Luke who traveled with Paul on his journey to Greece and accompanied him on his last and fateful voyage to Jerusalem. He is sometimes identified with the "beloved physician" referred to in Paul's letter to the Colossians.[7] This statement has prompted some to suggest that Luke was trained in medicine, quite possibly in Antioch in Syria, and that he only became a Gentile convert to Christianity under the tutelage of Paul. However, there is nothing in the Gospel text itself that suggests that the author was a doctor or even interested in medical issues, particularly when it comes to scenes of Jesus' healing.

Despite his obvious gifts as a writer, the author of Luke is not very familiar with Palestine or Palestinian topography. What's more, his Greek is heavily influenced by the "biblical" style of the Septuagint, the Greek trans-lation of the Hebrew Scriptures composed in Alexandria, Egypt. This would suggest that "Luke" wrote for a Diaspora Judeo-Christian commu-nity somewhere in the Mediterranean region.

The author of Luke is also traditionally credited with writing the book of the Acts of the Apostles; given the similarity in style and theological per-spective, this suggestion is usually accepted by scholars. Nevertheless, neither the Luke Gospel itself nor Acts provides a clue to the identity of its author, so that once again there is no certainty about who Luke was, or whether he should indeed be credited with these works.

In the case of Matthew, Christian tradition is even more specific. It attributes this work to the tax collector named Levi whom Jesus found in the customs house in Capernaum and subsequently called to join him as an apostle.[8] Levi was thereafter known as Matthew, which means "gift from God." But this attribution has problems as well. The Gospel text never iden-tifies Levi/Matthew as its author. What's more, the Matthew Gospel is written in an erudite and elegant Greek that bespeaks the hand of an edu-cated scribe, not a Palestinian tax collector in a small township like Capernaum. Bishop Papias of Hieropolis (Asia Minor) wrote in the early second century C.E. that Matthew had compiled a collection of sayings by Jesus, written in Hebrew. If this is true, then it is certainly possible, though not yet proven, that the anonymous author of Matthew had access to such a "sayings" document as one of his putative sources, which may have led to the Gospel's attribution to Matthew later on.

The thing we must remember is that our modern understanding of "author-ship" was utterly alien to the writers of antiquity. Ever since the Renaissance, those involved in the creation of an original work of art or lit-erature have typically insisted on "getting the credit." But in ancient times, artists seldom autographed their work, and writers (often professional scribes) were rarely identified by name. To the readers of antiquity, what mattered was not the man who wielded the pen but the authority with which he wrote or the literary tradition with which he identified himself. Consequently, all through the Old Testament we come across works that are attributed to notable biblical figures, even though historically, those figures could never have written those texts. The Song of Solomon, for example, was written not in the time of Solomon in the early tenth century B.C.E., but some seven hundred years later. Similarly, some of the verses attributed to Isaiah actually originated some three hundred years after Isaiah had died. To us this sounds confusing, even suspect. To the ancient reader, however, it made perfect sense. Who actually committed these verses to vellum was not important; what mattered was the wisdom and didactic value of the literary work, and if the unknown author sought an honorary attribution to a notable figure with whom he felt a particular kinship, so much the better.

Finally, we have the Gospel of John, which traditionally has been credited to either the apostle "John, son of Zebedee," or the apostle John, "the disciple (whom) Jesus loved."[9] Since most scholars usually date the Gospel of John to the last decade of the first century c.e., it is difficult to imagine that it could have been written by someone who was Jesus' contemporary. The Gospel itself makes no claim about its authorship, but it does state that its account of Jesus' Passion is based on the testimony of the apostle John, "the beloved disciple," and adds in its final paragraphs that "this is the disciple who is testifying to these things and has written them, and we know that his testimony is true."[10] There is, therefore, every reason to suggest that the author of the Gospel of John may have had access to a written testimonial attributed to an apostle from Jesus' immediate circle, though any evidence for this has so far eluded us.

Throughout his Gospel, John is not so much interested in creating a comprehensive "biography" of Jesus, nor of presenting him as the anointed "Messiah," the principal theme of the other Gospels; rather, John advances the case that Jesus is the Son of God, whose birth and death were ordained as part of God's greater plan for mankind—a divine figure, in other words, who came to earth in human form. As such, John's Gospel is perhaps the most elegant and erudite development of the creed originally developed by Paul.[11]

"John" was well versed in the structure of Greek oratory and makes his case with ease. In John, Jesus emerges as a transcendent being who manifests himself in Zen-like terms, like the Light of the World and the Bread of Life. With this Jesus, we are indeed far removed from the very human, down-to-earth figure who inhabits the Gospel of Mark.

✠ ✠ ✠

Significantly, none of the four evangelists were native Galileans. Christian tradition holds that "Mark" wrote in the city of Rome. "Matthew" and "Luke," who wrote their Gospels some ten or twenty years *after* that of Mark, also lived outside of Palestine. "Luke" probably worked for a community of Gentile Christians in Asia Minor (modern Turkey) or Greece—though, as noted, the sheer elegance of his Greek has led some scholars to suggest that Luke wrote in Alexandria. "Matthew" probably produced his Gospel in Antioch in Syria, since Ignatius (bishop of Antioch) is able to cite passages from his work as early as 110 C.E. Christian tradition places the author of "John" in Ephesus in Asia Minor. All four, therefore, were hundreds of miles removed from the small hamlet of Nazareth in Roman-occupied Palestine. The distance of time and space makes it very unlikely that the evangelists were able to "interview" those who knew Jesus personally.

It follows, then, that these authors must have drawn from a range of oral traditions about Jesus, passed from one person to another, from congregation to congregation, until they could be committed to paper. Luke, who of all the evangelists is most concerned about the historical context of his work, explicitly refers to certain accounts that "were handed on to us by those who from the beginning were eyewitnesses and servants of the word."[12] These accounts could have reached Luke in either oral or written form, and Luke makes the point that "many other authors" before him had tried to organize the reports of Jesus. This implies not only that Luke had access to *several* sources, but also that these traditions were, in one way or another, inadequate or conflicting, for Luke continues by saying that "after investigating everything," he saw the need to compose "an *orderly* account."[13] So what could these sources have been?

EARLY WRITINGS ON JESUS

As it turns out, the oldest written source about Jesus is not the Gospel literature, but the letters (or "epistles") written by Paul of Tarsus ("St. Paul" to Christians). These letters were addressed to early Christian communities throughout Asia Minor, Greece, and Rome, and dispatched by traders or friends using the rapidly improving sea and road network in the Roman Empire. The purpose of these missives was to bolster the faith and steadfastness of these congregations, and to adjudicate whenever tensions arose among their different constituencies. Some of these letters Paul dictated himself; others were written on his behalf or by anonymous authors eager to claim Paul's authority.

Unfortunately, Paul provides hardly any biographical information about Jesus. One reason may be that Paul never met Jesus, so knew only what the disciples knew. Most importantly, however, Paul believed that the cardinal significance of Jesus was not so much his life and his teachings, but his death on the cross. This, as Paul taught, was preordained by God to expiate the sins of mankind.

Fortunately, there are several other sources that shed light on Jesus' early life. Several of these were written by early Christians who did *not* embrace Paul's definition of Jesus as Savior by virtue of the cross. They, by contrast, believed that the point of Jesus' existence was not his death, but his life. Unlike Paul, they diligently studied Jesus' sayings, particularly those pertaining to Jesus' vision of the "Kingdom of God," and concluded that Jesus had been talking about a life of inner transformation by virtue of which one could eventually glean the secret knowledge of divine wisdom within oneself. Biblical scholarship has coined the rather unfortunate term of "Gnostics" for these Christians, based on the Greek word for (secret) knowledge, *gnosis.* Our understanding of these "dissident" Christian communities was largely based on scraps of papyrus coupled with fervent denunciations by church fathers, until in 1945 a pair of Egyptian shepherds went digging near the town of Nag Hammadi. They were delighted to discover an ancient earthenware jar, hoping it would contain gold. In fact, the jar contained no fewer than thirteen separate codices. (A *codex* is a set of papyrus pages bound in a book, rather than rolled up in a scroll.) Copied from Greek into Coptic, the language current in Egypt at that time, the books contained forty-five Christian texts that are not included in the New Testament, including a tantalizing document now known as the "Gospel of Thomas." This work is (or is based on) a collection of sayings that can be traced to the first century C.E. and, according to some scholars, may be as old as the oldest canonical Gospel.

What is so peculiar about the Gospel of Thomas is that it is not a "Gospel" at all. It is, quite simply, a collection of almost verbatim sayings by Jesus, without any attempt to place these statements in a theological context. Some of these quotes can also be found in the canonical Gospels; others are wholly original. In form, Thomas follows the popular "sayings" format by which writers in antiquity recorded the pithy teachings of philosophers, sages, and religious figures. The Book of Proverbs and The Wisdom of Solomon in the Old Testament are examples of such works, as are the books of famous sayings by wise kings, such as the *Instruction of Amenemopet,* that were popular in ancient Egypt. We have seen how the author of John claims to have had access to an "eyewitness account" of the Passion of Jesus. Thomas could thus—quite possibly—be a veritable "first layer" of source material, based on an oral source very close to Jesus.[14]

Unlike the Gospels, there is no doctrinal claim and—most significant of all—no reference to the Passion in the Thomas text. It is, rather, an unbiased and surprisingly modern portrait of a Jewish rabbi guided by the spirit of God.

THE "Q" DOCUMENT

Ever since the seventeenth century, scholars have noted that the Gospels of Mark, Matthew, and Luke have much in common, whereas these three differ substantially from the fourth Gospel, that of John. This is why the first three books are often referred to as the synoptic Gospels (from the Greek word *synoptikos,* meaning "seen together"). The reason why the first three Gospels are so similar is simple: Luke and Matthew both used the Gospel of Mark as a major source.[15] Clearly, as one scholar has suggested, Luke and Matthew were writing their account of Jesus with Mark's book "on their lap." If Mark is second-generation history, using primary oral or written sources, then Luke and Matthew must be considered a "third generation" of information about Jesus.

By the same token, however, there is a great deal of information in Matthew and Luke that does *not* appear in Mark. This new material is quite specific; it even contains extensive dialog that is quoted almost verbatim by both evangelists. Clearly, Luke and Matthew must have also used a written source *other* than Mark's. But what is this source?

Over the last century, many scholars-turned-sleuths have carefully perused the text of both Gospels in search of telltale signs that could identify this mysterious document. Using old-fashioned detective work, by rating the authenticity of a given phrase according to various criteria, they were able to piece together this source document which biblical scholarship refers to by the initial Q. This letter is derived from the German word *Quelle* or "source."

The format of Q is not a Gospel narrative, but a straightforward inventory of sayings, without any attempt to place these in a theological or chronological framework. In fact, the artificially constructed document of Q bears a strong resemblance to the Gospel of Thomas discovered in 1945. Neither Thomas nor Q says anything about Jesus' Passion and death on the cross (though some scholars believe there are allusions).

Even though Q is based on hypothesis, it has greatly advanced the archaeological search for Jesus and the actual record of his teachings. Some scholars have even gone as far as to translate Q back into the original Aramaic as spoken by Jesus, with sometimes stunning results.[16]

THE WORKS OF JOSEPHUS

Any investigation in the political, religious, and cultural conditions of first-century Palestine is unthinkable without the works of a Jewish historian who, by a twist of fate, became the protégé of the emperor Vespasian. Safely ensconced in Rome, he was able to write and publish several books at leisure, which have survived nearly intact to the present day.

This historian's name was Josephus. Of priestly stock, he reluctantly accepted a commission in the army of Jewish resistance fighters during the Jewish War of 66–70 C.E. Put in charge of a regiment in Galilee, he faced the Roman legions under the command of (then-general) Vespasian and was easily defeated. Josephus was captured and brought to Vespasian for interrogation. There, he adroitly saved his life by prophesying that the bald, corpulent general would one day become emperor. Vespasian laughed, then decided to call Josephus's bluff and hold him captive.

Fortunately for Josephus, Rome was passing through a brief period of civil war that would see three different emperors in eighteen months. In July of 69 C.E., Vespasian's own legions pronounced him emperor, and Josephus was released. He eventually joined the emperor's household in Rome, where he wrote a book about the Jewish War. He later published another book about Jewish history, *Antiquities of the Jews,* as well as an auto-biographical work. Since *Antiquities* features a short (though highly controversial) paragraph about Jesus, Josephus's works were meticulously copied by monks throughout the Middle Ages and preserved until modern times. It is to Josephus, therefore, that we will often turn to fill in the gaps of events during the years of Jesus' childhood and adolescence.

THE MISHNAH

For many centuries, Talmudic literature was considered the exclusive province of Jewish scholarship—until the twentieth century, when Christian scholars discovered that its earliest writings, and particularly the Mishnah, contained a lot of material that could shed light on the situation of early first-century Palestine (a period scholars refer to as Late Second Temple Judaism). The Mishnah (the word means "teaching") was first composed around 200 C.E., possibly by Rabbi Yehuda na Hasi ("the Prince"), in an attempt to codify the long tradition of rabbinical debate about the legislative precepts of the Hebrew Scriptures. The author's goal was to provide rabbis with a systematic reference of legal arguments, based on the Torah, to serve as a guide for everyday life. The Mishnah is organized around six basic subjects areas (subdivided into 63 tractates and 531 chapters), including *Seeds* (agricultural laws), *Appointed Times* (Jewish festivals), *Women* (marriage laws), *Damages* (civil law), *Holy Things* (sacrifice), and *Purities* (issues of what, from a Jewish cultic perspective, is ritually pure or not). On each topic, the Mishnah provides legal commentary, which is then illustrated by a rabbinical discussion of actual cases.[17]

Two decades ago, a backlash ensued. Jewish scholars, notably the eminent scholar Jacob Neusner, argued that New Testament scholars were using the material in the Mishnah uncritically, to suit their own purposes, without considering the fact that much in the Mishnah was colored by rabbinic ideals that did not always reflect actual practice. Furthermore, these scholars warned that the Mishnah was indelibly stamped by the traumatic experience of two ill-fated Jewish rebellions that took place well after the time of Jesus and changed the face of Judaism forever.

These caveats are sound. Recently, however, a number of authors have suggested a compromise. They argue that when trying to apply the Mishnah to the time of Jesus, we should separate theological arguments from descriptions of Palestine's social and economic environment, which appears to be closer to actual practice. David Fiensy, for example, has pointed to the enduring quality of many social and agrarian customs in Palestine from New Testament times to today, particularly among Israeli and West Bank Arabs. Fiensy has also shown that the relationship between wealthy landowners and (indebted) farmers in the eastern Mediterranean remained fairly constant from the Hellenistic to the Byzantine period, so

that precepts in the Mishnah reflecting these socioeconomic conditions may be quite accurate. Furthermore, as Ze'ev Safrai has argued, the recent discovery of a large number of rural roads fits the description in rabbinic literature and attests to the organizational ability of local villages. Similarly, the excavation of large cisterns near ancient villages appears to corroborate descriptions in the Mishnah. We will therefore use the Mishnah as another source for reconstructing the young life of Jesus, but with caution.

A MAN FROM GALILEE

Another important factor in our story is Jesus' unique cultural background. Jesus, we are told in the Gospels, hailed from a small village in Galilee. He was a Nazarene, a man from Nazareth. While at first glance this sounds innocuous, in first-century Palestine it had far-reaching associations. Galilee was different from Judea, in not only a geographical but also a cultural and socioreligious sense. For much of the preceding ten centuries, Galilee had been a distinct political entity whose historical record diverged significantly from that of the "heartland" of Judea. Galileans spoke a different dialect, shared a different ancestry, and hailed from a village culture that was quite distinct from either Samaria or Judea. Galilee was a land of peasant farmers, screened (if not insulated) from the rest of the world by mountain ranges on almost all sides. Over the centuries, these differences added up to a growing prejudice against Galileans, particularly in Judea, and this prejudice would follow Jesus whenever he strayed from his ancestral territory.

To begin with, the geography of Galilee was markedly different. According to the first-century Jewish historian Josephus (who wrote a scant fifty years after Jesus' crucifixion), Galilee was divided in two regions, Upper (or northern) Galilee and Lower (or southern) Galilee, following the natural contours of the region's geography.[18] Upper Galilee, said Josephus, ran from the Litani River in Lebanon to "Bersaba" (possibly Abu Sheba), and from "Meroth" in the west to "Thella" on the Jordan. A land of tall peaks and deep valleys, Upper Galilee was and still is far more rugged than Lower Galilee, with some of its limestone plateaus rising as high as 3,000 feet. Its mountains serve as the region's principal source of water, enjoying a rainfall of up to 44 inches per annum—far more than in any other part of Israel.

Below the natural boundary of the HaKerem Valley was Lower Galilee, the place where Jesus lived as a young boy. The borders of Lower Galilee,

according to Josephus, ran from the Plain of Ptolemais (or Akko) in the east to Mount Tabor and Beth She'an in the south and the Sea of Galilee to the west. Hence, from the period of the Israelite Settlement to the time of the young Jesus, the geographical boundaries of what people referred to as "Galilee" underwent very little change, save for the loss of some of the territory in the northwest to Phoenicia.

Within this territory, Galilee was a veritable Garden of Eden filled with a vast range of flowers, plants, and produce. "Its soil is so universally rich and fruitful, and so full of the plantations of trees of all sorts," wrote Josephus, "that it invites even the most indolent to engage in agriculture, because of its fruitfulness." Within Lower Galilee itself there were two distinct geophysical regions, each with a particular type of vegetation. The ridges surrounding the Allonim Hills were covered with lush shrubs that thrived on the alluvial soil of chalk and limestone. High on the ridges, some terebinth and evergreen oak (*Pistacia palaestina*) could be glimpsed, while the hillsides teemed with the dense brush of carob (*Ceratonia silqua*) and mastic trees (*Pistacia lentiscus*). In drier areas there were dense clusters of styrax.

On the eastern side of Lower Galilee, an entirely different picture presented itself. Here were highlands made largely of basalt, a forbidding element for natural growth, so that hillsides could stretch for miles without any prominent vegetation other than low-level brush and grass.

The true secret of Lower Galilee's fertility, however, was its abundant supply of water. In the region around the escarpment now known as the Nazareth Ridge, natural springs such as the Nahal Sippori provided a stable source of water all year round. These springs were fed by large subterranean aquifers of cool water, which made the region uniquely suited for the cultivation of fruits and vegetables. In his 1992 study, Israeli archaeologist Zvi Gal identified no fewer than twenty-five springs between the Nazareth Ridge and the Allonim Hills, some of which may have dated as far back as the Early Bronze Age.[19]

The bountiful presence of water and the outstanding quality of the soil all but guaranteed that the area around the Nazareth Ridge would attract the greatest density of settlement from the Early Iron Age and well into the Roman era. In fact, it is from Galilee that we have the earliest written testimony of human habitation in Palestine—or Canaan, as it was called—before the days of Joshua's conquest. During the fourteenth century B.C.E., when

Canaan was under the political and economic influence of Egypt, the sheiks of Canaanite city-states paid tribute to the Egyptian crown and received protection in return.[20]

CANAAN IN THE MIDDLE BRONZE AGE

When exactly the Exodus and Israelite "return" to the Promised Land took place is a matter of intense biblical debate.[21] What is clear, however, is that the region most coveted by the Israelite settlers was Galilee, for it held the most fertile valleys in all of the Levant—including the Jezreel (which in the Bible is also called Esdraelon, the Greek translation of "Jezreel").[22] Unfortunately, the region was already occupied by Canaanite farmers and herders whose culture, such as it was, owed much to neighboring Syria and northern Mesopotamia.

As the northernmost region of the Israelite realm, Galilee was surrounded by foreign territory. To the northwest was the Phoenician region of Sidon and Tyre, which in the centuries to come would serve as the main conduit of Hellenistic influence (the culture of ancient Greece), extending well into the days of Jesus. To the north was the land of Aram-Damascus, and to the east lay the territory of Ammon and Moab (today's Transjordan). Galilee was therefore an enclave of sorts, insular and landlocked, though with access to the Sea of Galilee. In sum, it formed an almost perfect circle of highly fertile land surrounded by foreigners—which is probably the root of the word Galilee (*ha-galil*), a presumed shortening of the Hebrew *galil ha-goyim,* meaning "circle of the peoples."[23]

According to the Book of Joshua, western Galilee was settled by the tribe of Asher, while the tribe of Zebulun was directed to central Galilee and that of Naphtali settled in eastern Galilee.[24] Meanwhile, the tribe of Issachar was moved to the volatile valley between Beth She'an and the Jezreel.[25]

New archaeological data has corroborated the claim in the Bible that the Israelites were gradually able to expand their presence in the north.[26] In the decades to come, these Israelites would devote themselves to building their settlements, raising their herds, and gathering their crops.[27] But the settlers faced renewed struggle when a third group, the Philistines, arrived to compete for the scarce resources of the land. In fact, the complete conquest of Galilee was not concluded until the days of King David, when David's commander Joab drove the Philistines back toward the coastal strip of Philistia. This marked the first time that Galilee, Samaria, and Judea were united in one political entity, the kingdom of David and Solomon.[28]

The unified monarchy of Israel was short-lived. Even during the reign of Solomon, tensions between north and south were simmering under the surface, not in the least over David's choice of Jerusalem, a Jebusite city with no Israelite pedigree, as the place of national worship, instead of long-established sacred precincts in the north. And so it was that when King Solomon died, the north seceded from Judah in the south and declared a new kingdom, the Northern Kingdom, proudly arrogating the name of "Israel." These tribal leaders then anointed their own king, King Jeroboam. The south, now shrunk to little more than the territory of Judah and Benjamin, would henceforth simply be known as the Southern Kingdom or "Judah."

Buoyed by the fertility of Galilee and surrounding regions, the Northern Kingdom now began to exploit its rich agricultural lands in earnest, focusing on the production of olive oil, wine, figs, dates, and cereals. The result was a growing agricultural surplus that boosted trade with surrounding regions.[29]

But up north, in Mesopotamia, a new colossus was rising. In 858 B.C.E., the Assyrian king Shalmaneser III decided to press his claims on the lands of the southern Levant and made the Northern Kingdom a vassal state.[30] The impact felt in Galilee was limited; the farmers were left alone to harvest their fields, provided the annual tribute was paid on time. But nearly a century later, the Assyrian king Tiglath-pileser III was no longer content with tribute. He conquered the fertile valleys of northern Israel and populated them with Assyrian settlers.[31] The proud Northern Kingdom was broken up into the separate Assyrian provinces of Dor (the coastal plain), Gilead (the Transjordan), and Megiddo (Upper and Lower Galilee). Most of the population in the Israelite townships was sent into exile to make room for Babylonian settlers. Galilean farmers weren't spared either; recent archaeological surveys have shown that by the eighth century B.C.E., much of Lower Galilee had suffered a considerable interruption in existing population patterns.[32] At the same time, the region received its share of eager Assyrian settlers. As Isaiah wrote, "[The Lord] brought into contempt the land of Zebulun and the land of Naphtali."[33]

THE "GENTILE CONTAMINATION" OF GALILEE

As a result of this foreign settlement, the character of Galilee underwent a profound change. What had once been a predominantly Israelite region now became a patchwork of cultures. Galilee had truly become a "Galilee of the nations."

For a brief period, during the reign of King Josiah (640–609 B.C.E.), Galilee was once again brought under the nominal control of Jerusalem.[34] King Josiah, whose rule coincided with the gradual disintegration of the Assyrian Empire, was driven by the elusive dream of restoring the kingdom of David and Solomon. Indeed, it was during his reign that the first effort was launched to collect and codify the *Torah,* the Five Books of Moses.[35] Josiah then set about to cleanse the formerly Assyrian possessions of Dor, Gilead, and Megiddo (Galilee) of every form of pagan worship and restored the rite of sacrifice at Solomon's Temple in Jerusalem. This is when we first hear of the prophet Jeremiah, the son of a priest named Hilkiah from the village of Anathoth, who was to have such a profound influence on the young Jesus. He poured scorn on those who benefited from Josiah's booming economy by hoarding "wealth unjustly,"[36] at the expense of the peasantry—an accusation that would return, almost verbatim, in one of Jesus' parables.

But Josiah's control of Galilee was brief. The king was killed in a battle with Pharaoh Psammetichus I. In 604 B.C.E., the new Babylonian king, Nebuchadnezzar, claimed the Israelite kingdom as a vassal state. Jerusalem fell in the summer of 586; its inhabitants were slaughtered or sent into exile.

Though this Babylonian Exile lasted only sixty years, it was to have a profound influence on the development of post-exilic Jewish society. Unmoored from their homeland, desperate to maintain their identity, the refugees felt an urgent need to record and preserve Jewish cultic life. The first division of the Bible, the Torah, was enlarged and refined, while work continued on the second division of the Hebrew Scriptures, the books of the Prophets.

In 553 B.C.E., the mighty Neo-Babylonian empire fell to the Persian king Cyrus II, who granted the Jews leave to return. Though many chose to stay in Babylon, having grown accustomed to its high standard of living, many hundreds of families made the thousand-mile trek to their ancestral homes. Here they found that Galilee, Samaria, and Judah had once again been divided into separate subprovinces under the fifth Persian satrapy, known as *Abar nahara* ("Beyond the [Euphrates] River").

Cyrus also provided funds for rebuilding the Temple in Jerusalem. As a result, the focal point of the Jewish restoration shifted inexorably to the south, to Judah, now named *Yehud*. Here, two Jewish officials from the Persian court, Nehemiah and Ezra, were expressly tasked with "purifying" Jewish society, removing all foreign elements, even to the point of forcing Jewish men to divorce their foreign-born wives.[37] But their restorative efforts were strictly limited to *Yehud;* when elders from Samaria petitioned to be included in the rebuilding of the Temple, they were rudely rebuffed.

While the south increasingly became a theocratic state, governed by the religious elite of the priesthood, Galilee remained a captive land, ruled by Persian officials. Much of the alienation that was to develop between Galilee, Samaria, and Judah in later centuries had its origin in this period.

THE ARRIVAL OF HELLENISM

The growing estrangement between north and south was exacerbated by the growing influence of Greek culture, known as "Hellenism," which percolated into Galilee with tradesmen, merchants, and craftsmen from Phoenicia. With its seductive art and sculpture, its highly developed polytheism, and its superb architecture and city planning, Hellenism found fertile ground in Syria and northern Palestine. The conquest of the Near East by the Macedonian king Alexander the Great only accelerated this process. Galilee (or *Galila*), Samaria, and Judah (now called *Judea*) became separate *hyparchies* in the Ptolemaic empire of Egypt-Palestine, founded by one of Alexander's generals, Ptolemy I Soter. This realm also included Idumaea (ancient Edom), a territory roughly analogous with southern Jordan and the Negev. A currency system was introduced, using coins bearing the Attic owl, which greatly facilitated international trade.

For Galilee, the advent of the Ptolemies brought prosperity and peace. The Ptolemies actively encouraged a restoration of the region's former agricultural bounty. A Greek official named Zenon, private secretary to the finance minister of Ptolemy II and III, traveled through Egypt, Palestine, and Syria, pausing in Galilee in 259 B.C.E. Here he carefully recorded its agricultural yields as part of a series of documents known as the *Zenon Papyri*.

21

Countless caravans passed through the region, bringing Galilee's oil, dates, figs, and wine to markets in Syria and Asia Minor. The region's wealth, in turn, encouraged the rise of a landed gentry that was soon to play a major political role in events to come. To purists in Judea, however, this growing interaction with Gentiles made the Galileans even more suspect.

Before long, Ptolemaic Palestine was threatened by the Syrian kingdom to the north, which likewise had been founded by one of Alexander's generals, Seleucus I. The growing tensions led to the outbreak of hostilities in 200 B.C.E., during which Galilee became the inevitable battleground. Ptolemy V ("Epiphanes") was defeated by his Seleucid opponent, Antiochus III, and, by his decree, Galilee and the rest of Palestine were annexed to the Seleucid Empire. Both Galilee and Judea were combined in the *eparchy* of Samaria, which in turn formed a part of the Seleucid province of Coele-Syria and Phoenicia.[38]

The Seleucid takeover was initially welcomed by the Galilean landed gentry, who fervently hoped that the Seleucids would reduce their tax burden; but this harmony did not last. As it turned out, Antiochus III had launched an ill-fated attack on Greece, which left the Seleucid Empire on the verge of bankruptcy. A successor, Antiochus IV, responded to the financial crisis by looting temples throughout his realm, including the restored (or "Second") Temple in Jerusalem, in the course of which he was assisted by the high priest Menelaos, a Seleucid stooge. A number of pious elders (called *Hasidim* or "the wise" in the books of Daniel and 1 Maccabees) rose in protest. Antiochus IV then demanded that all Jewish cultic practices be assimilated in the worship of Greek gods. Whoever refused to renounce Jewish cultic customs was in for severe punishment.

Horrified by this regime of terror, a priest named Mattathias from the village of Modein, located some twenty miles west of Jerusalem, revolted against the enforced worship of Greek deities and inspired a widespread rebellion. This movement, which was led by Mattathias's sons, became known as the Maccabean Revolt, and it succeeded beyond all expectations. In 164 B.C.E., Mattathias's son Judas was able to capture part of Jerusalem, cleanse the Temple, and rededicate it to Jewish worship—an event later to be commemorated by the Jewish festival of Hanukkah.

Galilee, however, remained firmly under Seleucid control. Western Galilee particularly had attracted scores of Syrians, Arameans, Phoenicians, and Greeks from Asia Minor, in addition to the Babylonian and Persian settlers who had been moved there in preceding centuries. Jewish farmers had, in fact, became a *minority*. Even worse, the outbreak of the Maccabean Revolt in the south provoked a strong anti-Jewish sentiment among Gentile communities in Galilee. According to the book of 1 Maccabees, a number of these Gentiles swore to erase the Jewish presence in Galilee altogether.[39] Judas, the ruler of the liberated south, sent a force of five thousand soldiers to rescue the beleaguered Jewish communities. After "many battles," these Galilean Jews were saved. But Judas was unable to break Gentile control of western Galilee, and he was forced to repatriate the Jewish farmers "and their wives and children" to Judea.[40]

During the next half century, the Maccabeans continued their struggle to also liberate Samaria and Galilee.[41] When at last they succeeded, their heirs, the Jewish dynasty of the Hasmoneans, launched a program of forceful Jewish conversion across all of Galilee, bringing in Jews from Judea for good measure.[42]

To what extent this "cleansing" program was successful in restoring the Jewish character of Galilee is a matter of intense scholarly debate. That such a program was even contemplated, less than ninety years before the birth of Jesus, may illustrate the deep suspicion harbored by conservative Jews in the south toward their Galilean brethren in the north. As it was, the conversion attempts failed to dislodge a large number of Gentile families that remained and prospered well into the era of Jesus. One example was the city of Sepphoris, only four miles distant from Nazareth, which had always had a mixed population. After the conquest of Palestine by the Romans in 63 B.C.E., Sepphoris became the seat of the Roman-controlled regional council governing Galilee.[43]

All this may explain why the Gospel of Matthew still refers to "the land of Zebulun and the land of Nephtalim" as "Galilee of the Gentiles" and why, in the Gospel of John, one of the Apostles' friends would scoff, *Nazareth?* "Can any good come out of Nazareth?"[44] Galilee, in sum, was not the type of place where pious Judeans expected to discover a "hasid" or "holy man" like Jesus.

GALILEE IN JESUS' TIME

Scores of coins and pottery fragments of Greek or Hellenistic origin, brought to light in recent excavations, bear out the enduring Gentile character of many enclaves in the Galilee that Jesus knew. They suggest that once the Gentile population no longer posed an acute threat to Jewish farmers and settlers, the daily intercourse of trade between Jew and Gentile could resume. The result was what the archaeologist Eric Meyer has called a rather "cosmopolitan and multilingual atmosphere" in Lower Galilee that, for better or worse, reached its apex during the boom times of the reign of King Herod. Many of the townships of Lower Galilee, says Mark Chancey in his Galilean study of 2005, were "no less Hellenized and urbanized than anywhere else in the Roman world."[45]

It was different in the hundreds of small rural villages found throughout the rolling hills of the region. Josephus tells us that there were no fewer than 204 such hamlets, most clinging tenaciously to their ancestral faith and customs, even as the world around them became first a Hellenistic and then a Roman preserve. This is why Talmudic literature would make a sharp distinction between a village (*kfr*), a township (*'yr*), and a city (*kerakh,* similar to the Greek word *polis*). Cities such as Sepphoris or Scythopolis (Beth She'an) could have a population of twenty thousand or more, usually a mixture of Jews and Gentiles. Townships, also mixed, numbered anywhere from two to five thousand inhabitants. Only villages were predominantly Jewish, though many were not larger than eight to ten *dunams* (each *dunam* representing ten families), living in huts and mud-brick homes over an area of no more than two and a half acres.[46]

Here, in these rural enclaves, the unique indigenous culture of Galilee had remained relatively constant through the preceding ages, even as foreign conquerors came and went. And it was this culture that would now produce a young boy from the village of Nazareth, a boy named *Yeshua*.

ONE

THE BETROTHAL OF MARY AND JOSEPH

Nazareth was a tiny hamlet, precariously perched on an outcropping that geologists refer to as the Nazareth Ridge. This ridge is made up of a soft, chalky rock, strong yet easily workable, which made it eminently suitable for settlement. From here, Nazareth's inhabitants could look north toward the Beth-Netopha Valley, the single largest valley in Lower Galilee, rich in minerals and nitrates. Because of the lack of drainage, its soil could draw from vast underground water tables, which in times of excessive rainfall would lead to flooding, keeping the valley floor moist and fertile. As a result, Nazareth and other villages in the area could pride themselves on some thirty-eight square miles of excellent farmland stretching across the Beth-Netopha and the Nahal Sippori valleys.

It was here, in this Jewish hamlet, that a man named Yosef (or Joseph) was betrothed to a young girl named Miriam (or Mary). It is not clear where Joseph came from, or whether his family lived in Nazareth as well. As we have seen, neither the oldest Gospel, that of Mark, nor the youngest Gospel, that of John, describes the events that led to the birth of Jesus. Both of these Gospels begin their story when Jesus is a grown man and has joined the movement of John the Baptist. Mark never even refers to Joseph, identifying Jesus merely as "the son of Mary."[1]

Matthew does refer to Joseph and even offers an extended genealogy, but this follows the largely symbolic formula, often used in the Old Testament, of establishing an august pedigree for the lead protagonist of a story. The purpose of creating such a birth list was to anchor him (or her) within the continuous narrative of Scripture and legitimize the historical role he (or she) was about to play. In Genesis, for example, Terah, Abraham's father, is traced back to Shem, the son of Noah.[2] In Matthew's text, Joseph is traced to the house of David, a prerequisite for any potential *Mashiach* or

Messiah, and ultimately back to Abraham.[3] To further illustrate the perfect symmetry of God's plan, Matthew makes the point that fourteen generations separate Abraham and David; fourteen generations lie between David and the Babylonian Exile; and fourteen generations again separate the Exile from Jesus, the "Messiah."[4] Once again this argument is rooted in allegory, for fourteen is the symbolic number often associated with the name of David.

Luke limits his information about Joseph to the fact that he was "of the house of David."[5] Later in the narrative, however, Luke also presents a detailed patrilineal genealogy of Jesus, although his birth list is markedly different from Matthew's. Joseph is identified as "the son of Heli, son of Matthat," followed by a list of over fifty generations, which end with Adam; most of the names mentioned are otherwise unknown and probably legendary.[6] Neither genealogy gives us any explicit clue as to where Joseph's residence might be, though Matthew implies that both Mary and Joseph originally lived in Bethlehem. Only John, writing several decades after the synoptic Gospels, specifically states that Joseph was "from Nazareth," but he offers no further details.[7]

Mary is clearly established in Luke's Gospel as a native of Nazareth.[8] Matthew, however, equivocates on the issue. Throughout his Gospel, Matthew is deeply concerned about providing scriptural precedent for the words and deeds of Jesus so as to eliminate any doubt about Jesus' pedigree in the Hebrew Scriptures. His oft-used formula "in fulfillment of the scriptures" is meant to establish that Jesus is a legitimate heir of the Covenant, and that he is the "Anointed One," the Messiah, of Davidic origin.

Matthew had a very specific motive for doing this. The evangelist wrote in a time when early Judeo-Christians found themselves ostracized from Jewish society, forbidden to participate in synagogue meetings, and sometimes even persecuted. The purpose of Matthew's use of scriptural symbolism is therefore to provide "evidence" for the rehabilitation of Jesus, to establish his honor as a bona fide prophet, and to "prove" that he is the Messiah.

For this reason, it was essential that the birth of Jesus be located not in Mary's home town of Nazareth, but in Bethlehem. Only then could Jesus fulfill the prophecy of the prophet Micah (late eighth century B.C.E.) that he "who is to rule in Israel" shall come from Bethlehem.[9] This prophecy is so pivotal to Matthew's story that the evangelist even quotes it in full.[10] He then refrains from providing any information about the birthplace of either Joseph or Mary, and simply states that Jesus "was born in Bethlehem of Judea."[11] Matthew then has the family make their home "in a town called Nazareth" *after* the birth of Jesus, implying that neither parent had lived there before.

Both Gospels do agree, however, that at one point Mary became engaged to Joseph to be his wife. As things went in first-century Palestine, this was most likely not the result of a spontaneous romance between two young people. Marriage was an extremely grave matter for Palestinian Jews, not least because it implied the transfer of a good part of a family's treasure (the dowry) to the young couple's home. It was of the utmost importance to establish beforehand whether the two families involved in this matter were compatible, of a similar background, observant, honorable, and trustworthy. It was equally crucial that the fathers of the two families could see eye to eye and establish the necessary rapport to bring the negotiations about the value of the deeded properties to a successful conclusion.

A marriage, then, combined two families and made them *kinfolk,* a cardinal element in the fabric of Palestinian society and indeed much of Israelite history. Kinship created relations that would affect the future of the family and the clan for generations to come. For all these reasons, a marriage was too critical an enterprise to be left in the hands of teenagers with their hormones raging. In rural Galilee as elsewhere in Palestine, marriages were arranged by the parents, often many years in advance of the happy couple reaching a nubile age.

The most important aspect of the wedding negotiations was the matter of the dowry, as well as (in many cases) the extent of the bridewealth. A *ketubba* or dowry was a deed of gifts that the bride's parents were prepared to present to the couple. This could involve money, cattle, land, or property. In the case of wealthy households, gold, silver, and even slaves could figure in the equation. Though theoretically this deed was given to the bride, in practice it was the groom who disposed of all of the bride's assets on her behalf. The dowry therefore consisted of everything that the bride's family was prepared to part with in order to establish a new household for the young couple. The *bridewealth,* on the other hand, was a gift or deed from the groom's family to the family of the bride—not the bride herself—to compensate the bride's father for the loss of his daughter and the expense of the dowry needed to make her marriageable.

A recent review of marriage contracts between the fourth century B.C.E. and the fourth century C.E., written in either Greek or Aramaic, reveals a broad array of terms under which such marriages were concluded. These contracts illustrate the care with which the families went out to identify suitable partners and then negotiate the most favorable arrangement possible. The study also shows that while the practice of a bridal dowry was widespread, the Greek custom of the bridewealth, of the groom's family presenting a share of their property and possessions to the bride's family, became more common in the last two centuries before the birth of Jesus. Third-century rabbinic texts, for example, suggest a pension of 200 *dinarii* for a virgin and 100 *dinarii* for a widow or divorced woman as part of the bridewealth, should her husband divorce her or die.[12]

A *dinarius* was roughly equal to a day's wages of a worker on a farm. In Jesus' time, it was most often a silver coin, sometimes stamped with the image of the reigning emperor, Tiberius. By comparison, a "scribe"—essentially a notary public who filled out forms of marriage, divorce, sale, credit, or rent—made twelve *dinarii* per week, roughly double a worker's wages. For a single *dinarius,* you could buy a large meal or a jar of olive oil of average quality. According to Luke, an overnight stay in an inn cost two *dinarii.*[13] A lamb cost four *dinarii,* and an outer garment between twelve and eighteen *dinarii.* Two hundred *dinarii* therefore represented a sum that allowed a frugal widow to live for about six to eight months, but not much more. Not surprisingly, Jesus says in the Gospel of Luke: "What woman, having ten silver coins, if she loses one of them, does not light a lamp, sweep the house, and search carefully until she finds it?"[14]

An interesting example of a Jewish marriage contract is the one between Shelamzion, the daughter of Judah, son of Eleazar, and Judah, son of Ananias. Both lived in the village of En Gedi in Judea in the early part of the second century C.E. As part of the agreed terms, the contract states, Shelamzion brought to the groom "for dowry women's jewelry in silver and gold, and clothing appraised by mutual agreement, as they both attest, to be worth two hundred *denarii* of silver." Judah, in turn, acknowledged that "he owes to Shelamzion his wife three hundred *denarii* which he promised to give her in addition to the sum of her dowry," subject to the understanding that this capital would be used to "his undertaking of feeding and clothing both her and future children." Since both Jewish and Greek custom dictated that the property remained in the husband's hands, the contract also stated that "his wife Shelamzion" would have the right at any time to "redeem" this cash value from her husband, "in silver secured in due form, at his own expense, interposing no objection," at failure of which his wife could charge a penalty equal to double the value.

Another marriage papyrus from Palestine, contracted just two years before the wedding between Shelamzion and Judah, has the Jewish groom pledging to his bride that "you will be my wife according to the law of Moses and the Judeans and I will feed you and clothe you and I will bring you [into my house] by means of your *ketubba* and I owe you the sum of 400 *denarii* . . . together with the due amount of your food and your clothes and your bed, provision fitting for a free woman." Thus, in both contracts, the primary concern (other than the bride's dowry) is for the provision of food, clothing, and shelter as well as conjugal rights. This was a reflection of Covenant Law, which states that "if [a man] takes another wife to himself, he shall not diminish the food, clothing, or marital rights of the first wife."[15] Similar guidelines concerning the provision of food, clothing, and conjugal rights would later resurface in the Mishnah. "A husband," says the third chapter devoted to "Women," "may not give [his wife] less than two *kabs* of wheat or four *kabs* of barley [every week]. . . . A *kab* of pulses . . . half a *log* of oil and a *kab* of dried fruits or a *mina* of fig cake," which together amounted to fourteen full meals per week, or two per day.[16] In addition, "he must also give her a cap for her head and a girdle for her loins and shoes at each of the three feasts," meaning the festivals of Passover, Shavuot, and Succoth. In return, the Mishnah says obliquely, "she should eat with him on the night of every Sabbath," which is code for the wife agreeing to sleep with her husband on that night.

Dowries could be quite substantial. Even among peasant families, who could not present the betrothed with silver, dowries often included substantial deeds of land, sufficient to sustain the young couple and their anticipated offspring. It is therefore not surprising that the peasantry was always looking for marriage partners among their kin, so as to keep their aggregate land holdings "in the family." Endogamy—marriage between close relatives, such as cousins or nieces, usually on the paternal side—was quite common in ancient Palestine (and is still practiced in parts of the Middle East today). This may come as a surprise to us who are used to the essentially exogamous character of modern marriages (marriage, that is, outside the principal family group). But for first-century Palestinians, the desire to keep property within one's family group was a powerful motive. The insular quality of Jewish observant villages within Gentile Galilee, the small pool of eligible partners within a village, the close bonds of family, and concerns about cultic purity also played an important role.

The custom of seeking marriage partners among the sons and daughters of one's siblings has a long tradition in Judaic culture. The Hebrew Scriptures give many examples in which parents seek a wife for their son among their kin. Abraham sent a trusted family servant to Haran, where his brother's family dwelt, to find a bride for Isaac, lest his son be forced to marry a local Canaanite.[17] Isaac's son Jacob likewise journeyed to Haran to find a spouse among his kin.[18]

As far as Joseph and Mary are concerned, however, we lack the necessary data to determine their ancestry and establish whether the young couple was in any way related. Suffice it to say that, at the very least, it was possible.

THE ENGAGEMENT

A Jewish girl like Mary was usually deemed to be of marriageable age after the beginning of her menses, at age thirteen or fourteen. This, too, may come as a shock to us. Modern science tells us that even though a child's body may be fully developed at an early age, a child's brain does not reach full maturity until age twenty-one. This is why, in our society, children are encouraged to focus on their education and develop the necessary intellectual and spiritual maturity before marriage can even be considered. But it was different in biblical times, not least because the average life expectancy of a man and a woman was forty years, compared to the seventy-plus years in First World countries today.

What's more, a young girl in a rural community like Nazareth had no educational opportunities to speak of. Instead, from about age six or seven on, Mary would have been taught to cook, to wash, and to take care of younger children in the family. In addition, a woman in rural Palestine was expected to make all the garments needed to clothe herself and her family. Mary's mother would therefore have introduced her to the art of weaving at an early age. First, her small, nimble fingers would have been trained in rolling coarse wool or flax into spinning yarn. Then she would have learned to weave the wool, using a simple upright loom of threads that were suspended with small wooden or clay weights. One such loom, dating from the first century B.C.E., has been discovered in En Gedi. In Galilee, looms could produce cloth of a width of three feet. Two of these lengths, joined together, produced a garment.

At the time of her engagement, Mary would have worn clothes that she or her mother had made. This would have consisted of a linen undergarment, which in turn was covered by a long, sleeveless tunic bound by two girdles: one under the young bosom, one around her waist. The bottom of her tunic would have had fringes to cover her ankles. When Mary went out (invariably in the company of her mother or another female relative), she would throw a long, rectangular cloak over her shoulder. This cloak was sometimes adorned with a simple geometric pattern near the shoulders and at the hem. For footwear, Mary would have worn sandals made of palm bark, fastened with straps of flax or rope. Fragments of human hair found in En Gedi suggest that girls like Mary wore their hair in plaits. Whenever she ventured outside, she would have covered her hair with a veil. At night, she would have combed out her hair with a two-faced comb, similar to the one found by excavators in the mountain fortress of Masada.

As far as Joseph is concerned, we do not know whether he received any form of education or not. Rabbinic sources from the late second and third century C.E. indicate that larger villages typically maintained a synagogue where young boys received some schooling. Synagogues were not sacred temples, but community centers where villagers would convene on the Sabbath to read and discuss Hebrew Scripture. At other times, they served a variety of other functions, including a rudimentary form of education where young boys were trained in Scripture, starting at age five or six. The Palestinian and Babylonian Talmuds, for example, tell us that Simeon ben Shetah (103–76 B.C.E.) decreed that every district and town have a *Bet ha-Sefer* or "School of the Book." The main purpose of this schooling was not to teach young boys to write, but to expose them to the Hebrew Scriptures and the precepts of Covenant Law. A late first-century inscription of a synagogue, found in Jerusalem and honoring the "donor" of the synagogue building, summarizes the functions of the building quite succinctly: "Theodotus, son of Vettenos . . . built this synagogue for the reading of the Law and the study [teaching] of the commandments, and the guest chambers, the rooms, the water installations for an inn for those in need from foreign lands." If large enough, the synagogue could also be used for local tribunals, as a collection point for tithes and taxes, and for community banquets.

Scholars, however, are divided on the issue of whether the schoolings described in rabbinic sources are based on actual practice, or rather reflect a pious ideal that could only occasionally be realized. Moreover, there is considerable doubt that any such schools would have existed in the Galilean countryside *before* the destruction of the Temple in 70 C.E. Luke tells us that Jesus returned to Nazareth at the beginning of his ministry and "went to the synagogue on the Sabbath day, as was his custom," but it is doubtful that Luke ever visited Nazareth. This description may simply be based on synagogue services Luke himself observed in Asia Minor in the latter part of the first century.

On the other hand, in 1955, a Franciscan archaeologist, Bellarmino Bagatti, began a series of excavation campaigns directly underneath the Church of the Annunciation in Nazareth—traditionally the site associated with the paternal house of Mary. He uncovered a number of architectural fragments from the second century C.E. that he identified as the remains of a village synagogue. This identification has been hotly contested, however, principally because the building is oriented toward the north, rather than toward Jerusalem, as was the custom for synagogues.

We are left with the conclusion that there is no evidence for the existence of a synagogue in Nazareth at the time of Joseph and Jesus. Village gatherings, such as they were, would have simply taken place in a central area, perhaps near the shade of a tree or the village cistern, or in the largest mud-brick house of the village. This also implies that most of the village boys would have received their vocational training at home, which almost invariably meant following in the footsteps of their fathers. By age thirteen, a boy was deemed to have reached adulthood. At that point, he would begin to work alongside his father full-time. In Galilee, this most often involved farming. While accompanying his father to the produce markets of the nearby townships, the boy could sometimes pick up a rudimentary understanding of Greek, which in first-century Palestine had increasingly become the *lingua franca* of everyday commerce and trade.

According to the Mishnah, a Jewish boy in Palestine was deemed to be of marriageable age by the time he reached eighteen, though his fitness for marriage would depend to a considerable extent on his ability to provide for his wife and his future offspring.

Tradition tells us that Jesus was a carpenter, which would strongly suggest that his father Joseph was a carpenter as well. The identification of Joseph as a carpenter, however, is based on the Gospel of Mark: when Jesus speaks in the synagogue on the Sabbath, people are amazed, saying, "Is this not the carpenter, the son of Mary?"[19] We must, however, qualify this statement on two grounds. First, Mark does not explicitly state that Joseph, Jesus' father, also worked as a carpenter throughout his life. Second, the Greek word Mark uses is *tektoon,* which, as we have seen, translates not as "carpenter" but as "laborer" or "worker."

Why is this so important? Simply put, because neither the Gospels, the Q source, nor the "Gospel" of Thomas give us the impression that Jesus was a carpenter at all. On the contrary, when Jesus searches for metaphors to explain his teachings in the form of parables, he uses not the language of the workshop, but the language of the field. This is surprising in a carpenter, for the lore of sawing, carving, and hammering would have provided him with a wonderful visual vocabulary of its own.

Instead, in the eloquent Gospel of Luke, Jesus speaks of a "grain of mustard seed, which a man took, and cast into his garden; and it grew, and waxed a great tree; and the fowls of the air lodged in the branches of it."[20] Casting a practiced eye on a fig tree that has not borne fruit for three years, Jesus counsels the owner to "let it alone this year also, till I shall dig about it, and dung it: And if it bear fruit, well: and if not, then after that you should cut it down." And to emphasize that the goodness of one's heart produces good, Jesus reminds his audience that it is not "for thorns that men gather figs, nor for bramble bush that they gather grapes."[21]

The impression we get is that Jesus was intimately familiar with agriculture and the careful cultivation of Galilean soil, which would suggest that

Joseph's principal occupation was farming. Josephus tells us that virtually everyone in Galilee was in some way or form involved with farming the land. Apparently, this was true for the small hamlet of Nazareth as well. While excavating underneath the Church of the Annunciation in Nazareth, the archaeologist Bagatti found granaries, olive presses, and wells, which attest to the existence of an agricultural hamlet as early as the first or second century C.E. We will therefore assume, for the moment, that Joseph was a farmer, and deal with the identification of Joseph and Jesus as *tektoi* later on.

MARY IS FOUND "WITH CHILD"

It is unlikely that Joseph and Mary would have been permitted to "date" in a modern sense, or even to engage in any lengthy courtship. Even the urbane and cosmopolitan Jewish philosopher Philo (20 B.C.E.–50 C.E.), a contemporary of Jesus, warned that a woman should "cultivate solitude," and urged her husband "not to let her be seen going about like a woman who walks the streets in the sight of other men, except when it is necessary for her to go to the temple." Nor should she be allowed to "go to the market at noon, when [it] is full, but only after the majority of the people have returned home." While according to the Mishnah a woman was allowed to leave the house occasionally, for example to visit a *mikveh* or ritual bath, to see friends, to shop, or to attend a feast, she was to behave decorously at all times. Loose hair, a torn dress, or washing in public was not tolerated and could, in fact, be grounds for divorce without alimony.[22] These prescriptions applied to a mature woman already wed, so we can imagine that, for an *unmarried* woman of nubile age, even stricter rules would have applied. Mary would never have been able to meet with Joseph unattended, only while a chaperone was present, and then only for a brief period of time. In all such matters, a girl of Mary's age invariably deferred to the male members of her own household, whether her father or her brothers. After all, it was they who were charged with protecting her chastity and thus safeguarding the honor of her family.

Despite the limitations of the courtship, both families looked forward to the wedding feast, which was the responsibility of the groom's father. Even in a small hamlet like Nazareth, a wedding could stretch over several days. All the members of the village, as well as many people from surrounding villages, would be invited. The festivities would begin with a procession of the bridegroom and his relatives to the house of the bride on the eve of the wedding. The veiled bride, decked out in white, would be received and carried back to the groom's house, where she was given separate sleeping quarters with her bridal attendants. The next day, the celebrations would begin in earnest with song and dance, culminating in a great feast. This was one of the rare occasions when the families of Joseph and Mary could indulge in the luxury of roasted meat, in this case one or several sheep that would be slaughtered for the purpose. All through the evening, the happy couple would be showered with seeds and flowers, until it was time for the bride and groom to excuse themselves. While they consummated their union for the first time, the party continued with renewed vigor. The feast could continue for several days, until finally the relatives returned to their homes and villages, leaving the couple to settle into their new home. This was usually a small one- or two-room hut made of mud brick and covered with a thatched roof.

But as the time of Joseph and Mary's wedding feast drew near, a dreadful thing happened: Mary was "found to be with child," even though she and her future husband were not yet living together in matrimony.[23] It would be difficult to overstate the impact of such a catastrophe on a small observant village such as Nazareth. A premarital pregnancy brought great dishonor and shame on the family—specifically (as things were those days) on the bride's family, for clearly the father and brothers of the bride had been remiss in their duty, failing to restrain the willful passions of the young woman. According to the Covenant Law, Mary's relatives would have been entitled to take her out of her parental house and stone her to death.[24]

So great was the shame attached to Mary's premature pregnancy that many scholars are prepared to assume that this was a historical event, based on an authentic tradition about Jesus' birth. This assessment is based on what scholars term the criterion of embarrassment—the idea that pejorative or potentially embarrassing stories in the Gospels were included nevertheless, because the underlying oral or written tradition was simply too persistent or well known to ignore. In this case, we can safely assume that no observant Jewish author would have dared to invent such a scandalous event as Mary's illicit pregnancy, regardless of the theological ramifications with which the evangelists seek to frame the story.

The potential for scandal was certainly foremost on Joseph's mind when he learned of Mary's pregnancy. According to Matthew, he "planned to dismiss her quietly" so as to contain the calamity of her condition and to preempt any bad blood between the two families. As befits an honorable young man, Joseph was "unwilling to expose her to public disgrace."[25]

This is the moment when both Luke and Matthew venture to explain the reason for the premarital conception of Jesus. Both state that Jesus was conceived not by man, but by the Holy Spirit. In building their case, they turn to Old Testament precedent, though each arrives at a different scenario.

THE NATIVITY ACCOUNT IN MATTHEW

In Matthew, Joseph is the real protagonist of the story. It is to him that an angel appears to explain the unusual circumstances of Mary's pregnancy. Matthew's model is the Genesis story of God's appearance to Abraham, telling him that he will be the father of a son by his wife Sarah. This story unfolds in three distinct parts. First comes the principal annunciation by the Lord:

> I will bless her, and moreover I will give
> you a son by her.

Second, to assuage Abraham's obvious skepticism, God insists that:

> . . . your wife Sarah shall bear you a son,
> and you shall call him Isaac.

Third, the narrative reveals the scope of God's greater plan:

> I will establish my covenant with him as an ever-
> lasting covenant for his offspring after him.[26]

Matthew's Annunciation story follows the Abraham formula almost verbatim. The angel appears to Joseph in a dream and opens with the annunciation:

> Joseph, son of David, do not be afraid to take Mary
> as your wife, for the child conceived in her is from
> the Holy Spirit.

The angel then reaffirms this astonishing news, and names the child:

> She will bear a son, and you are to name him Jesus.

The message then concludes with a prophecy that explains the child's future as part of God's plan:

> . . . for he will save his people from their sins.

To further underscore the authenticity of this event, Matthew avails himself of a favorite device, the *fulfillment* of a prophecy given by a prophet in the Hebrew Scriptures—in this case, Isaiah. "Look," Matthew says, quoting the Book of Isaiah, "the *virgin* shall conceive and bear a son, and they shall name him Emmanuel."[27] Matthew, however, spoke Greek. He therefore did not quote from the Hebrew Scriptures, but from the Greek translation of the Scriptures known as the Septuagint. And while the Septuagint uses the word *parthenos* (or "virgin"), the original Hebrew text does not refer to a *virgin* at all, but to an *almah,* meaning "young woman":

> "Look, the young woman is with child and shall
> bear a son, and shall name him Emmanuel."[28]

Isaiah, in short, was not talking about a virgin per se, but about a typical married young woman who was about to give birth. The point of his verse is not to announce a future Redeemer, but to describe the span of time—the period required for a baby to be weaned—within which Israel would be saved from her foreign enemies.

In the Gospel of Matthew, it is Joseph who receives these tidings, and it is Joseph who arrives at the decision to accept Mary as his wife-to-be after all. Mary's feelings on the matter are not discussed, in keeping with the patriarchal nature of Palestinian society. Of course, a lavish wedding is out of the question. No man, under these circumstances, would have proceeded with a public feast, given that the marriage would always be under a cloud. And so Joseph merely "took her as his wife," but did not as yet avail himself of his conjugal rights: he "had no marital relations with her until she had borne a son."[29]

THE ANNUNCIATION IN LUKE

Luke's version of these events is presented from an entirely different perspective, for Luke chooses to make Mary the protagonist of the story. Like Matthew, Luke takes his cue from the Abraham story in Genesis, but his narrative is modeled on two different prophecies: that involving the child of Abraham's wife, Sarah, and another involving the son of Sarah's handmaiden, Hagar. Since Sarah had been unable to present her husband with a son, Abraham decided to lie with Hagar, which was his right by Mesopotamian custom as a tribal leader. The slave girl conceived in due course. But, knowing that she now controlled the fate of the tribe, the surrogate mother started to put on airs. This upset Sarah to no end, as we can imagine, and she decided to send the impudent girl into the desert. Before long, an angel appeared to poor Hagar, declaring the now-familiar three-part formula:

(1) Now you have conceived and shall bear a son,

(2) you shall call him Ishmael, for the Lord has given heed to your affliction

(3) . . . and he shall live at odds with all his kin.[30]

Soon thereafter, three strangers appeared in front of Abraham's tent. They asked where Sarah was; when Abraham replied, "There in the tent," they said, "I will surely return to you in due season, and your wife Sarah shall have a son." Abraham was amazed, and Sarah laughed, saying, "After I have grown old, and my husband is old, shall I have pleasure?" To which the Lord replied, "Is anything too wonderful for the Lord?"[31]

In Luke's hands, the order is reversed. The prophecy to Hagar is the model for the Annunciation to Mary, whereas the episode with Abraham and Sarah forms the basis for the story of Elizabeth and Zechariah, the parents of John the Baptist. As Luke tells us, Elizabeth and her husband Zechariah, a priest at the Temple in Jerusalem, were also childless and advanced in age. But one day, while Zechariah was in the Temple, the angel Gabriel appeared and told him, "Do not be afraid, Zechariah, for your prayer has been heard. Your wife Elizabeth will bear you a son, and you will name him John." Zechariah responded with the same incredulity with which Abraham and Sarah greeted the news: "How will I know that this is so? For I am an old man, and my wife is getting on in years." The angel's reply, too, follows the Genesis model closely:

"I stand in the presence of God, and I have been sent to speak to you," meaning, *is anything impossible for the Lord?*[32]

Luke then adds a further refinement to the story, using as his source the story of Hannah and Elkanah from the Book of 1 Samuel. Elkanah, a man from the region of Ephraim, north of Bethel, had two wives: Peninnah, who had given him children, and Hannah, who was barren. One day, during their annual pilgrimage to the shrine of YHWH in Shiloh, Hannah prayed fervently to the Lord, promising that if God granted her a son, she would make the son a *nazarite*—a person who lives in solitude, devoted to the service of God. As a true nazarite, Hannah pledged, "he shall drink neither wine nor intoxicants, and no razor shall touch his head."[33] In Luke's story, the angel uses the same words to admonish Zechariah: "He must never drink wine or strong drink."

Now we understand the beauty of Luke's parallel analogy. In the Old Testament, Hannah gave birth to Samuel, the judge and prophet. In the New Testament, Elizabeth will give birth to John the Baptist. Like Samuel, John will live in solitude, in the desert, without a razor touching his hair. And just as Samuel once anointed David, the king of Israel and founder of the Davidic dynasty, so too will John the Baptist "anoint" Jesus as the Davidic Messiah in the waters of the Jordan. Neither Samuel nor John could touch wine or spirit, for they were filled with the Spirit of God.[34]

In sum, the purpose of Luke's elegant story is not to establish historical facts, but to provide a literary preamble to the life of Jesus that confirms him as a figure fully in line with the prophets of Scripture—indeed, as the capstone of that lineage.

We then come to the story of the Lucan Annunciation to Mary, which of all the Gospel texts ranks as the finest of New Testament literature. Six months after Elizabeth's conception, the angel Gabriel appeared once again, this time to Mary in her humble home in Nazareth. "Greetings, favored one!" said the angel; "the Lord is with you." Mary was "much perplexed" by these words, so the angel said, "Do not be afraid, Mary, for you have found favor with God." His words echo the consoling words spoken by "an angel of the Lord" to Hagar, after she had been cast out a second time, this time with her child. "Do not be afraid," the angel in Genesis had said; "for God has heard the voice of the boy."

In the Lucan scene, Gabriel now proceeds with the familiar formula: "You will conceive in your womb and bear a son, and you will name him Jesus. He will be great, and will be called the Son of the Most High." Still following Old Testament precedent, Mary expresses surprise and bewilderment. "How can this be," she asks, "since I am virgin?" The angel explains, "The Holy Spirit will come upon you, and the power of the Most High will overshadow you." The angel Gabriel then concludes with the remark that reiterates the Sarah prophecy (*Is anything too wonderful for the Lord?*): "For nothing will be impossible with God."[35]

MARY'S PREMARITAL PREGNANCY: A HISTORICAL ASSESSMENT

What historical information can be gleaned from Luke and Matthew's accounts? As we have seen, both evangelists draw heavily from Old Testament narrative to place the story in a theological framework. The purpose of this framework is to prepare the reader for the life of Jesus to follow. The miraculous power of God to create life where none was expected, and the device of angels to announce such news to unsuspecting women, are motifs found throughout the Hebrew Scriptures. But this demands the question: Are the Nativity cycles of Matthew and Luke purely motivated by the desire to anchor Jesus' birth in prophecy, or are they based on an authentic tradition? Is it symbolism for its own sake, or symbolism used to explain a historical occurrence?

To answer this question, the first thing we must remember is that the story of Mary's premarital pregnancy does not appear anywhere else in the New Testament literature. Paul, who as we have seen wrote the earliest extant texts of Christianity, does not refer to it at all. Granted, Paul generally does not show much interest in the details of Jesus' biography, but the idea of the virginal conception by the Holy Spirit would certainly have bolstered his argument that Jesus was the Son of God. The only other reference to the event is found in a hostile document, a polemic against Christianity called *True Discourse,* written by a pagan author named Celsus around 178 C.E.

Though this document has not survived, we can restore its principal thesis from extensive quotes in a retort written by the Church author

Origen around 248, titled *Against Celsus.* Celsus claimed that the story of the virginal conception was a myth, hastily cooked up to conceal the fact that Mary allegedly had an affair with a Roman soldier while she was engaged to Joseph. When Mary was found to be pregnant, the soldier and Joseph both abandoned her, and Mary wound up giving birth to Jesus alone. As a document, the discourse by Celsus is not unusual; by the late second century, there were several pagan authors taking aim at a religious sect that they considered un-Roman and hostile to the state.[36] What is remarkable, however, is that Celsus is somehow able to identify Mary's Roman paramour *by name.* He is called Pantera or Pandera.

The idea that Jesus was the result of an illicit liaison would return in rabbinical literature of the fourth century, when Judaism suddenly found itself on the defensive. By this time, the Roman Empire had embraced Christianity, and its former tolerance toward Judaism was rapidly waning. Prodded by the need to deny Christianity its foundation in Hebrew Scripture, one rabbinical text picks up Celsus's claim and gleefully refers to Jesus as *Yeshu ben Pandera,* Jesus, son of "Pandera."

Through the centuries, historians have dismissed the accusation by Celsus as an ill-disguised attempt at slander—until 1859, that is. In that year, the spade of a construction worker building a railroad in Germany hit a stone. When brought to light, it turned out to be a tombstone of a Roman archer of the I Cohort, which read:

TIBERIUS IULIUS ABDES PANTERA SIDONIA

ANN • LXII • STIPEN • XXXX • MIII • SIXS •

COH • I • SAGITTARIORUM

The tombstone referred to a man named Tiberius Iulius Abdes Pantera who lived from 22 B.C.E. to 40 C.E. According to the inscription, Pantera was born in Sidon in Phoenicia and served during the reign of the emperor Tiberius. Roman records further confirm that the I Cohort *Sagittariorum* was stationed in Palestine in 9 C.E. and then served in Germany from 40 to 70 C.E. It is thus conceivable that this archer *could* have been in the vicinity of Nazareth at the time of Mary's pregnancy.

The discovery would have given scholars pause, were it not for the fact that Celsus's accusation is not found in any other source from either the first or second century C.E. It does not appear in any of the polemic exchanges between Christian and pagan authors before 178 C.E., even though many a pagan polemicist would gladly have seized on it in order to substantiate his case against Christ. Moreover, Celsus's allegation originated not in Palestine but, most likely, in Egypt, where relations between Hellenists and Jews (and by extension, Judeo-Christians) had always been tense.

A further argument against the Pantera theory is that Joseph did not abandon Mary, as he most surely would have done if Mary (voluntarily or involuntarily) had been with another man—and a pagan at that. All available material indicates that Joseph did do "the right thing" and agree to take Mary as his wife. This is further evidenced by the fact that after Jesus, Mary had a number of other children. According to Mark and Matthew, Jesus had four younger brothers and an unspecified number of sisters.[37] How Celsus would have stumbled on the name of Pantera, however, remains a mystery.

JESUS AND THE HOUSE OF DAVID

Even though the Nativity narratives in Matthew and Luke diverge on key points, it seems that they—each in their own way—try to establish three salient ideas about the Young Jesus:

> (1) Jesus, through his father Joseph, was of the house
> of David, and therefore a bona fide pretender to
> the title of Messiah;

> (2) Jesus was conceived *before* his parents Mary and
> Joseph entered wedlock;

> (3) Jesus' conception occurred as a result of the
> intercession of the Holy Spirit, to substantiate
> Luke's claim that Jesus will be called "the Son of
> the Most High," the recipient of "the throne of
> his ancestor David."

Of all of these themes, only the first, the claim that Jesus was of the House of David, is echoed elsewhere in the New Testament. The other two appear only in the Nativity cycles of Matthew and Luke and, once dispensed with, never reappear anywhere else in these two Gospels.

By contrast, the idea of Jesus' Davidic lineage through Joseph is reiterated in several other Christian texts. It is attested, for one thing, in the epistles of Paul, which as we have noted are among the oldest extant Christian texts, dating from the 50s C.E., only twenty years or so removed from the crucifixion. In the opening salutation of his letter to the Romans, for example, usually dated around 58 C.E., Paul states that Jesus "was descended from David according to the flesh."[38] This statement is not further explained, which leads us to think that the community of Christians in Rome, whom Paul had not yet met, already held to this belief. In the second Epistle to Timothy, probably written by a disciple of Paul on his behalf, we are again exhorted to "remember Jesus Christ, raised from the dead, a descendant of David" (*ek spermatos David,* literally "from the seed of David").[39] Another pseudonymous letter, attributed to Paul, makes the case even more forcefully that "it is evident that our Lord was descended from Judah."[40] The Davidic claim is later reiterated in Mark and the book of Acts as well.

It seems therefore reasonable to assume that very shortly after Jesus' crucifixion, and possibly during his lifetime, his followers believed that Jesus had Davidic blood in his veins as a result of the parentage of Joseph and was thus a member of the southern tribe of Judah. It is impossible to determine whether this assumption was inspired by the belief in Jesus' Messianic role or based on an authentic tradition about Joseph's origins. Suffice it to say that even though Joseph most likely lived in Nazareth at the time of his betrothal, it is possible that his family traced their roots to Judah and ultimately to the House of David in Bethlehem.

With the themes of Mary's premarital pregnancy and the so-called "virginal conception," we confront the two most difficult and mysterious themes in the tradition about Jesus' birth. The issue is made even more enigmatic by the apparent differences between Luke's and Matthew's Nativity stories. On the one hand, the evangelists make the case that Jesus descends from the House of David through "the seed" of his father Joseph; on the other, each states (though not necessarily in unambiguous language) that Jesus was *not* conceived by Joseph having intercourse with Mary, but by the intervention of the Holy Spirit. By trying to have it both ways, the evangelists weave an almost impossible plot that over the centuries has generated streams of theological ink. But the bottom line remains that Jesus cannot be both the product of a divinely engendered virginal conception *and* the issue of Joseph's seed.

Perhaps a solution to this dilemma (and the source of these seemingly conflicting statements) is found in the book of 2 Samuel. Here we find God's promise to David that he will be the founder of a dynasty: "I will raise up *your* offspring after you, *who shall come forth from your body,* and I will establish his kingdom. . . . I will be *a* father to him, and he shall be *a* son to me."[41] This revealing statement tells us a few things. One, it shows that, to observant Jews, the idea that a child born from a mortal man of Davidic lineage could still be *like a son* to God, just as God could be *like a father* to him. The agency of this "adoption" by God is the Holy Spirit.

Throughout the Old Testament, we read of prophets favored by "God's Spirit," including Elijah,[42] Samuel, and David. It seems to me that Matthew, and particularly Luke, seized upon this verse in 2 Samuel to conflate two arguments: that Jesus (through Joseph) was a direct descendant of David, and that through the divine Spirit, Jesus was *like a son* to God, and God *like a father* to him.

The fact that both evangelists use this argument to "explain" the premarital pregnancy of Mary may suggest that her rather controversial condition is rooted in an authentic tradition too prominent to ignore. Joseph's decision to "take in" Mary despite her pregnancy is also an indication that from a strictly historical perspective, Joseph probably was the biological father, or that at least he may have thought he was the biological father. As far as the "virginal conception" is concerned, this is a spiritual matter that falls outside the scope of this book. If a virtual impregnation did occur, we lack the historical data to corroborate it. Instead, several scholars have argued that the idea of Mary conceiving as a virgin was inspired by the reference to "a virgin" in the Greek translation of Isaiah.

Regardless of these arguments, however, the *symbolic* meaning of the Nativity narratives is clear. With their stories, both Matthew and Luke forcefully make the point that the young Jesus, even before his birth, was favored by the spirit of God.[43]

TWO

HEROD AND
THE BIRTH OF JESUS

Perhaps the most amazing thing about Herod the Great's kingdom is that it was allowed to exist at all. His reign—remarkable for its thirty-three-year length, from 37 to 4 B.C.E.—coincided, after all, with Rome's decision to flex its muscle and bring a vast swath of the Near East under its control. The purpose of these new conquests was to provide Rome with strategic buffer states in the region—not only to contain the tiresome Parthians, heirs to the Persian Empire, but also to secure Rome's access to the granaries of Egypt. Syria and Palestine both fit that prescription to a T. And as it happened, Rome was presented with a perfect pretext to invade Palestine and make it the property of the emperor. The Hasmonean monarchy, established as a result of the Maccabean Revolt in the second century C.E., was tottering. After the aging Queen Alexandra's death in 67 B.C.E., two of her sons had vied for the throne: Hyrcanus II and his younger brother Aristobulus II. In order to boost his claim, Hyrcanus made the fateful decision of turning to outsiders for help. He appealed to an Arab people known as the Nabataeans, who occupied a territory roughly corresponding to southern Jordan today. The result was a messy civil war between the two rival pretenders and their forces, which dragged on for four years, from 67 to 63 B.C.E.

Their struggle coincided with the arrival of a redoubtable Roman general named Pompeius Magnus (Pompey the Great), who had just moved his legions into Syria after a successful intervention in the Third Mithridatic War. Pompey decided to take up residence in the Syrian city of Damascus, a strategic place, for it was the last major city on the north–south trade route between Persia and the Hasmonean kingdom. When news of Pompey's arrival reached Jerusalem, three separate Jewish delegations immediately set out to visit the Roman general and lobby for Roman support of their claims: the Aristobulus faction, the Hyrcanus faction, and a group of pious laymen called the Pharisees, who previously had led violent protests against the crimes of a former Hasmonean king, Alexander Jannaeus. The Pharisees urged a third alternative on Pompey: namely, to do away with the Hasmoneans altogether.

Pompey reflected on the situation and made up his mind: he gathered his armies and conquered the Hasmonean kingdom himself. Thus the flame of Jewish independence that had flickered for less than a century following the Maccabean Revolt was extinguished forever. Pompey then installed Hyrcanus II as a puppet king, a ruler in name only, for Judea had once again been reduced to the status of a vassal state.

THE RISE OF HEROD

These political developments were keenly observed by an Idumaean chieftain called Antipater. Idumaea was the southern region encompassing today's Negev and southern Jordan (the biblical Edom), which had been annexed to the Hasmonean kingdom by John Hyrcanus (135–104 B.C.E.). Following his conquest, John Hyrcanus had forced all Idumaeans to convert to Judaism, even though ethnically these people were Arab rather than Jewish. Antipater, a prominent man in the region and a close adviser to Hyrcanus II, figured that a show of support for Rome would boost his family's fortunes. In this he was not disappointed. No sooner had Pompey established himself in Judea than Antipater rushed to his side, pledging his wholehearted support for the Roman cause. Pompey, both surprised and pleased by this show of allegiance, invited Antipater into his circle, where he soon met a general by the name of Julius Caesar.

Antipater's lobbying efforts paid off when he was appointed *epitropos*, a position something like "prime minister" of Judea, under the nominal supervision of an increasingly enfeebled Hyrcanus II. Furthermore, Caesar granted Antipater Roman citizenship, an extraordinary honor in the late Republican period. In 47 B.C.E., Antipater was also able to secure two prominent positions for his sons: Phasael was appointed governor of Judea and Perea, and Herod was given the province of Galilee.[1]

The young Herod took to his new position with a vengeance. When Cassius, one of the assassins of Julius Caesar, appealed to Antipater for seven hundred talents so he could raise an army to fight Mark Antony, Herod squeezed the Galilean peasants with ruinous taxes until they produced the needed cash. Those unable to pay the tribute, such as the villages of Gophna, Emmaus, and Thamna, were sold into slavery.[2]

Young Herod, however, soon faced determined opposition in Galilee. A group of rebels, led by a man named Hezekiah, refused to accept the Roman occupation and was steadily building a resistance movement that could operate throughout the Galilean countryside. Josephus, writing at the behest of a Roman imperial house, calls Hezekiah a "bandit," an epithet given to most characters in his book who dare to challenge the sovereignty of Rome. It is quite possible, however, that Hezekiah was not an outlaw but a local nobleman, a member of the rural landed gentry who owed their wealth, title, and lands to the Hasmonean House. It is plausible that during the civil war between the two pretenders, Hezekiah had thrown his support behind the ill-fated claim of the Aristobulus faction. Naturally, these country sires would have bitterly opposed the regime of Hyrcanus and Antipater, who so openly collaborated with the Roman occupation. Staunchly loyal to the ideal of Hasmonean nationalism, they would have been determined to restore Jewish autonomy in Palestine before the Romans would be able to consolidate their control of the country.

However, Antipater's son Herod, the newly appointed governor of Galilee, was not prepared to take Hezekiah's rebellion lying down, not while he still had the loyalty of Rome. Fanning out across the hills and fields of Galilee, Herod's militia (which probably consisted of Roman auxiliaries or Greek mercenaries) was able to track the resistance leader down. Bloody clashes erupted at Sepphoris, Arbel, and a fortress in Northern Galilee, possibly Qeren Naftali.[3] Hezekiah was arrested, brought before a sham tribunal, and summarily executed. That would have been the last of it, had Herod's brutal tactics not been reported to King Hyrcanus.[4] On top of that, the mothers of the rebels who had been summarily slain by Herod rose in anger and decided to stage daily protest demonstrations in the Temple.

We can imagine the "publicity" this must have generated if we recall the weekly demonstrations by the mothers of the victims of the Argentine junta in the 1970s—a protest movement potent enough to ultimately contribute to the downfall of the regime. Standing in the Temple, the Jewish mothers, too, were determined to get satisfaction for their grievances. They insisted that Herod be tried by the Great Sanhedrin, the Priestly Council in Jerusalem, for it was the Sanhedrin that had the right to hear capital offenses—an interesting foreshadowing of what would happen to another Galilean dissident some sixty years later. Herod saw the writing on the wall and decided to cooperate—for the time being. He duly made an appearance in front of the Sanhedrin in Jerusalem, but was careful to surround himself with a private guard of well-armed soldiers. The members of the Sanhedrin, many of whom were deeply loyal to the Hasmonean House, were not intimidated. They heard the prosecution's case, deliberated its merits, and soon reached a consensus that the upstart governor should be condemned to death.

Tipped off to this development, Hyrcanus was filled with dread. He knew that Antipater, possibly the most powerful man in the land, would never allow his son to be put on the scaffold. Rather than risk a new civil war, Hyrcanus urged Herod to flee the city. Herod took his advice and raced to Damascus, where he knew he would be assured of Roman protection. Sextus Caesar, the Roman governor of Syria, did not disappoint him. Given Antipater's loyalty to the Roman cause, Sextus not only rebuffed the Sanhedrin's stringent demands for Herod's extradition but blithely appointed Herod as ruler of southern Syria and Samaria. Soon thereafter, when the dust had settled, Herod was quietly reinstated as governor of Galilee. No sooner had Herod arrived than he vented his wrath on the Galilean gentry that had opposed him.

What is significant about the Cassius and Hezekiah affairs is that they created a deep-seated enmity between Herod and the population of Galilee that would cast a long shadow over the adolescence of Jesus. Indeed, it is no exaggeration to say that the source of the terrible socioeconomic upheaval among the Galilean peasantry was rooted in Hezekiah's revolt and the brutal reprisal by an insecure and inexperienced governor, later to be known as Herod the Great.

And then fate intervened. The growing power of Antipater's family was temporarily thrown into disarray when, in 40 B.C.E., the meddlesome Parthians decided to invade Judea. Ostensibly, this intervention was at the behest of a more recent contender to the tottering Hasmonean throne, namely Antigonus, the son of Aristobulus II, though it is debatable whether the Parthians would have ever left Palestine. The invasion had its desired effect. The weak King Hyrcanus was ousted and Antipater's family was toppled from power. Gripped by panic, his son Phasael committed suicide. Young Herod, however, had no such intention. He quickly placed his family in the safety of a Hasmonean fortress on a high rock plateau near the Dead Sea, known as Masada, and then appealed for sanctuary in the Nabataean kingdom. The Nabataeans refused, after which Herod made a beeline for Rome.

Once in the capital of the Roman empire, Herod strenuously pleaded for Roman support. His oratory and genteel manners impressed the Romans, specifically Herod's patron, Mark Antony. Invited to address the Roman Senate, a rare honor, Herod was able to convince this august body that the Parthian invasion of Palestine was, in fact, a direct challenge to Roman sovereignty in the Near East. The senators agreed. They not only promptly voted him king and heir to the Hasmonean kingdom, but they also granted him a Roman army to ensure that he actually got to enjoy his throne.

Buoyed by this support, Herod, accompanied by his Roman forces, landed in Palestine in 39 B.C.E., steadily fought his way to Jerusalem, and besieged the capital city. Two years later, after a bloody battle, he was able to capture Jerusalem and oust Antigonus. The unfortunate boy-king was captured and later executed by the Romans. So were the judges of the Sanhedrin who had voted for Herod's execution following the Hezekiah affair.

Now all of Herod's ambitions had been realized. For the next thirty-three years, he would rule with greater autonomy than any other monarch in the region, backed by the awesome power of Rome, with jurisdiction over a territory that very nearly matched the legendary kingdom of Israel of David and Solomon.

There was only one problem: that Herod himself was not Jewish at all. This violated the kingly rule in Deuteronomy that only "one from among you brethren shall you set as king over you; you may not put a foreigner over you."[5] What's more, though outwardly Herod observed (or claimed to observe) the Covenant Law, in temperament the king remained an Arab, and a pro-Roman Arab at that. To counter the lingering questions about his legitimacy, Herod embarked on a vast campaign to adorn his country as few kings had done before him. A royal Roman vassal to the last, unencumbered by Jewish cultic scruples, he launched a grandiose construction plan that saw the establishment of Hellenistic temples, theaters, and even a gymnasium—an institution despised by Jews for the presence of young men working out in the nude. Herod's *Baulust,* his zest for construction, culminated in the creation, from scratch, of a city and harbor on the Mediterranean coast, named Caesarea in honor of Caesar's heir, Octavian, now called Caesar Augustus. The purpose of this technically ambitious enterprise was to give Judea its own industrial-sized harbor, reducing its reliance on foreign ports such as Sidon and Tyre. Josephus tells us that in order to create a breakwater large enough to accommodate Rome's huge grain ships and trireme naval vessels, Herod's architects created a vast breakwater with sluice gates, built by dropping huge blocks of stone, "fifty feet in length, not less than eighteen in breadth, and nine in depth," into water "twenty fathoms" deep.

Herod knew, however, that many of his subjects viewed him as an illegitimate usurper and a Jewish *poseur,* a man who had climbed to the throne on the back of an occupying army and had no royal pedigree whatsoever. He sought to wrap his ambitions in a cloak of legitimacy by marrying the Hasmonean princess Mariamne, granddaughter of Aristobulus II, in 38 B.C.E. The marriage had the additional benefit of preempting the ambitions of Mariamne's brother, Aristobulus III, who was the legitimate heir in the Hasmonean line.

To Herod's Jewish subjects, however, such chicanery mattered little. Many Jews not only resented Herod as an interloper, but also despised the king's embrace of Hellenistic—ergo, *pagan*—culture with the construction of opulent palaces, theaters, and Roman temples, often built (as in the case of Samaria, renamed Sebastos) on the ruins of ancient Jewish structures.

Herod's response was twofold. Whenever it suited him, he made a show of acceding to the peculiar cultic sensitivities of his Jewish population. He took pains to divorce his first wife Doris, before marrying Mariamne, lest his marriage give offense to conservative Jews, who in New Testament times were strictly monogamous. Moreover, he made sure that coins struck during his reign avoided the usual portrait of the Roman emperor, or any other representation of humans or animals that could offend the Jewish prohibition on graven images. When in 24 B.C.E. a severe drought led to an outbreak of famine, he organized a vast relief effort and imported large quantities of grain from Egypt. Lastly, in a bold strike to curry favor with his subjects, Herod launched a massive expansion of the Second Temple in Jerusalem, which had been rebuilt in 515 B.C.E. after its destruction by the Neo-Babylonian king Nebuchadnezzar in 586 B.C.E.

As part of this expansion, Herod created a vast esplanade around the original Temple precinct. Since the Temple area was perched on a hill known as Temple Mount, this ambitious design required the construction of massive support walls, which, in essence, created a vast platform towering high above the Lower City of Jerusalem. Covering no less than one-sixth the area of the city, this huge esplanade was accessible through two "floating" staircases on the west, each supported by arches. A small portion of one of these arches, known as Robinson's Arch, is still visible today, as are the monumental stairs that led to the Double Gate on the south. The Western Wall in Jerusalem, which today is the holiest place of Judaism, is in fact one of these mammoth Herodian supporting walls. Construction on the Temple expansion was begun in 22 B.C.E. and was still in full swing when Jesus visited the Temple during the Passover of 30 C.E. The Temple area was only finished in 62 C.E., and it stood for a mere eight years—until its destruction at the hands of the Roman general Titus in 70 C.E. near the end of the Jewish War.

On the other hand, the rising hatred of his subjects toward their sovereign prompted Herod to create a police state not unlike the totalitarian regimes of the mid-twentieth century. Prominent officials and citizens were ordered to swear an oath of allegiance to Herod. Everyone arousing even the slightest suspicion was closely watched by Herod's secret police. Citizens were encouraged to inform on one another; "even in the cities and on the open roads, there were men who spied on those who met together," says Josephus. Dissidents were caught and "disappeared"—they were dispatched to concentration centers in Herod's fortresses, such as the Hyrcania, and executed without trial.[6] Furthermore, Herod encircled his kingdom with a string of fortresses, both to keep invaders out and to defend against any dangers from within.

Herod's vast construction program, and the growing trade with Roman possessions on the Mediterranean through Caesarea, created a boom economy—but a boom that mostly benefited the upper crust of Jewish society: the merchants, the priestly elite of the Sadducees, and Herodian officials eager to collaborate with the Roman occupiers. Beneath the Herodian veneer of Hellenistic gentility, however, the country seethed with unrest. The majority of Jews, if not pressed into work gangs on Herod's projects, remained disenfranchised. They would soon be forced to bear a burden that would, quite literally, tear the ancient fabric of Israelite peasant culture to shreds.

THE SADDUCEES

Originally, the highly conservative, priestly-aristocratic families known collectively as the Sadducees had observed the rise of Herod with alarm. As we have seen, a priestly elite had governed Judea as a *de facto* autonomous government since the days of Cyrus the Great, when Ezra and Nehemiah struggled to restore a society based on Covenant Law. Even during Ptolemaic and Seleucid occupation, the colonial governors had gladly deferred the adjudication of civil matters and minor crimes to the priesthood, specifically the Priestly Council of the Sanhedrin, which had jurisdiction over both religious and domestic matters.

Ever since the Hasmonean period, control over the Sanhedrin was contested by two parties: the Sadducees on the one hand, and the predominantly lay brotherhood known as the Pharisees on the other (although many Pharisees were priests as well). The relations between the Sadducees and the Hasmoneans had been strained ever since the Hasmoneans had combined the role of king and high priest. This violated the tradition that the office of the high priest should be held by descendants of Solomon's high priest Zadok (hence the term "Zadokites," which may be the root of the name "Sadducees"). Faced with Sadducee opposition, the Hasmonean kings struck a compromise: the Sadducees were given majority control of the Sanhedrin as well as the administration of the Temple and its sacrificial system, in return for Sadducee support of the Hasmonean regime.

Of course, this did not sit well with the principal opposition to the Sadducees, namely the Pharisaic party. The Pharisees strenuously opposed the militaristic and Hellenistic tendencies of the Hasmonean rulers and objected to Sadducee control of the Temple. Things came to a head when the Hasmonean king Alexander Jannaeus, officiating as high priest, deliberately bungled a libation ceremony, pouring the water on his feet rather than on the altar. A crowd of protestors, many Pharisees among them, promptly pelted him with fruit. Furious, Alexander struck back by initiating a bloody persecution of Pharisees that by Josephus's count cost the lives of fifty thousand Jews. According to one story, some eight hundred Pharisees were crucified in public while Alexander and his concubines reclined to enjoy the spectacle.[7] Naturally, this development further bolstered the influence of the Sadducees, but during the reign of Alexander's successor, the Hasmonean queen Salome Alexandra, the pendulum swung back toward the Pharisaic party.

Herod knew all about the history of the Sadducees and Pharisees, but he firmly resolved that neither party would interfere with his plans. He allowed the Sadducees to retain control of Temple operations, but then slyly imported priestly families from Babylonia from which he could appoint high officials—including the high priest—whose loyalty to Herod would be unquestioned. One such family favored by the Herodian dynasty was the house of Ananas—a man whose son-in-law, Caiaphas, would soon sit in judgment of Jesus.

That Herod was an Arab rather than a Jew mattered less to the Sadducees than their continued grip on the Temple and its treasury. Now that the collection of the Temple Tax was protected and facilitated by the Romans, massive amounts of money flowed into the coffers of the Temple, bolstering the power of the Sadducees tenfold, for which they were heartily despised by Judeans and Galileans alike.

THE PHARISEES

These developments left the Pharisees not only bereft of political power, but also deeply resentful of everything that Herod stood for. The Pharisees were not primarily a priestly aristocratic faction; they were a group of pious laymen passionately devoted to the application of Covenant Law. Whereas the Sadducees (naturally) emphasized the sacrificial cult as the only redemptive activity in Jewish life, the Pharisees felt that man should please God in virtually every action of everyday life, particularly when it came to matters of purity. The Pharisaic concern for ritual observance, so often maligned in the Gospels, was really an attempt to transfer the priestly rules governing purity from the Temple to the home—giving, in effect, every man the opportunity to serve as a priest of God.

This explains the great popularity enjoyed by the Pharisees in Palestine, particularly in urban areas. Against the arrogant and haughty attitude of the Sadducees, the Pharisees offered a populist and progressive attitude toward observance of the Law. For example, whereas the Sadducees considered the written texts of the Hebrew Scriptures a closed book, the Pharisees continued to debate and interpret the application of Scripture to everyday life, a corpus of wisdom and exegesis that became known as the Oral Law. In the process, the Pharisees developed detailed rules governing food preparation, ritual bathing, tithing, and Sabbath observance—matters that, in later years, they would sometimes debate quite vigorously with a certain itinerant rabbi from Nazareth.

What is so interesting for our story is that the Pharisees embraced the Hellenistic idea of the immortality of the soul, as well as the belief in the resurrection after Judgment Day—two concepts that would return in the teachings of Jesus. It was the Pharisees who articulated the idea that immoral souls are punished, while righteous souls pass into immortality.[8]

Socially, too, the Pharisees were distinct from the wealthy priestly aristocracy dominated by the Sadducees. Pharisee support could usually be found among the professional "middle class," including scribes, teachers, tradesmen, merchants, and trained craftsmen. Their leaders formed a minority position on the Great Sanhedrin; but, because of their support among the urban elites of the country, their influence was still strong.

Despite the support of the Sadducees, despite the full backing of Roman power, despite all the wealth and glory of his kingdom, Herod still remained an intensely suspicious man. His innate insecurity, rooted in the illegitimacy of his house and his collusion with Roman ambition, needed an outlet. He found it in the chimera of conspiracy—not only among his subjects, but also among his family. In the inner circles of his Idumaean court, he could let his paranoia roam free without fear of provoking a rebellion. Aristobulus III, Mariamne's brother and heir to the Hasmonean throne, drowned under suspicious circumstances one year after Herod had him appointed high priest. The lad was only seventeen years old. The king then ordered the execution of the old Hasmonean king, Hyrcanus II, in 30

B.C.E., even though the man was nearing eighty and had long since given up hope of reclaiming power.

In the following year, Herod's distrust turned on his wife, Mariamne, by now the mother of five of his children, even though he loved her to distraction. Herod suspected her of having an affair, perhaps even of plotting against him, and ordered her freedom sharply curtailed. One day, when he lay down to rest, he called for her and asked her to sleep with him. Mariamne refused, which for Herod was the last straw. He ordered his wife to be put on trial on a trumped-up charge. There, she suffered the humiliation of seeing both her sister and her mother appear as witnesses for the prosecution. The outcome was never in doubt; Mariamne was convicted and executed. Herod then turned his wrath on Mariamne's mother, Alexandra, who was put on the scaffold in 28 B.C.E., followed by Herod's brother-in-law, Costobar. Many more family members would be put to death in the years to come.

Mariamne's death only intensified the king's desire for her. "He would wander around the palace," says Josephus, "calling for his wife and ordering the servants to bring her to him."[9] As he grew older, his insanity increased, as did his paranoia. He escalated the search for political dissidents among his population. Still distrustful of the reports of his agents, the king himself went out at night, dressed as a commoner, to learn what the people thought of him. The feedback could not have been any too favorable.

DATING THE BIRTH OF JESUS

The Gospels give us little insight into Herod's reign. One reason may be that at the time of Mark's writing, Herod's rule was nearly seventy years in the past and already a fading memory. Nevertheless, both Matthew and Luke place the birth of Jesus in exactly this time period, "in the time of King Herod," which we assume must be the waning days of Herod's reign.[10]

Luke, who is more concerned about the historical context of his story than any of the other evangelists, provides additional information about the moment of Jesus' birth. Unfortunately, his dating system has confounded scholars no end. "In those days," says Luke, "a decree went out from Emperor Augustus that all the world should be registered." By "all the world," Luke meant the Roman Empire; and, indeed, Roman governors occasionally did order a comprehensive census of subjects in their allotted territories. Such a census had but one goal: to create a comprehensive inventory of tax-paying individuals and their property, so that an accurate forecast of the region's tax yields could be drawn up. A forecast was important, because the Roman occupation authorities did not collect the taxes themselves. They "outsourced" this activity to free agents known as tax collectors or publicans. By making a comprehensive assessment of projected tax revenues from a given territory, therefore, the Romans were able to give these publicans a well-informed benchmark that they were expected to meet if they didn't want to be suspected of cheating.

Luke gives us additional information about this putative census by Augustus, telling us that it was "the first registration" (i.e., since the beginning of the Roman conquest of Palestine) and that it was taken on orders of "Quirinius, governor of Syria."[11] At first glance, this appears to be accurate. Even in Herod's day, as we have seen, Judea formed part of the greater Roman province of Syria, so that Herod, in effect, "reported" to the governor based in the Syrian capital, Antioch. The problem, however, is that in Herod's time, the Syrian governor was not Quirinius at all, but a man named Sentius Saturninus, who served in office from 9 to 6 B.C.E. He, in turn, was succeeded by Quinctilius Varus, who ruled from 6 to 4 B.C.E., the year of Herod's death. There *was* a governor in Syria named Quirinius, but he did not enter office until 6 C.E., a full ten years *after* the death of Herod.[12]

The link with Quirinius is not the only problem we have with Luke's dating system. Another, and more substantial, problem is the very mechanism of a Roman census. While Herod was still in power, it fell to Herod's government to collect the taxes in his realm, rather than to the Romans. It was only *after* Herod's death, and the subsequent dismissal of his son Archilaus as ruler of Judea, that the Romans decided to take charge of the administrative control of this region themselves. Judea became, in effect, a Roman sub-province under the supervision of a Roman career diplomat, subordinate to the Roman governor in Syria, with the title of prefect. This meant that the Romans now took direct responsibility for tax collecting in the area. Since they had no idea what Judea was worth in terms of projected tax revenues, the then-governor, quite possibly the same Quirinius referred to in Luke, ordered a census to be taken. The thing is, however, that this census pertained only to the sub-province of Judea and *not* to Galilee, for Galilee remained under the control of one of Herod's other sons, Herod Antipas. Therefore, the census would not have affected Joseph's or Mary's family in any way.

Lastly, even if there had been such a census, and even if by some stretch of the imagination Joseph would have been compelled to register, he would not have traveled to Bethlehem at all, even if—as the Gospels tell us—Joseph's family originally hailed from that village. The whole purpose of a Roman census was to update the mechanism of *taxation*. Therefore, the Romans would have wanted people to appear in their current place of residence, where the tax man could find them, rather than in the place of their ancestral home, which in some cases could have been many miles away. And as Luke makes eminently clear, Joseph and Mary resided in Nazareth, in Galilee.

THE IMPORTANCE OF BETHLEHEM

No matter how we look at it, there is no way to reconcile the double attestation by Matthew and Luke that Jesus was born during the reign of Herod the Great with Luke's suggestion that the birth was preceded by a Roman census. Why, then, does Luke introduce the story of the census to begin with?

The answer lies, once again, in the language of Old Testament symbolism with which Luke "illustrates" his story. As we have seen, both Matthew and Luke are at pains to place the birth of Jesus in the hamlet of Bethlehem, lest his birth fail to meet the criterion that he "who is to rule in Israel" shall come from Bethlehem, where King David himself was born.[13] To make this happen, Matthew and Luke avail themselves of different scenarios. Matthew avoids any reference to Mary and Joseph's place of residence, and obliquely implies that both were living in Bethlehem at the time of the birth. Luke, who is more concerned about historical authenticity, cannot bring himself to deny that Mary was a resident of Nazareth. But he still must find a way to get Joseph and Mary down to Judea, to the little town of Bethlehem, in time for her to give birth to Jesus. It is quite possible that Luke knew that at one point a Roman census had been conducted in Palestine, and he probably seized on this historical footnote as a pretext for getting Joseph and Mary to travel to Bethlehem.

It is possible that Luke may not have been aware that the governorship of Quirinius did *not* overlap with the reign of Herod the Great. On the other hand, he may have confused the Quirinius census with one that, according to the Roman author Tertullian, took place in Syria under the governorship of Saturninus, who ruled from 8 to 7 B.C.E. This census has not been attested anywhere else, however, and it is very doubtful that this Syrian census would have included the kingdom of Herod, which, as we have seen, was an autonomous tax-collecting territory at the time. But then again, historical accuracy was a relative concept in first-century Palestine. Outside the imperial libraries in Rome, Caesarea, or Antioch proper, there would have been few places where Luke (or his readers, for that matter) could have consulted any archives to verify the dates for his story.[14]

An interesting footnote to the question of Jesus' birth date is provided by Matthew. In his Gospel, three wise men (or "kings") are alerted to the birth of Jesus by the appearance of a bright star: "Where is he that is born King of the Jews? For we have seen his star in the east, and are come to worship him."[15] Some 1600 years later, on the evening of December 17, 1603, the astronomer Johannes Kepler pointed his rudimentary telescope to the night sky. His eye was soon drawn to a bright conjunction of the planets Jupiter and Saturn in the constellation of Pisces. Working his way backward, he calculated that a very similar phenomenon must have occurred in 7 B.C.E. A devout Lutheran, Kepler immediately identified this phenomenon with the "star in the east" described by Matthew.

Babylonian astrologers would have agreed. In 1925, the German scholar P. Schnabel deciphered a cuneiform inscription from the ancient astrological archives of Babylon that contained an observation of Jupiter and Saturn. Their convergence in Pisces had been recorded over a period of five months in the year 7 B.C.E.—exactly the date postulated by Kepler.

What makes this observation even more intriguing is its echo in the fifteenth-century writings of a rabbinical sage known as Abravanel (1437–1508), who prophesied that when Saturn and Jupiter conjoined in Pisces, the Messiah would come. This argument was based not on observation, but on ancient Jewish exegesis and astrology. In rabbinical writings, the House of Israel was sometimes identified with the constellation of Pisces as symbol of the Messiah. In this context, the planet Jupiter symbolized the royal star of the house of David, and Saturn was the protecting star of Israel.

There is no way of verifying whether the symbolic meaning of Pisces was already current in first-century Palestine, whether Matthew was familiar with such symbolism, or whether, indeed, the "star in the east" is in any way related to the conjunction of Jupiter and Saturn, which could have easily been observed with the naked eye. One only has to travel into the Judean desert to get an idea of how impossibly clear the unpolluted night sky over first-century Judea would have been, undimmed by the lights of today's urban centers. In such an environment, any planet, whether Venus, Jupiter, or Saturn, could easily have been taken for a "bright star."

An entirely different explanation for Matthew's "star from the east" comes from China, where Chinese astronomers during the Han Dynasty recorded their observation of what was probably a supernova in the year 5 B.C.E. This supernova, Chinese records show, was observed for at least "seventy days."

Clearly, it is impossible to date the birth of Jesus with any accuracy. The one date that most scholars do accept as definite, however, is the death of Herod the Great. Josephus tells us that the death of the monarch was accompanied by a lunar eclipse. Modern astronomers have ascertained that such an eclipse would indeed have occurred over Judea, sometime between Sunday, March 12, 4 B.C.E., and the Passover eve of Wednesday, April 11, 4 B.C.E.

In sum, if we assume that Matthew and Luke are correct and that Jesus was born in the waning days of Herod's reign, then it seems logical to assume that his birth took place sometime between 7 and 4 B.C.E.

WHERE WAS JESUS BORN?

The issue of whether Jesus was born in Bethlehem or not is one with which scholars tend to grapple rather gingerly, knowing full well how deeply the image of the manger, the stable, and the shepherds has entrenched itself in our Christian culture. Once again, we must try to separate the symbolic message from the factual one, and from that point of view the story of the manger in Bethlehem is no less valid than any historical reality. Luke was not only seeking a correlation with Micah's prophecy, but also trying to illustrate that Jesus came to this world in the most humble form possible, without any of the trappings of a traditional Jewish monarch. What's more, the image of the infant being rejected from Judea's inns must have struck a chord with Jesus' followers who, in Luke's time, were being ejected from communities all over Judea and Galilee.

From a strictly historical perspective, however, there is a growing consensus that Mary did not journey to Bethlehem in Judea as Luke would have us believe. The reasons are legion, but one stands out: such an arduous journey would have been unthinkable for a young, first-time mother in her last trimester. No sane individual, certainly not her husband, would have wished to impose the dangers and discomfort of such a five-day trek on her—least of all because, even if Luke is correct and there *was* a census, her presence would not have been required. It was the *man,* the head of the household, who went to be registered, not his wife.

The inevitable conclusion is that Jesus was probably born in Nazareth, either in Joseph's home or that of his parents. Bruce Chilton, author of *Rabbi Jesus,* has suggested an interesting variant of this possibility: namely, that Mary gave birth in a small hamlet located not more than two hours' walk from Nazareth,[16] called, of all things, "Bethlehem in Galilee." The idea that Mary could have gone to this village seems eminently plausible. Since the pregnancy was under a moral cloud, and possibly illegitimate, Mary would have preferred to give birth far away from the sneering stares of her neighbors. Perhaps her family had relatives in Bethlehem. And if this was indeed the case, then it is entirely possible (though not yet proven) that a stay in Bethlehem in Galilee could have inspired the tradition of Jesus being born in Bethlehem in Judea.

MARY GIVES BIRTH

The choice of where a young mother was to have her child was a very important decision, because in first-century Palestine, a peasant girl like Mary did not give birth in a hospital or under the care of a doctor. She instead had to rely on the people most qualified to assist her: the married women of the village, often under supervision of a midwife. Jewish customs recognized that women knew more about a woman's body than men—and with women in charge, no one needed to worry about modesty. So important was this collective obligation for women to help a mother-to-be that, according to the Mishnah, if a woman went into labor on the Sabbath, her female companions were given special dispensation to rush to her aid and assist her. Men were strictly out of bounds. They were left to hover in the distance until, as the book of Jeremiah suggests, someone "brought the news" to the father.

If Mary's mother was still alive, she would undoubtedly have assisted Mary as well. What's more, she would have done everything she could to prepare her teenage daughter for the tribulations of childbirth. Even so, the event would have been a harrowing experience, as it can be for any first-time mother.

There are few documents related to the practice of childbirth in Palestine. Much of what we know is inferred from Greek and Roman sources, including a tractate by a physician named Soranus of Ephesus in Asia Minor (today's western coast of Turkey). According to Soranus, who practiced in Ephesus some ninety years after the birth of Jesus, prenatal care began around the seventh month. At that time, linen bandages would have been tied around Mary's back and over her shoulders to relieve the burden of her growing abdomen. Soranus also recommended that expecting mothers massage their swollen bellies with olive oil and myrtle, so as to prevent stretch marks. After the eighth month, the support bandages were removed in order to let gravity take effect and allow the child to drop. Then, as the hour of labor approached, the woman was often bathed in warm, sweetened water to help her relax and let nature take its course.

When labor began at last, the midwife would be summoned. Casting a practiced eye on the rhythm of contractions, she would first set out the tools of her trade. This included a jar of pure olive oil; a large bowl for warm water; soft, natural sea sponges; clean linen; and special herbs. Then she would set to work. Mary would be placed on a soft blanket or straw mat on the floor. The midwife would dip her hands in the virgin oil spiced with herbs and gently begin to lubricate the birth canal. As the hours passed, the small room in which Mary lay would steadily begin to fill with excited women, enjoying this respite from their daily chores, each of them full of advice for the young mother-to-be.

At last, the moment came when the midwife pronounced the dilation nearly complete. The women gathered around Mary and gently helped the young girl to a special chair, known as a birthing stool. Essentially a sturdy wooden chair with special supports for the mother's arms, the stool had an opening in the seat for the delivery of the child. Once Mary was seated, the midwife placed a woman on either side of the chair and directed them to support Mary under her shoulders as the labor progressed. One other woman now used a sponge to wipe the perspiration off Mary's young body, while a fourth used olive oil to continue massaging the belly as the contractions increased. The midwife, meanwhile, crouched in front of Mary and whispered encouragement, steadily urging her to push.

Needless to say, Mary was in great pain, as any woman who has ever been in labor can attest. Modern pain medication was, of course, unheard of, although a discovery near Beth Shemesh may suggest that other methods could be used to assuage the discomfort: here, Israeli archaeologists found the burial site of a fourteen-year-old girl who had apparently died in childbirth. The tomb also contained a vial of seven grams of an unknown substance. Microscopic analysis, followed by a chromatography performed by the Hadassah Medical School, revealed that the material was *Cannabis sativa.* Such use is also documented in Egyptian papyri from around 1600 B.C.E. Apparently, hashish could be administered to mothers to increase their contractions, while also lessening the pain. A study by British medical researchers has corroborated the effectiveness of cannabis in "increasing the force of uterine contractions, along with a significant reduction of labor pain."[17]

If the birth was difficult, or if the baby was in breech position, the midwife could intervene by prodding the vaginal area and trying to move the baby down the birth canal. Once the head appeared, she would gently pull it downward until the child dropped cleanly into her waiting hands. A great sigh of relief from Mary would have been met with cries of joy from her female companions, followed by a prayer of thanks to YHWH.

The midwife now moved swiftly to cut the umbilical cord, first making sure that the afterbirth had separated from the uterus. She made the cut four finger-widths from the baby's belly with a sharp piece of iron, glass, reed, or other material, and tied it at the end with a string of woolen yarn. Next, she quickly wiped the blood off the infant Jesus with soft wool in order to proceed with the next step: to ascertain the baby's health and viability. She listened to his crying, checked his limbs, and prodded his body cavities for any sign of malformation—not unlike the Apgar scores given by nurses in modern birthing clinics. Once she pronounced Jesus a healthy boy—followed by another chorus of praise and thanksgiving—the baby was rinsed with warm water and sprinkled with a disinfectant such as powdered salt. The midwife's agile fingers cleaned the little nose, mouth, ears, and anus, and she gently washed the eyes with tiny drops of olive oil so as to wash off the birth residue.

Thus cleansed, Jesus was laid on the lap of the midwife and swaddled in wool or linen strips. The swaddling was tightened so that he was prevented from injuring his eyes with his fingers. Lastly, he was laid down on a pillow full of hay or on a mattress with a depressed channel, to prevent him from rolling over. Soranus's text advocated the use of a feeding trough as a cradle, since the trough's slight incline would prop up the baby's head— suggesting that Luke's portrayal of Jesus in a manger may reflect actual use. Mary, meanwhile, was gently moved from the birthing chair and back to her bed, there to lie back and rest while waiting for the moment to hold her newborn son in her arms.

This is the birthing scenario as Soranus presents it to us, and there is no reason to doubt that, by and large, the process would have been similar in a Galilean village. At this stage, however, the cultic precepts of Covenant Law took over.

For seven days after the birth of her male child, Mary was considered ritually unclean as her body slowly recovered from the strain of birth. (If her baby had been a daughter, the period would have been fourteen days.) Then, on the eighth day after birth, a male infant like Jesus was considered strong enough to undergo *berith,* or ritual circumcision, for at that point it was believed that the blood had developed the ability to coagulate. Luke, with his customary eye for authentic detail, confirms this: "After eight days had passed," his Gospel says, "it was time to circumcise the child." The circumcision usually took place in the center of the village, with all elders present.

The rite of circumcision also marked the moment when what had largely been a women's affair became the province of men. After the tiny foreskin of Jesus' penis was cut, the men rejoiced. The women, meanwhile, were busy laying out tables with fruits, barley cakes, and wine, and sometimes even a lamb or sheep was slaughtered to heighten the feast. It was also the moment for the father to formally accept the baby as his legitimate offspring. Joseph did so by giving the child its name, and he named it *Yeshu.* This is a shortened form of Joshua, the name of the great commander who conquered the Promised Land. Yeshu or "Jesus" was a very common name in first-century Palestine, similar to our John or Joe. Josephus mentions at least twenty men who are alternatively called "Jesus" or "Joshua"—ten of whom lived in the same period as Jesus of Nazareth.

For thirty-three days after the circumcision, Mary was exempt from all household chores. This was the period of "blood purification," which atoned for the impurity of her postpartum blood flow. It was also a special time for the young girl to revel in the joys of motherhood and bond with her newborn son, while the women in the village took care of her and her husband's needs. Though her impurity was no longer considered "contagious," she was still forbidden to touch anything holy, such as Scripture. What's more, Joseph was to abstain from having any sexual relations with her during the same period, not only because she was still impure, but also to allow her body to heal.

Once the thirty-three days were complete, Mary rejoined her young household as spouse and mother. In order to restore her purity, she offered sacrifice to YHWH. Leviticus prescribed a first-year lamb and a pigeon or dove for a burnt offering; but if the mother was poor, as young Mary probably was, she could substitute two pigeons or doves.

THE FLIGHT TO EGYPT

Matthew offers a coda to the story of the Bethlehem Nativity that does not appear anywhere else in the New Testament. As we have seen, the Matthew Gospel introduced "three wise men from the East" who wished to worship the newborn "king of the Jews" and were guided to Mary's "house" by a star. Before long, Matthew says, word of this extraordinary development reached King Herod, who right away was "troubled" and convened his "chief priests and scribes" in order to determine the location of this newborn child. These counselors readily recalled what was "written by the prophet," naturally the prophet Micah, that a prince would be born in Bethlehem, "who shall rule my people Israel." For Herod, a deeply suspicious man, this would have been very bad news indeed. Matthew clearly implies that Herod felt threatened by the birth of this putative "king of the Jews" and wanted to do away with the pretender while the babe was still in the cradle. Consequently, the child had to be located right away. But who knew where Mary's house was? According to Matthew, Herod decided on a piece of subterfuge, summoned the wise men (who had been the source of this birth story to begin with), and urged them to let him know when they found Mary's child in Bethlehem, "so that he could worship him also."[18]

Fortunately, both the wise men and Joseph (still the principal protagonist in Matthew's story) were warned of Herod's true intentions in a dream, whereupon the three sages immediately departed for their own country by using a different route. Joseph, meanwhile, gathered his young family and fled to Egypt posthaste, well outside the reach of Herod's henchmen.

In due course, Herod discovered that he'd been had, and that the wise men had fled to their own country without revealing the location of Mary's house. Matthew says that Herod exploded in anger and ordered that all the newborn children of Bethlehem, two years of age and younger, should be slain forthwith. And so it came to pass, the Gospel tells us; all the babes and toddlers of the village were put to the sword.

Did this extraordinary massacre take place? None of the other evangelists report this event; nor does the historian Josephus, who otherwise presents us with an exhaustive catalog of Herod's misdeeds. There is no question that Herod's reign, particularly near the end of his life, had become increasingly oppressive. Josephus calls him "a man of great barbarity toward all men equally, and a slave to his passion."[19] The Jewish historian also tells us that as Herod lay on his deathbed, knowing full well that his passing would elicit little mourning, he decided to make his death the occasion for great grief and sorrow, come what may. He ordered that all the "principal men" of Judea be rounded up and incarcerated in the stadium or "hippodrome" of Jerusalem. He then gave his military commanders strict instructions that the moment he gave up the ghost, all of the prisoners were to be shot with arrows.[20] In the end, nothing came of this insane order. Once Herod was pronounced dead, his sister Salome ordered the prisoners in the stadium released without delay.

Nowhere in the description of Herod's last days, however, does Josephus refer to a massacre of children in Bethlehem or to any other villainous act against the Jewish peasantry. There is no question that Herod was a pathologically suspicious man who never hesitated to preempt any challenge to his throne with instant arrest and execution. But the targets of his ire were the political elites: his immediate family; his court officials and counselors; and the leading families, the "principal men" in his kingdom, who were fed up with his repressive policies and heavy taxes. It is doubtful whether the birth of a child to a peasant family in Bethlehem would have merited his attention.

Since the Bethlehem Massacre of the Innocents, an outrageous act by any standard, is not attested anywhere else in the New Testament or in any other sources of antiquity, we are compelled to conclude that Matthew used the story to illustrate a deeper meaning, once again availing himself of the symbolic language rooted in the Old Testament. The immediate reason, naturally, was that Matthew somehow had to get Joseph's family to Nazareth, where all traditions agree that Jesus grew up. A lesser writer would have Joseph simply pack up his family and move north to Galilee. Matthew, however, takes advantage of the shift in location to weave an elegant story of Old Testament imagery, using Herod's well-known reputation for manic suspicion and cruelty. By having the Holy Family travel to Egypt in exile, only to return to Palestine when the evil king is dead, Matthew completes his Infancy Narrative in imitation of the story of Moses. As such, it is a fitting counterpoint to the beginning of his story, which hearkened back to the story of Abraham.

Matthew's symbolic message is simple: just as Moses led his people out of Egypt to the original Covenant with the Lord, so shall Jesus emerge from exile in Egypt to deliver his people in the New Covenant, the New Testament with God. And when Joseph thought it safe to return to Palestine, he did not go back to his ancestral home in Bethlehem, but decided to settle instead in Galilee. The evangelist explains this sudden change of residence by the fact that Herod had since been succeeded by his son Archilaus.[21] Why Archilaus constituted a particular threat to Joseph and his family is not explained; nor does Matthew give us the reason why Antipas, the new ruler of Galilee, who was also a son of Herod, was in any way less of a threat. To Matthew, historical facts served merely to sustain the theological thrust of the story. What matters is that at the end of his Infancy Narrative, Jesus, Joseph, and Mary are safely settled "in a city called Nazareth," and that from this point on, much of the story will unfold in the rolling hills around this tiny hamlet in Galilee.

THREE

GROWING UP IN GALILEE

As the reign of Herod entered its inevitable decline and various forces in Palestine prepared for the power vacuum that was to come, the infant Jesus grew up in the modest home of his parents. Like any other first-born baby, he delighted his young mother with his first smile, his first gurgled words, and his first attempts to walk on his own two feet. But the baby Jesus was growing up under a cloud. In the tightly knit community of Nazareth, the uncertainty of his paternity would have haunted him and his parents. According to Deuteronomy, such a child was designated a *mamzer,* doomed to be ostracized from the congregation and social life. The Mishnah, too, castigates *mamzers* as children born of an illegitimate sexual union.[1] The Talmud states that *mamzers* can have no voice in public congregations— they are supposed to be silent at all times.

The impact of being stigmatized as a "mamzer" in a small, gossip-ridden hamlet like Nazareth would have been devastating. Bruce Chilton believes that it would have had a profound psychological impact on the development of the young Jesus. The other children in the village would have been forbidden to play with him. If Jesus was allowed to participate in "synagogue" gatherings at all, he would have been prevented from speaking up. Quite possibly, he would not even have been able to attend.

Throughout Jesus' early years, Mary and Joseph lived in a humble peasant house. The house would have been built of stacked stone, either limestone or basalt, mortared with mud, then coated with stucco (clay and mud). In wintertime, rainfall and moisture seeped through the stucco, so that it needed a new application often. The roof would be made from a latticework of thin beams and branches, covered with palm fronds and leaves and packed with mud. Here, Mary and Joseph ate, played with their son, kept their stores, slept, made love, and shared their dreams about the future, as any newlywed couple would. They slept in the same clothes they wore during the day, on a mattress of dry straw covered with a mat.

Usually, dwellings such as these opened onto a small courtyard, where the animals where kept. Here, Mary had her "kitchen appliances," which consisted of a stone mill and an oven made of clay or brick. In many cases, the courtyard was surrounded by multiple one-room dwellings, each allotted to a particular couple (and their children) within an extended family. The remains of such multi-family residential units have been excavated in Hirbet Najar, Hirbet Yeqavim, Yattir, and Meiron.[2] So common was this layout that Talmudic literature would later refer to this type of residence as simply a "courtyard."

The unique composition of the courtyard residence, with all immediate kinsmen living in close proximity and sharing the same communal functions, underscores the role of the *family* as the Galilean peasant's principal support mechanism. The type of services offered by local, state, and national governments in our modern times were wholly unknown to first-century Galileans. The ruling elites, such as they were (including, as we shall see, the priesthood, the Herodian administration, and their Roman overlords), taxed the peasantry heavily without, in essence, giving anything in return—with the exception of the questionable "protection" offered by the nation's armed forces. Indeed, these elites looked upon the peasantry as merely an exploitable commodity with which to sustain their position of power and lifestyle of luxury.

Consequently, Galilean peasants would in essence have been left to fend for themselves were it not for two levels of support: their families first, their village second. The family provided a shared resource for food, clothing, companionship, and love. The village offered a resource for economic assistance and shared cultic facilities. In a way, the village served as a sort of farmers' cooperative, where the principal necessities of agriculture—water, farming tools, draft animals, and winnowing area—were maintained for collective use. A village often also produced its own pottery, though the quality was usually inferior to artisan-made ceramics sold in townships. A village was also responsible for the construction and maintenance of rural roads needed to reach its patchwork of fields and the nearest town, as well as for building cisterns to catch and collect rainfall. This water was needed both for agricultural use and to replenish its communal *mikva'ot* or ritual baths, used for purification rites prescribed in Covenant Law.

Josephus tells us there were over two hundred such tiny villages spread all over Galilee, some of which could typically house up to a hundred families. By comparison, Nazareth was a mere hamlet. It is not mentioned in any works by Josephus, though the historian himself was born in Galilee and later served as commander of the region during the Jewish War. Modern excavations suggest that Nazareth was first settled in the third century B.C.E. and in its heyday covered some sixty acres, sufficient to house 480 inhabitants; but in the time of Jesus it may have been much smaller.

While a village was in many ways self-sufficient, it could not exist without a large town in its immediate vicinity. Such a town offered a ready market for surplus produce, usually paid for in hard coin (which could then be used to pay taxes). Second, a town offered additional services that a village could not provide, such as a judicial court that could hear small-claims cases, presided over by a local Sanhedrin, or "council."

The Mishnah and other sources describe the activity of townships in great detail, though it is not clear whether the oral traditions of the Mishnah, which were first collected in 200 C.E., accurately reflect the situation of first-century Palestine before the Jewish War of 66–70 C.E. Talmudic literature distinguishes between a *city (kerakh)*, which was similar to the Greek *polis,* and a *town ('yr,* plural *'yyrot).* A *kerakh* was a fairly sophisticated place, often fortified and usually Gentile and Hellenistic in character. Here one could visit shops and stores along a central boulevard or *decumanus,* or spend an afternoon in a Roman-style bathhouse.

A *'yr,* by contrast, was a far more modest affair, primarily Jewish, and usually built on the location of older Israelite settlements. Quite often such towns were nestled in the sloping hills of Galilee or on their summits, as Nazareth was, with a commanding view of the countryside. Compared to cities, towns usually had populations anywhere from four hundred to a thousand families. The Talmudic literature indicates that these towns had at least one "general store" that sold items such as fruits and eggs, amphorae containing olive oil or wine, or fresh vegetables. At times, these stores also served as restaurants.[3]

Since neither the Romans nor the Herodian administration in Jesus' day had the means to administer each and every town and village, a town was given considerable autonomy to run its district, including the many satellite villages that were arrayed in its immediate vicinity. To do so, a town relied on a council (Sanhedrin), consisting of seven town elders, and an administrative unit of three executives known as *archons,* who in turn were led by a principal or "mayor." Decisions with great import for the town at large were taken in the presence of a town assembly. Councils were subject to the jurisdiction of the Great Sanhedrin, particularly when the council sat in judgment. This was certainly true for the rabbinical era (post-136 C.E.) but it may also have been the case in the time of Jesus.

Market day was held each Monday and Thursday. Peasants from all the surrounding villages would come to town to offer their surplus produce. Products intended for markets beyond the town were invariably "processed foods" that could be stored and transported without spoiling, such as wine and raisins (from grapes), olive oil (from olives), seeds (from wheat), and dried figs and dates. Religious services were held on market days as well, so as to benefit the peasants, whose villages usually lacked the requisite priests or facilities. Towns were also responsible for assessing and collecting taxes from the villages in their district, which deepened a peasant's dependence on the "mother-town."

As it happened, Nazareth lay in the district and jurisdiction of a place called Sepphoris, located just four miles away. In fact, Sepphoris was not a town but a true *kerakh,* probably the only city worthy of the name in all of Lower Galilee. It had been fortified as early as the Persian Period (sixth and fifth centuries B.C.E.) and still held a sizable Hasmonean garrison by the mid-first century B.C.E. that gave the Roman general Pompey no end of trouble. Though originally Jewish, Sepphoris had a growing Gentile community, which may have prompted the Romans, shortly after their conquest of the country, to make Sepphoris the capital of the province. As we will see, Nazareth's proximity to, and dependence on, the city of Sepphoris would have a decisive influence on the adolescent years of Jesus.

DAILY LIFE FOR MARY AND JOSEPH

Mary and Joseph would have lived like any other peasant couple in Lower Galilee. Every morning, while her family still slept, Mary rose to prepare breakfast. It would still be dark, cold, and damp in the house, so Mary dressed warmly and lit an oil lamp to work by. She entered the courtyard, checked on the animals, and then proceeded to make the daily portion of fresh bread. First, she took a jar that held the precious kernels of grain; it was tightly closed with flax rope to keep out hungry rodents and other trespassers. Then she poured out several cupfuls of grain onto the mill. This mill usually consisted of two round slabs of stone, anchored on a central wooden spike, which allowed the top to be moved back and forth across the bottom slab by way of a wooden handle. The motion crushed kernels and ground them into a fine flour that sifted down to the floor. It was hard work for a young girl of fifteen: one hour of grinding would typically produce only some 800 grams of flour. Mary then collected the flour in a bowl and added a bit of salt, a few drops of olive oil, and half a cup of water, kneading the mixture until it had the consistency of dough. She also added yeast—the spoiled remains of dough from two days back—to leaven the bread so it would rise in the oven.

At one point or another, the toddler Jesus might rise in search of his mother, only to find her busy at work kneading the dough. He must have observed her closely; later, in the days of his ministry, he would compare the Kingdom of Heaven to "yeast that a woman took and mixed in with three measures of flour, until all of it was leavened."[4] Once the dough was ready, Mary's agile hands quickly shaped it into thin round cakes, which baked more quickly and thus saved time and fuel.

Then it was time to fire the oven. Mary probably used animal dung to fire her oven, with branches and leaves for kindling. Once it was lit, Mary waited until the small clay chamber immediately above the fire was sufficiently hot. She then placed the cakes on a wooden baker's palette and slid the cakes into the baking chamber, checking regularly to ensure that the bread rose and baked to her liking.

After fifteen or twenty minutes, the cakes would be ready. By this time, Joseph would have risen and washed himself, either at the village well or from a nearby cistern that collected rainfall in winter months. As the sun rose, the family sat down to enjoy their first meal of the day—delicious hot bread, dipped in olive oil and seasoned with garlic. They ate the bread at a low table, sitting on rough woolen rugs. Mary made sure to save several cakes for Joseph's haversack, to serve as his lunch in the field. Other pieces were carefully stowed away to feed the family at suppertime, the second and last meal of the day, when the bread would be augmented with a cooked egg or vegetable. Only on the Sabbath would the family eat three meals. Later rabbinic writings specified that a Sabbath meal should include at least two cooked foods to underscore the festive character of this holy day—for example, fried fish, legume paste, or vegetables.[5]

In all, the daily process of preparing and baking the bread, the staple of a peasant's diet, would have taken anywhere from two to three hours. Jesus would later pay homage to this quintessential ritual of Galilean life by including the words "give us this day our daily bread" in the prayer he taught to his disciples. Thus fortified by the morning meal, Joseph rose, kissed his young wife and son, and headed for his fields to spend the rest of the day in cultivating the land.

How large was Joseph's plot? As far as we can determine, the land held by Galilean farmers depended on the extent to which ancestral property had been parceled out among family sons from generation to generation. The eldest son typically received double the share that was allocated to a younger sibling; but depending on the number of sons, even the largest share was often reduced substantially from the size of the father's original property. In many cases, younger sons were left with lots too small to sustain a family and were forced to sell their inheritance back to their eldest brother. If the farmer had no sons but only daughters, the land was usually transferred to the family of the groom as part of the dowry. What this meant was that over time, the acreage held by one single family was usually fragmented into separate plots, spread in a confusing patchwork in between the holdings of other farmers. Such individual plots were not fenced, but marked with boulders; olive orchards or grapevines, by contrast, were bordered by walls to deter roving animals and thieves.

As we have seen, the secret of Galilee's bounty was its soil and its access to water. Its bedrock of porous limestone was covered with fertile terra rossa topsoil, suitable for growing a variety of crops. Thus, Joseph and most Galilean farmers like him were able to sustain themselves and their families with mixed farming on their small plots. Separate patches of land were set aside to cultivate cereals such as wheat and barley; millet and rice; or garden vegetables such as onions, garlic, squash, radishes, beets, and leeks. Many farmers also had orchards to cultivate olives, figs, grapes, and dates. Talmudic literature lists no fewer than five hundred types of produce grown in Galilee, including 150 types of cultivated crops, eight types of grain, twenty legumes, twenty-four vegetables, and thirty types of fruits. Other farmers, particularly in villages around Sepphoris (including Nazareth), grew flax, since Sepphoris was known as the premier center of linen production in Galilee. So ingrained was this method of mixed farming that when Talmudic literature refers to times of difficulty, it says that "the world was injured—one-third in olives, one-third in wheat, and one-third in barley."[6] Any surplus that might occur at any time, of any given crop, was considered a bonus and could be sold for coin or bartered for other goods.

Modern analysis suggests that the land holdings of a farmer like Joseph probably ranged from four to eight acres, though, as we noted before, they were seldom contiguous. By comparison, Caesar gave veteran legionnaires with three children a plot of land covering some ten *jugura,* the equivalent of over six acres, which was considered the minimum with which the retired soldier could sustain a family of this size.[7] This is true even today. A modern United Nations survey of Southeast Asia recently concluded that 60 percent of rural families have access to under five acres of land, which, even using modern seeds and fertilizers, produces subsistence yields barely sufficient to feed an average family with 5.2 children.[8]

Joseph would start to prepare his soil for seeding in the month of *Tishri* (September–October) or *Marchesvan* (October–November), when the first rains of the season had softened the sun-baked topsoil. This is when plowing (as well as ground-clearing) could begin in earnest. To do so, a farmer used a curved hardwood plow equipped with an iron plowshare, which was pulled by one or two oxen. A pair of oxen (a "yoke") was a treasured possession, often owned by larger estates but lent out to individual farmers, perhaps against a share of the future harvest.

First, Joseph plowed the land lengthwise, then passed over it crosswise, continuously turning over the soil to prepare it for seeding. He then took a sack of seeds culled from his previous harvest and walked in straight lines across his land, throwing the seed with the full sweep of his arm, just as his father had taught him. As he strode across his field, showering the soil with seeds, little Jesus might have been sitting close by, following his father's movements with keen eyes. He must have watched the fall of the seed and, later on, as the seed sprouted, observed how some plants prospered, while others withered and died. Many years later, this vivid experience would inspire Jesus' parable of the sower: "Some [seed] fell on the road; the birds came and gathered them up. Others fell on rock, did not take root in the soil, and did not produce ears. And others fell on thorns; they choked the seed(s) and worms ate them. And others fell on the good soil and produced good fruit: it bore sixty per measure and a hundred and twenty per measure."[9]

The most important subsistence crops were wheat and barley, planted in late November. Wheat was used for bread, the most important staple of a farmer's diet, whereas barley usually served as fodder for farm animals, including sheep, goats, and sometimes cattle. Sometime in February, during the Jewish month of Adar, the first sprouts of barley would appear, and by April (Nisan/Iyyar) these ears would be ready for harvesting. The wheat harvest followed a month later. The reaping was done with a scythe, a difficult and exhausting task, after which the sheaves were stacked near the farmer's house, to await their turn at threshing.

Every observant farmer, as Joseph certainly was, left the stalks at the corners of his field intact, so that they could be reaped by the poor. By the same token, the "alien, the orphan, and the widow" had the right of trespass after the farmer had finished harvesting, free to scour the field for any sheaves that he had left in his wake.[10]

Every agricultural village typically had a "threshing floor," a plateau of hard-packed earth, usually placed in an elevated position, where the wind blew strongest. The threshing floor formed an integral part of village life. It was used for public gatherings and could sometimes acquire a special sacral significance. The threshing floor of a small Jebusite town known as Jerusalem, for example, was chosen by King David as the place to pitch the tent-like tabernacle that held the Ark of the Covenant. Later, the tent was replaced by Solomon's Temple; today, this "Temple Mount" is marked by the Dome of the Rock.

During harvest time in Nazareth, each of the village farmers would have waited for his turn to use the threshing floor. First, the harvested sheaves were dropped on a pile; then the pile was passed over with a device known as a threshing board, a wooden slab studded with jagged stones or iron bits on the bottom. The farmer hitched a donkey to the board and drove it across the grain in circles, often placing one of his children on the board to add weight. The repeated motion of threshing board steadily removed the kernels of grain from the stalks, so that in due course there remained a con-fused pile of grain, chaff (husks and stubble), and straw. It is not difficult to imagine the young Jesus standing on the board, his eyes full of delight while he ran across the golden sheaves over and over again under the watchful gaze of his father.

Next, to separate the grain from the chaff, Joseph took a winnowing fork. As the afternoon breeze picked up, he threw the harvested wheat up in the air, relying on the wind to blow the empty stalks and chaff away from the heavy kernels. This he continued to do until all of the chaff had been dispersed, and only the pile of precious grain (or "corn," as the King James Bible termed it) remained. This winnowing process would later inspire the exhortations of one of Jesus' most important role models, John the Baptist. Very soon now, John said, a Messiah would come whose "winnowing fork is in his hand, to clear his threshing floor and to gather the wheat into his granary; but the chaff he will burn with unquenchable fire."[11]

At last, the grain was sifted through a sieve to eliminate any remaining foreign matter, then stored in clay jars. A portion was set aside for the tax collector; another for religious tithes; and lastly, a share for use by the farmer's family. To mark the end of the grain harvest, Joseph and his fellow farmers celebrated the Festival of Weeks (*Hah ha-Shavuot,* also known as the Feast of Reaping, the Festival of First Fruits, or Pentecost). A small group would be chosen to bring the year's "first fruits" to the Temple. For this, the wife of each farmer would bake two loaves of breads of the finest grain, to be presented to the Temple as "show bread."

Shortly thereafter, the next growing season began. Leviticus refers to this season as "the season of vintage," the time when "the trees of the field shall yield their fruit."[12] Joseph would now tend to his orchard, carefully binding and propping the saplings while cutting weeds and pruning the branches of dead wood, in preparation for the growth of grapes, figs, and olives. By early summer, during the month of Tammuz, the vineyards were ready to be har-vested. Gathering the grapes and olives was a mammoth task, in which every member of a man's family was pressed into service. In later years, Jesus would vividly remember the time when swarms of workers descended on the vineyard to collect the ripened fruit before it spoiled. Luke, Mark, and Matthew all contain parables of the vineyard; the story of the landowner who leased his orchard to tenant farmers during harvest time belongs to one of the oldest strata of the source text known as Q.[13] A large part of the grape crop was pulped into juice for wine fermentation, while another portion was set aside for the production of raisins. Olives were pressed for varying qualities of olive oil.

During the critical weeks before the grape and olive harvest, a farmer's family usually moved out to sleep in their fields, where they could guard the ripening crop against thieves and marauding animals. While little Jesus ran around in the field, for once free of the confines of their tiny house, Joseph and Mary built a hut from palm branches. This improvised tent or "booth" was meant to protect the family against the sun during the day and offer a modicum of privacy at night. For young children like Jesus, this must have been a festive time, perhaps analogous to modern-day family camping trips. The whole family would once again build such huts during the Feast of Succoth, the Festival of Booths (or Tents), in commemoration of the years the Israelites spent in the wilderness before entering the Promised Land. Similar to our Thanksgiving, this was a time when even city folk built tents of palm fronds on their rooftops and everyone waved palm branches to give thanks to the Lord for that year's harvest. When all was done, it was time to harvest the figs and dates.

For generations, Galilean farmers had tilled the land in this manner. Favored by the soil, the balmy climate, rainfall, and wells, they had been able to feed their families a stable diet of bread, fruits, and vegetables while usually retaining enough surplus to raise a modest income. With this money, they bought and maintained their farming tools, their animals, and other necessities of life, including pottery and yarn with which wives like Mary could spin and weave their clothes. These same meager funds were used to meet the demands of the tax man and religious duties, such as the annual Temple tax and the so-called priestly tithes. Taxes and tithes had been part and parcel of Israelite life from the very beginning of the Davidic monarchy; but now, under the Herodians, that burden was to change dramatically.

TITHES AND TAXES

Tithing was a custom as old as the Hebrew Scriptures themselves. Abraham granted King Melchisedek tithes of everything he possessed, and Jacob promised YHWH a tenth of his property yields if only God would allow him to return safely to his ancestral home.[14] After the settlement in the Promised Land, tithing became an integral component of the Mosaic Laws. The fundamental basis for tithing was the belief that the land of Palestine was YHWH's, and that the Israelites were merely tenant farmers, tilling the land at the Lord's pleasure. Therefore, it was only proper that a share of the harvest should be returned to the rightful owner. This share was not offered in sacrifice; it was presented to YHWH's representatives, the priests and priestly assistants known as the Levites.

According to Scripture, during the settlement in the Promised Land the tribe of Levi, which was charged with maintaining the sanctuary of the Lord, was expressly designated a "landless" class, with no income of its own. The Levites were responsible for various activities at the Temple, including the maintenance of Temple facilities, the singing of Psalms during Temple services, the teaching of the Torah, and the policing of the Temple precinct as Temple guards. It therefore behooved the farmers of Galilee and Judea to see to it that a fair share of the harvest was used for the sustenance of these priestly servants. The Book of Numbers states that a full tenth of the harvest was to be handed over to the Levitical community.[15] Joseph and other farmers thus effectively lost a tenth of all of their harvest yields, be it wheat, barley, grapes, dates, or any other consumable product of the soil or tree. Only once every seven years, during the so-called Sabbatical year, were farmers exempt from paying the tithes since the land was supposed to lie fallow and "rest."[16]

Next, Joseph—like any other Jew in the Roman Empire—was obligated to pay the annual Temple tax. The basis for this tax is likewise found in Covenant Law, specifically Exodus 30:11–16, according to which each person twenty years or older was expected to pay "half a shekel" for the maintenance of the sanctuary of the Lord—in Joseph's time, the Second Temple in Jerusalem. Though at one point the tax needed to be paid only once, by the time of the Hasmoneans it was levied on an annual basis, no doubt to finance the restoration of full operations at the Temple in Jerusalem—and to cement the Hasmonean concordat with the Sadducee priestly aristocracy. Half a shekel (or *didrachma*) was equal to two Attic *drachmas* or two Roman *dinarii,* hence the equivalent of a worker's wages for two days—for a Jewish farmer, not an insignificant sum. In addition,

Joseph and Mary, like any other Jewish parents, were expected to pay five shekels (20 *dinarii*, equal to twenty days' wages) in thanksgiving and for God's blessing of their firstborn son, and the birth of Jesus would undoubtedly have compelled them to do so.[17]

The temple tax was collected from every Jew, both those residing in Palestine and those in the Diaspora communities throughout the Mediterranean region. In such foreign places, Temple tax funds were collected by synagogue officials and then brought to Jerusalem during one of the major festivals. An edict by Augustus, dated to 12 B.C.E., specifically authorized Jews to collect and transport such funds through the Roman Empire for this purpose, so that "their sacred monies shall be inviolable and may be sent up to Jerusalem and delivered to the treasurers in Jerusalem."[18] Those who tried to steal these temple shekels in transit faced stiff penalties.

In Palestine proper, the collection of temple taxes began in the month of Adar. Rabbinic sources suggest that money-changing tables were set up throughout the country, including Galilee, to change coins from local currency into half-shekels. This operation began on the fifteenth day of Adar and was usually concluded on the twenty-fifth of Adar, at which point the money changers returned to the Temple and served the needs of worshipers in the forecourt. Sustaining the Temple with the tax was a holy obligation; even the Essenes, who resolutely rejected the legitimacy of the high priest and his priestly elite, sent their contributions to the Temple. In later years, Jesus also willingly gave his contribution, notwithstanding his own issues with the priesthood and the sacrificial system.[19]

Even though the tithing and Temple tax system placed a considerable burden on the Jewish farmer, up until the Herodian era he by and large had been able to honor his obligations and feed his family with a varied diet at the same time. Recent studies have attempted to determine what a field like Joseph's might have yielded on an annual basis. Most economic experts agree that the farmer in antiquity, using manure to fertilize his land, probably realized a return of 1:5, that is, five times the original seed planted. Joseph, as we have seen, probably tilled a field of approximately four to eight acres. Since a good part (probably a third) of that acreage would lie fallow at any given time, we will for the moment assume that Joseph seeded approximately four acres of land per year. Douglas Oakman has estimated it probably took eleven bushels of wheat to feed an adult person for one year. What's more, he has calculated that during seeding, each acre absorbed around 1.8 bushels of seed. If we apply the 1:5 ratio, then Joseph would have realized approximately nine bushels of wheat per acre, or a total of thirty-six bushels from his entire arable plot in any given year. One fifth, or roughly seven bushels, would have been set aside to serve as seed for the next year; a further tenth, or some three bushels, would have been subtracted to serve as tithes.[20]

If this calculation is correct, then Joseph's labors would have yielded some twenty-six bushels of wheat per year—just enough to feed himself, his young wife, and their son Jesus. Naturally, there were other, smaller crops to supplement this diet—including olives, onions, and dates or grapes. In addition, Joseph would have grown barley to serve as fodder for his animals—and as the main ingredient of his family's bread, if the wheat harvest was poor. Nevertheless, this example illustrates that, as Donald Engels wrote, the peasants of antiquity lived at the margin of human existence and had little or nothing left over after they paid their taxes and their maintenance and rents on land, equipment, and draft animals.[21] As long as the rains came each winter, the water was plentiful, and the taxes imposed by the governing authority were modest, the Galilean farmer was able to survive, sometimes even prosper. But this careful balance of yields and needs was dramatically upset when Palestine became part of the Roman Empire and Herod ascended the throne of greater Judea.

THE TAX BURDEN UNDER HEROD

For the preceding seven hundred years, as we have seen, Galilee had either been ruled by a foreign power or formed part of an autonomous kingdom led by a Jewish king. Since Palestine was largely an agricultural region, with no other source of income to speak of, this meant that at any time during Israel's history—including the periods of Assyrian, Persian, Egyptian, and Seleucid occupation—the burden of paying tribute to a foreign power largely fell on the shoulders of Palestine's farmers. It was for this purpose that the foreign powers invariably organized their conquered lands into distinct administrative regions. During the Assyrian occupation, for example, Galilee formed part of the newly created Assyrian province of Megiddo. The Persians ruled Galilee as a subprovince of the fifth Persian satrapy known as *Abar nahara* ("Beyond the [Euphrates] River"), whereas the

Ptolemies in Alexandria cast Galilee as a hyparchy named Galila. After Ptolemy V was defeated by the Seleucid king Antiochus III in 200 B.C.E., the Seleucid Empire absorbed Galilee in yet another administrative unit, known as the eparchy of Samaria (which also included Judea), a part of the Seleucid province of Coele-Syria and Phoenicia.

In each instance, the sole purpose of the subdivision was to make the exploitation of local agricultural resources as efficient as possible, if not in moneys then certainly in the form of agricultural surplus. Josephus suggests that in the final years of Ptolemaic rule, the tax burden became so oppressive that many Palestinian Jews rallied to the Seleucid forces besieging Ptolemy's last holdout in Jerusalem. After the Egyptian forces were evicted, Antiochus III expressed his gratitude by immediately reducing the Ptolemaic tax burden.[22] Unfortunately, these concessions were mostly directed at the governing elites of Jerusalem, including Temple officials, so it is unclear to what extent Galilean farmers benefited from the Seleucids' generosity.

In any case, the kindness of the Seleucids was short-lived. After Antiochus's ill-fated attack on Greece, a vassal of an emerging power called Rome, the Seleucid Empire was on the verge of bankruptcy. Syrian tax officials scoured Palestine for any source of revenue, even going as far as to loot the treasury of the Temple in Jerusalem. This was part of the impetus for the Maccabean Revolt, which eventually restored Palestine as an independent kingdom, ruled by the Hasmonean dynasty. Nevertheless, the Galilean farmer continued to be taxed. More than likely, the Hasmonean kings simply restored the tax collection systems that had been in place during the Seleucid era.

But all this changed when Herod ascended to the throne. A new situation presented itself; for while Herod surrounded himself with the trappings of an autonomous monarch, he was still very much a vassal king, forced to pay tribute to Rome. As a consequence, the tax layer on his subjects doubled: instead of paying taxes to *either* a foreign ruler *or* a Jewish king, the Galilean farmer now saw himself compelled to support *both*. Palestine—like any other vassal state in the Roman Empire—was expected to remit its full share to the Roman treasury for partaking of the blessings of the *Pax Romana*. Herod, therefore, needed to extract sufficient funds not only to pay his masters in Rome but also to maintain the prop of his own government in Jerusalem. On top of that, Herod's tax collectors were always hard pressed to feed the king's lust for lavish construction.

Galilean farmers, says Richard Horsley, went "from one to three layers of rulers in the sixty years from the Hasmonean take-over to the imposition of Herod, with three layers of payments due: taxes to Herod, tribute to Rome, as well as the tithes and offerings to Temple and Priesthood." In addition, life in Galilee (as elsewhere in Palestine) was now further encumbered by a salt tax, custom duties for the shipment of produce from one region to the next, tax on property, fishing poles, and tax on other sources of "manufacturing," notably the production of salted fish. Palestine was occupied territory, and like any other Roman colony its primary purpose was to be exploited for the greater good of Rome.

Unfortunately, Palestine had no natural wealth to speak of. Unlike Spain, it had no silver mines or tin deposits; unlike northern Africa, it lacked any source of gold or silver; unlike Gaul, the Balkans, or Lebanon, it lacked dense forests that could feed the Empire's appetite for construction and shipbuilding. As Josephus put it, "we neither inhabit a maritime country, nor do we delight in merchandise . . . [but] having a fruitful country for our habitation, we take pains in cultivating that only."[23] The only resource Palestine did have were its fertile valleys, particularly the agricultural regions in the north that had always been the breadbasket of the Near East with its production of wheat, barley, olives, figs, and dates.

The upshot of all this is that the years preceding Jesus' birth saw a rapidly escalating tax burden placed on peasant families like Joseph and Mary's, propelled by the growing demands of Herod's kingdom. Scholars such as E. P. Sanders have estimated that as much as 28 to 33 percent of a farmer's harvest was used for meeting the combined demands of tithing and taxes—a crippling amount, given what we know about the average yields of a family plot.[24] Horsley believes it was even higher, closer to 40 percent. What's more, the burden was placed disproportionately on the *Galilean* farmer, not only because he tilled some of the richest land in Palestine but also because Herod had long since decided that Galilee should be exploited mercilessly to fund improvements elsewhere in the kingdom.

Herod's enmity toward Galilee ran deep. As we have seen, Hezekiah had led a successful revolt against the young Herod shortly after he was appointed governor of the region during the Hyrcanus/Antipater regime, when he bled the peasantry dry to pay tribute to Cassius. Herod had responded to Hezekiah's challenge with a brutal campaign of retribution, which would hardly have endeared him to the peasant population.

The situation repeated itself when, several years later, it was Mark Antony's turn to face the legions of Octavian. According to Josephus, he too turned to Herod for financial assistance so as to boost his forces prior to the fateful Battle of Actium. Herod, says Josephus, was in a position to do so because "the countryside had been yielding him rich crops for a long time." By the same token, when Palestine experienced a prolonged period of drought, Herod saw himself forced to reduce taxation levies by a third.[25] Clearly, Herod's financial fortunes were inextricably tied to the taxation base of the nation's agriculture.

We can begin to imagine the extent of the Herodian tax burden when we consider the fabulous fortune Herod had managed to amass near the end of his life. As Josephus reports, Herod's will bequeathed the staggering sum of ten million drachmae to his then-mentor and protector, the emperor Augustus. In addition, he deeded gold, silver, and precious garments for Augustus's wife, Livia, as well as another five million drachmae to "certain others," no doubt Roman officials, prelates, and military leaders whom Herod owed one favor or another. Even then, he still had sufficient funds to grant his sister Salome five hundred thousand drachmae, while also giving the rest of his surviving kin "sums of money . . . that left them all in a wealthy condition."[26] This, we should remember, was the fortune that remained *after* Herod had expended a good deal of his treasure on massive projects, including the construction of Caesarea, the acropolis of Sebaste on the ancient site of Samaria, and the expansion of the Second Temple. There is little reason to doubt, therefore, that Herod's regime was pushing farmers like Joseph to a socioeconomic crisis of a severity never before witnessed in the thousand-year history of Jewish Galilee. The results were dire and, for the purpose of our story, ultimately catastrophic.

PALESTINE AFTER THE DEATH OF HEROD

Not surprisingly, the death of King Herod was welcomed by his subjects with near-universal relief. The promise of change stirred the hearts of the elites and the peasant classes alike. Many of the old landed gentry in Galilee—Jewish landowners who had cultivated their estates since

Hasmonean times—may have quietly been hoping for a restoration of that Jewish royal house and the many privileges they had enjoyed during its rule. The peasants of Galilee, Joseph and Mary included, may not have cared who ruled after Herod, as long as his death produced a lessening of the tax burden. The last thing the country needed was to see the king succeeded by another megalomaniac Herodian who would squeeze his subjects in the pursuit of grand, vainglorious building schemes.

Of course, neither the farmers, the gentry, nor even the aristocratic families in Jerusalem had any say in the matter. The only man who did was Caesar Augustus, who at the time of Herod's death in 4 B.C.E. was the undisputed master of the Roman world. His empire stretched from the English Channel to the Euphrates, inclusive of a narrow strip of land known as Palestine. And Augustus remembered that Herod, whatever his faults, had been a faithful ally who could be relied upon to act in Rome's best interests. Augustus was therefore inclined to trust Herod's judgment in choosing his successor in his last will, should such a document be found.

One was found, and it was a curious document. Herod proposed that his kingdom be carved up. Perhaps he believed that none of his sons was up to the task of ruling his territory. Or perhaps, in a rare moment of concern, he recognized that unless he appeased his surviving sons with portions of his inheritance, a civil war might be in the offing. Whatever the case may be, Herod proposed a return to the traditional separation of Palestine's southern heartland, Judea, from the north, including Galilee. According to Herod's will, Judea—as well as Idumaea and Samaria—would be granted to his son Archilaus, the same Archilaus whom Matthew presents as the reason for Joseph's decision to settle in Galilee. Since this was by far the largest portion of Herod's territory, Archilaus naturally assumed that this bequest would also include Herod's dynastic title of *basileus* or "king"—subject, of course, to the consent of the emperor Augustus. In this, he was fatefully wrong.

The second largest portion, that of Galilee and Perea (the Transjordan), was intended for Herod's son Antipas. His son Philip, meanwhile, would become ruler of the Gaulanitis (the northern region in the Golan). Herod's sister Salome had to make do with the crumbs, a handful of cities including Ashdod and Phasaelis.

However, this disposition was merely Herod's *recommendation,* subject to confirmation by Augustus, which could take some time. Archilaus thus decided to do what any modern politician running for office would do: namely, to launch a "campaign" to win the hearts and minds of his putative subjects. He appeared in public, something that Herod had rarely done, and went to great lengths to present himself as a compassionate and honorable ruler.

He even took the daring step of inviting the people's comments. Not surprisingly, he received an earful. Some Jews petitioned Archilaus to release the scores of political prisoners that were even now rotting away in Herod's jails. Others seized the opportunity to beg him to "ease some of the annual payments"—that is, the heavy yoke of the Herodian taxes that were still in force. Some were so bold as to suggest that officers of the former regime who had willfully persecuted Herod's political opponents should now be brought to justice.

Truth be told, opposition to Herod's rule had been steadily building in the final months of his life—usually prompted by religious grievances, which in first-century Palestine were closely intertwined with social and political concerns. One opposition group was led by two scholars "of the Law," possibly Pharisees: Judas, son of Saripheus, and Matthias, son of Margalothus. Both were highly popular teachers, says Josephus, "well beloved by the people because of their education of their youth"; indeed, their lectures drew a crowd of students every day.[27] Knowing that the Herodian regime was on its last legs, these scholars began to inveigh against the numerous statues, bas-reliefs, and other forms of Hellenistic art so beloved by Herod but in violation of the Covenant prohibition against "graven images," man-made representations of living creatures made by God. In particular, Judas and Matthias railed against the most abominable sculpture of all, a large golden eagle, symbol of imperial Rome, that was perched over the "great gate of the Temple" of all places. In placing it on the Temple portico, Herod had sought to please his Roman masters. All he succeeded in doing, however, was to provoke pious Jews who were forced to see the wretched thing every time they came to the Temple to worship and sacrifice.

It so happened that in Herod's final months, a rumor rippled through the city that the king was dead. The two scholars rallied their students who, in a fit of idealistic fervor (not unlike the student demonstrations of our modern times), dashed to the Temple, climbed to the upper cornice of the gate, and cut the eagle from his moorings. It crashed to the Temple pavement, whereupon the students scrambled down and, surrounded by an enthusiastic crowd, cut the thing into pieces with axes. Unfortunately, it then transpired that Herod, though very ill, was still very much alive. The Temple Guard raced to the scene and arrested close to forty of the young perpetrators, as well as the instigators, Judas and Matthias. Herod flew into a rage and sentenced the whole lot to death—and not by the more usual stoning or beheading, but by burning at the stake.[28]

The memories of that horrific episode were still foremost in people's minds when Archilaus began his campaign among his future subjects. Now that Herod was finally dead and buried, the people demanded reparation. Matthias and Judas, they cried, should be granted an honorable funeral, and all those who had been involved in the persecution of these scholars and their courageous students should be tried.

And so Archilaus's short-lived experiment with *perestroika* led to protests. Gingerly testing their newfound freedoms, the public began to speak up, and with increasing vehemence they began to clamor for a redress of all the wrongs that had been committed by the Herodian regime. A good many, perhaps led by the Pharisees, demanded the immediate eviction of the high priest, appointed by Herod and universally regarded as one of his cronies. The people wanted a true high priest, one who would be genuinely concerned with justice based on the Covenant Law, as well as matters of purity, a pivotal issue for Pharisees. Archilaus, backed into a corner, granted their request, but then refused to accede to other demands. Alarmed by the sheer breadth of discontent, he claimed that until Augustus had confirmed him in office, he would not have the authority to make any further changes. This immediately raised suspicions about Archilaus's good intentions.

The prevailing mood of public discontent reached a climax during the Passover festival of that fateful year, 4 B.C.E. (This, it should be remembered, was the feast when Jews celebrated their deliverance from another despot: the Pharaoh in Egypt.) In the spirit of the moment, large crowds gathered in and around the Temple; soon, voices of protest rang out. The festival became a rallying point for demonstrations against the crimes of Herod's regime and the people's demand for change. Whether this rally actually led to acts of violence, as Josephus intimates, is not clear; we should remember that Josephus wrote at the behest of his benefactors, the Roman emperors Vespasian and Domitian, and that, through much of the first century C.E., Rome had favored Herod's dynasty as a staunch ally in a volatile region. But it is clear that Archilaus, in his eagerness to secure his succession, had vastly underestimated the mood of discontent among the people. When he sent emissaries to negotiate with the protesters in the Temple, the demonstrators refused to meet with them. The people demanded a restoration of a nation under the law of God, and they would settle for nothing less. In fact, one group of scholars and students went as far as to organize a "sit-down" strike in the Temple. Well provisioned with food and water, they refused to budge until their demands had been met.

And then Archilaus overreacted. His eagerness to please was replaced by a sudden fear that, unless he contained the spread of protest, he would be perceived by Rome as a weak, inept ruler who could not control his own people. The king-elect summoned "a regiment of armed men, and with them a captain of a thousand" just as the Passover sacrifice rituals at the Temple reached a fever pitch. These forces surrounded the Temple. The worshipers, aghast at the sacrilege, greeted the soldiers by throwing pebbles and stones. Since a large part of the Temple complex was still under construction, rocks of all sizes were in plentiful supply. The soldiers, stunned by this display of public ire, withdrew, after which the faithful returned to their sacrificial rituals.

Archilaus was now seized by panic, convinced that a genuine revolt was in the works. If allowed to spread, his chances of becoming king would be virtually nil. In response, Archilaus mobilized all of Herod's standing army, including the king's cavalry, and rushed them into Jerusalem. As the infantry pushed into the Temple forecourt and horsemen thundered down the narrow streets of the Lower City surrounding the Temple sanctuary, a bloodbath ensued. Those who ran from the forecourt were mercilessly cut down by the cavalry, with total casualties running as high as three thousand people. The survivors ran to the nearby hills.[29]

As the grim task of collecting the dead began, a deadly calm settled over the city. The illusion of a new era, the promise of a new and compassionate regime, had turned to ashes. Archilaus had proven himself every bit as ruthless as his father.

Herod's son had put Palestine on a course toward turmoil and war from which the land would never recover. With the king's princes preparing to carve up their father's inheritance in service to the predatory ambitions of Rome, the once-glorious Hasmonean kingdom, heir to the legendary realm of David and Solomon, was doomed forever. For the next few decades, Palestine—and specifically Galilee—would become a battleground in which Jew would turn on Roman, the rich on the poor, and the landowners on the peasants. And, as it happened, these were the formative years of a young boy named Jesus.

FOUR

REVOLT AND REPRISALS

Satisfied that he had restored public order, Archilaus prepared to embark for Rome to hear Augustus's verdict on the disposition of Herod's will. But word of the Temple Massacre had already begun to spread through the Jewish Diaspora communities of the Mediterranean. In due course, the news reached the ears of high Roman officials, including Varus, the governor of Syria-Palestine, and Augustus's *chargé d'affaires* in the region, a man named Sabinus. While Archilaus was placidly sailing across the Mediterranean to Rome, confident of being named Herod's heir, Sabinus had traveled in the opposite direction, to Jerusalem. There, he summoned all of Herod's senior officials and demanded that they give him a detailed accounting of the former king's properties and state income. The officials complied and, before long, Sabinus had a complete picture of what the kingdom of Palestine was worth. Unbeknownst to Archilaus and his immediate family, the groundwork was being laid for a complete takeover of Judea.

When Archilaus arrived in Rome, an unpleasant surprise awaited him. His siblings, notably his sister Salome and his brother Antipas, accompanied by their retinue of advisers, had also rushed to Rome. As Archilaus was soon to discover, they had formed a secret alliance to deny Archilaus the crown and to petition Augustus to make Antipas the legitimate heir of Herod instead. Thus began the struggle between Archilaus and Antipater for the glory of Herod's legacy that would have far-reaching consequences for the population of Lower Galilee.

Apprised of the arrival of this dysfunctional family, Augustus scheduled a hearing and invited his close advisers to attend. The son of Salome, named Antipater, "a bitter enemy of Archilaus," was invited to speak first. The young man immediately launched into a denunciation of his uncle Archilaus, calling him a usurper who had shed blood even before Rome had had the chance to confirm him as king. Archilaus, he railed, was a two-faced "actor" who pretended to shed tears for his dead father during the day, then threw parties to celebrate his takeover of the Herodian government at night. The Passover massacre, the "slaughter of all those in the Temple and the impiety of it all," said he, was clear evidence of Archilaus's tyrannical bent. But the biggest bombshell was saved for last. Herod's will, said Salome's son, was incorrect. When the king was still "of a sound mind," he had drafted an earlier and "more authentic" testament in which he had clearly designated his son Antipas as his legitimate heir.

All eyes now swiveled to Archilaus. In fact, Archilaus had come prepared. Knowing the odds he now faced, Archilaus had also enlisted the services of a skilled orator, who was none other than the renowned historian and philosopher Nicolaus of Damascus. A brilliant legal mind, Nicolaus was the author of a large library on world history, as well as a biography of the emperor himself. It so happened that Nicolaus, a trusted adviser of Augustus, had also been a close friend of King Herod. This may be the reason why the eminent historian had come to the defense of the Archilaus faction—in the hope of securing a lucrative appointment in the future.[1]

As far as Archilaus's intentions were concerned, Nicolaus began, everyone should be assured that he had only the best interests of his people at heart. Why, then, the incident at the Temple? The reason, Nicolaus said smoothly, was that Archilaus had faced not a peaceful demonstration but a rioting mob who had tried to take advantage of the uncertain political situation to upend the law. Why, all Archilaus had done was intervene so as to protect the innocent worshipers at the Temple. As far as the rebels were concerned, they had brought the bloodshed upon themselves. Indeed, said Nicolaus, availing himself of a legal ploy that would later be used against Jesus, the disturbance of the peace was not only directed against Archilaus but also against the sovereignty of Rome and Augustus himself. Condone these "tumults" and one, in effect, condoned violent opposition to the authority of Rome.[2]

It was a skillful defense, and it had its intended effect. Despite the damning evidence, Augustus could not bring himself to discard Herod's carefully crafted testament. He asked for time to think matters over.

THE REVOLT SPREADS

Back in Palestine, however, time was running out. Emboldened by Archilaus's absence, the country seethed with unrest. The heady scent of freedom was in the air. Passover was followed, fifty days later, by the feast of Pentecost, a time when thousands of Jews once again came together in Jerusalem. This time, a great many who were converging on the city raised their voices not only against Archilaus but also against the arrogance of the Roman legate, Sabinus, who had used Archilaus's absence to seize all of Herod's fortresses. Even now, the legate was avidly scouring the country for treasure "for his own personal gain." Word of Sabinus's actions ran through the Pentecost crowd like wildfire. It truly seemed like Rome was preparing a complete takeover of the Jewish nation.

Among the worshipers, says Josephus, were "a great number who had come from Galilee." Were Joseph and his kin among them? Unlikely; journeys such as this were expensive, and Jesus was only two or three years old. But, regardless, the growing protest over the looting by Sabinus and the prospect of another ruthless Herodian ruler would have dominated the conversation at the village cistern.

Sabinus was well aware of the growing popular opposition to his role as *de facto* governor. With the Pentecost festival looming, he had appealed for immediate reinforcements. Governor Varus, back in Syria, agreed—and not a moment too soon. As soon as the festival had officially begun, throngs of worshipers surged through the Temple complex and made for the scaffolding of the Temple porticoes, which were still under construction. From there, they proceeded to pelt the Roman soldiers, stationed in the adjacent Antonia Fortress, with anything they could get their hands on. Incensed, the soldiers broke into the Temple forecourt and set the porticoes to the torch.

Fed by the fresh pitch and timber, the flames quickly spread and soon engulfed not only the protestors, but innocent bystanders too. A holocaust ensued; all in the vicinity of the gates were "either burned alive or slaughtered by the enemy when they attempted to retreat." Then the soldiers stormed the Temple precinct proper, broke down the doors to the Temple, and made their way to the Temple treasury. This treasury, as we have seen, was the central repository of Temple tax proceeds, as well as being Judea's "central bank," swollen with deposits from wealthy families throughout the region. The soldiers broke into the coffers and helped themselves to as much silver and gold as they could carry; Sabinus himself, who stood and witnessed the event, made off "with 400 talents." A "talent" was not a coin but a measure of weight, roughly equal to fifty pounds. Assuming that the treasure looted by Sabinus consisted mostly of silver, we can safely infer that the Roman ran off with the equivalent of $2.6 million (at $6,500 per talent) or more. Thus sated with loot, the soldiers withdrew to Herod's former palace in the Upper City and barricaded themselves in, waiting for the inevitable Jewish backlash.[3]

It was not long in coming. Outraged by this sacrilege, thousands of worshipers laid siege to the Roman contingent inside the palace. The whole country, now effectively without government, erupted in violence. Entire regiments of Herod's standing army disbanded and spread across Judea, where they took to banditry.

This was the moment that Judas, the son of Hezekiah, had been waiting for. As we have seen, a half century previously, Hezekiah had led a rebellion in Galilee against the collaborationist regime of Hyrcanus and Antipater. His militias had been defeated by the forces of Herod, then Galilee's governor, and Hezekiah himself had been executed. Now that Herod's precious police state lay in ruins, his militias were on the run, and chaos reigned everywhere, the time had come for Judas to avenge his father. He organized his own band of resistance fighters and set out to "terrorize Galilee," waging guerrilla warfare on anything and anyone associated with either the Herodian regime or the Romans: officials, landowners, and ordinary soldiers.[4]

We do not know to what extent the peasants of Galilee rallied to his cause, but given their lot under Herod's regime, it would not come as a surprise to know that many of them threw their support behind Judas's cause. For years, their surplus and their meager profits had been sucked up by Jerusalem, there to further swell the coffers of Herod's elites. As the winds of freedom swept down from the hills, it would have been tempting indeed to heed Judas's rallying cry and get payback from the Judean puppet rulers and their Roman overlords.

What the rebels had in enthusiasm, however, they lacked in weapons. Judas knew that to withstand the Roman reprisals that were surely coming, his forces needed to be equipped with first-rate arms, and lots of them. As it happened, there was a cache of weapons right in the heart of Galilee, in the arsenal built by Herod in the still-fortified city of Sepphoris. Before long, Judas rallied his forces and succeeded in breaking into the city, where he headed straight for the Herodian administrative building. His men scoured the place from top to bottom and made off with all the weapons that were in store there, so that, as Josephus tells us, Judas was able to "arm everyone in his band of men."

News of this audacious act must have spread across Galilee, also reaching the village of Nazareth, which was only four miles distant from Sepphoris. Suddenly, Judas had become a force to be reckoned with. What's more, there were reports of other uprisings as well. In Jericho, a former slave from Herod's entourage named Simon had decided to exploit the general confusion to pronounce himself king. He gathered a following, burned down Herod's palace in Jericho, and proceeded to do the same to all of Herod's property throughout the area, until a patrol of Roman soldiers caught up with him and cut off his head.[5]

A third revolt was initiated by another character with royal aspirations, Athronges. This rebel leader was neither a former slave nor a landowner, we are told, but a simple peasant who had previously made a living as a shepherd. He and his brothers, four in number, decided to follow Judas's example and create a resistance force with the goal of ousting the Romans. Their stated aim was to create a kingdom, which, reading between Josephus's lines, probably meant a restoration of the former Hasmonean monarchy. Whether Athronges was really a "shepherd," as Josephus dismissively claims, or a member of the landed gentry with extensive herds, is subject to debate. Josephus allows that he and his brothers, "every one of them, were commanders," which may imply some form of military pedigree.

And so it happened that within a short period of time, all of Galilee and the surrounding regions, including the Jordan Valley, were seething with rebellion. What's more, there was no reason to think that these spontaneous uprisings would not have a chance of succeeding. After all, the Maccabean Revolt of the second century C.E. had prevailed over a very powerful and determined foreign occupation. Indeed, each of these rebel leaders may have seen himself as a new Judas the Maccabean, the hero of that revolution, who had succeeded in restoring full Jewish independence. And, if Josephus's records are to be believed, these resistance fighters were certainly as bellicose as the Maccabeans had been. Whenever an opportunity presented itself, they "fell upon the King's [Herod's] men . . . and killed a great many of the Romans and the king's forces."[6]

The sheer ferocity of these clashes is illustrated by the following example. One day, a band of guerrillas decided to prepare an ambush for a company of Roman soldiers that was about to pass through the township of Emmaus. Emmaus, located some seven miles from Jerusalem, would later gain fame as the place where, in the Gospel of Luke, Jesus appeared to two of his followers after the Easter events.[7] Josephus tells us that this particular Roman company was "carrying bread and weapons to the army," which means they were probably bringing badly needed supplies to the besieged Roman forces in Jerusalem itself. As the company entered the ambush, the guerrillas attacked. The centurion, Arius, was overwhelmed, and, after a fierce fight, forty of his unit's soldiers lay dead in the dust. The remainder fled, allowing the guerrillas to melt back into the Judean wilderness.

These and other successes of the rebel militias convinced the Roman governor Varus in Antioch, capital of Roman Syria, that a major response was needed. At that moment, Varus had three legions at his disposal. One was already in Palestine, for it had accompanied Varus and Gabinus during their original journey to Jerusalem. Varus, heeding the appeals of Gabinus, had ordered it to remain garrisoned in Palestine for the time being. Two more legions were in their home barracks in Antioch in Syria. Josephus does not give us the names of these legions, but it is likely that Roman strength in the area included the *III Gallica,* the *X Fretensis,* and either the *VI Ferrata* or the *XII Fulminata.*

The problem was that these legions were not stationed in Antioch to police this narrow strip called Palestine, but to serve as a deterrent force against the vast Parthian empire to the northeast. If Varus sent one or two of his remaining legions to Galilee and Judea, he would weaken his own position and essentially leave all of Rome's Near Eastern possessions exposed to attack. The danger was all too real; just thirty years previously, the Parthians had used the turmoil of the civil war for the Hasmonean throne to launch an invasion under the pretext of intervening on the side of Aristobulus. What's more, the Parthians, heirs to the Persian empire, were a force to be reckoned with: it had taken Herod, equipped with some of Rome's finest legions, a year of hard campaigning to drive them back across the border.

It is therefore a clear indication of Varus's concern over the situation in Palestine that he chose to dispatch not one, but *two* legions to the region, all of his remaining strength, in a desperate gamble to quell the uprising by force. And even these two legions, a force of eight thousand men, were apparently deemed insufficient: Varus also ordered his cavalry force into the Palestinian theater, "four troops of horsemen," and then appealed to all of Rome's vassal kings in the region to contribute auxiliary forces, as they were expected to do in times of crisis.[8]

His request did not fall on deaf ears. The community of Berytus rose to the occasion by mobilizing no fewer than fifteen hundred auxiliaries. "Aretas, king of Arabia" (or Nabataea) hastened to offer his forces as well. We assume that this was king Aretas IV Philopatris, the same Aretas who had given his daughter Phasaelis to Herod's son Antipas in marriage. Aretas may have sensed an opportunity to march into Palestine and stake his claim for the Transjordan area (today's West Bank), since his territory of Arabia Petraea Nabataea (roughly analogous to today's Jordan) consisted chiefly of desert.

Varus and the commanders of the Roman legions, their ranks now swollen with auxiliaries, then made their basic plan of attack. Governor Varus himself would lead the main force along the highway hugging the Mediterranean Coast, passing through Tyre and Ptolemais (Acco) before crossing the Jezreel Valley into Samaria and ultimately Jerusalem. In order to clear the way for his main column, Varus ordered King Aretas and his Arab soldiers, who were much closer to the main areas of guerrilla activity, into Galilee with the objective of capturing Sepphoris and suppressing the Galilean resistance fighters at all costs.

This strategy would have fateful consequences for the Galilean peasants. The Nabataean kingdom and Herod had been at loggerheads for much of the past forty years. A small kingdom with few agricultural resources, Nabataea—famous for the rock-hewn city of Petra—derived most of its revenues from trade caravans bringing spices and luxury goods from India and Arabia to Rome. For the Nabataean soldiers, the prospect of plunging into the fertile valleys of Galilee, looting their way from village to village, must have sounded like a dream come true.

And this is precisely what happened. Unfettered by any Roman authority, yet with Rome's explicit sanction, Aretas pushed into Galilee with relish. Rather than pursuing the guerrilla bands in their natural hiding places—the limestone caves and hills of Galilee's highlands—the king embarked on a series of reprisals, moving his forces from village to village and raping, looting, and burning as he went. Varus, who arrived in the region a short while later with his main army, was surprised to find that most villages had been burned to the ground. As it happened, the Arab king's ultimate objective was Sepphoris, the largest urban center in the area. This placed Nazareth directly in his path.

We do not know what happened in Nazareth, nor how the rampage by Aretas affected Joseph's family. We do know, as Josephus tells us, that "along their march nothing escaped them, but that all places were full of fire and of slaughter." The vision of these Arab soldiers, pillaging their way through the fields of Nazareth, must have traumatized Joseph's young family. Though clearly they escaped with their lives, it is likely that much of Joseph's land would have been destroyed or burned, dooming that year's harvest and plunging the family into economic hardship.

It was Jesus' first exposure to the vulnerability of the peasants under Roman occupation rule. Though it is questionable whether the child, who was probably two or three at the time, would have remembered, the fear and destruction must have made an indelible impression on Joseph, and it is possible that Joseph imparted the horror of these reprisals and the futility of opposing Rome to his son. Throughout his later years, Jesus would never advocate a confrontation with the Romans. Instead, he would urge his followers to "give Caesar what belongs to Caesar."[9] The Gospel of Luke even tells us that Jesus once consented to heal the servant of a Gentile "centurion" stationed in Capernaum.[10] A centurion commanded a troop of one hundred soldiers and was a very prominent symbol of the collaborationist regime of Antipas.[11] For Jesus to associate himself with such a figure was clear evidence of his belief that, onerous though it might be, violent resistance was not the way to cope with the Roman occupation.

In due course, the looting hordes of Aretas moved on, with the forces of Varus following in their wake. It soon became clear that in his lust for pillage, Aretas had failed in his primary objective, and that it was up to the Roman forces to track down and capture the various rebel leaders operating in the area. Jerusalem, too, was invested and pacified. Varus then set out to exact his vengeance. In a reprisal reminiscent of Nazi brutality, the village of Emmaus was burned to the ground as punishment for the ambush that had occurred in its vicinity, even though none of the villagers had been involved. The captured resistance fighters were next. Though a few were released, some two thousand men (and possibly women) were condemned to death, using Rome's favored method of punishing rebels: by crucifixion.

Even while these mass executions went on, the ragtag army of auxiliaries and "allied" forces continued their rampage in the countryside, flouting attempts by Varus to bring them to heel. Only gradually was the Roman governor able to disband these foreign militias and to send the soldiers and mercenaries back whence they had come, sated with loot. Galilee's fields and villages were left in ruins.

AUGUSTUS REACHES A DECISION

Meanwhile, back in Rome, Augustus had still not decided what to do with Archilaus. The matter may not have been foremost on his mind: the most pressing item on his agenda was, once again, how to deal with the Parthians. Just two years earlier, in 6 B.C.E., Rome's loyal vassal king of Armenia, Tigranes, had been ousted in a coup. Armenia had previously been Parthian territory, and had been ceded by the Parthian king only with the greatest reluctance in a treaty painstakingly negotiated by Augustus himself. On the Palatine Hill, it was widely believed that the Parthians were behind the coup, bent on reclaiming their influence in the region by subterfuge. Exasperated, Augustus ordered his stepson, Tiberius, to lead a military expedition to Armenia and reinstate the toppled king Tigranes. Tiberius, Augustus's future successor, was an obvious choice, for it was he who at age twenty-two had marched into Armenia to invest Tigranes to begin with.

Surprisingly enough, Tiberius flatly refused to go. It mattered little to him that since the death of Augustus's son-in-law, Agrippa, he was clearly marked for the succession. Truth be told, Tiberius was fed up with the politics of Rome, just as he was fed up with the antics of his famously promiscuous wife Julia, whom he had been forced to marry. Instead, Tiberius retreated to Rhodes, there to brood in peace. Since Agrippa's sons, Augustus's grandsons, were only in their teens, the fifty-seven-year-old emperor faced the prospect that his carefully laid succession plans would come to naught, and that if he died now, Rome might once again be plunged into civil war.

Sometime late in that tragic year of 4 B.C.E., however, the matter of who should rule in Palestine was once again moved to the front burner. The reason was the arrival of a new embassy from Palestine. These, interestingly enough, were not members of the Herodian family, but rather noblemen and private citizens who, with Varus's permission, had come to apprise the emperor of the latest upheaval in their native land. The embassy had one goal: to persuade Augustus to appoint neither Archilaus nor Antipas, and to do away with all pretense of a Herodian kingdom altogether, "so that they may live by their own [i.e., Mosaic] Laws." To press their case, the Jewish delegation rallied the Jewish community of Rome and mustered eight thousand people, all fervently anti-Herodian, to lend further support to their petition.

The embassy was received in the temple of Apollo, the patron god of Augustus, which the emperor had ordered built on the Palatine Hill, next to the temple dedicated to the goddess Cybele. The spot, it was believed, had been identified by Apollo himself by helpfully hurling a bolt of lightning to earth.[12] For Augustus, the setting had a symbolic significance that would not be lost on the various delegations from Palestine. The temple, only located and excavated in the 1960s, commemorated the emperor's victories over both Pompey in 36 B.C.E. and over Mark Antony in 31 B.C.E.—two battles that had sealed the emperor's control over the Near East. Built of white Luna marble, with a façade of graceful Ionic columns, it was topped by Apollo's attribute, a splendid chariot of the sun.[13]

It was in this building that Augustus brought the latest embassy from Judea face-to-face with Herod's sons and their advisers. The citizens were invited to speak first. A long discourse followed as to why the Herodian dynasty should be discarded, substantiated by an extensive list of Herod's misdeeds. The most grievous of the king's crimes, the embassy stated, was that Herod "had found a nation in flourishing condition, and had left it in a state of abject poverty." Herod, the delegates said, had extorted leading men of property, taken their estates, and then threatened to take their lives as well unless they paid a handsome ransom in gold and silver. It was therefore no surprise that the country had welcomed Herod's death, in the belief that any change could only be for the better. This is why, the ambassadors said, they had been ready to accept Herod's heir, Archilaus, provided that "he would reciprocate with a fair degree of moderation."

Alas, how their good faith had been betrayed! Archilaus, the delegation attested, had been anxious "to prove himself a worthy son of his father," and had given his subjects a foretaste of "his future virtue." At the very earliest opportunity, he had slaughtered "three thousand of his own countrymen at the Temple." Was this what lay in store for Judea—another thirty years of brutal dictatorship? "Deliver us from these royal forms of government," the Jews beseeched the emperor, and urged that Palestine be added to Roman Syria, to be governed by the Roman legate—*as long as they would be allowed to live according to their laws*.[14]

The delegation fell silent, the echo of their words fading beneath the rafters of the temple. The *imperator* nodded, absorbing their arguments. With growing apprehension, Archilaus realized that his chances of becoming king were in acute jeopardy.

Then Nicolaus of Damascus begged to be heard one more time. In a devastating retort, Nicolaus skillfully refuted everything that the Jewish delegation had said. Herod was dead, he said; consequently, one could accuse the man of any form of slander, knowing full well that he could never defend himself. If all these crimes had been committed, why had the people of Judea not spoken up any sooner? Why had they waited to appear before Caesar until now, with Herod safely in his tomb?

Augustus was impressed. What's more, he may have been relieved. Herod had always acted in the best interests of Rome and the Julian House. And as for the massacre in the Temple, Augustus himself understood the value of preemptive violence if it suited his plans; he knew that Palestine was an unruly nation with a long history of revolt. Nicolaus's speech had merely helped him to make up his mind.

And so, a few days after the meeting, the emperor's verdict was made public. To the despair of the Jewish embassy, Archilaus was confirmed as Herod's principal heir. He was to rule over a territory encompassing Judea, Idumaea, and Samaria, as well as a handful of Greek cities in Palestine's coastal region. However, Augustus attached one condition—perhaps an attempt to soften the blow to Archilaus's subjects. The emperor refused to grant Archilaus the much-desired title of *basileus* or "king." Archilaus would have to earn it. If, said Augustus, he proved himself to be a just and compassionate ruler and governed his territory "virtuously," he might gain the royal title in due course. Until then, he was effectively on probation and only permitted to use the title of *ethnarch,* a Greek word meaning "ruler of a people."

At the same time, Augustus confirmed Herod's younger son Antipas as *tetrarch* of Galilee and Perea—another Greek term, meaning "ruler of one fourth." Herod's other son Philip was likewise invested as tetrarch of the Gaulanitis and surrounding territories, just as Herod had ordained in his will. The Gaulanitis was the area to the north and east of the Sea of Galilee, extending further eastward into Batanea, Trachonitis, and Auranitis, an area roughly analogous to today's southern Syria and northern Jordan.

As we would expect, this arrangement pleased no one. Archilaus returned to Judea bereft of the coveted title of king and incensed over the way his own subjects had denounced him in front of the emperor. Antipas was disappointed that he had not been chosen as his father's heir in Archilaus's stead, despite the fact that his brother's short period of rule had been such a disaster. And the Jewish people were stunned to find that they were once again facing a government of Herodian despots. Only Philip, half-brother to Archilaus and Antipas (his mother was Cleopatra of Jerusalem), was content with his lot. He retired to his designated territory, built a modest capital in Caesarea Philippi (formerly known as Panias) near the source of the Jordan, and by all accounts ruled justly and peacefully. As it turned out, his region had a predominantly Gentile population, so that Philip was spared the simmering mood of Jewish nationalism that would continue to vex his brothers to the west.

ARCHILAUS TAKES REVENGE

Immediately upon his arrival in Jerusalem, Archilaus decided to exact his revenge on those who had sought to sabotage his throne. The first target of his wrath was the high priest, Joazar, son of Boethus, whom Archilaus accused of secretly plotting his overthrow. The high priest was summarily removed from his position; in his stead, Archilaus appointed Joazar's brother, Eleazar ben Boethus. He barely lasted a year; then Eleazar, too, was removed in favor of Joshua, son of Sie, who remained in office until 6 C.E.

Archilaus then embarked on a reign every bit as "tyrannical and barbarous" as that of his father. Whereas Herod had always maintained a modicum of consideration for the piety of his subjects, Archilaus flaunted his disdain for Scripture and the Law. His eye fell on the widow of his deceased brother Alexander, son of the Hasmonean princess Mariamne. The widow's name was Glaphyra. Archilaus decided to marry her, though his motive is unclear. Perhaps he was genuinely in love with her. On the other hand, her dead husband Alexander, in whose veins had once flowed Hasmonean blood, had been highly popular, which surely figured in his decision as well.

The problem was, however, that Glaphyra had three young children by her first husband. To marry one's brother's wife after she had borne children by her first husband was a violation of Mosaic Law; one could take a sister-in-law in marriage only if she had been childless.[15] Archilaus proceeded with the marriage nevertheless. The Judeans were scandalized by the union, but Archilaus ignored them. Instead, he turned his energies to construction projects in a deliberate effort to emulate his father. His first endeavor, funded by a renewed levy of taxes, was the development of a lavish palace near Jericho, sited close to the large palm and balsam plantations for which the area was famous. These groves had originally been developed by the Hasmoneans and later given by Mark Antony to his lover, Cleopatra, who in turn had leased them to Herod. Since their yield was highly profitable, Archilaus decided to expand the plantations. This required a large influx of water, so Archilaus ordered that the water supply of a nearby village be rerouted to his plantations, leaving the villagers dry.

After ten years of Archilaus's misrule, the nobles of Judea were fed up. They (along with Archilaus's "brethren," which we can assume means Antipas and Philip) took ship for Rome and requested an audience with the emperor, remembering what Augustus had said about the ethnarch's "probationary period." As soon as they were ushered into Augustus's presence, the delegation launched into a tirade about how Archilaus had broken every promise he had made only a decade ago. Archilaus had been told by the emperor himself to rule "with virtue," the noblemen recalled, but he had done the opposite. Consequently, Archilaus was no longer fit to hold office, for "he had broken the commands of Caesar."[16]

Augustus was in no mood to be indulgent. In the last four years, his grandsons and designated heirs, Lucius and Gaius Caesar—the former still in his late teens, the latter in his mid-twenties—had died under mysterious circumstances. Much later, Roman historians would point the finger at Augustus's wife, Livia, who had continued to lobby for her own son Tiberius. Livia got her way in the end; with both of Augustus's grandsons removed from the scene, Augustus had no choice but to reluctantly appoint the dour Tiberius as the rightful heir, despite his misgivings on the subject. Thus the path was cleared for the man who would rule the Roman Empire throughout Jesus' adulthood. Interestingly enough, three years later, in 9 C.E., Tiberius resumed his rank of general and rode to suppress a revolt that had broken out among several Germanic tribes. During this campaign, he was accompanied by general Varus—the same Publius Quinctilius Varus under whose auspices, as governor of Syria, the Roman army had undertaken the murderous reprisals in Galilee and Judea in 4 B.C.E. Varus met his end when, during the Battle of the Teutoburg Forest, he was ambushed by Germanic tribes and killed.

Now the weary Augustus had to face the hard fact that his decision concerning Herod's will had been ill advised. He angrily summoned Archilaus's representative at his court, who had the misfortune of being called Archilaus as well, and ordered him to bring his master to Rome at the earliest opportunity. The diplomat sped away and duly arrived in Jerusalem, only to find Archilaus immersed in one of his favorite pastimes, a drunken feast with his circle of cronies and friends.

The news of Archilaus's summons must have put an abrupt end to the revelry. The ethnarch had three choices: he could ignore the order, a most unwise course of action; he could flee with whatever he would be able to carry; or he could return to Rome and face the music, relying on his charm to sway Augustus as he had done previously. He chose the latter.

From Caesarea, the gleaming white new harbor city built by his father, Archilaus set sail for Rome. Once arrived, he was ushered into the presence of Caesar Augustus, who had surrounded himself with skillful *delatores* or accusers. These prosecutors proceeded to plead their case against the Judean ethnarch, and the verdict was swift. Archilaus was summarily banished to Vienne, a city on the left bank of the Rhône River in Gaul (modern France). Lest this not be punishment enough, Augustus also voided Archilaus's title and his holdings, "took away his money," and ordered that all his estates be seized—including the plantations in Jericho on which he had lavished so much care.

JUDEA BECOMES A ROMAN PROVINCE

Archilaus's fall from grace would have fatal consequences for the history of the people of Israel. In fact, we could go as far as to say that it established the conditions that would ultimately lead to Jesus' death. For Augustus resolved not to hand the territory of Judea and Samaria to Herod's other sons, the tetrarchs Antipas and Philip, nor to return the sovereignty of this ancient territory to its legitimate dynasty, the Hasmonean House. Perhaps Augustus was led to this decision by the sober fact that there was no unblemished Hasmonean House to speak of, and that the only surviving Hasmoneans were also descendants of Herod. Agrippa, Herodias, and Herod of Chalcis were all grandchildren of King Herod and the Hasmonean princess Mariamne. What's more, the sixteen-year-old Agrippa was not in Palestine but in Rome, of all places, there to be educated at the imperial court, as his grandfather Herod had requested. Agrippa's time would come, but not in Augustus's lifetime. And so Augustus made the fateful decision for the annexation of Judea, making it a subject province of Rome known as Iudaea, part of the territory of Greater Roman Syria. This region, as we have seen, was ruled by a Roman governor based in Antioch.

Interestingly enough, this was precisely the solution for which the Jewish delegation had argued back in 4 B.C.E. But their motives at that time had been specific. First, by doing away with the useless prop of the Herodian royal house, they had hoped to eliminate that heavy layer of Herodian taxation that was bringing the nation to ruin. Second, by submitting themselves to the sovereignty of the foreign power itself, the delegation fervently hoped to arrive at an accommodation similar to the one reached with Cyrus the Great, emperor of Persia, after the Exile. Cyrus had agreed that the Jewish people would be left to administer themselves, by virtue of a theocracy made up of prominent priests in Jerusalem, provided the annual tribute was paid on time. We can only speculate what turn history would have taken if their dream had been granted. If Roman Judea had indeed been administered by a reform-minded priesthood, genuinely dedicated to eliminating the contaminating influence of Hellenism and the restoration of Covenant Law observance, perhaps the history of Israel, and the career of a young rabbi from Nazareth, would have taken a different course.

But this was not to be. Augustus did not return power to the Jewish people—nor, for that matter, to the Jewish priesthood. Instead, he chose what he believed was the best option, namely, to place the governance of the territory in the hands of a professional diplomat, a Roman *prefectus,* who in turn would report to the governor in Syria. As it was, the current governor of Syria had finished his term, so the post was vacant. A new diplomat was needed to govern both Syria and the newly minted Roman province of Judea.

Augustus's choice fell on a man named Gaius Publius Sulpicius Quirinius. A Roman aristocrat by birth, Quirinius had first come to the attention of Augustus during his service in the legion that defeated the emperor's nemesis, Mark Antony, at the Battle of Actium in 31 B.C.E. In the years to follow, Quirinius's career followed an upward trajectory typical of a Roman nobleman destined for great things: overseas service in Spain, followed by promotion to governor of Crete and Cyrene. Along the way, Quirinius brutally suppressed a revolt by a marauding tribe of desert warriors known as the Marmarici, which made his reputation as a man devoted to law and order.

It also boosted his career, for soon thereafter Quirinius reached the highest and most coveted post in the land (after the emperor's), that of consul. Though this office was already becoming a mostly honorary position, bereft of the power it once had held under the Republic, it was nevertheless a mark of great favor. Quirinius then went on to serve as governor of Galatia and Pamphylia, the same region where, some fifty years later, Paul would be active as missionary.

By the year 1 C.E., Quirinius's career had reached its apogee. He had become a member of the imperial household and principal adviser to Gaius Caesar. No doubt, if the young man had lived, Quirinius would eventually have attained a prominent position in the new emperor's administration. But it was not to be. Two years before Archilaus's banishment to Gaul, the twenty-four-year-old Gaius, eager to drench himself in military glory, insisted on participating in the campaign in Armenia (the very expedition that, fatefully, Tiberius had refused to lead). Gaius was injured in battle and shortly thereafter died of his wounds. The news plunged Augustus into grief. It also, quite suddenly, left Quirinius without a formal position at court.

For the next few years, his career was on hold. He made overtures to the party of Tiberius, the newly designated heir of the empire, but his advances were rebuffed. This all may serve to explain why, when Augustus appeared to offer him the post of Syria–Palestine, Quirinius accepted, even though by the standards of the Roman diplomatic service the position was a considerable step down. Compared to Galatia and Pamphylia, two deeply Hellenized regions in booming Asia Minor, Syria was a backwater with little opportunity for military distinction or personal enrichment. But Quirinius swallowed his pride, complied with the emperor's wish, and took to his task with a vengeance.

High on his list was the need to find a *prefectus* who could govern the new territory of Judea on his behalf. With Augustus's consent, he chose a Roman diplomat named Coponius. Coponius was not of senatorial rank, but was rather a member of the equestrian class—a knight, in other words, as was common with the rank of prefects. *Equites* formed an upwardly mobile subset of middle-class Romans who pursued diplomatic postings for the purpose of getting rich quick. With any luck, one could use the post of prefect to accumulate the requisite fortune of a million sesterces (roughly a quarter of a million dollars in today's currency), which qualified one for acceptance in the senatorial class.

The immediate question that needed to be settled was how much this dry patch of land called Judea was worth. By eliminating the Herodian administration and making Judea a subject territory of Rome, Augustus had also done away with the Herodian system of tax collection—including the tribute due to Rome. This responsibility now ultimately fell on the governor of Syria–Palestine. As we will recall, Roman officials did not collect taxes themselves, for a number of reasons. They did not know the villages nor the seasons when produce was harvested; they usually didn't speak the local language (Aramaic); and even if they did, they lacked the manpower to go to all the threshing floors in agricultural regions and be present when the harvest was brought in. Hence, the Romans relied on subcontractors to collect the taxes for them—the local townships and the infamous "publicans" of the New Testament.

To ensure that these contractors passed on to Rome whatever they received from taxpayers, it was important to determine what each district was worth. This, as we saw in Chapter 2, was the reason why Quirinius, upon assuming control of Judea, immediately ordered a census. The purpose of this census was not to count heads and families, as would be the case with a modern census, nor to have people register in the place of their birth. The sole aim of the Roman census was to assess the value of property a man might have, and to calculate the projected yield of his land. It was, in the words of Fabian Udoh, a straightforward "registration of property." Significantly, the new census required the population to declare their property in its cash equivalent, rather than in terms of land size or projected harvest yields.[17]

Naturally, the prospect of opening their books to the new occupation authority was not something that Judeans looked forward to. But the high priest at the time, the same Joazar, son of Boethus who had been appointed by Archilaus, decided to collaborate with the foreign takeover of his nation. He pledged his full support, doubtless in the hope of maintaining his office and thus control of the Temple operations. According to Josephus, the high priest also urged his fellow Jews to cooperate and to freely provide Roman officials with whatever information they required. Most Jews—specifically the upper elites—took his advice, "giving a full account of their estates without protest." They did this despite the fact that the new Roman tax rate, which has been estimated at 20 percent, was high by the standards of antiquity—so high, in fact, that, as Tacitus reports, Judeans would appeal for tax relief only a decade after the census was completed.[18]

THE JUDAS REVOLT

Some, however, took exception to this census. Their leader was a man called Judas the Galilean. Whether this is the same Judas, son of Hezekiah, who had organized a rebellion ten years earlier upon the death of Herod the Great, is a matter of debate. What is clear, however, is that this new Judas movement was motivated by religious principles rather than a thirst for revenge. The Roman census, Judas claimed, was illegal because the land to be assessed did not belong to Rome but to God. It was God who had given the Promised Land to his people, for them to till as tenants. To submit to the census and accept the Roman occupation as a fait accompli was therefore tantamount to accepting the yoke of slavery and rejecting the Lord's title to one's property. Consequently, Judas urged the populace to simply refuse any dealings with the Roman authorities, at any level, whether involving the census or any other form of contact.

Josephus presents this Judas movement as an outlaw force simply by virtue of their opposition to the Romans, as is his habit. Yet it is far from clear whether the Judas group was indeed an active resistance force or merely a civil-disobedience movement. Obviously, Judas's ultimate goal was to free the land of any foreign occupation and to create a nation governed by the laws of Moses. But nowhere do we hear about this Judas actually instigating attacks on Roman patrols, as Judas, son of Hezekiah had done a decade earlier, or in any other way resorting to violence to realize his goals. He may have done what Gandhi did in postwar India—paralyzing the foreign administration by organizing widespread nonviolent resistance.

Josephus claims that the Judas movement ultimately evolved into a full-fledged party, known as the Zealots. This is an interesting suggestion that, for the purpose of our story, deserves some explanation.

The Zealots were the "fourth philosophy" known in Palestine during the early years of the Roman occupation. The other "schools" were the Pharisees and the Sadducees, as we saw earlier, as well as a third movement called the Essenes, which we shall encounter when Jesus joins the group of John the Baptist.

At face value, the philosophy of the Zealots had much in common with that of the Pharisees. Like the Pharisees, they were devoted to a literal interpretation of the Mosaic Laws as a way to sustain the Jewish character of daily life. Indeed, says Josephus, the Zealots embraced "almost everything that the Pharisees believed in," with the exception that the Zealots were devoted to liberty and would not accept any notion of foreign occupation, including the idea of Palestine as an autonomous state beholden to Rome. By contrast, Judas and his party accepted only one ruler, and that was YHWH.

Judas's aim, in short, was to create a Kingdom of God—ruled by Covenant Law rather than the laws of Rome. This objective, as we will see, was not dissimilar to a manifesto propagated some twenty years later by a rabbi from Nazareth.

Recent scholarship, however, has questioned whether Judas the Galilean was indeed the force behind the Zealots—a movement that would become increasingly militant as the century wore on and would ultimately precipitate the outbreak of the Jewish war in 66 C.E. God, these later Zealots claimed, was fully behind their cause; therefore, the Jews should not shrink

106

"from the slaughter" that inevitably came with a struggle for freedom. By contrast, Judas "reproached the Jews for recognizing the Romans as masters when they already had God," but nowhere do we hear that Judas resorted to violence. In fact, in one of Josephus's other books, Judas is described as merely a "teacher" who told his fellow countrymen that they were "cowards if they submitted to pay a tax to the Romans."[19]

✣ ✣ ✣

History is written by the victors. In our case, the history of Palestine in the first decade of the first century C.E. was written by a man writing for the Romans on behalf of a Roman sponsor. Consequently, Josephus's story is almost exclusively preoccupied with the actions of the powerful elites who ruled Palestine during the years of Jesus' childhood. The peasants and day-workers who made up the vast majority of Galilee's population rarely figure in his narrative; and when they do appear on his radar, it is usually as a group of "bandits" or "outlaws" who choose to terrorize the citizenry and challenge the sovereignty of Rome.

It is not surprising, therefore, that Josephus rarely bothers to ask himself *why* the peasants of Galilee would be involved in not one, but several desperate revolts against the ruling regime in the span of a mere ten years. The fact is that Josephus couldn't have cared less about the lot of the Palestinian peasant. As a member of a priestly aristocratic family, raised in a world of privilege, Josephus looked upon the world as one inevitably divided between the haves and the have-nots. In Palestine, the vast majority of peasants toiled in poverty so that their betters could administer the state in the comfort that they thought was their due. This had been the way of the world since the earliest days of Israel; to question such an arrangement was to question nature itself.

Hence, in Josephus's worldview, anyone who strove to upset the order of things was by definition a bandit or a terrorist. That is why Hezekiah was "the head of the robbers," even though modern scholarship has argued that Hezekiah may have been a Hasmonean nobleman. This is also why Judas, the son of Hezekiah, as well as Simon, Athronges, and other resistance fighters against Roman oppression—why all these men were invariably branded as terrorists, whose hopeless revolts accomplished nothing but to provoke the inevitable and just reprisals at the hands of the Romans.

What is so astonishing about Josephus's story is that the Galilean peasantry was galvanized to revolt at all. Ever since the earliest days of the kingdoms of Israel, the nexus of resistance against foreign oppression was not in Galilee, but rather in Samaria and Judea. There, Israelites struggled in vain to resist the inexorable onslaught of Egyptian, Assyrian, or Babylonian powers. In Galilee, by contrast, the peasantry shrugged and focused their struggle on the soil. Consoled by the constancy of land and kin, they had little incentive to light the torch of resistance. It took almost half a century before the Maccabean Revolt—that great revolution that liberated all of Judea—would reach Galilee and incorporate it into the newly independent Jewish kingdom.

And yet, as we just saw, three leaders from Galilee were able to instigate resistance movements in the ten years following the death of Herod. In two cases, these revolts were so widespread that they could only be suppressed by the combined might of all of Rome's military assets in the region. This may give us an idea of the vast socioeconomic despair that Herod's rule had wrought among the hamlets and villages of Galilee—an upheaval that would now profoundly affect the adolescence of a young peasant boy in Nazareth.

FIVE

JESUS AND JOSEPH IN SEPPHORIS

Life in Galilee had always been bound up in land. Land brought a family stability and anchored it to the soil of its ancestors. Land encouraged fathers and mothers to seek marriage partners for their children among their kinsmen, so as to keep the ownership of that land within the clan. Land was more than just soil to be tilled and harvested; it was the source of a farmer's pride, his sense of dignity, as it had been for his father and his father's father before him. Take it away, and you took away the very purpose of his existence.

But Herod, unlike the Hasmoneans, was utterly indifferent to the ancient patronage in Galilee, to the tribal legacy of land ownership that went back to the very origins of Israel. Nor did he pause to consider the ancient Jewish belief that the land was the Lord's to give and to take; that that land was only given to the farmer in tenancy, to cultivate at the Lord's pleasure; and that no man should call himself an owner of what was rightfully the property of YHWH. The idea of the land as the property of God is enshrined in the books of Joshua and Deuteronomy, but it was equally valid in the Hellenistic period, as evidenced by the books of the Jubilees and Sirach.[1] In all these writings, no man but God is recognized as the ultimate landlord of Israel. By ignoring this core precept of Covenant Law, Herod proved himself the consummate Idumaean ingenue: the Arab who only paid lip service to Jewish beliefs to the extent that it suited him. And so Herod ravaged Galilee as no king, foreign or domestic, had ever done before him.

Traditionally, Galilean society consisted of three distinct groups: Jewish small farmers, tilling patches of land that had been held by their families across generations; Gentile farmers and artisans, living on the periphery of Gentile cities; and owners of larger agricultural estates. Many such landowners were Jewish landed gentry with historical ties to the Hasmonean House, or wealthy priestly and aristocratic families in

Jerusalem (including, for example, the Sadducees) who did not live in Galilee but used the estates as a source of income. These priestly families relied on managers (or "stewards," as the Gospels call them) to run the estates on their behalf.

Historically, the relationship between peasant and landowner was to a certain degree symbiotic. Whereas the small farmer focused on mixed subsistence farming for the specific purpose of feeding his family and paying his taxes, larger estates used their greater access to capital to focus on the production of surplus crops for the marketplace. Until the Herodian era, this "market" was mostly regional, including townships and cities such as Capernaum and Sepphoris as well as the hungry mouths of Jerusalem. Many estates therefore did what the subsistence farmer could not: specialize in the cultivation in bulk of certain types of produce, whether wheat or barley; olives or grapes; melons, figs, or dates. David Fiensy, who made a special study of these estates, has identified large agricultural operations in the Jezreel Valley, Gaulanitis, western Samaria, and even Jericho during the Hasmonean era. Such large estates often had oxen yokes and farm implements that could be rented out to small farmers during harvest time, against a rental fee or a share of the harvest.

Estates of this type could be quite extensive. The Zenon Papyri, which date to the time when Galilee (and the rest of Palestine) formed part of the Ptolemaic Empire in Egypt, describe the estates of a finance minister, Apollonius, near the Galilean village of Bet Anat. The minister's holdings included extensive fields of wheat in addition to a vineyard of some eighty thousand grapevines, large enough to require a work force of twenty-five laborers.

These large aristocratic *villae* proved irresistible to Herod and his inner circle of courtiers and sycophants. Shortly after assuming power as king of all of Palestine, and without any attempt to legitimize his actions, Herod began to systematically terrorize families of property with known ties to the Hasmonean court. He first arrested scores of aristocratic supporters of the ousted Hasmonean king Antigonus—including forty-five high-ranking noblemen in Jerusalem itself. Their estates were confiscated and brought under control of Herod's privy purse. Prominent officers and administrators of the former regime with land holdings in Galilee were next; their lands and property were likewise expropriated and granted to either Herod's family members or his political cronies. This included high-ranking members of the priesthood. After the last Hasmonean-appointed high priest had been killed off, Herod appointed other, more pliable high priests, usually by inviting prominent members of priestly families from Persia and Egypt. Their loyalty was bought with gifts of appropriated land.[2]

As we have seen, the tax burden on the peasantry—taking into account the tithes levied by the priesthood as well as the taxes charged by the Romans and the Herodian regime—escalated to around 30 to 40 percent of a peasant's harvest yields, compared to a tax rate of around 9 to 12 percent elsewhere in the Roman Empire, such as Egypt.[3] Unlike landowners, however, the Palestinian peasant did not have the surplus to absorb these exorbitant taxes, for he practiced subsistence farming rather than bulk agriculture. Virtually every crop he raised was used to feed his family first and to barter for seeds and other necessary goods second. His margin for taxation, allowing for bad harvests, droughts, and the ravages of war, was therefore extremely limited—certainly not more than between 10 and 15 percent of yields.

THE SPIRAL OF DEBT

This created an insoluble dilemma for Galilean peasants who, like Joseph and Mary, had the misfortune of living through the turbulent years of Herod's passing and the reign of his son Antipas. They simply lacked the means to satisfy the demands of the governing elites. The only way to survive and stave off the inevitable was to *borrow* the money, then hope for a bumper crop that would let them hold off the tax man and creditor for one more year.

For Galilee, this was an unprecedented development. True, a farmer had always lived with a measure of debt, but it had largely taken the form of barter, of exchanging one's goods or services for that of another, without any cash being involved. Now, however, the very existence of the native Galilean peasantry was threatened. With their backs to the wall, farmers were essentially forced to mortgage their harvests so as to live another day.

To do so, they turned to the only people in the region with capital. These were in many cases the very landowners who had only recently taken possession of estates in Galilee and therefore looked upon their holdings as investments. Most of them were Judeans with no social or cultural ties to the peasantry. The peasants' fate was of no consequence to them. What did concern them was the pledged collateral, which inevitably was a peasant's harvest, guaranteed by his ancestral land.

It then dawned upon many of these landowners that the perilous state of the overtaxed peasantry provided an opportunity. They began to grasp that these peasants were bound to enter a spiral of ever-increasing debt from which they could never recover. And so, inevitably, there would come a moment when the peasant was no longer able to pay off the principal or the interest. At that instant the estate owner could demand the collateral, oust the peasant and his family, and confiscate his land. It was, all told, an irresistible proposition: lend capital at a hefty interest rate, while positioning oneself to vastly expand one's estates—at a fraction of the cost. So attractive was this opportunity that many landowners hedged their bets and drafted agreements with debtor farmers that made confiscation all but certain. The Midrash Rabbah reveals how a group of small farmers from a village called Bethar found themselves cheated with loss of fields or vineyards as a result of fraudulent contracts.[4]

The Mosaic Laws had anticipated this possibility since, as we have seen, a similar situation had taken place in the boom years following the return from Exile. In keeping with its concern for social justice, the Law had made provisions for a sabbatical year, when the land was supposed to lie fallow. In that same year, the Law stipulated that all debt should be forgiven and that debtors who had been enslaved should be released, so that the farmer could start with a clean slate.[5]

But the protection offered by the sabbatical year backfired in the Herodian era. What happened was that most creditors who only lent money for interest (and not for eventual confiscation) became increasingly reluctant to offer peasants loans as the sabbatical interlude drew near, for fear that their investments would come to naught. The eminent Pharisaic rabbi Hillel tried to circumvent this problem by providing for a special arrangement known as the *prozbul,* a special warrant that assured creditors that their loans would be repaid regardless of the sabbatical year.[6] While this made loans easier to obtain in the months and years just before a sabbatical, it had the unintended effect of removing whatever protection the Law still offered to indebted peasants.[7]

The opportunity of buying land cheap from bankrupt farmers soon attracted a new class of *nouveaux riches,* officials or cronies of Herod's court, who wasted no time in building and enlarging their own estates. The essential difference between them and the old landed Hasmonean aristocracy was that these *arrivistes* actively supported Herod and Roman rule. Consequently, these newly created landowners, many of them Judeans, were not burdened by any sentimental feelings toward the Galilean peasantry. They gladly took control of the confiscated plots, small as they may have been, and offered the unfortunate farmers work as tenants, cultivating the land they knew so well for little more than the wages of a day laborer. Many farmers, faced with the urgent need to feed their families, accepted and continued to break their backs on their former lands for the greater wealth of their new patrons. Others couldn't bear the heartbreak and the humiliation and instead flocked to the working pits of Herod's vast construction projects in Jerusalem, Caesarea, or Samaria. They, too, became day-laborers or "workers"—a vast throng of the poor and marginalized captured in the term *am ha-aretz:* "people of the land."

THE RISE OF A PEASANT PROLETARIAT

What was the response of the Roman occupiers to this growing crisis among the peasantry? The Romans welcomed it. Throughout the Empire, it had been standard Roman policy to encourage the consolidation of small, private plots into large estates, for it made cultivation more efficient and ultimately more profitable to the state by way of taxation. Augustus himself set an example by granting large swaths of the most fruitful land in Egypt to members of the imperial family and to court favorites. In addition, land that could not be tilled without a considerable investment in materials and labor (such as clearing and the provision of irrigation) could sometimes be assigned to qualified individuals with the proviso that they would make the necessary expenditures to make it profitable.[8] As we will see, the growing tension between the traditional farmer, staunchly defending his family plot against all odds, and the ever-growing "capitalist" estates, owned by Gentile and Herodian collaborators alike, would strongly color Jesus' "New Kingdom" vision of social and religious justice.

So the Palestine of Joseph and Jesus evolved into what we might describe as a proto-capitalist economy, not dissimilar to the agrarian societies in today's Africa: a society consisting largely of a peasant and day-laborer proletariat, whose output together supported a very small group of economic elites. The traditional socioeconomic milieu of Galilee, founded on the principles of economic equality and justice, was replaced by an exploitationist model that emphasized profit, creating in essence a class society. Fiensy, along with Heinz Kreissig, estimates that the peasant class accounted for a full 90 percent of the population of Palestine in Jesus' time. This included both small landowners who tilled the land to sustain their families; tenant farmers who worked the land at the behest of wealthy estate owners; and day-laborers who roamed the countryside in search of work and lived at the very margins of life. Their labor sustained an upper class of elites, consisting of Herodian officials and courtiers; the religious aristocracy, specifically the Sadducees; and other prominent constituencies, possibly including some Pharisees.

In sum, the relationship between the countryside and the major cities, between the peasantry and the elites, became increasingly parasitic: peasants like Joseph slaved to pay taxes that sustained the lavish lifestyle of a tiny affluent minority. The Roman annexation of Judea in 6 C.E. only accelerated this process. In fact, after the ouster of Archilaus, the Roman occupation authority made a point of assuring Herodian family members that they could retain the large estates they had acquired (largely by illegitimate means) under the regime of Herod the Great.

The accumulation of land in the hands of a small group of wealthy landowner–speculators also changed the nature of agricultural production in Galilee. Previously, as we have seen, peasants like Joseph cultivated a broad spectrum of produce in small quantity—enough to provide their families with a varied diet of bread as well as vitamin-rich vegetables such as onions, cabbage, squash, and beets, and occasionally grapes, olives, or figs. The compartmentalization of land into tiny crop-defined plots inevitably left the peasant with little surplus to sell. This is why before the Herodian era, agricultural production for markets outside of the immediate vicinity of peasant villages was limited.

With the rapid growth of other "capitalist" landholdings, owned by the new elites around Herod and his offspring, the percentage of diverse subsistence farming in Galilee dropped precipitously in favor of dedicated cultivation specifically for urban markets in Galilee and beyond. Land that had previously sustained the growth of many different crops was now seeded exclusively for popular export products such as grains. Orchards were combined to become vast production regions of olives (and olive oil), dates (and date wines), or grapes (for wine)—three key products for which there was a high demand in the Eastern Mediterranean as well as in Rome itself. This had been the whole point of Herod's plan to build a vast new harbor at Caesarea. Under the Hasmoneans and earlier rulers, Palestine had never had a major harbor, since there was no compelling need—much of its output was consumed by the Galilean producers themselves.[9]

Now that small landowners were increasingly subject to land confiscation, a growing number of urban elites saw an opportunity for profitable investment in commerce. They—unlike the Galilean peasant—had a keen understanding of the power of the marketplace in the Roman Empire; they understood that the Pax Romana established by Augustus had created unprecedented opportunities for international trade throughout the Mediterranean. This "boom" in Mediterranean trade was fueled by the growth of cities in Roman-occupied Asia Minor and on the Italian mainland, which brought with it an escalating demand for food. With Palestinian agricultural regions unlocked by Herod's great harbor, and with Palestine itself, as a vassal state of Rome, "plugged in" to the dense network of Mediterranean seaborne trade, these speculators understood that a lot of money was to be made—by selling Palestine's durable crops in quantity to markets throughout the basin and even as far as Rome itself.

In the Gospel of Thomas, Jesus denounces the futility of such agricultural hoarding at the expense of others. "There once was a rich man who had much money," Jesus tells his followers. "He said, 'I shall put my money to use so that I may sow, reap, plant, fill my storehouse with produce. . . . Such were his intentions, but that same night he died.'"[10] His scorn for wealthy landowners and speculators also inspired his comment, so disturbing to his followers, that "it is easier for a camel to go through the eye of a needle than for someone who is rich to enter the kingdom of God."[11]

More often than not, these wealthy speculators lived not in Galilee proper but in urban centers in Judea, relying on hired managers (*oikonomoi*) to run their Galilean estates on their behalf. These managers and stewards were heartily despised by the peasantry, exposing the ancient fissures between Judea and Galilee. Josephus states explicitly that Judas, son of Hezekiah, had been able to raise a guerrilla force in 4 B.C.E. by recruiting "a large number of desperate men." Indeed, one of the first actions the Galilean peasants undertook at the beginning of another revolt, the outbreak of the Jewish War of 66 C.E., was to exact their revenge by unceremoniously drowning these *nouveau riche* aristocrats (or *dynatoi*) in the Sea of Galilee.[12] Meanwhile, another group, led by *Sicarii* or "daggermen," broke into the public archives in Jerusalem, where the records of all indebted land and property were kept, and burned the building to the ground. The objective, says Josephus, was not only to erase all record of these hated debts but also to "persuade the poorer sort to join in their insurrection with safety against the more wealthy."[13]

✣ ✣ ✣

Thus, the years in which the young Jesus grew into adolescence were also a period of unprecedented economic change in Galilee. Large numbers of peasants whose families had held their land for many generations now saw themselves faced with the unthinkable: the loss of the very land that had sustained them and their kin for centuries. All in all, the displacement of the peasantry from their ancestral land was a crisis of untold economic, social, and psychological proportions.

We don't have to look far to try to imagine the impact of this process on the peasantry. There are plenty of regions in the world today that closely resemble the situation in first-century Palestine. A 2007 UN report estimated that in Southeast Asia alone, there were three million peasants who had become internally displaced as a result of economic pressures. One key example is the state of Burma, or, as its current rulers call it, Myanmar. Like ancient Palestine, Burma is predominantly agrarian, with over three quarters of the population deriving its livelihood from agricultural activity. For centuries, Burma's 150 ethnic tribes managed their land while respecting communal and family interests. But after it achieved independence from British colonial rule in 1948, its economy became almost exclusively driven by the need to sustain its army. The Burmese forces have, in fact, become one of the largest standing armies in the region, absorbing fully half of the national budget.[14] The purpose of this army, in the absence of any territorial disputes with Burma's neighbors, is solely to buttress the power of the ruling military junta, just as the Galilean peasantry supported the lavish lifestyle of the Herodian elite.

As in ancient Palestine, the principal instrument of peasant oppression in Burma is taxation. The junta forces peasant farmers to sell part of their harvests to the government at prices far below market rates. Harvest quotas are fixed even before the harvest is brought in, much as Galilean peasants were expected to meet yields established as a result of the Roman census.[15] A World Bank study of the 1994–1995 season estimated that these forced sales amount to a tax of 25 percent of gross income. Peasant households unable to meet the state quota face arrests, beatings, and confiscation of their paddy land. Another report has documented numerous instances in which land was seized from indebted peasants and then "rented" back to the original owner at stupendous rates.[16]

In an eerie replay of what took place in ancient Galilee, many of these paddies are subsumed by a small number of "entrepreneurs" or corporate estates that are on excellent terms with the government. The reason is that unlike the subsistence agriculture practiced by the peasantry, these large estates export up to 50 percent of their crops, thus earning the government hard currency. What's more, the situation is hardly unique. In Latin America, the wealthiest 20 percent of the population owns 90 percent of the land. In Brazil specifically, 1 percent of the Brazilian population (or approximately 1.8 million people) holds title to 43 percent of Brazilian land. In addition, Brazilian ranchers have been accused of killing more than 750 farmers in disputes over land in just the past thirty years.[17] Elsewhere, in Guatemala, a 2004 report has accused large haciendas of forcibly moving indebted farmers to unproductive farmland where they are unable to feed their families.

The case of Burma also gives us an indication of what the health conditions in Palestine would have been like. Only 40 percent of all peasant households are currently taking in sufficient calories necessary for normal sustenance. UNICEF reports that 18 percent of the 1.3 million children born in Burma each year do not survive past age five.[18]

In Galilee, the impact of these same rapacious policies would reverberate for decades and permeate Jesus' teachings. His parables are filled with "landlords," as well as the "stewards" who manage large estates on their behalf. In the Gospel of Luke, we learn of debtors who owed their creditors the staggering amount of "fifty measures of oil" or "fourscore measures of wheat," suggesting interest rates of anywhere between 25 and 50 percent.[19] Such extortionate terms were all but designed to bring the peasant to his knees, shortening the time it took for the landlord to foreclose on a peasant's land. At the same time, the story of the wicked tenants in Mark and Matthew suggests that Jesus was well acquainted with the way in which payment of interest was enforced. Landlords would rush "inspectors" to their tenant farmers at the beginning of the harvest season, lest any crops escape their surveillance and wind up in the farmer's pockets. The fact that, in Jesus' parable, the unfortunate "inspector–slaves" were unceremoniously beaten by their tenants clearly shows the deep resentment and hatred felt by these farmers toward the over-lords in whose power they now found themselves.[20]

✢ ✢ ✢

Once a farmer's land was confiscated, the landlord sometimes allowed him to continue working the soil he knew so well, in return for either a mod-est wage or a small share of the harvest. Other landlords accepted the peasant as a "tenant" farmer on his own ancestral land, paying "rent" to the landlord in the form of agricultural produce. Either way, this form of employment drastically reduced the farmer's standard of living, already primitive by our modern standards.

More often than not, however, the peasant was simply dismissed, given the abundant supply of cheap day-labor (mainly consisting of displaced peasants) from which the landlord could take his pick during the sowing and reaping seasons. In the Gospel of Matthew, we hear of a householder who was delighted to find day-laborers for "a penny a day," well below the going rate; even then, he found scores of other laborers "standing idle in the marketplace" at any given time of the day.[21]

Life in Galilee, historically the breadbasket of Palestine, had become a bat-tle for daily survival, and one with which the young Jesus was becoming all too familiar. In another segment from Q, he consoles the peasantry by saying, "Don't worry about 'What will we eat,' or 'What will we drink,' or 'What will we wear?'," voicing the vexing questions his audience faced on a daily basis. And he adds: "*Everyone* does that, and your father knows that you need these things," showing that the struggle for survival in Galilee was all but universal.[22]

THE CRISIS IN NAZARETH

How did the economic situation affect the young Jesus himself? What impact did the crushing burden of taxes, tribute, and tithes have on the young family that Joseph was trying to raise? The Gospels are silent on the issue, so we can only speculate. But the circumstantial evidence is compelling. For one thing, we have seen how Nazareth must have been swept up in the vicious reprisals that followed the peasant revolt of 4 B.C.E., when Jesus was two or three years old. The destruction of land, tools, and draft animals would have had a major impact on Joseph's harvest yields for several seasons, perhaps starting him on the inevitable spiral into debt. We have seen how Jesus' parables are layered with rich and vivid allusions to agriculture, so it is conceivable that Joseph continued to cultivate his land—at least long enough for the young Jesus to observe his father at work and remember the minutiae of daily life on a farm. Then again, we should not readily conclude that Joseph was still a freeholder, that he *owned* the land he was tilling; he may have already been reduced to the status of tenant farmer, working the land on behalf of a large estate to which he had become indebted.

The Gospel literature, as we have seen, refers to Joseph as a ΤΕΚΤωΥ or *tektoon*. Many scholars accept this to mean "(skilled) worker," as opposed to the role of an unskilled day-laborer (*ergates*), a title that appears numerous times in the New Testament, including six references in Matthew and four in Luke. As far as we can determine, a tektoon was engaged in various types of building. Elsewhere in the Greek world, the word "tektoon" could also signify a man skilled in the working of wood. This led to the unfortunate translation, starting with the King James Bible, of tektoon as "carpenter," which in our Western culture—as the painting by our Pre-Raphaelite artist suggests—is often taken to mean "cabinetmaker," or at least someone with the requisite skills to craft objects in wood.[23] What this translation failed to take into account was that Palestine did not have the large forests that Europe had. Even in Galilee, as we have seen, wood crops were sparse. Consequently, wood was a very expensive material. The popular image of Joseph contently carving doors or cabinets for his fellow villagers is a fantasy, for none of the villagers could have afforded it. What little workable wood that existed was cut down and transferred to wood shops in or near Jerusalem itself, there to be worked by skilled craftsmen for the only clientele who could pay for such luxury—namely, the Temple and the owners of palatial mansions going up in Jerusalem's Upper City.

How then did Joseph earn the label of "[construction] worker"? The first clue can be found in Josephus. There, we read that sometime in the first decade of the first century C.E., Tetrarch Antipas of Galilee decided that his territory was in need of a proper capital. I would venture to suggest that Antipas did not arrive at this conclusion until sometime after 6 C.E., the year in which Archilaus was summarily removed from his position. Antipas must have observed the events leading to his brother's downfall with interest. As we have seen, Antipas himself, as well as his sister Salome, had lobbied hard for his own elevation as heir of Herod the Great. It is possible that the emperor's decision to put Archilaus "on probation" kept alive Antipas's hope that one day, Archilaus's misrule would lead to his downfall—which is exactly what happened. Antipas may even have abetted the negative perception of Archilaus's rule—though we have no evidence to support this. Either way, it was only natural for Antipas to assume that, once Archilaus was removed from the scene, Augustus would turn to *him* as the next in line to rule as ethnarch of Judea and Samaria. Since Antipas was always careful to do Rome's bidding, it would not have been inconceivable for the emperor to permit him to continue as ruler of Galilee too—thus becoming the king of a reunified Palestine by default.

Augustus certainly had never given him any reason to think otherwise. The emperor had always favored the Herodian dynasty, as his adoptive father Julius Caesar had done, and there is no indication that Augustus would have considered any other pretender to the throne, including the now-scattered Hasmonean dynasty. If all this had come to pass, then Antipas would have inherited not only Archilaus's title and territory but also the biggest prize of all, Jerusalem. While that pleasant prospect was still on the table, there would have been little reason for Antipas to contemplate building a capital city in Galilee.

But as we have seen, Augustus broke with precedent and decided *not* to grant Antipas the former territories of his brother. Instead, Judea became a Roman province, to be ruled by a prefect reporting to the Roman governor of Syria. This must have come as a rude awakening to Antipas. In fact, it is quite plausible to think that Antipas decided to take revenge and assuage his bruised pride by behaving *as if* he were the only rightful heir to the glory of Herod's kingdom. First, he assumed his father's name, so that from now on he was known as *Herod Antipas*. And second, he decided to do what his father had done: to mark his reign by building something spectacular—an all-new city from scratch, like Herod's Sebaste or the port of

Caesarea. This, I believe, is when Antipas set his mind on the construction of a grand capital—a little "Jerusalem" in Galilee—almost as if he wanted to get even with Augustus and give himself that which the Roman emperor had denied him.

For the next fourteen years, Antipas's administration in Galilee was wholly focused on making the tetrarch's fantasy a reality. He summoned the finest architects from the Greco–Roman world. These experts explained to him that cities in the Roman Empire typically followed the design of a grid (inspired by the layout of a Roman military camp or *castrum*), anchored on a main north–south axis known as the *cardo,* which was bisected at right angles by another axis known as the *decumanus.* Both avenues, bordered by the bustle of shops and offices, would ultimately lead to the administrative and commercial heart of the city, the forum.

No one had ever built such a city in Galilee. Towns were usually a haphazard affair of modest commercial facilities surrounded by residential clusters, with serpentine alleys connecting one block to the next. Central planning was unheard of. Even Jerusalem, the greatest city in all of Palestine, was a warren of labyrinthine streets and byways. But Sebaste had been built on a Roman grid pattern by Antipas's father Herod, and so the new city of Antipas was to have this latest innovation as well.

What's more, Antipas knew exactly where he wanted his new capital city built: on the site of the city of Sepphoris. Located in the heart of Lower Galilee, almost equidistant from the Mediterranean and the Sea of Galilee, Sepphoris (or *Zippori* in Hebrew) had been a center of Galilee's provincial administration in the earliest days of the Roman conquest. Archaeologists have uncovered evidence suggesting that it actually may have been quite a bit older than that. Though there is evidence of habitation during the pre-exilic period, the first significant remains date from the Persian era. The town then appears to have been fortified in the early first century B.C.E. during the Hasmonean era, to judge by the plethora of coins from the period of Alexander Jannaeus. One recently discovered structure had walls nearly six feet in width, which fits with Josephus's claim that the Egyptian king Ptolemy VIII once launched an attack on Sepphoris during Alexander Jannaeus's reign, but was rebuffed by the city's stout defenses.[24] Later, after the Roman conquest of Palestine, the relative prominence of Sepphoris prompted the Roman governor in Syria, Gabinius, to make the city the residence of the council governing Galilee. So Antipas's choice was not without precedent.

The site was fortuitous for another reason as well. Around 4 B.C.E., the legions sent by the Roman governor Varus to suppress the revolt of Judas, son of Hezekiah, had done Antipas the favor of razing the old city to the ground.[25] Sepphoris was a *tabula rasa*—a clean slate on which his Roman architects could design a city at will. Like a Nero after the great fire of Rome, Antipas had the luxury of creating a capital virtually from scratch.

Thus Herod Antipas set out to make Sepphoris "the ornament of all Galilee," in the words of Josephus, just as his father, King Herod, had rebuilt and adorned Jerusalem beyond all recognition. A vast enterprise such as the construction of a city must have sucked resources and manpower from every corner of Lower Galilee. It is therefore inconceivable that the inhabitants of the tiny hamlet of Nazareth would have been unaffected. Nazareth lay only four miles from Sepphoris—a two-hour walk at most. Nevertheless, for the peasants of the village, the project would have been a mixed blessing. On the one hand, Antipas's zest for construction necessitated the continued levy of heavy taxes, just as Herod the Great had financed his great monuments with the sweat of Galilean peasants. On the other hand, the project also offered the thousands of landless and disenfranchised peasants an opportunity to find long-term employment. Better, certainly, than standing in the square each day, waiting for a landlord to drop by and offer work for mere pennies.

As it was, the construction of the new city of Sepphoris took fourteen years. Scores of peasants would have been needed to provide the muscle for hefting beams, hoisting smooth-hewn blocks of stone, or pounding slabs of pavement. But the project would also have employed hundreds of skilled workers—those experienced in chiseling stone, sawing wood, or polishing marble. These were the *tektoi* described in the Gospel of Mark.

It is quite conceivable that Joseph and his oldest son found their way to Sepphoris in precisely this manner. We have no proof that Jesus worked on the construction of the city, but the circumstantial evidence is compelling. We have seen how his early years probably took place on a small farm, rather than in the imaginary "carpenter's workshop" for which one would have searched in vain among the tiny hamlets of Galilee. But perhaps Joseph was skilled at repairing or even fashioning farming tools; then, as now, small farmers often supplemented their income with a second trade. And given what we know about the escalating tax burden in Galilee, it is quite possible that Joseph, too, succumbed to the inevitable spiral of debt and final forfeiture.

One reason is that, as the Gospels somewhat reluctantly attest, Jesus' was not the only mouth Joseph was looking to feed. In the years since Jesus' birth, Mary had presented her husband with a steady succession of children. As Mark attests, Jesus had four brothers, including James, Joses, Juda, and Simon— proper Jewish names from what clearly was an observant and pious home. In addition, there were sisters; Mark does not tell us how many, since for him, apparently, girls did not rate as highly as men, but the plural indicates that there were at least two.[26] There is no reason to doubt that Mark's description is based on an authentic source, simply because Mark would have had little to gain from presenting Jesus as coming from a large home. What's more, the existence of Jesus' brother James is also attested in Acts of the Apostles, where he is described as the leader of the Jesus movement in Jerusalem.

What this tells us is that by 6 C.E., some twelve years after the birth of Jesus, the small, ramshackle home of Joseph and Mary in Nazareth would have been filled with the cries and laughter of a number of young children—at least seven—aged anywhere from two to twelve. All of these looked to their father to feed them. Given the circumstances of subsistence farming in Galilee at this time, it would have been very difficult for him to do so solely by means of his ancestral plot—unless Joseph's family had large land holdings itself, which is nowhere attested in the Gospel literature.

Consequently, I do believe that sometime after Jesus reached his twelfth birthday, when a Jewish boy was considered old enough to undergo his *bar mitzvah* and join his father in whatever craft he was engaged in, he and Joseph made their way to Sepphoris to join the throngs of peasants and workers in search of work. Whether this was entirely of their own volition, or whether they had been conscripted into construction gangs, is not clear. When governing Bithynia for the emperor Trajan, the younger Pliny found that public construction relied on a large amount of men who had been sentenced *ad opus publicum* by way of penalty for crimes or misdemeanors.[27] In many cases, however, such convict labor was not sufficient to build large construction projects. The town of Urso in Roman Spain, for example, passed a decree expressly authorizing it to conscript its population for building works if no adequate source of forced labor could be found.[28]

Conscripting the peasantry into building his new city would not have freed Antipas from the obligation to pay them, though he would have been able to set wages that reflected the depressed economic condition of the peasantry at the time. Roman records from Africa suggest that it cost between sixty and seventy thousand sesterces to build a modest temple, whereas the construction of a theater ran around six hundred thousand sesterces. These budgets would have been difficult to maintain if all workers assigned to the project were paid the usual one *dinarius* per day.

It is pointless to speculate what building project Jesus and Joseph would have been assigned to, as some scholars have attempted to do. But the current excavation of Sepphoris, which at the time of this writing was still ongoing, has revealed the sheer scope of the city Antipas was trying to build.[29] The archaeological evidence indicates that, stylistically, the tetrarch was also following in the footsteps of his father. True to Roman precedent, the new Sepphoris would be equipped with a bathhouse and a basilica (a Roman meeting hall used for civic functions) in addition to other, multistory buildings, connected by well-paved streets and sidewalks such as a stone pavement from around the time of Jesus that was only uncovered in 2006. Fresco fragments and Corinthian capitals attest to the Hellenistic elegance of the city's public buildings.[30] The 2006 expedition also uncovered a *decumanus* dating from the Late Roman or Byzantine period. There was even a sophisticated sewage system underneath the stone pavement.

Antipas had not neglected to consider the entertainment needs of his future subjects. He thus indulged in the extraordinary expense of building a Roman-style theater, in imitation of the famous amphitheater of Jerusalem built by his father. Though the dating of this theater is the subject of a spirited and ongoing scholarly debate, it is quite possible that Antipas originally built a theater accommodating some fifteen hundred spectators, which in the third or fourth century C.E. was expanded to a capacity of forty-five hundred viewers.[31]

Based on African records from the early principate, Richard Duncan-Jones has estimated that to build an average Greco–Roman city in the provinces, including temples, baths, forum, and theater, as well as the additional costs of sewers, roads, and gates, would have cost a sum equivalent to between 120 and 140 years of tax revenue from that district.[32] This is why such cities were usually built over an extended period of time; the pace of construction was set by the cash flow the city was able to generate. As it was, Antipas completed Sepphoris in the extraordinarily short time span of less than fifteen years. This merely illustrates the heavy tax yoke that Herod's son must have continued to place on the Galilean farmers—that is, those whose land holdings were still intact.

JESUS' STAY IN SEPPHORIS

Jesus' purported sojourn in Sepphoris is important for two reasons. First of all, in the Gospels Joseph disappears from view, never to be heard from again. When compared to ancient literature, including the Hebrew Scriptures, this is unique. The death of a father in ancient times was a significant event, for inevitably it made the oldest son the new head of the household. One would thus expect the Gospel literature to tell us when Joseph, a major character in the Gospel of Matthew, passed from this world, leaving the care of his family to his oldest son. But it doesn't, and so we are left to speculate about what happened to Joseph and why we are not given information about his death. One thing is clear: Joseph did not live until old age, as Mary did.

It is not impossible to imagine that Joseph was the victim of a construction accident in Sepphoris. In the ancient world, accidental deaths of workers were quite common. Safety concerns of the type that govern our modern building sites were unheard of. Workers were cheap and plentiful, certainly in Herodian Galilee, and therefore expendable. What's more, construction methods were primitive, and working with heavy masonry was inherently dangerous. Though Antipas availed himself of Greco–Roman architects, he may not have had access to the more sophisticated hoists and tools that we know were being deployed in Augustus's blossoming empire.

If this suggestion is true, then Jesus would have brought the body home to Nazareth, there to be buried before sundown. Mary would have wept; Jesus would have consoled her; and the next day he would have returned to Sepphoris, knowing that the burden of supporting his family now fell entirely on him.

The distance between Nazareth and Sepphoris would have made it impractical for Jesus (and Joseph, while he lived) to return home after work ceased at the end of the day. More than likely, they would have lived in a

125

workers' camp, in tents or huts erected for the purpose just outside the city proper. It would have been primitive living, without women or children; it would have been too costly to feed them as well. Instead, the men would have only returned to their villages in time for the beginning of Sabbath on Friday evening at sunset, to return to the work pits when the holy day was over.

✦ ✦ ✦

The second reason why a reconstruction of Jesus' stay in Sepphoris is important is that it may answer the question of when, if at all, he received any form of formal schooling. As the son of a peasant from a hamlet like Nazareth, his opportunity to learn anything beyond a few lines and phrases from Scripture would have been extremely limited. We can make a comparison with the thousands of illiterate adolescents in the Middle East of today, whose only education consists of phrases from the Qur'an, learned by rote. Yet all of the Gospels suggest that Jesus was not only well versed in Scripture but also highly articulate in debating the finer points of Covenant Law. In Luke, for example, Jesus reads from Isaiah in the synagogue of Nazareth, and all in attendance "wondered at the gracious words which proceeded out of his mouth." That this was unusual for the son of a villager is attested by John, who notes that "the Jews marveled, saying, How does this man read letters, given that he has never had any formal learning?"[33]

Where, indeed, would Jesus have received this training? Until recently, popular works about ancient Palestine often showed young Jewish boys like Jesus at the feet of their village rabbi, being schooled in a *bet Talmud,* a "house of learning."[34] Today, however, most scholars no longer presume that the claim in rabbinic sources of a synagogue in every Palestinian town and village should be applied to the early first century C.E. Nor should we blithely accept, as many postwar publications have done, that teachers or *rabbis* were conveniently at hand in each of these villages, no matter how small, to teach Scripture to the children of the local peasantry. Such may well have been the case in a later, post-Temple era—or at least as the rabbis of the third and fourth centuries envisioned it—but not during the Late Second Temple Period in which Jesus lived.

The archaeological record on this issue is quite specific. As of the time of this writing, no synagogue from the time of Jesus has been excavated anywhere in Galilee. The word "synagogue" is derived from the Greek word *synagogè*, which literally means "assembly" or "gathering of people." It does not necessarily denote the *building* in which such an assembly takes place; the common word for this is *proseuchè* or "prayer house." Evidence of such a prayer house has been found in Diaspora territories outside Palestine, but not in Galilee proper. The remains of two buildings in Magdala and Gamla that were previously identified as synagogues have now been shown to be mere homes.

THE JEWISH COMMUNITY OF SEPPHORIS

There is, however, a tantalizing reference in Josephus's autobiography, *Vita*. Here, Josephus states that during the early months of the Jewish War, the citizens of the city of Tiberias "assembled in the prayer house [*proseuchen*], a huge hall [*megiston oikema*] which was capable of accommodating a large crowd."[35] Tiberias, like Sepphoris, was a "planned city" built by Herod Antipas. If Tiberias had a prayer house, then it is certainly conceivable that Sepphoris had one, too.

Ever since the first excavations of the city in the late 1960s, scholars have assumed, given its Hellenistic appearance, that Sepphoris was largely Gentile and not Jewish. Recent finds and research, notably by Mark Chancey and Eric Meyers, have now shown that the opposite is true.[36] The presence of ritual baths or *mikva'ot* from the late second century B.C.E. indicates that the city had a sizable Jewish community as early as the beginning of the Hasmonean period. Furthermore, an analysis of an ancient "garbage dump" near the western summit of the site by Billy Grantham of Troy State University has identified a remarkable absence of pig bones, in contrast to such remains found near Gentile communities. Though the principal layout and architectural style of Sepphoris was Roman, there were no sculptures, sculpted friezes, or any other form of graven images that might have given offense to the Jews. Similarly, coins struck in Sepphoris in the first century C.E. scrupulously avoid the habitual portrait of the emperor. This evidence suggests that the Jewish community of Sepphoris continued to be a dominating presence through the early Roman era.

I would go one step further and argue, based on the archaeological evidence recovered over the last fifteen years, that the city of Sepphoris comprised not only a majority of observant Jews, but a substantial Pharisaic community as well. The evidence for this is manifold. First, as we have seen,

Pharisees were very concerned about applying the priestly rules of cultic purity to their own daily lives. This not only included repeated ritual immersion in "living" (that is, non-stagnant) water, but also the taking of great care in determining which vessels, plates, or utensils were ritually clean. Interestingly enough, archaeologists were able to recover over a hundred fragments of stone vessels in the residential area of Sepphoris. This is significant because stone, unlike pottery, glass, or metal, could never become impure. Stone vessels, though expensive, were in great demand by pious and relatively affluent Jews—precisely the socioeconomic group among whom the Pharisees enjoyed great popularity.

As we have seen, the Pharisees were a pious group of religious laymen who rejected the idea that the only path to a Jew's salvation led through the rite of frequent sacrifice at the Temple.[37] They believed that, in contrast, a purification of mind and body could be realized by the meticulous application of Mosaic ritual purity on everything that a person touched, from the moment he got up to the time he went to sleep. The Pharisees are often depicted in the Gospel literature as people hopelessly obsessed with the minutiae of the Law; but in practice they represented a strong reformative element in Second Temple Judaism that continuously sought solutions for situations that the Mosaic Laws had never anticipated. The foreign occupation of Palestine's land, the need to pay taxes to a pagan power, the necessity of dealing with Gentiles on a daily basis challenged the most essential tenets of the Law and demanded answers. Unlike the Sadducees, who considered the Pentateuch a closed book, the Pharisees led the ongoing debate to apply the *principles* of the Law to the changing circumstance of Palestinian Judaism—a process known as the development of the Oral Law. Indeed, one of the more revolutionary concepts that the Pharisees were prepared to accept from Hellenistic thought was the very idea of a life after death—an idea that would resonate with our rabbi from Nazareth.

The Pharisaic movement consisted of two "houses." The House of Hillel followed the milder and more liberal teachings of the great rabbinic sage Hillel (30 B.C.E.–10 C.E.). The House of Shammai followed a harsher and more radical school of thought. The House of Shammai had, in fact, thrown its support behind the "tax revolt" of Judas in Galilee in 6 C.E. Both movements would continue to figure prominently in the great debate of the Law that would ultimately produce the Mishnah of 200 C.E.

What is important for our story is that in contrast to the highly conservative and elitist outlook of the Sadducees, the Pharisees were essentially populist in character. They formed a "middle class" of semi-educated tradesmen and merchants as well as literate scribes, teachers, and legal professionals. Though predominantly urban—only in the cities could employment for their skills be found—the movement was far from limited to Judea. In fact, after the Sadducees had succeeded in excluding the Pharisaic party from the power circles in Jerusalem in the late Hasmonean period, many Pharisees may have simply packed up and left for townships outside of Judea.

I believe it is reasonable to assume that the development of Sepphoris as the preeminent administrative center in Galilee would have attracted a large number of Pharisaic professionals. As Josephus attests, Antipas established his court as well as the administration of his tetrarchy in the city, including "the archives and bank."[38] These facilities would have served as a magnet for educated professionals—precisely the group in which support for the Pharisaic cause was strongest. Indeed, based on the most recent archaeological measurements, scholars believe that, by about 20 C.E., Sepphoris was once again a sizable city, ranging anywhere from 12,000 to 30,000 inhabitants.

✢ ✢ ✢

Why is this significant? Simply put, because I believe that only in Sepphoris could the young Jesus have found an opportunity to be educated to the extent attested in the Gospels; and that the only group willing and able to give Jesus that level of learning would have been a group of Pharisees working in Antipas's newly built capital. Why would some of these Pharisees have taken this young boy under their wing? The answer may be that Jesus had recently lost his father. What's more, the young Jesus was an intelligent, inquisitive, and attentive young man. It is eminently plausible that in the course of his building tasks, he would have come in contact with Pharisees. Once invited into their midst, he would have been intrigued by the Pharisaic idea that the Torah was *not* an immutable codex of human behavior: that one, in fact, had the freedom to interpret and debate the tenets of the written Covenant Law; that God encouraged such interpretation and sent his divine Spirit to guide such deliberations, as his Spirit had guided prophets of days past; and that, lastly, the cumulative wisdom of these discussions, this "Oral Law," could help Palestinian Jews to better cope with the great social inequities of their time. All of these ideas, which are cornerstones of Pharisaic thought (as well as the core principles of the Pharisees' spiritual heirs, the postwar rabbinate), would resonate strongly in Jesus' teachings. Furthermore, Jesus may have observed something that he had never encountered in the humble home of his parents: a group of literate people, eager to engage each other in stimulating debate. His quick mind must have leaped at the opportunity to learn from—and match wits with—these highly articulate men.

The Pharisees, for their part, were devoted to educating the young. While they may not yet have created the "Sunday School" system of synagogue education that was to emerge after the destruction of the Temple, they may nevertheless have anticipated the idea in Talmudic literature that by applying the Mosaic Laws in everyday life, a Jew could "restore" that Temple by turning his home into a living sanctuary. Hence, the education of young Jews in the tenets of these Mosaic Laws may have been a high Pharisaic priority, for only through knowledge of the Law could a Jew attain the level of piety to which YHWH called him.

How Jesus would have been educated in Sepphoris is open to speculation. Perhaps he frequented the local synagogue or "prayer house," assuming that such a place existed at the time, where his quick mind may have caught the attention of a kind Pharisaic scribe or teacher. Conversely, a Pharisee may have taken pity on the boy still mourning for his father and taken him into his family home. This would explain why Jesus not only became an expert in Scripture but also a close observer of Pharisaic life and customs, as countless parables would later attest.

For many readers, the idea that Jesus was tutored by Pharisees may sound far-fetched. After all, the Gospel literature presents a very different picture. There, we read that the Pharisees would harass Jesus at every turn, trying to outwit him and "catch" him in an act or utterance that would disqualify his credibility as a teacher. Many scholars, however, now accept that the confrontational relationship between Pharisees and Jesus in the New Testament is a deliberate distortion by the evangelists. In the period when we believe the Gospels were written, the decades after the destruction of the Temple in 70 C.E., Jewish followers of Jesus' teachings were increasingly ostracized from Jewish social and religious life. The reason was not that the teachings of Jesus were in any way subversive in and of themselves: on the contrary, Jesus himself had always taught that he had not come to destroy the Law, but to uphold it.[39] What did change, however, was the growing popularity of a certain *interpretation* of Jesus' life and death, namely the teachings of Paul (which scholars refer to as the Pauline *kerygma*). Beginning in the late 40s and 50s C.E., Paul argued that Jesus was not only the Messiah, but also the only Son of God, sent to Earth to offer salvation to all of mankind. This doctrine offended and enraged observant Jews, who could not conceive of any man claiming to be of the divine substance of YHWH. What's more, Scripture spoke of the Messiah as a Davidic king who would come to cleanse Israel from foreign occupation and restore its people under Zion; Jesus, by contrast, had been executed as a common criminal. If he ever did harbor messianic ambitions, he had clearly failed.

Hence, the more Paul's teachings spread, the more Jewish "Christians" were considered a dangerous sect who violated the very principles of Jewish monotheism. As it happened, the people leading the charge to eradicate Christian "sectarianism" from Jewish towns and villages were the new religious leaders, the rabbis, who strongly identified with the Pharisaic movement before the destruction of the Temple. The result was an inevitable schism between "Christian" Jews and "traditional" Jews, forcing the split of Christianity as a separate cult.

This was the religious and political atmosphere in which the Gospels came about. The evangelists, in short, wrote for a community of early Christians who believed themselves to be under siege by traditional Judaism. In response, the evangelists consoled their readers by showing that rejection and confrontation had been a constant theme of the Jesus movement from the very beginning. They "rear-projected" the situation of the late 70s and 80s into their tale of Jesus, using every opportunity to place hostile Pharisees in Jesus' path.

Luke goes so far as to place this theme of Pharisaic confrontation at the very beginning of his Gospel. There, we learn that when Jesus was twelve years old, his mother and father brought him to Jerusalem for the feast of Passover. Once the rite of sacrifice had been concluded, his parents returned to Galilee, only to discover that Jesus was not in their midst. They rushed back to Jerusalem, and were astonished to find Jesus in the Temple, engaging the "doctors of the Law" in sharp debate.[40]

In fact, all of the Gospels are replete with incidents in which a group of Pharisees, usually a delegation "from Jerusalem," tries to set a "trap" for Jesus. It is highly improbable that the Pharisees—who, as we have seen, were a professional class—would have bothered (let alone found the time) to chase a peasant teacher up and down Lower Galilee in an effort to "entrap" him. What's more, the various scenes in which the Pharisees appear to "challenge" Jesus' teachings betray a fundamental misunderstanding among the evangelists of the way in which the Pharisaic community interacted. Spirited debate on matters of Law was the bread and butter of Pharisaic life; lively discourse was their method of probing Scripture and, they believed, finding divine revelation of solutions for the pressing issues of their day. Indeed, the Mishnah is essentially an almost verbatim account of rabbinic debate on the same issues that would return in the oldest saying traditions of Jesus: social justice, compassion, love, marriage, agriculture, and faith. If a group of Pharisees did seek out Jesus for his views on these matters, it would have been a mark of great respect rather than an attempt at entrapment. If the tradition of these debates is authentic, then clearly certain Pharisees must have recognized a kindred spirit and would have eagerly sought Jesus' opinion on matters pertaining to the Law.

✦ ✦ ✦

That many of Jesus' teachings were consonant with prevailing Pharisaic views at the time, as we will see in the next chapter, can only substantiate, in my view, the idea that a Pharisaic group was responsible for Jesus' education. It may also explain why the Gospels are completely mum about the so-called "lost years" of Jesus' puberty and early adulthood. One reason, as we saw earlier, was that the biographical material of the young Jesus was of little relevance to the evangelists; they would rather emphasize the unique and unprecedented nature of Jesus as the son of God, untainted by interference from mere mortals.

What's more, Sepphoris was indelibly linked with the Herodian dynasty, most notably Herod Antipas, who in the Gospels is portrayed as one of Jesus' adversaries. Thirty-six years after the death of Jesus, following the outbreak of the Jewish War, its population refused to choose the side of the rebels and declared itself on the side of Rome. It readily accepted a small garrison of Roman soldiers, dispatched in haste, and later opened its doors to the legions of Vespasian. The city's allegiance to Rome is further documented by two coins struck at Sepphoris in 68 C.E., honoring Vespasian and calling the city, in Greek, *Eirenopolis* or "city of peace." Significantly, Antipas had named the city "Autocratoris," in a veiled tribute to the Roman emperor. Later, in the second century C.E., the city would become known as Diocaesarea, an allusion to the emperor Hadrian, who was identified with the Greek supreme god, Zeus.

In sum, by the latter part of the first century C.E., when the evangelists first began to write, Sepphoris was perceived as hopelessly pro-Roman and collaborationist. Exactly what the Galilean population thought about the inhabitants of Sepphoris is vividly illustrated by Josephus's account of the assault on Sepphoris at the beginning of the Jewish War. "The Galileans," says Josephus, "took this opportunity for venting their hatred on them, since they detested that city. They then set out to destroy them all, even those who had sought refuge there. And so they descended upon them and set their houses on fire."[41]

If the evangelists had known about Jesus' education in the city, there would have been little incentive to associate him with a community of such questionable character.

But perhaps the most important reason why the role of the Pharisees of Sepphoris in Jesus' life was erased from the record is that the evangelists, writing for a Greco–Roman audience outside of Palestine, chose to make the Pharisees the ultimate villains of the Jesus story. They, rather than the Romans, are cast as the evil opponents of Jesus at every turn; they are the architects of Jesus' arrest and ultimate downfall. The possibility that these very same Pharisees would have figured in Jesus' education certainly did not fit that scenario.

Thus, it is quite possible that the young *tektoon* from Nazareth, the son of a small and illiterate village, was introduced by the Pharisees to the great mysteries of Hebrew Scripture. By the first century C.E., the canon of the Hebrew Bible consisted of two divisions: the *Torah* or Law (of Moses), also known as the "Pentateuch"; and the books of the Prophets, or *Nevi'im*. The

Torah included the books of Genesis, Exodus, Leviticus, Numbers, and Deuteronomy. The "Prophets" covered all the books from Joshua through 2 Kings. The third division, that of the "Writings," was still evolving in Jesus' time, even though many texts contained in this grouping were at least as old as some contained in the Prophets (including, for example, the book of Psalms). This is echoed in the Gospel of Luke, where Jesus refers to the "law of Moses, the prophets, and the psalms."[42] Thus we can safely assume that the Pharisees also taught their novice in the writings of the Prophets.

The Hebrew canon traditionally distinguishes between the so-called "Former Prophets" (the historical books of Joshua, Judges, Samuel, and Kings) and the individual books of the so-called "Latter Prophets," who were active in the period of the divided monarchy. These prophets—Isaiah, Jeremiah, and Ezekiel, as well as the "Minor Prophets"—were all active across a span of four hundred years while the twin kingdoms of Israel and Judah faced the dual threat of pagan cults and foreign occupation. Needless to say, this made the writings of the prophets eminently relevant to Jesus' day, when Galilee suffered not only the Roman boot but also the pernicious influence of Hellenistic culture. I believe that Jesus absorbed the writings of these prophets and, in the process, found a role model that was to guide him for the remainder of his life as a social activist and religious reformer.

THE END OF THE SEPPHORIS PERIOD

When did Jesus leave Sepphoris? It is impossible to say with certainty, for we lack any record on the issue. But once again we may be permitted to speculate, based on the available evidence. And the first date that looms large in this regard is 14 C.E., when the emperor Augustus, who had ruled the Roman Empire for the better part of forty-five years, breathed his last. An extraordinary period of relative peace in much of the known world—the celebrated *Pax Romana*—had come to an end. The future loomed with uncertainty, even as Augustus's reluctant heir, his stepson Tiberius, assumed the throne.

Antipas, too, observed the passing of the torch with interest. Augustus had always been keenly interested in the affairs of Roman territory in the Near East. Consequently, Antipas had (rightly or wrongly) believed himself to be on a short leash, eager to show himself to be an obedient vassal of Augustus, lest he be banished into oblivion like his brother Archilaus. With Augustus dead, Antipas felt himself freed of such unwanted scrutiny. It is possible that Antipas, who was educated in Rome, was careful to cultivate contacts with the Tiberius party in the last years of Augustus's life. Josephus was later to write that "the tetrarch . . . was in great favor with Tiberius."[43] Antipas may therefore have felt himself unleashed to build another and even greater city.

This city, unlike Sepphoris, was to be conceived entirely in the Hellenistic style, unfettered by Jewish cultic concerns. Indeed, Antipas intended to populate it entirely with Gentiles, imported for this purpose from the various towns west of the Jordan, the region known as the Decapolis (Greek for "Ten Cities"), which was predominantly non-Jewish. None of the scrupulous attention to Jewish sensitivities that had constrained the construction of Sepphoris would matter; here, Antipas could indulge in the building of baths, temples, and a gymnasium—institutions detested by observant Jews since they were frequented by people in the nude—with total abandon. As luck would have it, Antipas believed he had found just the right spot, on the southeastern shore of the Sea of Galilee, close to the location of some mineral springs. And just to ensure that the new emperor would be in agreement with these rather ambitious plans, Antipas piously dedicated the new city to Tiberius, calling it *Tiberias.*

Whether the construction of Sepphoris was actually complete is subject to debate. What matters is that funding must have slowed to a trickle, as most of Antipas's tax revenue was now channeled to the creation of the new city on the Sea. And so, one by one, the stonemasons, roofers, plasterers, and artisans who had worked on Sepphoris packed their bags and prepared to leave the workers' camp. Many, mostly Gentile workers, may have left for Tiberias. Most of the Jewish labor, however, would have refused to follow Antipas to his new city. The reason is simple: Antipas, a man never bothered by Jewish purity laws, had picked a spot which, according to local lore, had once been a Jewish cemetery. Consequently, in Jewish eyes the site was unclean; by building on its soil, a worker would defile himself. Jesus, and many observant Jews like him, would have never accepted work in such a place.

And so the day arrived when Jesus, too, gathered his meager belongings and left to find his destiny among the rural villages of Galilee. What he found there would shock him to the core and determine the course he was to take for the remainder of his life.

SIX

THE ITINERANT
WORKER AND HEALER

Jesus was now twenty-five years old. Except for periodic trips to Nazareth to spend the Sabbath with his mother, brothers, and sisters, his entire adult life would have been spent in Sepphoris. Here he had worked from dawn to dusk until his hands were callused, his arms swollen with muscle and sinew, and his skin tanned to a deep brown.

What would he have looked like? In our culture, we imagine Jesus as a tall, slender, pale-skinned man with flowing long hair and moist blue eyes. But that portrait of Jesus is a projection of our time, as it has been throughout the centuries.

For example, frescoes from third- and fourth-century catacombs in Rome portray Jesus as an Apollo, the Roman god he most resembled: a handsome, virile young man, beardless, topped with golden hair, shining like the sun. Then, as the focus of Christianity shifted toward Asia Minor, Jesus changed from a Roman god to a Greek philosopher. He grew a beard. His handsome, godlike features became more marked, and he dressed in a toga, like countless philosopher statues that dotted the Greek landscape.

Under the Byzantine emperor Justinian, the divine nature of Jesus gained new emphasis. That meant that Jesus could no longer be portrayed like a Greek philosopher, dressed in the cloak of Greek naturalism. Jesus became an ephemeral, supernatural character, rendered as a luminous, shimmering figure in the deliberately non-naturalistic medium of the mosaic. At the same time, the face of Jesus became more stern, as if scornful of the sinful world that beheld it. From this Byzantine paradigm, the Orthodox Church developed the image of the *Pantokrator* that would remain emblematic in Eastern Christianity for centuries to come. Painted in strict two-dimensionality, against a backdrop of gold that symbolized heaven rather than earth, Jesus was an omnipotent leader, a stern father gazing down on humanity.

Then Christianity moved to Europe. Here, sensibilities were different. Europeans embraced the suffering of Jesus, and in the process produced the iconographic archetype of the Passion: Jesus on the cross. He was now portrayed as an ascetic with hollow eyes and sunken cheeks, deprived of love and sustenance, quietly enduring the endless torment that a cruel and heartless world chose to inflict upon him.

Finally, the portrayal of Jesus entered the Renaissance. A new element crept in: the *sweetness* of Jesus. Buoyed by the new Maria cult (one of the many ways in which the Church fought the Reformation), the innate goodness and love of Jesus became the paramount qualities of his portraiture. The result was the warm, handsome-featured, pale-skinned Jesus, smiling indulgently at his accusers, that endures to this day.

Of course, the reality was quite different. The Gospels imply that Jesus looked like any other Galilean worker, for on the evening of his arrest in the Garden of Gethsemane, the Temple Guards had to rely on Judas to point him out. If this is true, then Jesus would have been about five foot two to five foot four in height—the average size of a Galilean peasant. He would have had brown eyes and brown or black hair that fell to his shoulders. Like any young pious Jew who had attained full manhood, he would have worn a beard with pride. His clothes were the garments of a peasant worker: a simple loincloth, over which he would wear a tunic of rough flax, tied with a linen girdle or leather belt with thongs at the ends for fastening. The belt was sometimes also used to hold a leather drawstring purse. These were his only garments: he wore them during the day and slept in them at night. In colder seasons, Jesus would throw a heavy cloak of undyed lamb's wool over his tunic, perhaps decorated with fringes and tassels as described in the Talmud. His footwear was a pair of simple, open leather sandals of the type still used in the Middle East today.

Like virtually all other Jewish peasants in Galilee, Jesus spoke Aramaic, though it is possible that he could have picked up a few words of Greek in Sepphoris.[1] The Gospels contain no fewer than twenty-six words in Aramaic spoken by Jesus, no doubt to bolster the authenticity of the Gospel record. What's more, Jesus most likely spoke with a strong Galilean accent, which marked him as a man from "the sticks." Matthew notes that Peter was promptly recognized as one of Jesus' followers, because "your speech gives you away."[2]

✝ ✝ ✝

One of the first things Jesus would have done upon leaving Sepphoris was to return to Nazareth to see his mother and the rest of his family and decide on the next stage of his life. By now, all his siblings would have been in their teens, and the little house of Mary would have been teeming with the rough-and-tumble of Jesus' younger brothers and sisters. James, the brother nearest to Jesus' age, would already have been at work, as either a tenant farmer or day-laborer.[3] About Jesus' other siblings we know little. His sisters would have been approaching marriageable age, so that Mary's priority would have been to identify appropriate husbands for them from her immediate circle of relatives. If there ever was a wedding, and if Jesus attended it, we will never know. The only reference to a wedding attended by Jesus (as well as Mary) is the enigmatic wedding at Cana, which only appears in the very late Gospel of John, written near the end of the first century C.E. According to John, this is where Jesus changes water, stored in six stone jars or *pithoi,* into wine. The bride and bridegroom are not identified, but since Cana was located close to Nazareth, it is not inconceivable that the wedding may have involved one of Jesus' relatives, possibly even one of his siblings.

By this time, the role of *paterfamilias,* the head of the household, would have been assumed by James. Even though James was a younger brother, Jesus' prolonged sojourn in Sepphoris would have made James the oldest male in the family by default. Naturally, James would have been concerned that his status as head of the household could be challenged by Jesus' return. But there was no need, for Jesus never planned to move back to Nazareth. His youth as a *mamzer* and his many years as a worker in Sepphoris had made him extremely self-reliant, content to roam the fields by himself, far away from the social life of the village, from which he was automatically excluded.

Reading between the lines of the Gospels, we sense a certain alienation between Jesus and his family. In Q we hear Jesus say wistfully, "Foxes have dens, and birds of the sky have nests, but the son of man has nowhere to lay his head."[4] When, many years later, some people want to follow Jesus but worry about what to tell their families, Jesus angrily rebukes them, saying, "Whoever does not hate his father and his mother cannot become a disciple to me. And whoever does not hate his brothers and sisters . . . will not be worthy of me."[5] Strong words, of course, spoken in a moment of passion, and amplified by oral transmission. Nevertheless, this is a Jesus for whom family life meant little, who rarely tasted the simple pleasure of

138

running around the village with friends or basking in the love of his mother and siblings. This is the son who was taken away from home and hearth to work in the construction pits of Sepphoris, to chafe his hands on sharp rock and brick, day after day, in the burning heat of the sun. Many years later, after he had become a famous figure, Jesus was speaking to the crowds when some people told him that "his mother and his brothers were standing outside," no doubt expecting him to rush over. But in that moment, all of the resentment about his youth, buried for so long, may have welled up inside him. "Who is my mother, and who are my brothers?" was Jesus' devastating reply; and pointing to his disciples, he said, "Here are my mother and my brothers!"[6] The outburst speaks volumes about Jesus' experience as a child; it is hard to imagine anyone with fond memories of his childhood being capable of such harsh words.

Modern psychological models may help us to better understand Jesus' rather shocking attitude toward kinship, which ran against the very grain of Galilean village culture. Over the last decade, developmental psychologists have begun to focus more closely on the mechanisms of resilience and coping in children—or what some psychologists call "post-traumatic growth." By our standards, there is no question that Jesus' youth was "traumatic." As a young child, he would have witnessed the terrible reprisals that followed the tax revolts of 4 B.C.E. and 6 C.E. As a *mamzer*, he would have experienced the distress of being denied normal contact with other boys in the village. This pain would have been compounded by his father's desperate attempts to both satisfy the tax collectors *and* feed his growing family. This experience was followed by many years of hard labor in Sepphoris, toiling alongside his father. At Sepphoris, no quarter would have been given: at age twelve, a young boy was considered an adult and expected to work accordingly. The conditions in the work pits and the workers' camps nearby would have been appalling. Finally, shorn of the love of his mother since age twelve, Jesus was then deprived of his father when Joseph, already a broken man, suffered a fatal accident.

In 2002, researchers Trang Thomas and Winnie Lau identified classic symptoms of post-traumatic stress disorder (PTSD) in children who had experienced "the violent death of a parent . . . witness of murder/massacre . . . witness of parental fear and panic, famine, forcible eviction, separation and forced migration and . . . the endurance of political oppression."[7] All of these children were found struggling to develop coping mechanisms that would help them assimilate the terrible emotional upheaval of those experiences. The research concluded that children exposed to prolonged stress must summon tremendous psychological stamina and truly behave like "trauma survivors who are simultaneously suffering and surviving."[8] Furthermore, Richard Tedeschi has argued that social isolation in early childhood, while undoubtedly stressful, may actually give children greater freedom to observe, cope, and re-create the world around them. In this context, Jesus' isolation as a *mamzer,* no matter how traumatic, would have mobilized his inner strength as an individual and prepared him for a coping mechanism unfettered by social or familial obligations.[9]

Personality theorists such as Albert Bandura and Abraham Maslow agree. In their view, post-traumatic stress is not so much a coping mechanism focused on the past as it is an agency of healing and resilience through restorative action. Kenneth Pargament has described it as a "search for significance." In the face of stressful change, these authors argue, traumatized people often cope by mobilizing a new reality—by aggressively seeking to rearrange the world around them.[10]

All this may perhaps explain why Jesus chose not to stay in Nazareth. Young people who suffer from PTSD tend to avoid places that remind them of recent pain or trauma. What's more, there was nothing to keep him in the village—neither memories nor friends nor economic opportunity. He was eager to break away, to roam through Lower Galilee in search of work—repairing roofs, walls, and fences—and in the process, perhaps, find the peace to heal himself. He was, after all, a *tektoon;* chances were good that in the larger villages of Lower Galilee, particularly around the Sea of Galilee, he would find an opportunity to put his skills to work. And so, for the very first time in his life, Jesus set out to go where his own heart told him to go. He took nothing with him. He was a young and able worker, and he trusted in his ability to work for food.

The Mishnah tells us that it was common to see such young men wandering from village to village in search of opportunity. There were, for example, journeymen and craftsmen of every ilk, including "traveling salesmen" (*rochlim,* singular *rochel*), who sold luxury items such as spices, ointments, and perfumes. These "*rochlim* who travel throughout the towns," says Mishnah Ma'asrot, "eat until they come to a place to sleep. R. Judah says—the first house [which he reaches] is his house." Elsewhere we hear of the "[*rochlim*] of Kefar Hananiah who go out and sell in four or five villages, and come and sleep in their own houses." Jesus certainly would not have looked out of place.[11]

Fortunately, as mentioned earlier, there was a widely developed network of rural roads in Galilee, built by the local villages to access the patchwork of ancestral lands and link the village to the market of the nearest "mother" town.

In some villages Jesus would have been welcomed, given the chance to fix the odd thing here and there, and paid with shelter and a meal. In other locales, all but eviscerated by debt and grinding poverty, there would have been little to do; but rarely was he turned away without at least a cup of water. This itinerant lifestyle of moving from one village to the next, trusting wholeheartedly in the innate hospitality of the Galilean, would become the *modus operandi* of Jesus' ministry in later years. No doubt he reveled in the freedom and the wonder of what each day might bring. Years later, he would insist that his followers live the same way, taking "nothing for their journey except a staff; no bread, no bag, no money in their belts."[12]

The experience of traveling the length and breadth of Lower Galilee had a profound impact on the young Jesus. It changed the future course of his life—something that could not have happened if, as tradition has always assumed, Jesus remained in his ancestral village until his "call" to ministry. For the journey through the towns and villages of the region brought Jesus face to face with the devastation wrought by the preceding four decades of economic exploitation. Villages once populated by freeholders were now poverty-stricken hamlets, crowded with families rent by hunger. Town and village squares were filled with unemployed men, waiting listlessly for the offer of a day's wages that might never come. The once-proud peasantry that had survived centuries of foreign occupation, that had withstood the encroachment of Gentile culture since the age of the Ptolemies, had finally succumbed to abuse by men of their own kind. The Judean political elites, shielded by Roman law and Roman arms, had succeeded in grinding the Galilean peasants into submission, taxing them into debt, and then converting that debt into land appropriation. The ancient social fabric of Galilee was torn beyond recognition.

THE OUTBREAK OF DISEASE

Now, some forty years after the beginning of the Herodian regime, the long-term effects of this economic exploitation were becoming evident, and Jesus could not fail to take notice. For the fact is that as the living standard of the peasant had plunged, so too had his diet and his health.

Traditionally, as we have seen, the subsistence farmers of Galilee had been able to provide their families fairly balanced sustenance of starch, vegetables, and fruit. This is important, for today we know that growing children need to have a diet of dietary fiber, low-fat grains, and vitamin-rich fruits and vegetables. Modern science can tell us that a healthy and active child between four and eight years old needs to take in anywhere from 1,500 to 2,000 calories per day, including 20 to 30 percent protein, 45 to 65 percent carbohydrates, and 25 to 35 percent fats, as well as 800 milligrams of calcium and 1200 milligrams of sodium.[13] While such modern concepts of nutrition were of course wholly unknown in Jesus' time, farmers may have had an intuitive sense of the need for such a balanced diet, which they met by growing wheat or barley (for calories), vegetables (for vitamins and dietary fiber), and fruit (for vitamins). Even in Rome, as Peter Garnsey has argued, the poor could usually supplement their diet with a modicum of cheap legumes (cabbage, leeks, beets, and onions) as well as wine, olive oil, and low-quality fish.[14]

But when they lost their land, the Galilean peasantry also lost the ability to provide their families with balanced nutrition. With what little they made as tenant farmers or day-laborers, their daily diet was reduced to bread, occasionally relieved with a piece of salted fish if they were lucky. What's more, the bread they ate was no longer made from emmer wheat but from barley, previously grown as fodder for farm animals. The quality of this barley bread was considerably more primitive than, for example, the bread baked by professional bakeries and consumed by the poor of Rome. Because many displaced peasants were deprived of their village mills and ovens, the cereal would have been poorly sieved and improperly leavened, impairing the absorption of vital minerals, producing coarse bread of poor quality.

Modern studies bear this out. A 2002 report by the World Health Organization revealed that in the developing world, 206 million children under five years of age are stunted (low height for age), 50 million are wasted (low weight for height), and 167 million are underweight (low weight for age). All of these conditions are invariably the result of a poor diet or malnutrition. In 1995 alone, 6.3 million of the 11.6 million deaths among children aged under five years were directly the result of malnutrition.[15]

We find ample evidence of these conditions beneath the theological layer of the Gospels. When the disciples worry about the need to feed the multitudes who have come to hear Jesus speak, they find "a young lad who has five *barley loaves,* and two *small fishes*"—exactly the type of substandard food, in miserable portions, to which the peasantry of Galilee had been reduced. There is no reference anywhere to the staples that had figured so prominently in the Bible from the earliest days of the Israelite settlement: olives, grapes, wheat, figs, dates, and pomegranates. All this was now grown behind the walls of the large private estates, cultivated on large single-purpose plots. Their yields were destined not for the Galilean villages but for the urban markets of Sepphoris, Tiberias, Jerusalem, and countless other cities in Palestine and beyond, where they would fetch top rates. And so, by singling out *barley loaves and small fishes,* Jesus not only exposes the conditions to which the peasantry had been reduced; by *multiplying* this humble meal into a veritable banquet, he also exalts the innate dignity of the peasant and holds up an example of how the riches of the earth should be shared rather than hoarded.

The rapid deterioration of the peasant diet in the time of Jesus has been vividly illustrated by the detailed study of ancient fecal matter, preserved in household "toilets" excavated in areas of human habitation. In one study, paleoanthropologist Jane Cahill was able to identify evidence of a healthy diet of fruits, vegetables, and herbs from specimens dating *before* the Roman occupation. Later archaeological finds, however, reveal not only a far less balanced diet, but also a dramatic increase in parasites and infectious agents, including traces of the parasite *Echinococcus granulosus.* This shows that the disenfranchisement of peasant families inevitably produced malnutrition throughout the region. This malnutrition, in turn, weakened the human immune system, leading to an outbreak of disease on an unprecedented scale.[16]

Barley bread, the staple of the peasantry in Jesus' day, is notably deficient in vitamins A, C, and D, as well as minerals such as zinc. Vitamin A deficiency would have inevitably led to eye disease, which is still common in developing countries today—including xerophthalmia, keratomalacia, and, in the worst cases, blindness. A 1998 study in Latin America concluded that no less than 25 percent of children under the age of five in this region suffered from some form of vitamin A deficiency, with eye lesions and irreversible blindness being the most common manifestations. In rural areas, the incidence was as high as 41 percent.[17] In the Middle East, these conditions would have been exacerbated by the intense sunlight, heat, and blowing sand. Significantly, the Gospels contain *eighteen* references to the blind.

A group of researchers at the University Clinic of Zurich has identified another affliction linked to vitamin A deficiency. Their research shows that it can also produce layers of bony tissue in the periostal capsule of the labyrinth, as well as advanced suppuration of the middle ear, inevitably leading to partial or complete deafness. The deaf, too, play a prominent role in the Gospels.

In addition to vitamin A, a lack of vitamin C can also have severe consequences. One particular condition is known as osteomalacia, a bone disease that can have a devastating effect on pregnant and lactating women whose condition is aggravated by the loss of calcium inherent in pregnancy and breast feeding. It can also attack the formation of healthy bones in young children, in essence crippling them.[18] The study of two skeletons from the Villa Gordiani near Rome has shown a strong link between low mineral counts (such as zinc) and bone disease.[19]

The extent to which the development of rural children is affected by nutrition was also demonstrated in a recent paper in the *Journal of the American Medical Association*, which revealed a connection between the incidence of stunting among children in rural areas and the size of the plots owned and cultivated by their parents. Most of the affected children (84.7 percent, in fact) lived in families cultivating two hectares or less of redistributed land.[20] By comparison, there are at least six instances in the Gospels where the evangelists refer to "the lame."

The sharp reduction in vitamin intake among children and adults would also have lowered their resistance to some of the most virulent infectious diseases circulating in first-century Galilee. Today, we know that the human body relies on its stored reserves of vitamins A, C, and E as well as minerals

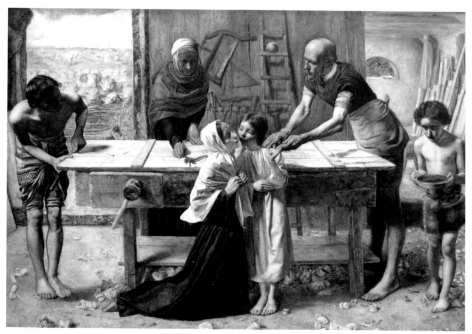

"Christ in the House of His Parents," by John Everett Millais, 1849.

View of the southern region of the Sea of Galilee. This view has changed little since the days of Jesus.

View of the northern shores of the Sea of Galilee, near the putative location of Jesus's "Sermon on the Mount."

The remains of the Roman bath "resort" of Gader, east of the Sea of Galilee.

One of the first Christian sarcophagi carved after Constantine's Edict of Milan (313 C.E), making Christianity a *religio licita* in the empire. This panel shows the entry of Jesus into Jerusalem.

Part of the original stairway that led from the east and the Valley of Kidron to the Herodian Temple. It is almost certain that Jesus would have used these steps to enter the temple sanctuary.

The Coenaculum or Hall of the Last Supper, located on Mount Zion, is traditionally associated with the place where Jesus and his disciples shared their last meal.

A possible location of the Garden of Gethsemane on the Mount of Olives, with a view of Temple Mount beyond.

Part of the Antonia Fortress underneath the Church of the Sisters of Zion. The Antonia Fortress is one of two possible locations of Jesus's indictment by Pontius Pilate; the other is Herod's Palace. The round stones were fired by Roman catapults during either the First or Second Jewish War, when the Antonia was held by the Jewish resistance.

A "Basilinda" game board scratched in the pavement (lithostrotos) of the Antonia Fortress, in the Convent of the Sisters of Zion. Though the date of the board is uncertain, it is quite likely that Jesus was held in this area prior to his crucifixion.

What was Jesus' reaction to the deteriorating conditions he witnessed as he moved from village to village? While in Sepphoris, he would have been shielded from the food crisis overtaking the peasantry at large. *Tektoi* were skilled workers, not slave laborers, and it was in Antipas's best interests to see to it that these men were well fed, lest their output diminish. He may therefore have ensured that the workers' camps had access to plenty of produce at affordable prices. No doubt Joseph and Jesus, as well as scores of other workers, used their privileged access to ensure that their families back in Nazareth had enough to eat as well.

Once Jesus left Sepphoris and began to move through the villages of Lower Galilee, however, the confrontation with the growing proletariat of hungry and displaced families must have come as a shock. More than that: it may have stirred in him the first wellspring of compassion, the will to *do something,* to come to the aid of these unfortunates, to comfort them and to lessen their suffering in any way he could. I would even go as far as to suggest that his individual coping mechanism may have identified an opportunity to transform his inner trauma into positive, transformative change. Matthew puts it best when he writes that "when [Jesus] saw the multitudes, he was moved with compassion for them, because they were harassed and helpless, like sheep without a shepherd."[23] Matthew is writing about his months of ministry, but I firmly believe that Jesus' social compassion did not appear, like a deus ex machina, from one day to the next—or, as the Gospels frame it, as a result of Jesus' anointing by the Holy Spirit in the waters of the Jordan. On the contrary, Jesus' uncanny ability to *resonate* with the Palestinian proletariat, to speak their language, to understand their suffering, and to give voice to their innermost hopes must have been nurtured during many years among the Galilean peasantry—long before his sojourn with John the Baptist.

These were the years when, I believe, Jesus discovered his talents as a social *worker,* well before he became a social *activist.* But what could Jesus do for these unfortunate people? He was a poor man himself; he had no money, no land, nor any food surplus to give. He was undoubtedly a young man of great kindness, and kindness is a highly prized virtue in the Near East; but beyond that, what tangible comfort would he have been able to offer?

The answer, I believe, is clearly attested in the Gospel literature. Jesus *did* have something special and something tangible to give. It was precisely this special talent that probably motivated him to engage in social work to begin with; to move among the poorest of the poor, knowing that he had something concrete to offer, something that could improve their lot in a significant way. For Jesus had discovered that he had the ability to heal.

THE "MIRACLES"

Regardless of what modern research makes of the "miracles" of Jesus, biblical scholars by and large agree that these stories belong to the oldest sayings strata about Jesus. Not only are the canonical Gospels replete with miracle accounts, but so are source documents such as Thomas and Q. About a third of the oldest Gospel, that of Mark, is devoted to miracle stories. Even Josephus, in his brief and highly disputed reference to Jesus, notes that he was "a doer of wonderful works (*paradoxa*)."[24] For some reason, the memory of Jesus was closely intertwined with the tradition of his miraculous abilities. It is, quite simply, not something that we can ignore.

We must recognize that Jesus lived in a society that, unlike ours, strongly believed in otherworldly phenomena and set great store by them. For contemporaries of Jesus, for example, the boundary between magic and miracle was almost nonexistent. Extraordinary men, that is, men possessed by the spirit of the Divine, were expected to be able to do extraordinary things. It validated their claim of prophecy; it corroborated their ability to speak the word of God—or gods.

This is as true for Egyptian, Greek, and Roman literature as for the Scripture of Judaism. Egyptian papyri from the second century B.C.E. to the fourth century C.E. abound with treatises on magic spells, while, in the book of Exodus, Moses engages in a contest with Pharaoh's magicians to see who can pull off the greatest stunts. The Old Testament tells us that during a prolonged famine, the prophet Elijah was able to sustain himself—and the family of a widow where he had found shelter—by multiplying a small vial of meal and olive oil. When the widow's son fell ill and died, Elijah raised the boy from the dead.[25] The prophet Elisha performed similar miracles, also including the resuscitation of a dead child and the feeding of hundreds of people with just twenty loaves of barley bread. He also cured Naaman, a Syrian commander, of leprosy.[26]

These, as skeptical critics have argued, are suspiciously similar to the miracles with which Jesus is credited:

ELIJAH/ELISHA	JESUS
Elijah multiplies the meal and oil of the widow at Zareohath.	Jesus multiplies the loaves and fishes to feed 4,000 (Matthew/Mark).
Elijah raises the son of the widow from the dead.	Jesus raises the daughter of Jairus from the dead.
Elisha cures Naaman, the "leprous" commander of the Syrian army.	Jesus cures the ten lepers.
Elisha cures contaminated water in Jericho.	Jesus converts water into wine in Cana.
Elisha multiplies barley loaves.	Jesus multiplies the loaves and fishes to feed 5,000 (Matthew/Mark/Luke/John).
Elisha raises the late-born son from the dead.	Jesus raises Lazarus from the dead.

In addition, these scholars have pointed to the similarity between the following excerpts from Isaiah and Matthew:

> Isaiah: "Your dead shall live, their corpses shall rise. . . . On that day the deaf will hear . . . the eyes of the blind shall see. The meek shall have joy in the Lord, and the poor shall exult in the Holy One."[27]

> Matthew: "The blind will receive their sight, the lame will walk, the lepers will be cleansed, the deaf will hear, and the dead are raised; the poor will have good news brought to them."[28]

In the view of these critics, the evangelists "grafted" the miracle accounts of Elijah and Elisha onto the words and deeds of Jesus so as to underscore the validity of Jesus as a prophet in his own right, walking in the footsteps of the greatest figures in Jewish history. Could this be true? Are the miracle stories of Jesus an incidence of literary symbolism, or are they based on historical fact?

Let's take a look at the precedent of miracle workers who are closer to Jesus' time. In the first century B.C.E., there lived a rather mysterious figure known as "Honi the Circle Drawer," who appears in Josephus as well as in rabbinic writings of a later age. Apparently, Honi (or Onias, as Josephus calls him) was "a just man, beloved of God, who once during a drought prayed that God would bring the drought to an end. Hearkening to [Onias], God caused rain to fall."[29] As it happened, Honi's activity coincided with the unfortunate struggle between Hyrcanus II and Aristobulus II for the Hasmonean throne, which places the story around 65 B.C.E. Hyrcanus, hearing of Honi's miraculous powers, prevailed upon him to cast a curse on the opposition party. Honi refused, and for this he was stoned to death.

The Mishnah reiterates the miracle story and embellishes it. In this version, Honi draws a circle in the sand and places himself inside it. He then swears that he will not step out of the circle until the rain begins to fall. The story is remarkable, because it is the only reference to a *hasid,* or "holy man," able to perform nature miracles in all of the Mishnah—although, much later, the Babylonian Talmud will credit numerous rabbis with the ability to produce either rain or drought through prayer.[30]

Other references in Josephus show that in first-century Palestine, people firmly believed that a prophet claiming to speak on God's behalf could only authenticate himself by showing a sign (*semeion*). One popular form of "evidence" was the ability to perform exorcism—driving a "demon" out of one possessed. Josephus here speaks from personal experience. "The ability to [exorcise] remains very strong among us even to this day," he writes, and adds that he once witnessed an exorcism performed by a Jew named Eleazar.[31] As we know, exorcism is a frequent theme in the Gospel literature. Miracles, therefore, were seen as a seal of divine approval. Those unable to work miracles or pull off amazing deeds were, by default, branded as false prophets.

Scholars such as David Aune and John Meier have tried to make some sense of the miracle traditions about Jesus. For one, they make a careful distinction between the so-called (1) *healing miracles,* (2) *exorcisms,* and (3) *nature miracles* in the Gospels. The last category includes such phenomena as the feeding of the five thousand, the stilling of the storm, the change of water into wine, and Jesus' ability to walk on water. John Meier has shown that unlike the healing stories, which follow a predictable vocabulary and literary form, the nature miracles have no recognizable pattern.[32] What's more, the Gospels never explicitly state that Jesus is the *agent* of these miracles. Furthermore, nature miracles have fewer multiple attestations. The story of the miraculous catch of fish, for example, occurs only in Luke, and the story of the miraculous conversion of water into wine at Cana appears only in John. Many scholars are therefore inclined to ascribe the nature miracles to the enthusiastic imagination of oral transmission and a desire to underscore the unprecedented nature of Jesus, lest the message somehow be lost on future generations.

Others believe that nature miracles were added in the process of transmission or redaction to emphasize the symbolic significance of Jesus' life and deeds. We have seen how the story of the miraculous multiplication of loaves and fish exalted the meager staples of the poor to the level of a glorious banquet. The miracle at Cana has a symbolic element as well. Rudolf Bultmann has pointed out that the early Church celebrated this miracle on January 6— the Feast of the Epiphany. In antiquity, this date was associated with the feast of Dionysus, when empty jars at every temple and shrine dedicated to the god were filled with wine. Bultmann believes that the Cana story sent a message to John's Hellenistic audience that Dionysus had now been upstaged by a far more powerful deity, namely Jesus, the Son of God.[33]

Yet others believe that the Cana story may have had special significance for Jewish Christians. As we have seen, in Jewish cultic practice, water was associated with ritual purification. Jesus, however, injects water with the new and vital component of wine, symbol of life. The message of the story is that in Jesus, the ancient laws of Moses gain a whole new dimension. Such symbolic significance may be largely lost on us, but for a first-century audience it may have been instantly recognizable.

THE HEALING MIRACLES

We are left, however, with the incontrovertible fact that *healing* miracles are consistently reported across all three synoptic Gospels, as well as, in some cases, the Gospel of John. In fact, *healing* is the very first miracle that Jesus is credited with in the oldest Gospel, that of Mark, when Jesus cures a man with an unclean spirit. This segment is immediately followed with an account of Jesus healing Peter's mother-in-law.[34]

We must therefore conclude that Jesus' ability to heal is an authentic attribute of the oldest sources about Jesus. Naturally, for Christians, Jesus' healing powers are accepted as a matter of faith. From a purely historical viewpoint, however, we must ask if it is possible to explain his supernatural powers with the range of medical, pathological, and scientific tools at our disposal. If Jesus truly had the ability to heal the sick, where did these powers come from? And does the Gospel material provide us with sufficient diagnostic information to verify the healing procedures attributed to Jesus?

Countless experts, authors, and scholars have attacked this issue, and some of their arguments are quite compelling. John Meier, for example, has identified the consistent formula by which the healing miracles are described. According to this paradigm, Jesus typically begins the healing process with the statement "Your sins are forgiven," the very words spoken to one of Jesus' first patients in the Gospel of Mark, the paralytic in Capernaum.[35]

To a modern reader, this sounds rather strange. What does sin have to do with a medical condition? The answer is: quite a lot. In ancient Palestine, illness and disease were routinely regarded as God's punishment for sins. If a child was born blind or deaf, for example, it was assumed that the infant had been conceived in sin and thus bore the penalty for his parents' immorality. This concept was rooted in the book of Exodus, in which God insists that the people of Israel not bow down to other gods, at the risk of punishment: "for I the Lord your God am a jealous God, punishing children for the transgressions of parents, to the third and fourth generation."[36] The Psalms praise the Lord "who forgives all your iniquity, [and] who heals all your diseases."[37] In the Gospel of John, as the disciples follow Jesus, they see a man who has been blind from birth. Their first question is, "Rabbi, who sinned, this man or his parents, that he was born blind?"[38]

People with chronic diseases were therefore ostracized as sinners and often lived in squalor on the periphery of the village. In the Mishnah, Rabbi Yohanan bar Nappa'ha forbids anyone to come within forty feet of a leper. Elsewhere, the Mishnah states that "when a leper enters the house, all possessions therein become unclean up to the rafters." For the sufferer, the strain of chronic illness was thus compounded by the emotional stress of being excluded from the culture and comforts of the village.

Jesus, however, broke with Jewish precedent. He rejected the idea that illness is by definition the product of sin. In John, Jesus answers his disciples, "Neither this man nor his parents sinned; he was born blind."[39]

This belief is fundamental to Jesus' approach to healing. He begins by telling his patients that *they are no longer sinners.* In Mark, Jesus tells a paralytic, "Son, your sins are forgiven."[40] From a psychological perspective, Jesus thus initiates the critical first step of the patient's recovery. Removing the stigma of sin offers the patient the prospect of being accepted back into his community, giving a powerful stimulus to the will to heal.

The Gospels report that Jesus' unorthodox strategy of forgiving a patient's sins provoked angry outbursts from observers. Inevitably, these are "scribes" and other learned folk whose function it is to prepare the collision course between Jesus and the Pharisees. "Why does this fellow speak in this way?" they cry out; "It's blasphemy! Who can forgive sins but God alone?"[41] Nevertheless, the Hebrew Scriptures show that forgiving a man's sins could be the right of legitimate, divinely inspired prophets. Nathan forgave David for seducing Bathsheba and plotting her husband's death.[42] Jeremiah told his audience, "I will heal your faithlessness."[43] Consequently, as a prophet who hewed close to the model of seventh-century B.C.E. prophets like Jeremiah, Jesus believed he had God's sanction to absolve as well. "So that you may know that the Son of Man has authority on earth for forgive sins," he tells his skeptical audience, and then commands the paralytic to walk.[44]

The second phase of the healing formula is Jesus' recurrent question "Do you have faith?" With this query, Jesus seems to ascertain whether the patient has the requisite faith in Jesus' ability to work as a divinely inspired healer. The implication is that the sick *cure themselves* by placing their full and complete trust in Jesus' words. This is borne out by a third aspect of Jesus' healing formula: the statement "your faith has made you well."[45]

The last phase of Jesus' healing methodology is his touch. Jesus made a point of touching or embracing the ill, thus explicitly rejecting the prevailing notion that the diseased were ritually unclean. For someone bereft of human intimacy for years, or possibly most of his life, the physical touch of Jesus must have been an electrifying experience. Jesus' deliberate proximity to the patient, his assurance that any presumed sins are null and void, and the comfort of a physical embrace all amount to powerful stimuli to the natural healing process.

This line of interpretation has prompted some to claim that many of Jesus' healings can simply be ascribed to the power of suggestion. Some scholars believe that further "reverse evidence" of this theory is found in the Gospel materials themselves. The evangelists admit that Jesus was unable to perform miracles in Nazareth. The reason may be that in his home village, people knew him as simply the son of Joseph, a peasant farmer and construction worker, and had a hard time accepting Jesus' authority as a *hasid*.

152

But the fact is that Eastern medicine has long known a truth that Western medicine has only recently embraced, namely, that the organ that plays the greatest role in a person's health and recovery is the human brain. Practitioners of Eastern techniques such as chakra healing argue that 40 percent of the human healing process is physical, but 60 percent is driven by mental factors. Clinical psychiatrist Stacy Davids cites a recent statistic that upwards of 80 percent of the illnesses in our high-pressure society are psychosomatic and, further, points to studies in controlled clinical trials in which on average 35 percent of patients appear to respond positively when given a new drug, even if it is a placebo. Even physicians in conventional hospitals know that the *will to live* is a hugely important factor in a patient's recovery.

A NEW THEORY OF JESUS' HEALING ABILITY

But such explanations serve to explain only part of the healing enigma. If Jesus' healing prowess can truly be explained as confidence-boosting therapy, then why did the apostles have only qualified success when they tried to apply the same formula? Eyewitnesses who observed Jesus certainly believed that he had extraordinary powers. This leads us to consider quite a different reason why Jesus' reputation as a charismatic healer was so well entrenched.

This idea is rooted in the growing body of scientific evidence that there are unseen forces affecting our health that our five senses cannot normally ascertain. In 1925, for example, the Russian scientist Georges Lakhovsky postulated that all living cells (including bacteria and animals as well as people) possess attributes similar to electronic circuits, namely resistance, capacitance, and inductance. When in perfect balance, these electrical properties will cause the recurrent generation or "oscillation" of high-frequency sine waves, a phenomenon known as resonance. Lakhovsky argued that this resonance exerted as great an influence on human wellness as any biochemical process in our body. For example, Lakhovsky found that when he increased the amplitude of healthy cell oscillations in a human patient, this increase could dampen and ultimately overwhelm the oscillations produced by disease-ridden cells, ultimately defeating the pathogens.[46]

Lakhovsky's research prompted the University of Southern California to appoint a Special Medical Research Committee to study the effects of electromagnetic energy waves on sixteen patients with terminal cancer. These patients were then treated with a special mitogenic impulse-wave technology, developed by Royal Raymond Rife. After four months, the Committee reported that all sixteen of the patients appeared cured. The Rife Frequency Instrument was subsequently put to use in the University of Southern California clinic of Dr. Virginia Livingston-Wheeler between 1968 and 1983. Approximately ten thousand patients were treated, with a success rate of 80 percent.[47]

For anyone with even a glancing familiarity with Eastern medicine, a knowledge base spanning some three thousand years, this will come as no surprise. Both the Ayurvedic philosophy of the chakras and the Chinese concept of *qi* identify energy concentrations in the human body. Both relate to energy systems that must be kept in balance in order to safeguard a person's well-being. Chinese practitioners maintain, for example, that *qi* flows through twelve primary organs of the body via twelve key channels or meridians. If the *qi* flow is blocked or unbalanced, disease results. To counter such imbalances, acupuncture or shiatsu massage is practiced; both modalities aim to restore the harmonious balance of energy or *qi* meridians.

In the United States, such alternative practices (including electromagnetic oscillation) remained on the periphery of medical practice until recent years, when a number of reputable scientific bodies began to investigate the matter. Premier among these is the National Center for Complementary and Alternative Medicine (NCCAM), established in 1998 by the National Institutes of Health, which in turn is a unit of the U.S. Department of Health and Human Services. One of the NCCAM's areas of research is energy field medicine. While this research is still ongoing, the NCCAM has declared that electromagnetic energy *is* a known quantity in the human body. More significantly, there appears to be sufficient empirical evidence to suggest that some individuals are capable of producing the same type of oscillation exchange as initiated by machines such as Rife's Frequency Instrument.[48]

The focus of this book does not permit us to dwell on the issue of electromagnetic oscillation and its benefits in patient wellness with any depth. Suffice it to say that mainstream science, including the U.S. health authorities, is now prepared to accept that electromagnetic phenomena may be a necessary complement to our conventional paradigm of biochemical medicine, and moreover, that certain individuals appear to be capable of reading and manipulating such magnetic field phenomena in patients.

In 2006, I had the rare opportunity to observe the application of electromagnetic healing (EMH) in therapy. This technique has been practiced for years by Dr. Rick Levy, a Ph.D. in clinical psychology with five board certifications in his field. As such, Dr. Levy has been able to integrate alternative medicine techniques such as EMH with an otherwise traditional psychotherapy practice. With Dr. Levy's permission, I observed individual sessions with some twenty-five patients, many of whom had come to see Dr. Levy for the first time. The results were astonishing. By repeatedly moving his hands in close proximity to specific areas of pain or disease (thus directing concentrated waves of energy into the patient's body), Dr. Levy was able to alleviate anywhere from 60 to 100 percent of the pain sensations reported by the patient. Most sessions did not last more than twenty minutes. In one such session, a woman suffering from debilitating back pain was able to stand up straight, free of pain, for the first time in thirty years.

✢ ✢ ✢

Who are these people, endowed with this gift of electromagnetic healing? What predisposes them to a superior understanding and manipulation of the energy flow in our bodies? We don't know. What we do know is that such individuals have existed for many centuries.

I believe that there is a strong probability that Jesus was endowed with the gift of electromagnetic healing, and that he only became aware of this gift when confronted with the epidemic incidence of disease during his journeyman travels through Lower Galilee. The people around him may have felt the unique power of his magnetic presence intuitively. Mark describes a situation where, unbeknownst to Jesus, a woman who had been suffering from hemorrhages for twelve years moved up behind him to touch his cloak. She thought, "If I but touch his cloak, I will be made well." Indeed, her hemorrhaging stopped. More importantly, Mark reports that Jesus was immediately aware "that power had gone from him."[49] Some form of energy had spontaneously surged from Jesus' physical presence, even though he himself did not direct it.

There is no precedent for this form of healing in either the Old or New Testament. Other healing episodes are invariably the result of a prophet consciously praying or invoking the power of God to bring a miraculous event about. The idea that healing could take place through physical touch

155

between two human beings and the resulting—unwitting—transfer of energy is simply unique. This may be why people were ready to ascribe special, "magical," or miraculous power to Jesus, even though he might not have been aware of it for much of his young adult life.

For five years, Jesus traveled through lower Galilee, visiting village after village while steadily gaining a reputation as a charismatic healer. Throughout this period, the social condition of the peasants grew steadily worse. Antipas was fully engaged in developing Tiberias and devoting every possible resource to the construction of magnificent homes, temples, and baths, so the triple tax regimen must have continued unabated. But the Tiberias project was of little benefit to Jewish workers and artisans, for, as we have seen, the site was considered ritually unclean. Hundreds, perhaps thousands, of laborers who had previously found employ in Sepphoris now inevitably joined the ranks of the homeless, landless, and unemployed.

These years of social work and healing are reflected in the oldest strata of the Q sayings document. "John [the Baptist]," says Q, "heard about [the healings] and sent his disciples to ask, 'Are you the one to come, or should we look for another?' Jesus said, 'Go and tell John what you hear and see: the blind recovered their sight, the lame walk, lepers are cleansed, the deaf hear, the dead are raised, and the poor are given good news.'"[50] This segment clearly implies that Jesus' healing activity took place *before* he joined John the Baptist in the Jordan wilderness. The story also suggests that word of his healing had traveled so far and wide that even the Baptist, in his remote spot in the desert, became aware of it.

This brings us to the next question: Why did Jesus decide to abandon his social work in Galilee to join the movement of John? What precipitated this decision? And when did the change take place?

SEVEN

IN THE FOOTSTEPS
OF JEREMIAH

Sometime between 20 and 28 C.E., Jesus' role as a social worker and charis-matic healer changed. Rather than merely ministering to the poor and the sick, he began to formulate a vision for rectifying the great injustice he was witnessing. He changed, quite literally, from a social *worker* to a social *activist*. From an observer, he became an agent of change.

As we saw in Chapter 6, modern psychology has often traced an indi-vidual's desire to make the world a better place to a prolonged traumatic experience. Jesus, arguably a highly intelligent child with an early expe-rience of social isolation in an otherwise close community, had experienced a traumatic youth on multiple levels; but he absorbed these assaults by channeling his resolve to resist destruction and to heal and protect others. Now he was ready to move on to a higher level of per-sonal engagement: to try to restore the socio-religious village society of Galilee and save the peasantry from the grip of the region's economic elites.

Richard Tedeschi, Crystal Park, and Lawrence Calhoun have dubbed this phenomenon, which has been observed in both children and adults, "posttraumatic growth" (PTG). In many cases, they argue, traumatized individuals develop coping mechanisms that inspire them to some form of redemptive activity, be it social or religious.[1]

Psychologists can point to a number of recent studies. A survey of young Sudanese children, for example, who were parted from their homes and families as a result of the civil war showed that 90 percent retained their faith in God and, in effect, believed that God would redeem their loss and suffering; 16 percent of these youths planned to become priests.[2] A 2006 report from the Secretary General of the UN indicated that one third of a group of Ugandan boys who suffered post-traumatic stress disorder from being forced to serve in rebel armies believed that prayers and a return to faith would help them cope with their ordeal.[3]

In another revealing study, traumatic stress was credited with motivating individuals to devote themselves wholeheartedly to socially redeeming activity. Several case studies have shown that personal post-traumatic suffering could be sublimated into social or artistic action and thus can serve as a powerful agent for social change.[4]

✝ ✝ ✝

Of course, studies such as these do not tell the whole story. Surveys of displaced children in other areas of conflict, notably Gaza and the West Bank, show that continued exposure to violence, military action, and displacement of home and school can produce a wide range of coping responses, not all of them constructive.[5] But these modern models do help us to better understand this next phase in Jesus' life. And for Jesus, the agency of cathartic activism was his faith.

In our modern society, we are used to a clear separation of the professional, social, and religious spheres of our lives. One may influence or inform the other, but from both an ethical and a practical point of view, these activities occupy distinct spaces. In first-century Palestine, the opposite was true. The social, economic, and religious experience of a peasant was deeply and closely intertwined, to a degree that we would find hard to fathom.

The foundation of this close relationship was the belief that the land of Palestine, the very soil on which Galilean farmers had worked and lived for so many centuries, still remained the property, the *kingdom,* of God; Jews were merely tenants, working and living at the Lord's pleasure. This was one of the fundamental tenets of the Covenant Law, enshrined in the words of God to Moses: "If you will obey my voice and keep my covenant, you shall be my own possession among all peoples; for all the earth is mine, and you shall be to me a *kingdom* of priests and a holy nation."[6] The idea that everyone was essentially a debtor to God, grateful to till the plot he had been allotted, not only formed the core of the Jewish identity but also guaranteed every Jew the equality and social justice that lie at the root of the Mosaic Laws. No one was more equal than the other. Hence, to hoard land and riches at the expense of others was not only an offense toward one's fellow man, but also an egregious breach of the covenant with YHWH. ⱳⱳⱳ

This may serve to explain why the indignation Jesus felt over the great social injustice perpetrated against the peasantry had a strong religious dimension from the very beginning. The integrity and harmony of the Kingdom of God had been violated; it was through God that this harmony should be restored.

The Gospels represent the moment of Jesus' call to activism in allegorical terms: in the form of a dove, symbol of the Spirit of the Lord, descending upon Jesus. The immediate setting is the River Jordan, where John the Baptist is about to immerse Jesus in the waters. As Mark depicts it, it is not John's water but the divine spirit that is *anointing* Jesus for his ministry. The idea of a man of God being anointed with the Lord's spirit is not a Christian invention, but an ancient Jewish motif; it is the process by which YHWH commissions his chosen ones. "The spirit of the Lord God is upon me," says Third Isaiah; "because the Lord has anointed me; he has sent me to bring good news to the oppressed, to bind up the brokenhearted, to proclaim liberty to the captives."[7] In his Gospel, Luke has Jesus read out Isaiah's commission as his own: "The Spirit of the Lord is upon me, for he has anointed me to preach the Gospel to the poor; he has sent me to heal the brokenhearted, to preach deliverance to the captives."[8]

To further validate the commission of Jesus, the Gospels describe "a voice from heaven" that speaks the words: "This is my Son, the Beloved, with whom I am well pleased." This formula, too, does not have a Christian source, as we might assume, but a Jewish one. Any anointed one (the very meaning of the word *mashiach* or "messiah"), such as a king, was by definition a "son of God." As we saw before, in 2 Samuel we hear of the Lord's promise to David's offspring that "I will be a father to him, and he shall be a son to me."[9] "You are my son" is the Lord's decree to Israel's Anointed according to Psalm 2; "today I have begotten you." Psalm 42 summarizes the formula and gives it purpose: "Here is . . . my chosen one, in whom my soul delights; I have put my spirit upon him; he will bring forth justice to the nations."[10]

The evangelists deliberately place the moment of Jesus' anointing by God's Spirit at the moment of John's baptism, for reasons that we will examine shortly. But Jesus' spiritual awakening to the plight of the poor, and his decision to fight on their behalf, must have come well before his encounter with John. It may have come about when Jesus realized that to heal the body was not sufficient. He had to give the peasantry *hope:* hope that their condition would improve; hope that together, as a nation, they had the power to end the crisis and rebuild a just rural society. It took time, but by the latter part of the 20s, Jesus' idea was slowly being forged into a plan of action, a manifesto for change.

The ideological foundation for what we could tentatively call Jesus' "program" was laid by Scripture, and specifically the Pharisaic approach to Scripture. As we saw earlier, the Pharisees passionately believed that all the children of Israel should function as priests of God, finding salvation in prayer and cultic practice—a view contrary to that of the Sadducees, who held that salvation was possible only through the sacrificial system of the Temple. The Pharisees also insisted that the Covenant Law governing the practice of Judaism was not frozen in an immutable canon, as the Sadducees believed, but in need of ongoing exegesis. In this continuous refinement, they believed, man was as blessed and guided by God's Spirit as Moses had been on Mount Sinai. Furthermore, though the Pharisees had largely relinquished the political role they had once played in the Hasmonean government, they still harbored the messianic hope of a restoration of Zion, of a nation under YHWH, a kingdom of God freed from the bonds of foreign servitude. Later rabbinic literature refined this idea as not an eschatological dream or the result of divine intervention, but as a deliberate choice by man. "From whoever accepts upon himself the yoke of Torah," says the Mishnah, "do they remove the yoke of the state and the yoke of hard labor."[11]

Lastly, the Pharisees believed in the Resurrection. This was a relatively new concept in Second Temple Judaism. Traditionally, Jews believed that the dead would dwell in a dark and featureless underworld known as *Sheol.* Though there are inklings of a hope of resurrection in Third Isaiah, it is the Book of Enoch that boldly sets forth the idea that on the day of God's final judgment, the just will receive the afterlife—as spirits, rather than in bodily form—while the wicked will be punished.[12] The book of the Wisdom of Solomon, tentatively dated to the first century B.C.E., goes a step further, arguing that the souls of the righteous enter God's heavenly realm imme-diately after death. "The righteous live forever," says its anonymous author, "and their reward is with the Lord."[13] Unlike their opponents, the Sadducees, the Pharisees wholeheartedly embraced this view. Josephus con-firms that the Pharisees believed in the immortality of the soul, while later rabbinical writings suggest that the righteous would be resurrected in *body* and welcomed in heaven.

These three ideas—that every man is responsible for working God's Kingdom in everyday life, that the Law needs constant reinterpretation, and that the spirit of the righteous will inherit eternal life—would form the ideological basis for Jesus' activity as a social activist and religious dissident.

JEREMIAH AND JESUS

While the *Torah* or Law, the first division of the Hebrew Scriptures, was the great legislative corpus of Jewish life, in itself it did not offer an executive strategy for restoring the great vision of Zion in first-century Palestine. Fortunately, the second division, the Books of the Prophets (*Nevi'im*), is quite different. As the chronicle of Jewish history from the beginning of Israel through the Exile, "Prophets" is filled with the thoughts and actions of men who confronted a situation very similar to the social upheaval of the first century C.E. Paramount among these were the prophets Amos, Micah, Hosea, and Jeremiah.

The prophet Amos was a herdsman from Tekoa, a village a scant six miles south of Bethlehem. He was active in both the southern kingdom of Judah and the northern kingdom near the end of the reign of King Jeroboam II (786–746 B.C.E.). Living in a time of economic prosperity, Amos denounced the growing power of rich landowners who steadily encroached on the property of small farmers and peasants. Amos's criticism of Israel's social injustice was taken up by the prophet Micah, who was active "in the days of Kings Jotham, Ahaz, and Hezekiah of Judah," hence from 742 to 687 B.C.E.[14] Micah came from Moresheth-gath in the Shephelah and spent most of his time arguing the plight of the poor to offi-cials in Jerusalem. Like Amos, Micah believed that the kingdom's social ills violated the fundamental precepts of the Laws of Moses.

While Amos and Micah were active in the south, the prophet Hosea operated mostly in the north. His activity coincided with the reigns of

Jeroboam through Hoshea, up to the fall of the Northern Kingdom to the Assyrian juggernaut in 721 B.C.E. Hosea railed against the growing popularity of pagan worship, particularly the cult of Baal, and accused his contemporaries of failing, "as an unfaithful wife," in their covenantal obligations to YHWH. He warned of the coming destruction of Israel as a nation, but held forth God's promise of a new beginning.

Jeremiah lived in the late seventh and early sixth centuries B.C.E., at a time when the last remnant of the great kingdom of David and Solomon, the small state of Judah, faced the oppression of the tyrants of Babylon. In a verse that must have resonated with the young Jesus, Jeremiah described how at age eighteen, "in the thirteenth year" of the reign of King Josiah (627 B.C.E.), he felt the calling of the Lord. "The Lord put out his hand and touched my mouth, and the Lord said to me, . . . Today, I appoint you over nations and kingdoms, to pluck down and to pull down, to destroy and to overthrow, to build and to plant."[15]

I believe that Jesus must have sensed a very special affinity with Jeremiah. There are obvious parallels between the Judah of the sixth century B.C.E. and the Palestine of the first century C.E. Like Palestine, Judah had been reduced to a vassal state, paying tribute not to the Roman emperor Tiberius but to the Babylonian king Nebuchadnezzar. What's more, after a brief period of reform initiated by King Josiah, Judah had lapsed back into religious laxity. The worship of pagan gods was creeping back into favor, abetted by King Jehoiakim himself, just as Herod and his son Antipas were keen to erect temples to Roman deities throughout their realm. Most significantly for Jesus, Jeremiah railed against those who stood to profit from these chaotic and perilous times—by hoarding vast riches, including land, at the expense of Judah's peasantry. Like Amos before him, Jeremiah poured scorn on wealthy landowners and castigated those who "amass wealth unjustly; in mid-life it will leave them, and at their end they will prove to be fools."[16] By forsaking social justice and true faith, Jeremiah said, the people of Israel had violated Covenant Law, and they would soon feel the wrath of the Lord.

Jesus knew, of course, that the inexorable slide of Judah into moral and social depravity would end in the most traumatic event in Jewish history: the capture of Jerusalem, the destruction of the Temple, and the dispersal of thousands of Jews across the Babylonian Empire. This cataclysm loomed large over Jeremiah's prophecies and lent his writing an intense, almost apocalyptic sense of urgency. Over and over again, Jeremiah appealed to his countrymen to "repent" and to abandon their hedonistic *après nous, le deluge* attitude.[17] Jeremiah urged his audience to return to the fundamental tenets of the Lord's Covenant—social justice, compassion, and observance of not only the letter but also the spirit of the Mosaic Laws. His sermons challenged his listeners to reform Judaism, to redefine what it meant to be called a member of God's chosen people in the difficult times of his day.

Did Jesus read the Book of Jeremiah? And if so, where and when? As we saw before, there are compelling reasons to think that he must have received his first instruction in the Hebrew Scriptures from Pharisees during his stay in Sepphoris, including the Books of the Prophets. It is impossible to say with certainty whether the Scriptures he used were written in Hebrew or Aramaic, but there undoubtedly were numerous scrolls to be found among the Pharisaic community. During the subsequent years of his wandering, the most obvious place to consult the Scriptures would have been private or public prayer rooms in larger Galilean towns such as Capernaum or Magdala. It is very likely that the scrolls in these places would have consisted of a *Targum* (a translation of Scripture written in the Aramaic of Palestine). We know that one such Targum, of the Book of Job, is mentioned in the time of Rabbi Gamaliel I, a contemporary of Jesus who died in 63 C.E.[18] Other evidence that Jesus consulted such *Targumim* is provided by the Gospels, who quote him crying out the opening verse from Psalm 22, in Aramaic, during his last moments on the cross: *Eloi, Eloi, lema sabachthani?* ("My god, my God, why have you forsaken me?"[19])

We are not quite sure which Targum Jesus would have read, though it may have been similar to the Targum compiled by Jonathan ben Uzziel, who reportedly was a disciple of the great Jewish sage Hillel (active 30–10 B.C.E.), and thus lived near the time of Jesus. The Dead Sea Scrolls, furthermore, have revealed that the Book of Jeremiah as it was known in its *Masoretic* or Hebrew form is quite similar to the version in the Septuagint, which in turn formed the basis for the Old Testament that Christians use today. Hence, we can be fairly sure that the Book of Jeremiah in modern Christian Bibles is close to the version that Jesus knew.

That *Targumim* were made freely available for consultation may be inferred from rabbinic writings, which state that "a person should always review his portions of scripture along with the community, reading the scripture twice and the *Targum* once."[20] The apparent facility with which Jesus is able to quote scripture, not only in the Gospels but also in source strata, suggests that Jesus continued his study of *Targumim* from his youth to the beginning of his ministry.

The example of a charismatic man like Jeremiah rousing the people of his time to change the path of Jewish history must have struck a chord with Jesus. There were other prophets who had called for repentance, but none had faced quite the immense threat that Jeremiah confronted. The very survival of the Jewish community was at stake—threatened not only by foes from abroad but also by enemies from within. For Jesus, therefore, reading the book of Jeremiah may have felt like hearing the words of an alter ego. Modern hermeneutics, which have shown that Jeremiah's works were heavily edited long after his death, were unknown to Jesus. In the first-century text that Jesus would have known, Jeremiah spoke to Jesus as if from the grave, and Jesus closely identified with those words.

Like Jesus, Jeremiah was a social outcast, a lonely but deeply sensitive figure, doomed to spend much of his life in solitude. He was not a *mamzer* like Jesus but the son of a Levitical priest, born in a rural village called Anathoth in the tribal country of Benjamin. Though culturally and spiritually in tune with the northern tribes, Benjamin had always been controlled by its neighbor in the south, the kingdom of Judah. What's more, Jeremiah was a descendant of Abiathar, one of the two chief priests from the time of King David; the other was Zadok. Since Abiathar was implicated in efforts to contest Solomon's claim to the throne, Abiathar and his house were ostracized and banished. The house of Zadok—the Zadokites, from which the term "Sadducees" is probably derived—henceforth controlled the position of high priest. Jeremiah was thus always viewed with suspicion by the people of Judah, both as a Benjaminite and as an Abiatharite—not unlike the suspicion that Jesus had experienced through much of his youth. Like Jesus, Jeremiah was a *krtny,* a rural figure; Anathoth was Jeremiah's Nazareth.

What's more, Jeremiah's resentment of the sacrificial cult in the Temple must have resonated with Jesus. Jeremiah had never accepted the idea that God could be appeased with piles of scorched meat. "Thus says the Lord, . . . In the day that I brought your ancestors out of the land of Egypt, I did not speak to them or command them concerning burnt offerings," Jeremiah declares in his famous Temple address. "But this command I gave them, 'Obey my voice, and I will be your God, and you shall be my people.'"[21] Jesus' teachers, the Pharisees, had said much the same thing: that sacrifice was meaningless unless it was matched by good deeds. It was, in fact, one of the roots of the great antagonism between Pharisees and Sadducees.

But Jeremiah would not have agreed with the solution as formulated by the Pharisees many centuries later. He would not have subscribed to a scrupulous observance of cultic purity, as the Pharisees did. What mattered, said Jeremiah, was a man's intimate communion with God—an idea that strongly influenced Jesus' later teachings. To Jeremiah's mind, YHWH was solely concerned with what went on in a man's heart, a theme that reverberates in his poems and sayings, faithfully recorded by his scribe, Baruch. "I, the Lord, test the mind and search the heart," reads one of Jeremiah's verses, "to give to all according to their ways, according to the fruit of their doings."[22] In this, he echoed the words of the eighth-century prophet Micah, who—not surprisingly—was also a rural figure. "Will the Lord be pleased with thousands of rams?" Micah asked sarcastically; "Shall I give my firstborn for my transgressions, the fruit of my body for the sin of my soul?" On the contrary, Micah argued; "what does the Lord require of you but to do justice, and to love kindness, and to walk humbly with your God?"[23]

This idea of God desiring man's heart, rather than the carcass of a sacrificial offering, hit home. The Gospels indicate that Jesus himself had always felt the same way about God. To him, YHWH was not some austere deity to be placated with animal flesh, but a loving father, an *Abba,* to whom he could confide his innermost fears and dreams. This feeling of intimacy with the divine, this sense of YHWH as a personal guide, had been nurtured by Jesus' deep sense of estrangement from his family and village. But it would truly blossom in the long months and years of solitary wandering from village to village.

YHWH was Jesus' confidant. He was a father on whose shoulders Jesus could rest his weary head, no matter where he found himself. And here now was a prophet, a man in a time very similar to Jesus', who had experienced the same close bond with God. What's more, here was a program for a different experience of Judaism, a simpler, purer form of Judaism that went back to the very roots of its raison d'être: to be a community of equals under the eyes of a compassionate God. Jeremiah wanted to return Judaism to its core spirituality, albeit a "naked spirituality," in the words of one of Jeremiah's biographers, devoid of the pitfalls of wealth, power, and inequality.[24] "I remember the devotion of your youth, your love as a bride," says the Lord in the wistful poetry of the prophet, deeply saddened by the betrayal of Israel, "how you followed me in the wilderness, in a land not sown."[25]

The theme of Israel as an unfaithful bride of YHWH haunted Jeremiah. It may have been instrumental in his decision not to have a wife and children. His life, he felt, should be fully dedicated to the cause of repentance to which God had called him. Thus, Jeremiah was doomed to live an itinerant life not unlike the one we have inferred about Jesus: a life of solitude, of aimless wandering without a home. Indeed, Jeremiah is the only Old Testament prophet who would never marry; and, as far as we know, neither did Jesus.

By contrast, Jeremiah sought consolation in nature, in much the same way that Jesus did. He looked up and marveled at the gracious swoop of birds across the firmament. "Even the stork in the heavens knows its times," reads one of Jeremiah's poems, "and the turtledove, swallow, and crane observe the time of their coming, yet my people do not know the ordinance of the Lord."[26]

Jesus' embrace of Jeremiah's teachings marked the beginning of his awakening as a *hasid* in his own right. At the same time, it initiated a critical process that led him away from the Pharisaic principles inculcated in him as a young man in Sepphoris. His mature mind, stirred by his indignation over the plight of the peasants, began to absorb, to parse, and to distill, building on the wisdom and experience of the Hebrew prophets.

But one question loomed large. How did one go about putting Jeremiah's great blueprint for reforming Jewish Palestine into action? How could one "re-spiritualize" Judaism and return the land to the core principles of its ancestral faith? Alas, here Jeremiah's book fell short. By his own admission, Jeremiah had largely failed in his pursuits. Indeed, much of Jeremiah's personal poetry is rent by doubt, brought on by years of excoriation, persecution, and humiliation that ultimately led to a severe crisis of self-loathing. "Cursed be the day of my birth," the prophet cries out in one abject moment; "cursed be the man who brought the news to my father, saying, 'a child is born to you, a son,' making my father glad."[27] Never-theless, his ideas were sound. Jeremiah, like Micah and Hosea before him, had put his finger on the issue: Israel had defiled itself by surrendering itself to wealth, greed, and pleasure at the expense of others. The question was, how to rectify the situation? How to motivate the people to repent, and realize Jeremiah's vision of a great Jewish spiritual revival?

JESUS IN JERUSALEM

I believe it is this question that compelled Jesus to travel to Jerusalem, possi-bly between 25 and 28 C.E. The immediate occasion may have been one of the three great religious festivals, when members of the more affluent villages and towns in Galilee would have set out to visit the Temple in Jerusalem. These three feasts, as we have seen, were: (1) Passover, celebrated in the month of Nisan (March/April); (2) Shavuot, or the Festival of Weeks, which followed fifty days after the beginning of Passover; and (3) Succoth, the Feast of Tabernacles, which came in the month of Tishri (September/October).

Jesus may have traveled in a group with villagers; or, more likely, he may have set out by himself. His later parables have several anecdotes about trav-eling the length and breadth of Palestine as a single sojourner. The parable of the Good Samaritan, for example, describes a solitary wanderer passing from Jerusalem to Jericho, where he is set upon by thieves. In the Gospel of John, there is an enigmatic reference to Jesus' brothers going to Jerusalem for Succoth and inviting Jesus to come along. Jesus refuses, saying that "my time has not yet come." But after his brothers have left, he decides to go after all, and travels "in secret."[28] The historicity of this passage is in ques-tion, and many scholars suspect that it is an example of John crafting episodes to illustrate a specific theological point—namely, that Jesus con-sidered Judea hostile territory, since "Jews were looking for an opportunity to kill him."[29] Nevertheless, the notion that Jesus traveled down to Jerusalem on his own, before "his time had come," may be based on an authentic source.

There were two principal roads leading from Galilee to Jerusalem. One was the more direct route that led from Sepphoris through the Jezreel Valley past the fortress of Megiddo and down to Shechem, the place where Abraham had erected the first altar to God in Canaan. Shechem was called Sychar in New Testament times. It was, however, located in the heart of Samaria. Later, it would be the location where John placed the story of a Samaritan woman drawing water from Jacob's well.[30] If this story is historical, it would suggest that Jesus was, at the very least, familiar with the route. From Shechem a larger, more frequently traveled route led to Jerusalem, for the road now became an artery of the great King's Highway. This was the principal caravan route from Damascus that connected Syria and Mesopotamia with Lower Palestine, Idumaea, and Egypt. This road crossed the boundary between Samaria and Judea shortly before Lebonah, close to the Old Testament site of Shiloh. Here was the location of an old shrine to YHWH where the prophet Samuel had served as priest. From there, the road scaled the Judean highlands and led the traveler to the northern walls of Jerusalem.

There was, however, a second route. This led from Capernaum along the western shore of the Sea of Galilee, past Magdala and the springs of Hammath to Beth Shemesh. It then followed the River Jordan through the territory of the Decapolis (the Gentile territory of the "Ten Cities" in the tetrarchy of Philip) and through the Judean desert, past Scythopolis (Beth She'an), Salim, the vineyards of Keruchim and the palm orchards of Archelais, ending at Jericho. Jericho, the world's oldest city, was located some 850 feet below sea level, with the shimmering waters of the Dead Sea just visible on the horizon. From there, travelers like Jesus faced a steep climb along a serpentine road, right through the sun-baked Judean hills to Jerusalem, arriving from the east. At any time in the year, this was easily the most arduous part of the journey. Fortunately, just two miles before reaching the walls of Jerusalem, Jesus would have passed the village of Bethany, located on the eastern slopes of the Mount of Olives. Here lived two relatives, Mary and Martha, to whom Jesus (uncharacteristically) appears to have been close. From Martha's house it was but an hour's walk to the walls of Jerusalem. It was thus a convenient place for Jesus to eat, to rest, to cleanse and mentally prepare himself for the final ascent to the Temple.

✦ ✦ ✦

Recovered from his long journey (which in the best of times would have taken at least five days), Jesus finally made for the city. He must have been amazed, as any country bumpkin would have been, upon setting foot in what was then the most cosmopolitan city in all of Palestine. Even Pliny, an experienced globetrotter, called Jerusalem "by far the most famous city, not only of Judea, but of the whole East." It was perhaps the first time Jesus had ever gazed upon the glittering marble walls of the Temple complex, rising majestically above the ochre-tinted hubbub of the Lower City—certainly the first time since his infancy. The way I envision it, pilgrims would have been pouring down into the valley of Kidron, streaming toward the shining promontory of the Temple. The roads were so clogged that Jesus had to take care not to trip over other people's feet. Nevertheless, the mood of the crowds was upbeat; the mere sight of the Temple, its marble as bright as snow against the indigo sky, was enough to fill their hearts with pride.

Eventually he arrived at the *mikva'ot* below the eastern steps, where Pharisees insisted that worshipers undergo ritual immersion, but neither the heat nor the long lines would have dampened the pilgrims' spirit. Jesus, too, waited patiently for his turn, paid the obligatory shekel to the Pharisee running the baths, then headed for the men's section, where he stripped to his loincloth. He followed the man in front of him through the wonderfully cool and cleansing waters of the *mikveh* and emerged refreshed, as cleansed as a newborn babe.

From there, Jesus once again joined an immense throng of the pilgrims, now pressing toward the city gate. A number of enterprising traders had set up a row of stands from which they sold water, fruits, devotional items, and souvenirs. Jesus ignored them and allowed himself to be carried through the gate, only to be caught up in an even greater maelstrom of humanity swirling through the small alleys and passages of the Tyropoeon Valley, on the way to the Temple. At every corner his ears, used to the stillness of the fields, were assaulted by the bleat of sheep, the cries of hawkers, the wails of beggars, and pilgrims speaking in every language imaginable. Through it all, mothers called for lost children, shoppers bargained and argued, and deliverymen with stupendously laden donkeys struggled to carry their produce to nearby stalls. And then there was the smell: the stink of rotting fruit, animal dung and sweating bodies in the hot midday sun, permeated by the odor of burnt flesh wafting down from the Temple complex.

Wherever he looked, Jesus saw huddles of peasant families and their grimy children, crowded under the overhang of a shop or simply squatting in the dirt, prepared to defend their precious perch at all costs. High above them rose great columns of thick oily smoke, rising from the altar beyond the great walls, casting thin flakes of ash on the crowds below.

At last, Jesus turned a corner and there it was: the "stupendous mass" of the Temple's walls, in the phrase of Josephus, eighty-four feet high, built up of huge hewn blocks of limestone that were fitted so tight that not even a knife could be pushed through the joints. He allowed himself to be carried along, up the long flight of stairs that led to the Double Gate, also known as the West Huldah Gate, leading to the Temple sanctuary. He stumbled, nearly fell, and discovered the reason: the steps of the stairway were uneven. A bystander may have explained that the steps were cut to different heights so that pilgrims were forced to ascend slowly and carefully, each tread reminding them that they trod on sacred ground.

The throng now entered a long tunnel lit by smoky, sputtering torches. A thousand voices echoed against the smooth Herodian stone as Jesus followed the crowd up a long flight of steps, his eyes adjusting to the sudden darkness. There, up ahead, a light blazed with such brightness that Jesus had to avert his gaze. As he came closer, he realized what it was: the bright white pavement of the Great Court, that vast esplanade of white marble that surrounded the actual Temple complex.

Now a new barrage of sounds assaulted him: the din of a thousand hammers and saws. The Stoa, the building under which he had just passed, was still partly under construction, encased in scaffolding, as were parts of the colonnade that ran all along the forecourt. Marble and limestone dust was everywhere; Jesus could taste it on his lips. And yet the space was vast. Even though the tunnels kept spewing forth crowds of people onto the forecourt, all were soon lost in the immense stretch of the esplanade. It was the largest thing built by man that he, or any of his contemporaries, had ever seen. Even by the inflated standards of imperial Rome, the Herodian Second Temple was a marvel, a monument to man's genius, a throne worthy of the Lord.

Some pilgrims had brought sacrificial animals that would soon meet their fate under the knife of the priests. Most peasants, however, could not afford this luxury; from them, the priests were content to accept a dove instead.

Jesus turned and moved toward the entrance of the Temple precinct proper. He first passed the *soreg*, a wooden fence some ten handbreadths high that marked the line beyond which Gentiles as well as those considered ceremonially unclean (such as some of the chronically ill) were not allowed to pass. For a moment his gaze fell upon one of the marble tablets, placed at intervals of a hundred paces, that warned that any Gentile found beyond this boundary would be stoned to death. The text was repeated in Latin and Greek for good measure, lest some dim-witted tourist stray beyond the fence and find himself facing a death sentence.

Just beyond the soreg, Jesus climbed the twelve shallow steps that led to what the Book of Acts calls the Beautiful Gate, a set of double doors that opened up into the first of two courts. The first was called the *ezrat nashim,* the Court of Women, beyond which no woman was allowed to pass. It was surrounded on all sides by a colonnade with gilded Corinthian capitals. Each of the four corners was taken up by a pavilion. One was used for the storage of wood to fuel the altar oven; the other was destined for "lepers," those afflicted by any skin diseases, after they had been cured and cleansed. In another pavilion, known as the Chamber of Oils, the oils and wine for sacrificial ceremonies were kept.

Many people had gathered here, for a variety of reasons. Sacrifice was not the only reason why a devout Jew would go to the Temple. Many worshipers came to offer their first fruits, tithes, or other obligatory offerings; to pray; to study the Torah or question priestly scholars on matters of the Law; or simply to receive blessings.

The colonnade surrounding the Court was topped by an open terrace or portico—the same portico from which worshipers had pelted Roman soldiers during the riots of 6 C.E. Whenever the Court was used for actual ceremonies, such as the celebration of water libation on the first day of Succoth, the men stood in the Court while the women observed the proceedings from the galleries above. As Jesus paused and observed the comings and goings of worshipers, he may have realized that it was near here, in the original forecourt of the First Temple, that Jeremiah had once stood to deliver his dramatic Temple appeal to the worshipers of his day. "At the beginning of the reign of King Jehoiakim son of Josiah of Judah," says the book of Jeremiah, "this word came from the Lord: Stand in the court of the Lord's house, and speak to all the cities in Judah that come to worship in the house of the Lord." And Jesus may have remembered God's oracle: "If you will not listen to me, to walk in my law that I have set before you ... then I will make this house like Shiloh."[31] Shiloh had once been an important sanctuary to YHWH, but it had been destroyed in the eleventh century B.C.E. Right on this spot, in other words, Jeremiah had predicted the imminent destruction of the Temple.[32]

Jesus turned. Just ahead of him, fifteen curved steps led to the magnificent brass double doors of the Nicanor Gate, which led to the sacrificial area proper. He waited for his turn to enter, then followed a group of men inside.

He now stood in the second or inner court, facing the Sanctuary proper, the Second Temple. A rectangular building originally constructed in 515 B.C.E. with funds from the Persian treasury, the Second Temple had been built on the foundations of the First Temple. This original Temple, as tradition went, had in turn been constructed by King Solomon in the tenth century, though it was destroyed after the capture of Jerusalem by Nebuchadnezzar II in 586 B.C.E. We are not quite sure to what extent Herod altered the sixth-century structure, but we do know that he covered the exterior with gold leaf that reflected the light of the sun in all directions. As a result, it was difficult to gaze at the Temple directly, especially in the morning hours when the sun, rising over the Mount of Olives, splashed the Temple in a golden halo of light. Jesus knew that no one except a priest was allowed to enter the Temple proper. Deep inside the Temple was an even more sacred place, the Holy of Holies, where the Ark of the Covenant had once been kept. Though the room was now empty, only the high priest was allowed to enter it, and then only once a year, during the Feast of Atonement, Yom Kippur.

The court was divided into two sections. The narrow strip in which Jesus and other worshipers stood was called the Court of the Israelites, from which they could observe the sacrificial ceremonies. These took place in a slightly elevated section, which was known as the Court of the Priests. This area was dominated by the huge altar that rose some twenty-five feet in the air. The altar was really a huge oven, stoked by sweating assistants on all sides, while priests standing on its summit threw large chunks of meat on the fire. Even on normal days, a variety of sacrifices would be made, presented by worshipers from all over Palestine and beyond. These included burnt offerings, peace offerings, offerings for thanksgiving, sin offerings, and purification offerings. While the meat was being roasted by the flames, some priests busied themselves pouring oil, wine, and blood on the embers, while others, standing on the steps to the sanctuary, sang hymns and blessed the worshipers. The liquids hissed, the meat fats popped, and all was consumed in billowing clouds of smoke that slowly rose from the altar and darkened the skies over Jerusalem.

✣ ✣ ✣

Of course, we do not have any hard evidence that Jesus did visit the Temple in this time frame. But the Gospels suggest that Jesus was familiar with the Temple district—certainly more familiar than his followers were. It is on this spot, in the outer court, that we find Jesus again in the Gospel of Mark, taking his disciples on a tour of the Temple. At one point, they pause near the Treasury where people pay the half-shekel of their Temple tax. His followers are amazed at what they see. "Look, Teacher, what large stone and what large buildings!" marvels one.[33] Jesus is not impressed. One day, while debating the sanctity of the Sabbath, he says, "Something greater than the Temple is here." And then he paraphrases the verse by Hosea quoted above: "I desire mercy and not sacrifice."[34] Clearly, Jesus shared Hosea's and Jeremiah's views of the sacrificial cult. Nowhere in the Gospels do we ever hear of him making a sacrifice during his visits to the Temple.

Back in the Court of the Israelites, Jesus finished his prayer, opened his eyes, and looked around. To his right, he could see the crenellated towers of the Antonia, the large Herodian fortress looming high over the Temple precinct. There, on the parapet, were not Temple Guards but Roman soldiers, reminding the worshipers that they stood in occupied territory. In fact, though Jesus may not have realized it, tensions between the Romans and their Judean subjects had been building steadily. The reason was the arrival of a man who would have a profound influence on the course of our story: a Roman from the house of Pontii, named Pilatus.

THE ARRIVAL OF PILATE

The Pontii were a minor family of Roman equites, or knights, whose burning ambition, shared by almost all other knightly clans, was to join the true aristocracy of Rome: the senatorial class. For a knight to gain the rank of Senator, however, he not only had to have successfully completed a distinguished military and political career; he also had to show assets in excess of a million sesterces. For many knightly families, this was an almost insurmountable problem. By law, senators (and aspiring senators) could not engage in commerce and trade or in any other form of financial speculation. Most Senators, in fact, owed their wealth to large agricultural estates, which is why the Roman Senate was traditionally composed almost exclusively of landed peerage. For a knight whose family did not have impressive land holdings, or who did not have the fortune of having married a wealthy widow, there remained only one avenue for advancement: the diplomatic service.

Serving in the office of prefect in one of the empire's far-flung possessions, one could do very well for oneself. Not by virtue of the salary, that is, which was a pittance, but by leveraging one's right, as Roman governor, to sell lucrative franchises. This included all sorts of licenses, including fishing, tax-collection, mining, and manufacturing rights, which inevitably were granted in return for a hefty bribe and a share of the profits. One such plum posting was Caesarea Augusta, in Roman Spain, where many a governor had sat back to enjoy the region's famous honeyed dates while the locals outbid and outfought each other for the rights to Hispania's mines. Or Athens, perhaps, where a fellow could make a fortune with the export of genuine Greek olive oil, deemed the world's finest. Or, if nothing else, in Gallia, where minerals were sparse but wood could be had by the boatload, and millions were made selling timber to cities sprouting throughout the Roman Empire. Some, like Gaius Verres, the governor of Sicily, had raised the pursuit of wealth to an art form. During his four-year term, Verres amassed a fabulous fortune by taxing the farmers, plundering the estates of the aristocracy, and extorting huge amounts of cash from the rich—using the simple expedient of threatening his victims with death by crucifixion. So powerful was the position of governor, and so prestigious its sway, that it took the oratory of Cicero to expose Verres for the rake that he was.

Pilate was undoubtedly aware of the benefits of a governorship and, like most other equites, must have coveted a posting in one of the more lucrative corners of the growing Empire. Under normal circumstances, these appointments were the prerogative of the emperor. But things had changed. Since 20 C.E., Tiberius had been growing weary of his crown. Initially he had found comfort in sharing the burdens of office with his son Drusus, but in 23 Drusus had died under mysterious circumstances. This tragedy had come on the heels of the loss of his former wife, Vipsania, whom Tiberius still loved to distraction. In the wake of these events, Tiberius began to rely increasingly on his secretary, a man named Lucius Aelius Sejanus, commander of the Praetorian Guard, which served as the emperor's bodyguards. Already Tiberius had moved the Guard from its traditional location outside the city to the heart of Rome proper, thus magnifying the power of Sejanus tenfold.

As it happened, Sejanus was an equestrian like Pilate, and just as ambitious. As it was, the more Tiberius withdrew from public life, the more he deferred to his solicitous commander. When, in 26 C.E., Tiberius chose to retire from political life altogether, Sejanus became the *de facto* ruler of the Empire. For the next four years, he would use his power to establish a regime of terror, extorting and eliminating rivals while favoring men of his own station, all the while plotting to become Rome's next legitimate emperor.

As fate would have it, in that same year of 26 C.E., the position of Prefect of Judea became vacant. The choice fell upon Pilate. Should we therefore conclude that Pilate was one of Sejanus's *amici* or "close friends"? As far as we can determine, Pilate was an individual with no known military or diplomatic record, a prerequisite for overseas service. Even so, Pilate may not have been any too pleased with his assignment. As everyone on the Palatine Hill knew, Judea was a rotten posting. Unlike many regions in the Mediterranean, it had no mines, no manufacturing, and no trade to speak of—nothing to sell or extort. Judea was a backwater, plain and simple, cursed with a hellish climate and populated by a tiresome and rebellious people. According to the Roman geographer Strabo, Judea was a "third-class" imperial province, of little value in terms of colonial exploitation and taxation.[35]

A more experienced diplomat would have sighed and retreated to his villa in Caesarea, the Roman headquarters in Judea, there to sit out his term and wait for better times. Pilate, however, was a different commodity. Ambitious, obstinate, eager to assert his newfound authority, the new prefect decided to make his mark by teaching these restless Jews a lesson. As it happened, fate had granted him the means to do so. Shortly before his retirement, Tiberius had begun an experiment in centralized government. Instead of sending his senior governors to their territories, as Augustus and former consuls had done, Tiberius decided to keep them in Rome, where he could summon them at a moment's notice. Because of this unusual arrangement, Pilate's immediate boss, Lucius Aelius Lamia, governor of Greater Syria, was not in Antioch but far away in the Roman capital.[36] This gave Pilate considerable freedom of movement and may well have emboldened him to take certain steps that would not have been tolerated if his superior had resided in Antioch, a mere five days' ride away.

✣ ✣ ✣

As it was, Pilate must have been surprised to hear that these unruly Judeans enjoyed privileges unheard of elsewhere in the Roman Empire. Many years before, Augustus had deferred to Caesar's close and most profitable friendship with Herod the Great by excusing the Jews from obeisance, and sacrifice, to a statue of the emperor. While this pledge of allegiance to Roman sovereignty was everywhere else deemed essential to safeguarding law and order, Augustus had respected Jewish sensitivities about idolatry and was content to let matters lie.

Pilate had no such compunction. Shortly after his arrival in Judea, he decided on a deliberate provocation to test the Jewish mettle. He sent a cohort of Roman soldiers into the Antonia Fortress in Jerusalem, and specifically ordered that the soldiers carry their ensigns in full view. These, as Roman custom demanded, prominently displayed the image of the emperor. As the citizens woke up and entered the Temple precinct, they were shocked to find these idolatrous standards posted right opposite the Temple proper. An outcry ensued. When it transpired that the new prefect was not in Jerusalem but safely ensconced in his villa in Caesarea, a protest march was organized. This demonstration soon brought "multitudes of Jews" to Pilate's doorstep.

For the first five days, the prefect pointedly ignored the protesters. When at last it became clear that the marchers were not going anywhere, Pilate decided to make a personal appearance. Placing himself on a throne in full view of the crowd, he pretended to listen to their petition while his soldiers secretly formed a ring around the marchers. No sooner were the soldiers in place than Pilate stood and declared that unless the crowd left Caesarea *at once,* he would order his soldiers to move in and kill everyone in sight. At this, the protesters threw themselves on the ground and bared their necks, ready to take the blade. They would rather accept death, their spokesman said, than to see their ancient laws trampled.

Pilate immediately knew he was outfoxed. He wanted to be known as a man of authority, a man of law and order; but it would not do to begin his term with a bloodbath of such proportions. He ordered that the ensigns be removed and returned to Caesarea. But he never forgave the Jews their victory. From that day forward, he secretly plotted his revenge. As we shall see, it was not long in coming.

The standoff in Caesarea coincided with the presumed period of Jesus' wandering as a social worker and healer. Word of Pilate's provocation must have traveled far and wide and, no doubt, stirred the anger of Palestinian youth. Some writers have intimated that Jesus was one of the protestors who marched on Caesarea, though there is no evidence that this was indeed the case. But we may, perhaps, consider that Jesus would have been as indignant as any other young, idealistic Jew. And so it is not unreasonable to think that the mass demonstration in Caesarea galvanized many young people in Judea to action.

The question was, to do what? Military action against the Romans was, as yet, not contemplated. No one wanted to revisit the horrible retributions that had followed on the heels of the rebellions of 4 B.C.E. and 6 C.E., which were still fresh in the memory of many. And so many of Judea's youth may have cast about for a rallying point, a common cause, a leader they could follow. If it is true that Jesus stayed in Judea during this period, then he would undoubtedly have heard what many others were talking about. There was a buzz about a charismatic dissident in the wilderness of the Jordan, a prophet with blazing eyes and fiery rhetoric, who was gathering people from all over this troubled land of Judea. His name was Yehonan the Immerser—better known to us as John the Baptist.

EIGHT

A DISSIDENT NAMED JOHN

Much of what we know about John the Baptist is derived not from the Gospels but from Josephus. John, says Josephus, "was a good man, who commanded the Jews to exercise virtue, both in terms of righteousness toward one another and piety toward God, and so come to baptism."[1] People came to John in droves, says Josephus, "for they were very greatly moved by his words." It is not difficult to see why. John believed that a great cataclysm was on the horizon, a deluge more terrible than anything Israel had witnessed in its thousand-year history. And this time, God's wrath would be more devastating than ever before. The end of time—the *apocalypse*—was near. Jews, said John, should make a total break with their sinful past, and do so with the symbolic act of an all-cleansing submersion in water.

By espousing these ideas, John tapped into a number of apocalyptic currents that had been steadily building over the previous two centuries. Scholars refer to these ideas as eschatological visions—prophecies, in short, about a catastrophic change in the near future that would end the world as we know it and leave only the righteous untouched. In Jewish treatises of the late Second Temple period, eschatological visions typically talk about one final cataclysmic battle between Good and Evil. Only after this great struggle would all of Israel's foes be swept away; only then would the day dawn of a New World Order. The head of this new order would be the Lord, and he would rule again over all the land of Israel.

The Intertestamental Writings—books written by Jewish authors in the era between the Old and New Testaments—are full of apocalyptic visions, a genre rarely seen in earlier times. One such book is the Psalms of Solomon, written (despite its title) in the first century B.C.E. "[God] shall judge peoples and nations in the wisdom of his righteousness," says its author, "and he shall have the heathen nations to serve him under his yoke."[2] Elsewhere, the author expresses his generation's urgent desire for a "cleansing" of the nation by the firm hand of the Messiah: "May God cleanse Israel against the day of mercy and blessing, against the day of choice when He brings back His anointed (*mashiach*). Blessed shall be they that live in those days, for they shall see the goodness of the Lord which He shall perform for the generation that is to come, under the chastening rod of the Lord's anointed, in the fear of his God, in the spirit of wisdom and righteousness and strength."[3]

Another example is the Book of Daniel. This book tells the story of a sixth-century Jewish exile in Babylon, though it was actually composed in the mid-second century B.C.E., when much of Judea suffered under the yoke of the Seleucid king Antiochus IV Epiphanes. The purpose of Daniel's story was to console Jews and explain that they themselves were to blame for all the depredations they were suffering. "All Israel has transgressed your law and turned aside, refusing to obey your voice," says Daniel,[4] but if the nation repents and returns to its faithful observance of Covenant Law, it will be redeemed. A new ruler will appear who will vanquish the foreign enemy, reestablish the kingdom of God, and restore God's control over Jewish history.

John the Baptist took Daniel's prophecy and extended it into his own time. He replaced the villains of Daniel's story, Antiochus IV and the Seleucid Empire, with Tiberius and Rome, but the core of the vision remained the same.

At some time after the Caesarea demonstration of 26 C.E., Jesus must have learned about John and decided to join him. The four canonical Gospels don't give us a motive for this decision; they simply have Jesus appear on the scene. Luke, assuming the role of the Greek historian, places this moment "in the fifteenth year of the reign of Emperor Tiberius, when Pontius Pilate was governor of Judea, and Herod [Antipas] was ruler of Galilee."[5] The fifteenth year of Tiberius's reign equates to 28 C.E., but Luke does not explain the significance of this very specific date.

Josephus, on the other hand, gives us a clear impression of what was happening in the volatile period between 26 and 28 C.E. "Many others came to crowd about [John]," says Josephus, "for they were greatly pleased by hearing his words." And, says Josephus, "they seemed ready to do anything he should advise."[6] John, in sum, had mass appeal. He was a star, an idol, a Palestinian Che Guevara who preached action, a form of protest that emphasized individual transformation in anticipation of the great revolution to come. His name must have been all over Jerusalem and the villages of Judea where, we assume, Jesus was staying at the time. Even the Gospels, which have little to gain from glorifying John at the possible expense of Jesus, admit that "the people of Jerusalem and all of Judea were going out to him, and all the region along the Jordan."[7] No wonder that we find Jesus, at this critical juncture in his life, gravitating to this great figure in the desert. For Jesus, too, his head full of ideas, was in search of a role model, a teacher, who could guide him into the next and pivotal phase of his life.

Where was John at this point? Mark places him "in the wilderness," where he baptized "in the Jordan river." Luke adds that John moved "into all the region around the Jordan."[8] The Gospel of John goes a step further and says that the Baptist operated, among other places, "in Bethany, across the Jordan."[9] This was not the village of Bethany located some two miles east of Jerusalem, but Bethany on the *eastern* bank of the Jordan; its exact location is unknown. Later on, we find John baptizing "at Aenon near Salim, because water was abundant there."[10] This location, too, has not yet been identified with any certainty, though some have placed it southeast of Beth She'an. Today, this spot is a flourishing tourist destination, where scores of modern pilgrims can be seen immersing themselves in the water.

The juxtaposition of desert, wilderness, and river appears to be a contradiction, but in truth it isn't. The Jordan Valley runs in a deep depression that is part of the Rift Valley, a fault in the terrestrial surface running from Turkey through Syria, Lebanon, Israel, and Jordan to the Dead Sea and into the Gulf of Aqaba. For much of its course, the Jordan is flanked by the Judean Desert in the west and the Jordanian Hills in the east. Such areas of cultivation as do exist are limited to groves, including the palm groves of Jericho, where once the large royal estates could be found. Jericho, located just a few miles from the Jordan River, was also conveniently located near the nexus of roads leading from Jerusalem, Shechem, and Scythopolis (Beth She'an) to Philadelphia and other cities of the Transjordan, with easy access to both banks of the river.

If indeed "all of Judea" swarmed down to see the Baptist, as the Gospels attest, then it would have made sense for John to operate in this area, within easy reach of "day trippers" as well as those who wanted to remain with John for a period of time. Significantly, this stretch of the Jordan formed the dividing line between two distinct territories: Roman-occupied Judea, governed by Pilate, and the region of Perea, which now formed part of the Tetrarchy of Herod Antipas, the ruler of Galilee. What's more, at this point the Jordan River was only twelve miles distant from the Dead Sea and a mysterious place known to archaeologists as Khirbet Qumran.

WAS JOHN THE BAPTIZER AN ESSENE?

In the late winter months of 1947, a Bedouin shepherd named Muhammad el-Hamed was looking for a lost goat in one of the hillside caves on the northwestern shore of the Dead Sea. He threw a rock to force the recalcitrant animal to reveal itself, and instead was rewarded with the sound of breaking pottery. Intrigued, he climbed up to the cave and made a discovery that would change the world of biblical research forever. For inside the cave were several jars containing ancient scrolls, among which are the oldest known versions of the Hebrew Scriptures. In the years to come, scores of other ancient "Dead Sea Scrolls" would be found in and around the caves, mostly written in Hebrew. Some of these have been carbon-dated to between 21 B.C.E. and 61 C.E.—straddling the time of Jesus.

Among the scrolls were other texts not related to the Bible, purporting to be the rules of some sort of cultic community. These include the so-called Community Rule and a foundational text known as the Damascus Document. It did not take a leap of faith to imagine that this mysterious sect was probably responsible for copying and storing the Dead Sea Scrolls.

The texts launched a search to see where this sect could have lived. In 1951, Roland de Vaux began excavating the remains of a large settlement near Khirbet Qumran, right in front of the rocky outcroppings where nearly nine hundred scrolls were found. This elaborate complex, guarded by a tower, was soon recognized as one of the most exciting archaeological discoveries of the twentieth century. It contained what has sometimes been identified as a library, a dining hall, a potter's workshop, kilns, ovens, and an elaborate system of stepped cisterns that could have been used for ablutions as well as storage of water. Though some scholars insist that the settlement was a private villa or a military fortress, the majority opinion is prepared to accept that this was the place of the cult that wrote the Dead Sea Scrolls.

But who were these people? The presence of what some have identified as ritual baths or *mikva'ot,* combined with an obvious interest in studying and preserving biblical texts, would suggest that they were Pharisees; however, Pharisees were usually merchants, scribes, and professionals found in urban areas, not in the depths of the desert. So some scholars made the suggestion that this might be a settlement of a community described in some detail by Josephus, namely the group known as the Essenes.

The Essenes, as we remember, were one of four influential "schools" identified by Josephus in the Late Second Temple Period (second century B.C.E.–first century C.E.), the other three being the Sadducees, the Pharisees, and the Zealots. The Essenes probably originated among a group of pious men who emphatically rejected the decision by the Hasmonean House to combine the offices of king and high priest in one man. The high priesthood, the Essenes maintained, was a holy office, to be held only by a man of Zadokite descent. Resentment over Hasmonean arrogance bred disillusionment and ultimately prompted a faction of deeply pious men to break away. Far away from Jerusalem, these Essenes devoted themselves to building a monastic community based on asceticism and full observance of the Law—specifically, its rigorous rules of cleanliness. The purpose of their ascetic lifestyle was to bring them closer to God. "They despise riches," Josephus writes, "and it is a law among them, that those who join must let whatever they have be shared with the whole order."[11] There were around four thousand members of this movement, Josephus claims, all living in a commune that practiced the strictest egalitarianism, keeping neither servants ("which tempts men to be unjust") nor wives ("which may lead to domestic quarrels").[12] "They reject pleasures as an evil," Josephus says elsewhere, "but esteem continence and the conquest over our passions to be a virtue."[13] A more apt description of a monastery was seldom written.

When we take Josephus's description of the Essene cult and compare this with the archaeological evidence found in Qumran, a number of parallels are immediately apparent. Josephus said that at the fifth hour, after "they have clothed themselves in white veils, they then bathe their bodies in cold water." This would explain the network of cisterns at the site, designed to catch rainfall or channel water from the Jordan, enough to allow members to submit to ritual immersion at set times of the day. After this ritual ablution, Josephus continues, the Essenes then enter a communal "dining room, as into a certain holy temple," where they say grace and share their meal. Exactly such a "refectory" has been tentatively identified in Qumran.

Furthermore, the Essenes "take great pains in studying the writings of the ancients, and choose out of them what is most for the advantage of their soul and body." In that respect, the Qumranites would certainly qualify, since they copied almost all of Hebrew Scripture. When not in use, these scrolls were placed for safekeeping in large clay jars. When, in 68 C.E., the Roman army moved closer to crush the Jewish revolt, the Qumran community must have hastily gathered the jars and placed them in caves in the craggy cliffs nearby. There they remained as the centuries rolled on, preserved in the dry air of the desert, until our young Bedouin shepherd stumbled upon them. When Josephus tells us that "[the Essenes] equally preserve the books belonging to their sect," he may very well mean the "Community Rules" documents that were found among the Dead Sea Scrolls.

And yet a heated debate has been raging about whether or not the Qumran "monastery" should be considered Essene. Opponents of this view point to the fact that in the works of Josephus, the Essenes are described as an urban phenomenon rather than a community of hermits in the desert.[14] The Jewish philosopher Philo also notes that the Essenes lived "in many cities of Judea and in many villages and grouped in great societies of many members."[15] The Roman explorer and scholar Pliny the Elder (23–79 C.E.), on the other hand, placed the Essenes near the northwestern shore of the Dead Sea, which is exactly where archaeologists discovered the remains of Khirbet Qumran.[16]

In more recent years, the pendulum has swung back to the identification of Qumran as essentially Essene, though with a caveat: it is now believed that the Qumran community may have been a splinter group that at one point broke away from the "urban" movement of the Essenes. For them, a desert sojourn may have had the symbolic significance of a return to the wilderness, there to prepare for the eventual entry into the Promised Land, just as the Israelites had once done. Interestingly enough, Josephus himself tells us that there was at least "another order of Essenes." This breakaway splinter group, says the historian, "agrees with the rest as to their way of living, and customs, and laws, but differ from them in the point of marriage." Significantly, graves uncovered near Qumran have yielded not only male but also female remains.[17]

✦ ✦ ✦

Just as the scholarly community has been fascinated by the putative relationship between the Essenes and Qumran, so too have many authors pointed to intriguing similarities between the Essenes and the life and deeds of John the Baptist. The "community texts" clearly show that the Qumranites thought of themselves as the only community in Palestine still living in full compliance with Covenant Law. Their task, as they saw it, was to prepare for the inevitable final struggle between the forces of good and evil, of "Darkness" and "Light"—terms that would later return in the Gospel of John. Furthermore, the Qumran community anticipated the arrival of a genuine Messiah, "the Prince of Light," a king of the line of David. This ruler would herald the new dominion of God, a reign of political freedom and strict observance of the Mosaic Laws. In preparation for this moment of truth, the Qumran community practiced repentance though prayer, scriptural discussion, abstention, and daily "baptism."

John the Baptizer also envisioned the coming of a Messiah, though perhaps a *mashiach* in the classical Jewish mold—a military genius who would not hesitate to cleanse the Jewish nation with all the powers at his command. "The winnowing fork is in his hand, to clear his threshing floor and to gather the wheat into his granary," the Baptist says in Luke; "but the chaff he will burn with unquenchable fire."[18] Like the Qumranites, John warned that only a complete and radical rejection of Israel's sins could save the Jews from utter destruction. Among these sins was undoubtedly the Hellenistic lifestyle that many urban Jews had begun to embrace, as well as the pursuit of individual wealth at the expense of others. When some followers asked John what this form of repentance should entail, he said "Whoever has two coats must share with anyone who has none; and whoever has food must do likewise"— echoing the Essene prescription that "there is no appearance of poverty, or excess of riches, but every one's possessions are intermingled with every other's possessions."[19] This egalitarianism is also reflected in the Qumran "Rules of the Community," whereby a novice had to agree that "his property and his possessions shall be given to the hand of the man who is the examiner over the possessions of the many."[20]

There are further parallels between the Baptist and Qumran. Both John and the Qumranites chose to exempt themselves from contemporary (urban or rural) society in favor of an ascetic lifestyle, living on a spartan diet in the Judean desert. Both eschewed Temple sacrifice. Both explicitly hearkened to the words of the prophet Isaiah to be a voice in the wilderness, to "prepare the way of the Lord, make straight in the desert a highway for our God"[21]—the same reference with which John is introduced by all four canonical Gospels[22]. Significantly, both John and the Qumranites practiced ritual immersion as an integral element of their teachings, as a symbol of repentance and renewal.

But there are also important differences. The members of Qumran preached a communal lifestyle of self-negation, prayer, fasting, and extreme purity in absolute isolation—even to the point of withholding one's bodily functions on the Sabbath. Theirs was an exclusive circle, open only to those who had successfully completed a prolonged period of initiation. The Baptist, by contrast, reached out to the entire nation, whether peasants, publicans, or professionals—or anyone else willing to listen. While the Essenes and Qumranites practiced ablution in special *mikva'ot* available only to members of the group, John invited anyone to step forward and be immersed. His *mikveh* was not a private bath, but the most democratic source of living water available: the River Jordan. John's message, in short, was inclusive, not exclusive. What's more, whereas the Essenes practiced immersion on a daily basis, as did many Pharisees, John immersed his disciples only once—as a single life-altering event.

Nevertheless, the similarities suggest the possibility that John had been raised by the Qumran community, only to break away and pursue his own path, his own *halakah,* at a later date. Josephus confirms that the Essenes did adopt children and train them in their customs and lifestyle while they were still young.[23] The idea that John spent most of his childhood in the desert is also intimated by the Infancy Narrative of Luke, which we encountered earlier. "The child," says Luke, "was *in the wilderness* until the day he appeared publicly to Israel."[24] Luke does not seem concerned over the obvious question of how a child of a priestly family in Jerusalem—Elizabeth's husband Zechariah was, according to Luke, a priest in the Temple—somehow wound up in the desert. The answer, as we saw earlier, may be that the characters of Zechariah and Elizabeth are the protagonists of a Lucan allegory, rather than historical figures in their own right. Some scholars have opined that John could have been the son of a priestly family, as Luke suggests, and that he became orphaned at an early age precisely because, as we have seen, Zechariah and Elizabeth were advanced in years. But that does not explain how the Essenes, who were notorious for their opposition to the Temple priesthood, could have gotten their hands on the young child, particularly because John would likely have been adopted by any of the other priestly families in order to safeguard his priestly heritage. It would seem more plausible that John's parents were rural figures in Judea and that John was adopted by the Essenes after both his parents died while he was still young.

JOHN'S HALAKAH

Jesus' sojourn with John the Baptist could be seen as the third stage in his intellectual development. The first stage, as we have seen, was a grounding in essential Mosaic Law by the Pharisees, including matters of cultic purity, Sabbath observation, and the question of eternal life. The second stage coincided with Jesus' identification with the writings of the eighth- and seventh-century B.C.E. prophets, specifically Jeremiah. The sojourn with John would complete Jesus' intellectual journey as he absorbed John's ideology as well as his unique brand of leadership.

We must qualify this statement, however, with the acknowledgment that we know very little about John's actual teachings. What we do know is gleaned from either the Gospel and sayings traditions or from the writings of Josephus. Based on these sources, we know that John had an urgent eschatological vision of Israel, and that he spoke of one "who comes after me." This latter was arguably an agent of God's wrath who was greater than John and would "baptize with fire" rather than water.

John's view that Israel faced a cataclysm of untold proportions is wholly in line with Old Testament prophecy of the eighth and seventh centuries. Like these prophets before him, John taught that God's wrath had been kindled by the social injustice committed by the people of Israel, as evidenced by the same growing gap between rich and poor that had invoked the ire of Hosea, Amos, and Jeremiah. This is obviously the thrust of John's teachings in the Gospel of Luke, where he exhorts his listeners to share their clothes and their food. The same segment also has John berating the "publicans," the tax collectors, to "collect no more than the amount prescribed to you"—meaning the target amount that the Roman census had assigned to each property, house, and village. By the same token, soldiers are warned not to "extort money from anyone by threats or false accusation, and [to] be satisfied with your wages"—implying that such extortion was a common practice at the time.[25]

John delivered his sermons with a fiery rhetoric that lifted the hearts of the oppressed and gave them both a vision and a purpose. It was a vivid, down-to-earth, and often violent rhetoric, using simple metaphors—such as the winnowing fork, the ax, and the burning fire—that John knew most Judeans would understand. What's more, he never shrank from direct attack to force his audience to sit up and take notice. Once, a group of newly arrived, well-meaning followers was promptly greeted as "a brood of vipers." Don't think you're special, or that you will be saved, simply because you "have Abraham as [your] father," he railed; just claiming your Jewish heritage is no longer good enough![26]

John's calculated attack on the smug self-confidence of his contemporaries was meant to shake the listener from his complacency and force him to reassess his values and assumptions. These denunciations were not born of anger or contempt, as later Church fathers have intimated, but of a deep desire to provoke an immediate and lasting change of heart. Later we will see that Jesus used the same tactic, particularly when addressing an audience other than the Galilean poor.

Furthermore, John's clever use of immersion in the waters of the Jordan gave the poor and downtrodden a tangible instrument of personal empowerment, of individual transformation, of rejecting contemporary society and the chokehold of the exploitative elites.

It is this quality of John that must have resonated with Jesus. In the Baptist, Jesus had his first opportunity to observe a bona fide charismatic leader up close and personal. It was as if Elijah, Jeremiah, or Isaiah had been beamed down from heaven for Jesus to witness in the flesh. This notion was quite real. In Matthew, Jesus speaks of John as the "Elijah who is to come." Significantly, the New Testament portrays John as a man dressed in a tunic of camel hair with a leather belt, eating locusts and wild honey, in a clear allusion to the prophet Elijah, who was similarly attired.[27] John was the Old Testament prophet personified, brought to life to pronounce on the unique circumstances of Jesus' time. In the years to come, Jesus would often pay homage to John as the great model of his movement. Was John a prophet? some asked. "Yes," Jesus replied in Luke, "and I tell you, more than a prophet." In fact, he continued, "no one among those born of women is greater than John."[28]

Another aspect of John that would make a profound impression on Jesus was his behavior toward his *followers*. Old Testament prophets had rarely cultivated a following. Their activity was targeted to ruling members of the nation's elite, quite often the king himself. In the Late Second Temple period, both Greco–Roman philosophers and Jewish sages and rabbis did surround themselves with students, but at the end of the day these followers would return to their homes. John's followers, by contrast, prayed, ate, and slept with him in the open desert. They went where he went. This rather unusual entourage gave John both social stature and an ideological gravitas. It enabled him to teach and inculcate his students at far greater length, thus sowing the seeds of his teachings and ensuring that his voice would be carried far beyond the banks of the Jordan.

This idea of a social movement being led by a rabbi or teacher was a Qumranite concept through and through. According to the Damascus Document, the Qumran community was formed in the mid-second century B.C.E. under the leadership of a "Teacher of Righteousness." This rabbi derived his position from his authority in interpreting the Torah and the Prophets in all aspects of life. It was "the Teacher of Righteousness," says one document, "to whom God has disclosed all the mysteries of the words of his servants the prophets."[29] It is quite possible, as we saw earlier, that this rabbi was a Zadokite whose chance of becoming high priest had been negated by the Hasmonean usurpation of that office.[30]

What the document tells us is that this Qumranite Teacher was no mere religious instructor or exegete, but a man *endowed with prophetic authority*. Like a prophet, he had arrived at his position by virtue of a *divine calling*. God had chosen the Teacher to explain the mysteries of the Law and to serve as a beacon of enlightenment to his community. In addition, the Teacher of Righteousness is presented not only as a prophet but also as an agent of salvation. By following his example of repentance, fasting, and prayer, the people would find renewal of Israel's covenant of God. "I am . . . healing to all who turn from sin," read one of the Thanksgiving hymns; "the foundation of truth." Those who rejected the Teacher implicitly rejected God himself, and therewith forfeited their possible salvation in God. "Because at the judgment you will condemn all who assail me," reads another Qumranite source, "separating the righteous and the wicked through me."[31]

Even the casual reader will grasp the similarities between the Qumranite Teacher and the role that Jesus was to assume at the beginning of his ministry. Jesus, too, would eventually become known as a Rabbi (Teacher), likewise called by the spirit of God to be a *prophet* and bring *salvation* to the people of Israel. The intermediary between these two models is, arguably, John the Baptist, who on two occasions is himself called "Teacher" in the Gospel text.[32] Like the legendary founder of the Qumran community, John is both Teacher *and* Prophet, the herald of the Messiah, a modern-day Elijah restored to life.

THE BAPTISM IN THE GOSPELS

The Gospel tradition, however, gives us an entirely different view of the relationship between the Baptizer and Jesus. Rather than Jesus' teacher, John serves as his herald, the Samuel who anoints Jesus as the Davidic Messiah. This act of anointing is affirmed by God's Spirit descending on Jesus at the moment of baptism, with a voice that speaks: "You are my Son, the beloved; with you I am well pleased."[33] In depicting this scene, the evangelists relied on Old Testament prototype. As we have seen, in the Book of 2 Samuel, God tells David that "I will raise up your offspring after you, who shall come forth from your body, and I will establish his kingdom. . . . I will be a father to him, and he shall be a son to me."[34]

The problem with the Gospel depiction of Jesus' baptism by John is that, unlike Samuel, the historical John the Baptist was not in the habit of anointing aspiring kings at all. On the contrary: John's business was to baptize people who were self-confessed *sinners,* who had seen the error of their ways and were prepared to change their lives. John's practice of immersion was therefore first and foremost an act of *forgiveness,* a form of absolution whereby past misdeeds were washed away in exchange for the sinner's determination to repent. Baptism, in this context, symbolized the mind-altering, *soul-cleansing* experience that they had undergone.

So why did Jesus come to John to be baptized? Did he believe himself to be a sinner? It is a question of profound theological implications—which may be the reason why in the Gospel of John, where the theology of Jesus as the only Son of God is fully developed, the actual act of baptism is not mentioned at all.

The obvious answer, it seems to me, is that Jesus underwent his baptism to signal his readiness to join John's activist campaign—a campaign, that is, to restore the socioeconomic and religious universe of Israel's peasantry by restoring their self-esteem and empowering their vision of a just society. Hence, we may be able to distinguish four layers of symbolic meaning in the story of John baptizing Jesus. In the top layer is the Christian view of God introducing his divine Son at the beginning of his ministry. The secondary layer illustrates this scene by using the Old Testament iconography of a prophet anointing a king of Israel. Both these layers are, in turn, grafted onto what we assume is a historical event, namely, Jesus being accepted in the ranks of John's followers through the ritual of initiation. The fourth layer may be a psychological one, the final act of catharsis with which Jesus brought closure to the traumatic experience of his youth. For from the cool green waters of the Jordan rose a new man: a social activist, dedicated to transforming the people of Galilee into the nation under God they had once been.

We do not know how long Jesus stayed in the company of John's disciples. If we accept that Jesus joined John's movement sometime between 26 and 27 C.E., it is plausible to think that he remained with John for at least a year, possibly longer. If we accept Luke's chronology and place the encounter between Jesus and John in 28 C.E., then his time would have to have been considerably less. Should we assume that Jesus himself became a long-term disciple of John's movement? We don't know, and scholars have offered arguments both ways. Unlike the Qumranites (or Jesus, for that matter), John did not, as far as we know, impose any membership conditions on his followers. He did not tell them to go and sell all their property; abandon their families, their crafts, or their trades; and follow their leader, come what may. Perhaps he collected followers as he went along, moving up and down the Jordan, crossing from one bank to the other. People may have hung on for a certain period of time before the harvests, their families, or the discomfort of living in the wilderness drove them home. Though we never hear of John having anything akin to the "core" of the twelve apostles,

Josephus clearly states that John did have a deeply committed and loyal following "who were prepared to do anything that John should tell them."

What we also know is that in the course of his travels along the Jordan, John garnered what today we would call massive "publicity." It was probably this publicity that brought Jesus in contact with John to begin with; it was this same word of mouth that would be the prophet's undoing, as we will see shortly. But this publicity also posed a serious challenge to the evangelists. For them, the question came down to who was more famous: John or Jesus. Josephus, who clearly has no preference for either figure, makes no bones about it. In Josephus's book *Antiquities of the Jews,* Jesus merits only one short (and highly controversial) paragraph, while the historian dedicates half a page to the works of John. More importantly, the two references are many pages apart, without any obvious connection to one another. Had the segment about John been "edited" by a Christian scribe, there would have been a very strong temptation to relate, if not subjugate, the story of John's deeds to that of Jesus. This is another reason to accept the material about John in Josephus as reliable.

We also know for a fact that John's movement continued after the Baptist's own death and survived well into the late first century, not only in Palestine but also in Asia Minor, posing a continued challenge to the legitimacy of the "rival" Jesus movement. The Gospel of Mark tells us that when John the Baptist was killed, long after Jesus and his followers had begun their campaign in Galilee, "[John's] disciples heard about it, . . . took his body and laid it in a tomb."[35] The Book of Acts reports that many years later, during his travels in and around Ephesus, a major port city on the coast of Asia Minor (modern Turkey), Paul came in contact with some disciples who professed themselves to be baptized by John.[36] Interestingly enough, in 1999 the archaeologist Shimon Gibson discovered a cave with a pool near Kibbutz Tzova at Ain Karim, which he tentatively identified with the cult of John; however, few scholars have come out in support of this claim.[37]

The evangelists countered the challenge of John's prominence by seeking to subordinate John's ministry to that of Jesus. John often spoke of the coming of "one who is stronger than I, whose sandals I am not worthy to touch."[38] This sentence is so well attested that many scholars accept it as genuine. However, it is less clear to whom John is referring. Some believe it is a Davidic *mashiach,* the Messiah as warrior-king, who would vanquish God's foes, both Jewish and foreign. Others, however, strongly believe that the description "one whose sandals I am not worthy to touch" is a reverential reference to YHWH, God himself. This fits with the interpretation of John as the Teacher/Prophet of Qumran: the original Teacher had also spoken of the wrath of God with the authority of one sent by God as his designated herald. What this implies is that, from a historical perspective, John's statement did *not* refer to Jesus. Nevertheless, the evangelists seized on this sentence as a prophecy of Jesus, not in the least because John's humble words "whose sandals I am not worthy to touch" removed any doubt as to who was greater, Jesus or John. Matthew, moreover, has John *refusing* to baptize Jesus, saying that it should be the reverse, that "I need to be baptized by you."[39]

The Gospel of John makes the "lower ranking" of John the Baptist even more explicit. Here we read that one day, the Baptist pointed out Jesus to his disciples, saying, "this is he of whom I said, 'After me comes a man who ranks ahead of me because he was before me.'"[40] This unspoken sense of competition between Jesus and the Baptist is also acute in another verse from the Gospel of John, in which the Pharisees "had heard that 'Jesus is making and baptizing more disciples than John.'"[41]

JOHN'S ARREST

The Gospels then tell us how John fell afoul of Herod Antipas, the Tetrarch of Galilee. This may further support the theory that the Baptist and his followers spent most of their time on the *eastern* side of the Jordan, in the territory of Perea, rather than on the *western* side, which formed part of the Roman territory of Judea, governed by Pilate. As we have seen, Perea had, strangely, been granted to Antipas's tetrarchy, even though it was not contiguous with Antipas's "home" territory of Galilee.

The Gospels, and particularly Luke, tell us why Antipas decided to issue orders for John's arrest. Apparently, John had rebuked the tetrarch for marrying his brother's wife, Herodias. Josephus confirms the unusual circumstances of this marriage. Antipas was originally married to the daughter of Aretas IV Philopatris, which is the hereditary name of the kings of Nabataea (later known as Arabia Petrea, the region roughly analogous to modern Jordan). This Aretas, or perhaps his predecessor, had many years earlier plundered his way through Galilee, ostensibly in pursuit of the leaders of the "census rebellion."

Antipas had been raised in Rome, and he made a habit of returning to that city whenever he could to meet old friends. During one of these periodic visits, he was introduced to the lovely Herodias, the wife of his half-brother Philip.[42] To complicate matters further, Herodias was also the daughter of another half-brother, Aristobulus (son of Herod the Great and Mariamne). Despite this rather delicate situation, Antipas persisted in pursuing the charms of Herodias, and eventually proposed to her. She accepted, though on one condition: that Antipas divorce his first wife, the daughter of King Aretas IV. In this (as in the case of Antipas's father, Herod the Great), we see the influence of the Hellenistic customs. Rather than taking Herodias as a second wife, as Jewish law certainly permitted him to do, Antipas and Herodias cleaved to the more enlightened Greco–Roman practice of having only one spouse (at one time, at least).

Unfortunately, Antipas's wife, the daughter of Aretas (the poor woman is not named in Josephus's account), found out about the machinations of her husband, as wives often do. Without letting on that she knew what Antipas was up to, she sweetly asked him to let her retire to one of his fortified palaces, called the Macherus fortress. Antipas, glad to have his wife out of the way, gave her leave to go.

The fortress of Macherus was located right on the border between Antipas's territory and that of the Nabataeans, and with good reason, for there were long-running territorial disputes between Perea and Nabataea, which the marriage between Antipas and Aretas's daughter had only partly resolved. No sooner did Antipas's wife arrive at the Macherus stronghold than she was whisked over the border by a rescue party of the Nabataean army. From there, the aggrieved wife made her way to her father's palace and gave King Aretas a full report of her husband's scheming. Aretas, roused in righteous anger, mobilized his army and prepared for war.

The fortress of Macherus still stands; it is the only Herodian fortress east of the Jordan River and the Dead Sea. Located close to the Jordanian town of Makawer, it was built by the Hasmoneans on a high natural mount, then expanded by Herod the Great. As such, it bears a close resemblance to Herod's other great Dead Sea fortress, that of Masada. Significantly, both Masada and Macherus would be captured by Zealots during the Jewish

War; they would be the last rebel-held outposts long after Jerusalem had been taken by the Romans.

With tensions at an all-time high, it is not difficult to believe that John's criticism of Antipas's second marriage would have stirred the ire of the tetrarch. Antipas would have been under intense pressure to defend his kingdom against the superior forces of Aretas; the last thing he needed, in this situation, was to be berated by some eccentric in the desert. And, as we know, John often operated in Perea, dangerously close to the Nabataean border.

From the perspective of the evangelists, however, John's criticism was motivated not by political but by moral and ethical considerations. John, according to Matthew, accused Antipas of violating Covenant Law, saying that "it is not lawful for you to have your brother's wife," specifically if this wife had borne children to her first husband (as Herodias evidently had done). This denunciation was motivated by the command in Leviticus that "you shall not uncover the nakedness of your brother's wife; it is your brother's nakedness"—the same command that had rendered Archilaus's marriage to Glaphyra unlawful.[43] & MiRiAM with Alphaeus

John's attack on the legitimacy of the marriage to Herodias then set into motion the train of events that would ultimately lead to the Baptist's death. John was arrested and thrown in a cell in the nearest military outpost, which, as it happened, was the same fortress of Macherus to which Antipas's spouse had fled. There he remained while Antipas debated what to do with him. In fact, the Gospel of Mark suggests that the arrest was really prompted by the new First Lady of Galilee, Herodias herself. She obviously felt that her newfound *majestas* as the tetrarch's consort had been impugned by this insolent preacher from Judea. "Herodias," says Mark, "had a grudge against him, and wanted to kill him." Antipas, on the other hand, is shown to harbor misgivings about the whole situation. "Herod feared John," Mark asserts, "knowing that he was a righteous and holy man, and he protected him." In fact, Mark continues, "Herod liked to listen to him."[44]

Nevertheless, when Herodias's daughter (by her first marriage) charmed her stepfather on his birthday with her dancing, Antipas impulsively offered her anything she wanted. The daughter, whose name was Salome, conferred with her mother. Herodias didn't think twice; she told her daughter to ask "for the head of John the Baptist on a platter." Antipas was "deeply grieved;

yet out of regard for his oaths and for the guests, he did not want to refuse her." An execution detail was hastily formed and dispatched to the prison. John the Baptist was unceremoniously beheaded. Herodias got her wish.[45]

Why Antipas deserves this rather sympathetic treatment is not clear. It is possible that Mark's model for this drama is the story of King Ahab,[46] the ruler of the Northern Kingdom whose domineering wife (the Phoenician princess Jezebel) also engineered the death of an innocent man—the poor Naboth, whose vineyard had caught Ahab's eye. The portrayal in the book of 1 Kings of a weak ruler manipulated by an imperious and unscrupulous spouse (likewise of foreign descent) may have appealed to Mark.

✢ ✢ ✢

Josephus, however, has an entirely different version of events. As we have seen, tensions in the region of Perea must have risen to a fever pitch after the Nabataean king Aretas IV had begun mobilizing for war over the ignominious removal of his daughter as the Tetrarch's Consort. Perea was "landlocked," ruled by Antipas but surrounded by foreign territories on all sides: Roman-held Judea on the west, the Decapolis on the north, and the kingdom of Nabataea itself on the east. The Decapolis formed part of the Tetrarchy of Gaulanitis, ruled by Antipas's half-brother Philip, who may have been the first husband of Herodias. It was thus unlikely that Antipas could expect any sympathetic feelings from that corner.

So while all this is going on, while the Perea becomes a hotbed of intrigue and warmongering and preparation for war, here comes this eccentric preacher clothed in camel hair, followed by a crowd of people. The preacher, as it turns out, has "great influence" over these people, who seem ready to do "anything that he will tell them to." For Josephus, the conclusion is obvious: Antipas feared that John would be tempted to exploit the region's instability, since in his eyes John had the "power and inclination to raise a rebellion." Matthew appears to agree when he states that "[Antipas] feared the multitude, because they counted [John the Baptist] as a prophet."[47] The difficulty of communication with Perea, and the sheer distance between that region and Antipas's home territory of Galilee, may have made his paranoia even more acute.

Though in Josephus's account John has not done anything untoward (yet), Antipas decides to preemptively order his arrest, then has him killed.

In doing so, Josephus explains, Antipas "thought it best, by putting him to death, to prevent any mischief he might cause, rather than get himself in difficulty by sparing a man who might make him regret it when it would be too late."[48] In other words, Antipas believed that John was about to incite a revolt among his following, and, in order to prevent this from happening, he had the Baptist killed.

Given the political situation of the moment, Josephus's account rings true. The "crime" of berating Antipas for marrying his sister-in-law/niece, as the Gospels have it, was a moot point because the entire Herodian dynasty was built on endogamous relationships. The figures speak for themselves: over the span of eight generations, thirty-nine members of the Herodian line were married, and *seventeen* of these marriages were between blood relatives. What's more, as we saw in Chapter 1, most marriages in Galilee were endogamous, for the simple purpose of retaining one's property within one's group of kin. The books of Tobit, Judith, and Jubilees attest that marriages between parallel cousins (a father's son marrying the daughter of his father's brother) had become quite common by the late Second Temple period, if not the norm.[49]

I believe, however, that there may be another reason why Antipas felt emboldened to move against so popular a dissident. The reason is an incident involving the prefect, Pontius Pilate, that few scholars have interpreted in this context but that may very well have had a major impact on subsequent events. This incident took place in Jerusalem sometime in 28 C.E., probably during one of the principal festivals, when Jesus may already have joined the Baptist movement in the Jordan.

As we have seen, Pilate had been outfoxed by the protestors in Caesarea and was no doubt waiting for an opportunity to exact his revenge. At the same time, he must have been eager to attend to the principal reason why he had taken an overseas posting to begin with: namely, to make his fortune. Alas, there was not a lot of commercial opportunity in Palestine. Much of the agricultural production in Palestine was based in the Tetrarchy of Galilee, outside Pilate's jurisdiction. On top of that, the Judean economy was still recovering from the excess of Herod's building program some twenty years earlier. Worse, the local trade that did exist was to a great extent based on barter rather than coin. There was, consequently, hardly any concentration of hard cash in the country—with one exception: the

Temple treasury, known as the *korban* (a word synonymous with "gift" or "sacrifice").

This treasury, as we have seen, was located in the Court of the Women of the Jerusalem sanctuary. It consisted of thirteen chests with tapering tops (*shoparoth*), akin to the shape of a trumpet—which is what the chests are called in the Talmud. Each of these chests was earmarked for a particular use: nine were for prescribed offerings, and four were used for non-specific donations.[50] In the Gospel of Luke, Jesus uses the setting of the *shoparoth* to expound on the social divide between rich and poor. First, he saw rich people putting their gifts into the treasury; he then observed how a poor widow dropped two small copper coins in one of the chests. "Truly I tell you," he said, "this poor widow has put in more than all of them; for the others contributed out of abundance, but she in her poverty has put in all she had to live on."[51]

At intervals, the proceeds of these chests were carried to a nearby treasury chamber, to be counted by cashiers known as *gizbarim* and deposited in what we assume were the Temple vaults. The capital contained within the Temple must therefore have been enormous. We know from a celebrated case defended by Cicero that in 62 B.C.E., the Roman proconsul of Asia Minor, Valerius Flaccus, tried to steal the proceeds of the annual Temple tax collection among some of the Jewish communities in his jurisdiction. One Jewish community from the town of Laodicea in Phrygia had collected twenty pounds of gold; another wealthy Jewish group in the Phrygian city of Apamea came up with no less than a *hundred* pounds of gold.[52] We can only imagine what the total take from all the Jewish communities in the far-flung Diaspora would have amounted to. Indeed, after the turmoil surrounding the death of Herod the Great, the Romans were able to steal more than four hundred talents (the equivalent of some 9.6 million sesterces) from the Temple treasury.[53]

Naturally, the operating budget of the Temple, including salaries, maintenance, and materials, would have been considerable. In addition, the Temple was still very much under construction, which would have required a vast outlay in additional salaries for skilled and unskilled workers, supervisors, architects, and craftsmen, as well as huge quantities in marble, stone, gold, wood, draft animals, and tools. Nevertheless, we may assume that the treasury operated on a surplus, not least because the Temple also functioned as a central bank. Apart from issuing its own currency, the shekel, the Temple also invited wealthy families to maintain savings accounts in the Temple treasury. Rabbinic sources repeatedly refer to a positive balance rather than a deficit.[54]

And so it is not surprising that Pilate would fasten his attention on this treasury, simply because it was the single largest concentration of capital in his realm. The problem was how he could get his hands on it. Simply confiscating part of the money would have been too crass and might have precipitated a rebellion. Intercepting the Temple tax funds before they reached Jerusalem was not an option either, given the recent criminal case against Valerius Flaccus. Instead, Pilate had to come up with a plan that not only guaranteed him a substantial share of the take but also ensured the tacit collaboration of the people in charge of the Temple: the high priest and his circle of senior prelates, who were mostly Sadducees. Perhaps Pilate knew that many of these wealthy priests maintained sumptuous homes in the elevated area southwest of the Temple, known as the Upper City. Most of these mansions were comfortably equipped with fountains, pools and, above all, *mikva'ot* or ritual baths. The excavation of the first-century "Priestly House" by Israeli archaeologist Nahman Avigad bears this out. This lavish 2,000-square-foot palace, located in the Upper City, featured an elaborate entrance bordered by *mikva'ot* or ritual purification pools; a large courtyard with a hearth; and a main residence, including a large, 33-by-21-foot reception hall for meetings and audiences. Many of its walls were decorated with stucco in the Roman style, simulating meticulously hewn and bossed masonry.

The problem was that all of these facilities required water; and not stagnant water, but running or "living" water. To serve these needs, Herod had built a channel from Solomon's Pools to the Upper City of Jerusalem, but this conduit was wholly inadequate. What's more, Judea was an arid land, and rainfall was uneven at best.

This, then, was the opportunity Pilate had been waiting for. It was time for Roman technology to intervene. He, Pilate, would build that great Roman invention, the aqueduct, which would carry fresh water from the mountains to the city and beyond. Who would fund this noble venture? Where to find the necessary capital? Why, in the Temple treasury, of course. After all, the priests were the ones who stood to benefit most from this rich new supply of fresh water.

On the surface, the arrangement may have looked legitimate. Later rabbinic sources indicate that the Temple treasury did pay for various municipal needs, including the maintenance of Jerusalem's waterworks, towers, and city walls.[55] The difference was that these services were funded and supervised by Jewish Temple officials. In the case of Pilate's aqueduct project, the whole enterprise would have been under Roman management. Only Rome had the technical and creative expertise to undertake such a complex venture. And as a Roman enterprise, it would naturally be supervised by Pilate himself, no doubt enabling him to take a significant "commission" on the funds flowing from the treasury to the construction zones.[56]

And so it came to pass. As Pilate had expected, the Sadducees proved to be amenable, and Pilate helped himself to the building funds. Construction was begun. But inevitably, the source of funding became known. The Judeans rose in uproar. Tens of thousands of protestors jammed the streets, denouncing the blatant theft of their hard-earned and sacred donations by the godless Romans. They demanded that Pilate cease and desist. But this time, the prefect was prepared. He knew that if he confronted these demonstrators head-on, he was likely to get the same results that he had gotten from the protestors in Caesarea. So he had to outsmart them. He ordered his soldiers to don anonymous black cloaks, big enough to conceal sharp daggers. Thus camouflaged, the soldiers dispersed throughout the crowd and waited for a signal. As soon as his forces were in place, Pilate appeared to the demonstrators, only to be greeted with boos and loud denunciations. Pilate smiled and gave the signal. In an instant, the soldiers threw off their cloaks and raised their daggers on whoever happened to be standing nearby. Once the killing began, the soldiers were gripped by a murderous frenzy. "They slew not only those that had participated in the demonstration," says Josephus, "but even innocent bystanders who had nothing to do with it." Since the protestors were unarmed and their attackers were professional soldiers, "a great many were killed; many others were wounded."[57]

I believe that the Aqueduct Affair is important for two reasons. One, it galvanized those who resented the Roman occupation, particularly the heavy-handed rule of Pilate. Many of us may remember the wave of protests that followed the massacre of student protestors at Kent State

University on May 4, 1970, when many Americans felt that a line had been crossed. The same may have happened in 28 C.E., when even law-abiding citizens in Judea would have felt that Pilate had gone beyond the pale. A wave of revulsion must have swept over Judea; on the crest of this wave, many Judeans may have decided to join the most famous and outspoken dissident of their day: namely, John the Baptist.

In this context, it is not difficult to see why Antipas would have considered John's massive following a political liability. An important clue to this line of reasoning is that Josephus himself specifically distinguished between those "sincere" followers who accepted baptism as a remission of sins and "many others [who] flocked to him"—thus implying that these "many others" had quite a different motive in mind. Furthermore, Josephus tells us that it was only when *these others* began to flock to John that Antipas feared a rebellion, precisely because of the great influence that John seemed to be having over these people.

The other consequence of the Temple Affair was that Pilate had signaled a new policy toward the maintenance of law and order in Palestine. Dissent was not to be tolerated in any form, and any means could be used to prevent dissent from erupting into a revolt. None of the demonstrators in Jerusalem had posed a danger to Pilate or his troops; none of these protestors had resorted to violence in any way, other than "clamoring against him," which we assume involved shouting rather disagreeable slogans about Rome and Pilate's person. Yet Pilate had responded with utmost brutality, with *terror*, killing and maiming men, women, and children without discrimination.

Until this time, Rome had represented the rule of law; a harsh law, certainly, but not a rule without an innate sense of justice. The Roman *Ius Gentium,* the codex of law pertaining to non-Roman citizens in occupied territories, explicitly granted subject peoples the law of petition: the right to make their grievances known to their governing body, provided this was done in an orderly and nonviolent fashion.[58] With his bloody strike, Pilate had dispelled the pleasant fiction that Rome's occupation of Judea was essentially a benevolent one, governed by the rule of law. What's more, his actions signaled to Rome's other vassal rulers in the region—including Antipas—that Rome fully sanctioned the use of preemptive terror to maintain public order.

Pilate's precedent-setting action, and the sheer number of people now swelling around John the Baptist in Perea as, quite possibly, the result of that action, may have convinced Antipas that to strike preemptively was his best course of action as well. I believe it is unlikely that Antipas would have acted against John under any other circumstances.

Josephus's interpretation of the events is so valuable because it speaks volumes about the political atmosphere of the time. Note, for example, that Antipas moved against John, by all accounts a popular charismatic figure and "prophet," certainly a *Tzaddik* or righteous man, without involving the seventy-two-member Jewish Council of the Great Sanhedrin. Though the Sanhedrin was based in Jerusalem, in Judean territory, it is believed that the Council had authority throughout Palestine in religious matters. For example, the tractate *Sanhedrin* in the Mishnah specifically describes the conditions under which a "false prophet" ought to be put on trial.[59]

For many years, the Temple massacre remained on people's minds. At one point, a group of people told Jesus that there had been Galileans among Pilate's victims who had traveled to Jerusalem to make an offering in the Temple, and "whose blood Pilate had mingled with their sacrifice." Jesus pondered the subject and said, "Do you suppose that because these Galileans suffered in this way, they were worse sinners than all other Galileans?" At that point, his theological program had matured sufficiently for him to provide the answer: that suffering was not the exclusive province of sinners, and that only heartfelt repentance, rather than sacrifice, would offer true salvation.

In the meantime, the invasion by the Nabataeans was postponed. It took altogether some five or six years before Aretas IV was ready to move. Perhaps the king needed time to build up his armed strength; perhaps he hoped for a face-saving conciliatory gesture from Antipas. And so it was not until 34 or 35 C.E. that Aretas ordered his generals to invade, and Antipas's forces were roundly defeated. The reason, Josephus says, was treachery committed by a fifth column from Philip's tetrarchy who had attached themselves to Aretas's army.

Josephus also adds that when word of the defeat spread, people nodded and "thought that the destruction of Herod's army came from God, as just punishment for what he had done to John [the Baptist]." This illuminating statement underscores the popularity of John among the masses and the fact that many years after his death, his memory remained a potent presence.

John's arrest marked the end of Jesus' stay in Judea. We will never know if Jesus felt that his apprenticeship under this charismatic teacher was complete, or what would have happened if John had lived; perhaps history would have taken a very different turn. But once John was taken away to the fortress of Macherus, there was no point in staying near the Jordan any longer. No one knew if Antipas's soldiers would return and hunt down John's followers as well. Many scattered, though a small group of John loyalists remained. Jesus wasn't one of them; the Gospels state unequivocally that "Jesus withdrew to Galilee after John had been arrested."[60] In fact, the Gospel of John intimates that a small number of the Baptist's followers crossed over to Jesus and called him their new Teacher, their new Rabbi, instead. Significantly, this group was composed of Galileans, including Simon Peter, his brother Andrew, and Philip, who were all from Bethsaida. They packed what meager belongings they had and set out for the long journey north.

The years of preparation had come to an end. Jesus was ready to return to his native land and embark on his great campaign for the restoration of Israel.

NINE

IN THE KINGDOM OF GOD

As many of John's followers fled across Judea, Jesus returned to his native Galilee. He was ready; ready to embark on his great campaign to bring hope to the peasantry, guided by his vision of a great new society. The date is uncertain, but it may have been the fall of 28 C.E. A small number of John's disciples followed Jesus. We know of three: Simon Peter, Andrew, and Philip. John the evangelist makes a point of telling us that all three were from Bethsaida. This has led some scholars to suggest that Bethsaida was the group's first destination, and for a very good reason: Bethsaida was located east of the Jordan River, near the northeastern shore of the Sea of Galilee, a short distance from a fisherman's village of the same name. What made the town special was that it lay just inside the lower Gaulanitis, the territory of the tetrarch Philip. In Bethsaida, therefore, Jesus and his small group of followers could expect not only to find shelter among relatives, but also to be relatively safe from any of Antipas's roving patrols, if any of these were still looking for John's followers. Here the group may have remained until it became apparent that Antipas no longer posed a threat.

Bethsaida was a bustling place. Two years later, in 30 C.E., Philip elevated the town to the rank of a *polis,* a city, and called it Julias in memory of Julia, the only natural child of Augustus and the estranged wife of the emperor Tiberius.[1] Even so, archaeologists have never been able to identify the town with any certainty. Some believe it was located on a mound called et-Tell, a mile distant from where the Jordan enters the Sea of Galilee. In any case, Bethsaida could not have been more than a short walk away from another major city on the sea, Capernaum.

Capernaum, located in the Tetrarchy of Antipas west of the River Jordan, was the home town of Peter's wife and her family. Known as *Kfar Nahum* or "Nahum's village," it was a prosperous town. Coins excavated on the site indicate that it was founded sometime in the second century B.C.E.

203

during the Hasmonean period. It owed its prosperity to its location, straddling the road from Damascus to Jerusalem, right on the border between
Galilee and the Gaulanitis. It therefore had a tollbooth as well as a military
garrison, while its location on the Sea of Galilee made it a convenient
jumping-off point for shipping traffic across the entire lake. Lastly, it was a
city known for its basalt industry, which was found nearby; most of the
town's residences were, in fact, built with basalt stone.

Once he felt it was safe to move about, Jesus decided to make this pleasant seaside town the launch platform for his Galilean campaign. It was here
that he chose to reveal himself as a Teacher/Prophet in the mold of John.
The obvious place to do so, says Mark, was the local synagogue. And so,
"when the Sabbath came, he entered the synagogue and taught." Naturally,
the townspeople were "astounded at his teaching, for he taught them *as one
having authority*, and not as the scribes."[2] We can imagine their surprise: the
self-effacing youngster from Nazareth, known for his charitable work
among the poor, had suddenly metamorphosed into a Rabbi who spoke
expertly and confidently, even though he was not a professional interpreter
of the Law. The lessons of Jesus' role model, John, had been well absorbed.

To further underscore Jesus' authority, Mark has a man possessed by a
"demon" appear in the synagogue. Jesus rebukes the unclean spirit and it
leaves the man. As Josephus has told us, exorcisms were generally considered persuasive evidence that a man was a prophet, divinely inspired. This
exorcism sealed Jesus' new role as not only a teacher, but also a man with
power over *demons*—symbol of Satanic power. By exorcising evil spirits,
Mark seems to tell us, Jesus showed himself capable of taking on the great
eschatological battle between the forces of good and evil.[3]

The ancient remains of Capernaum were first identified in 1838 by an
American explorer named Edward Robinson, but it was not until 1905 that
excavations began in earnest. The two German archaeologists in charge of
the dig, Heinrich Kohl and Carl Watzinger, were astonished to discover the
remains of an ancient Jewish synagogue. It was built on a slight rise and
divided by two rows of seven columns, each with Corinthian capitals, in
addition to a two-column row in the back. The three doors leading into
the synagogue were adorned with exquisite motifs, including vine
branches, grapes, and palm trees. Against the wall ran steps leading to
benches for the worshipers to sit. A nearby fragment depicts a four-wheeled

wagon, which may be the Ark of the Covenant. The wealth lavished on the synagogue is further attested by the fact that it was built of expensive limestone, rather than basalt, which was available in abundance.

Naturally, speculation was rife. Was this beautiful building the location for Jesus' first public appearance as Rabbi/Prophet? Could the site of such a seminal moment in Jesus' life be so well preserved? As excavations continued, a sobering realization set in. Coins found on the site indicated that the synagogue was probably not built until the late third or fourth century C.E., when Capernaum was at the peak of its wealth. But in 1969, Franciscan monks, who owned the site, resumed excavations underneath the synagogue. They found the remains of an older structure with a supporting wall made of basalt. Based on pottery shards and coins, some authors have recently identified this as an earlier synagogue that may be as old as the first or second century C.E. Whether this structure was already in place in the time of Jesus, well before the destruction of the Temple, is not clear.[4]

Near the synagogue, excavators also laid bare a continuous block of one- and two-story dwellings, known as an *insula*. Potsherds indicated that some of these houses could date to the first centuries of our era. One particular dwelling, in fact, had several layers of construction. The upper layer contained the remains of an octagonal church, built around the middle of the fifth century. Parts of its mosaic floor were still visible, including the motif of a peacock, symbol of eternity. Underneath this church was the outline of a large house, dating from around the fourth century. It had a stone arch that supported a tiled roof, covering a large central room. But the real surprise was waiting underneath. Here, under the remains of two successive buildings, was a modest dwelling. It followed the typical Palestinian layout of the first century: a haphazard arrangement of small rooms, built around a small inner courtyard, which held a small hearth. Its walls were made of local basalt and cement, covered with plaster. Such walls could not possibly have supported a pitched roof with tiles; more than likely, the house was covered with a shallow latticework of thin beams, covered with palm fronds and leaves, held together with mud. This appeared to resonate with the Gospel of Mark, which describes how Jesus, upon returning to Peter's house, was mobbed by crowds. A small group came, carrying a paralyzed man. When they saw that "they could not bring him to Jesus because of the crowd, they removed the roof above him; and after having dug through it, they let down the mat on which the paralytic lay."[5] Today, in Jericho, there are still houses that are roofed in exactly this way.[6]

As the excavators dug deeper, tantalizing clues came to light. First, they found a number of ancient fishhooks in the lowest layer of the house, which would indicate that the house had been occupied by fishermen. Next, the workmen discovered various inscriptions hidden under the plaster of a later era, with several references to the Greek word *Ichtos*. *Ichtos* was a code word among early Christians. While it simply means "fish," it also forms an acronym, in Greek, of the phrase *Jesus Christ Son of God Savior*. Today, the Franciscans in charge of the site confidently claim that this was the house of Simon Peter's wife. Whether this is true or not is perhaps not significant; what is important is that the structure may have been recognized as a place of pilgrimage by early Christians as early as the late first century C.E.

What appears to be beyond doubt is that in casting about for additional followers, Jesus targeted the fishing industry of Capernaum. Mark describes how Jesus walked along the shore of the Sea of Galilee, where fishermen were busy cleaning and repairing their nets. There he found "James son of Zebedee and his brother John, who were in their boat mending the net." Jesus called to them, and immediately "they left their father Zebedee in the boat with the hired men and followed him."[7]

This segment raises a number of questions. Unlike John, Jesus did not wait for disciples to approach him; he went after disciples himself. Jesus was clearly in a hurry. He knew that he could not organize his campaign and make a significant impact in Lower Galilee all by himself. He needed a group of *talmidin,* of followers who could serve as the core support of his movement. Fully versed in the Teacher's program and ideology, they would be able not only to propagate his ideology but also to assist him in arranging for food, shelter, and security. In sum, the followers that Jesus had in mind would not be students in the Platonic tradition, nor disciples in the Johannine mold, but *delegates,* fully empowered to assist the Teacher and to speak on his behalf. "Delegate" is, in fact, the exact translation of *shaliach,* which in the New Testament is translated as *apostolein* or "apostle."

So why fishermen? In antiquity, sages and wise men typically surrounded themselves with bright young pupils who were not yet married or vested in a given profession. Yet Jesus chose as his disciples working men who had a clear vested interest in staying close to the Sea of Galilee. So why was it that these men were both able and of a mind to simply get up and walk away from their boats, their nets, and their families?

Modern research has begun to answer some of these questions. The first thing we must recognize is that fishing in the Sea of Galilee was far from the lucrative occupation that traditional scholarship has always assumed it was. As we have seen, the dislocation of the peasantry from their ancestral land had resulted in the growth of a vast proletariat without homes or means of support. Bereft of the chance to inherit a piece of their fathers' property, many of these men, both young and middle-aged, would have converged on the Sea of Galilee. Here, they reasoned, was still a harvest to be had, a harvest of fish, from which no Roman or landowner could bar them.

Thus, hundreds of untrained amateurs began competing with the tightly knit group of professional fishermen who had plied these waters for generations. Many of these new arrivals may have tried to catch fish from the shore, with little effect. To get to the principal feeding ground, one needed a boat—specifically, a boat big enough to hold the usual complement of fishermen needed to cast and draw nets—and a crew adept at navigating the sometimes treacherous waters of the lake. Boats were expensive, but they could be leased out to multiple teams working in shifts. And this is precisely what happened, resulting in a virtual explosion of fishing activity on the Sea of Galilee.

As John Dominic Crossan has shown, excavations below the waterline have revealed no fewer than fifteen different harbors around the lake from the first century C.E. Certainly Bethsaida, Capernaum, Tabgha, Gennesaret, Magdala, and Ammaus, all cities referred to in the Gospels, had berths for fishing boats. But modern surveys have also revealed harbor structures in Tiberias, Sennabris, Beit Yerah, Tel Samra, Duerban, Sussita, Ein Gofra, and Gergesa. Each of these ports followed the same model, with varying degrees of sophistication: a short pier, protected by a long, curved breakwater to shelter the fishing boats at anchor.

Consequently, the lake in Jesus' time must have been teeming with fishing boats both large and small. Inevitably, this vast increase in activity led to over-harvesting and the gradual depletion of the fish population. We find further evidence of this depletion in the Gospel of Luke, in which a morose Simon Peter tells Jesus that they have "toiled all night long, and not caught anything." Jesus urges him to throw his nets one last time. And lo, Simon Peter and his crew bring in such a huge catch that his nets nearly break. Luke says that at that moment, "many ships from nearby" rushed to the scene to help and to get their share of this unexpected boon.[8]

Israeli scientists have established that there are still some twenty-seven species of fish in the lake, many of which are also described in ancient sources. The apostles, like all the fishermen of their day, would have been looking for three specific types of edible Galilean fish. The first were common sardines, which may be the "few small fish" that "a small boy" brought to the feeding of the four thousand in the Gospel of Mark.[9] As we have seen, these "small fish," together with barley bread, constituted the main source of protein for the Galilean poor, usually consumed on the Sabbath.[10] The second species is a fish known as "Barbels," so called because of the barbs at the corners of their mouths. The third and most popular type is today called Galilee tilapia (*amnun* in Hebrew), more popularly known as "St. Peter's Fish." This fish has a long, comb-shaped dorsal fin and can grow to 1.5 feet in length and 3.3 lbs in weight.[11]

To catch such fish, fishermen set out in crews of eight or ten, each tasked with manning the rudder, trimming the sails, or gathering in the nets. There are some twenty references in the Gospels to fishing vessels, each large enough to hold that many people. Matthew tells us that when Jesus "entered the ship, his followers followed him."[12] Obviously, such a vessel was no mere rowboat; it must have been able to accommodate at least ten men. Scholars once questioned whether the fishermen of Galilee could have used barges of such size, but their doubts were silenced by a spectacular discovery in 1986. In that year, a severe drought hit northern Israel, forcing water levels on the lake to unprecedented lows. Around that time, some locals walking along the shore spotted the outline of a large boat. It appeared to be in excellent condition, fully preserved in the mud, at a distance of no more than five miles from the ancient city of Magdala, located on the western shore where the Sea is at its greatest width. Archaeological experts quickly rushed to the scene, but the water had already begun to rise. Israeli archaeologist Shelley Wachsmann launched a heroic effort to preserve the wooden boat and carry it to the safety of a nearby museum.[13] Here, restorers used carbon-14 dating to assess its age. They were astonished to find that the vessel was built sometime between 50 B.C.E. and 50 C.E.—precisely the period of Jesus' lifetime.[14]

The "Galilee Boat" is an impressive example of ancient craftsmanship, twenty-six feet long and seven and a half feet wide—large enough to comfortably accommodate ten people and pieces of equipment, such as nets. The planks are carefully bonded together with joints, fastened with pegs— the construction method favored by Greek shipbuilders throughout the Mediterranean. With its sleek profile, the Galilee Boat is the very image of agility and speed. It is a far cry from our previous perception of ancient fishing boats as small, unwieldy, primitive craft.

Once loaded with fish, boats such as these would return to port and deliver the catch to agents waiting to inspect, weigh, and purchase the fish. Some of the haul was cleaned and shipped right away for sale in the markets of major towns nearby, such as Tiberias and Sepphoris. Other fish was destined for various fish workshops around the lake, there to be pickled and preserved or processed into fish sauce, a popular condiment in antiquity. The center of the Galilean fish processing industry was Magdala, also known as Tarichaeae (literally "fishing-town"), where the Galilee Boat was found. Its fish gravies and salted fish remained popular well into the fourth and fifth centuries C.E., as rabbinic sources show.[15]

Catching these fish, however, was not the open enterprise that many authors appear to believe it was. One could not simply push off and fish to one's heart's content. On the contrary: fishing rights on the Sea were held by the tetrarch, Antipas, and leased to fishermen by brokers. These brokers were probably the same publicans who also held the monopoly of collecting taxes among the fishing communities, and would thus be eminently familiar with everyone working in the industry.

What's more, fishing in volume for the marketplace required capital, not only to acquire the boats and nets but also for the tools and materials to maintain them. This is why most fishermen would have worked in cooperatives. Luke confirms this when he refers to "James and John, sons of Zebedee, who were partners (koinoonoi) with Simon."[16] Such cooperatives would be in a position to borrow capital by using their boats and future catch as collateral. This capital was, in turn, available from the same brokers who sold the fishing rights and extracted taxes.[17]

The result was a complex web of obligations between fishermen and tax collectors/brokers that under normal circumstances would have kept fishermen from simply dropping everything and leaving with Jesus, as the

Gospels suggest. The evangelists may simply have used the image of spontaneous surrender to Jesus as an allegory of the unconditional faith and commitment to Christ that they were advocating to their audience. On the other hand, it is possible that these fishermen-followers were not the principals in the fishing cooperatives, but rather newly arrived labor on the scene. These "for-hire" fishermen could move from gang to gang and pick up work whenever they could—mending and cleaning nets, repairing leaks, applying new pitch to bottoms. As such, these workers were not unlike the day-laborers in Galilee's agriculture. Such fishing "part-timers" would certainly be free to move with Jesus from village to village, unencumbered by financial obligations to brokers or fellow partners.

✢ ✢ ✢

Jesus' choice of fishermen as disciples now makes sense. From his past experience as a social worker in the region, Jesus must have known that there was a significant surplus of non-attached day-laborers who would be in a position to assist him on his travels. His introduction to Simon Peter and the sons of Zebedee, both hailing from generations of fishermen, offered the perfect opportunity to connect with this community and thus select his companions with care. Most importantly, as a "principal," Simon Peter must have had access to a cooperative boat. Jesus knew that a boat would give him unprecedented freedom of movement, enabling him to cross the lake in any direction and visit multiple villages in one day. Perhaps Peter's cooperative fished in the evening or by night, when the air was cool and fish could be lured to the surface with a combination of lamps and bait. This would explain why Jesus was able to use the boat by day, without any concern that this valuable commodity was being kept from gainful work.

THE KINGDOM OF GOD

Now equipped with a following of his own and the means to traverse the region, Jesus dedicated the remaining eighteen months of his life to propagating his great plan for social renewal in Palestine. This plan was a manifesto that Jesus himself referred to as "The Kingdom of God," although in Matthew we also hear it described as "The Kingdom of Heaven," and Thomas sometimes refers to it as "The Kingdom of the Father." With this manifesto, Jesus aimed for a general *levée en masse,* a grass-roots surge of renewal that would end the social and economic exploitation of the poor by the nation's elites and restore Israel as a nation governed by YHWH.

Various scholars have pointed out that the term "Kingdom of God" is relatively unknown in Hebrew Scripture, and therefore could be construed as a concept original to Jesus—and, by extension, to Christianity. Indeed, in Christian theology the "Kingdom of God" would later become a program of universal salvation, available to all, Gentile and Jew alike, who agree to be baptized in the Holy Spirit. For Christians, the physical manifestation of the "Kingdom" is the *ekklesia,* the Church on earth, preparing the faithful for the heavenly Kingdom that awaits after death.

But even a cursory reading of the Old Testament makes it clear that the idea of "Kingdom of God" was a deeply rooted principle of post-Exilic Judaism, certainly in the growing apocalyptic yearning of Late Second Temple Judaism. From the very first, the twelve tribes who settled in the Promised Land believed themselves to be a nation, or a *kingdom,* of God. Unlike the Christian God, the God of Hebrew Scripture was always a political and historical force, actively steering Israel's history. Time and again, YHWH would intervene in history to safeguard his people, whether to engineer their release from bondage, to plot their strategy of conquest, or to appoint a dynastic rule of Davidic kings. The books of the Bible that scholars refer to as Deuteronomistic history continue to breathe the fundamental principle that while kings may come and go, God is the ultimate ruler of Israel's destiny, just as the land on which the settlers live—the Promised Land—is God's land. The "Kingdom of God" therefore is the physical manifestation of God's plan for Israel, as a community of settlers who cleave to the three principal tenets of Covenant Law: compassion, social justice, and faithful observance of the Law.

The way Jesus saw it, this was the raison d'être of the Jewish commonwealth; without it, the nation had no moral compass, no manifest destiny. But Palestine had strayed far from the ideals of its original founding. One reason was the seductive influence of Hellenistic civilization, a culture rooted in pagan motifs. Another was the growing schism between rich and poor, accelerated by the economic exploitation by the Romans and the collaborationist elites. Yet another was the Herodian policy that encouraged the confiscation of small ancestral plots in order to create hugely profitable private estates. And all this was exacerbated by the blatant indifference of the priesthood to the plight of the poor.

It had not always been that way. After the return from Exile, a priestly elite had risen to the occasion to lead the restoration of Israel as a religious entity. Ezrah and Nehemiah had not only rallied the people behind the newly codified precepts of the Law; they had also urged social justice, actively protecting the people from the excess of economic growth. Once, during a severe famine, owners of small plots complained that they had to mortgage their fields and vineyards to buy grain and pay the Persian king's tax, thus enabling nobles and officials to confiscate the mortgaged land for their own estates. Some were even driven to sell their children into slavery. Nehemiah became very angry. "Restore to them, this very day, their fields, their vineyards, their olive orchards," Nehemiah demanded, and the oligarchs complied.[18]

Now compare this with the priesthood of the early first century. In Jesus' day, the chief priests had ossified into an aristocratic elite, oblivious to the massive social crisis in the land. They preferred to preoccupy themselves with cultivating their prerogatives and control of the sacrificial cult. Even worse, many of these same priests were deeply involved in acquiring confiscated land from displaced peasants so as to further support their lavish lifestyle. Talmudic literature has revealed that the high priestly families such as the houses of Boethus, Phiabi, and Kathros were among the wealthiest in Palestine, as was the house of Hanin, which had produced Annas and the current high priest, Caiaphas. All of these families, the literature reveals, used their position of prestige to amass fabulous fortunes with which they built veritable palaces in Jerusalem's Upper City. A rabbinic sage known as Abba Saul ben Batnit, who lived in Jerusalem some ten years after Jesus' crucifixion, claimed that the high priests appointed their sons as treasurers of the Temple and ordered their servants to go out and beat debtors with their fists and staves.[19]

 Rather than serving as pastors to the nation, as shepherds of their sheep, these chief priests actively collaborated with the Roman occupation so as to keep their grip on the sacrificial and financial operations of the Temple. Not surprisingly, perhaps, at the outbreak of the rebellion in 66 C.E., the feared *Sicarii* immediately moved to kill the high priest while sending many other wealthy citizens fleeing for their lives through the sewers of Jerusalem. In the end, all of the chief priests were unceremoniously put to the sword. Their homes, including the palatial mansions of former chief priests such as Annas and Caiaphas, were burned to the ground.[20]

Many Jews before Jesus had recognized the illegitimacy and moral corruption of the priesthood during the Late Second Temple period. Some, as we have seen, fled to the desert, where they created their own idea of a Kingdom of God in the form of a monastic community. Others, notably the Pharisees, transferred the idea of the Kingdom of God to their homes, and the traditional role of priestly sanctity to themselves, by observing priestly conventions about purity and Sabbath observance in their own daily lives.

But Jesus had come to understand that the method of transformation advocated by the Pharisees was wrong. It was all well and good to be obsessive about the purity of the food one ate, the water with which one cleansed oneself, or the things one was or was not allowed to do on the Sabbath. These, Jesus acknowledged, were legitimate concerns enshrined in Laws of the Kingdom. What was wrong, however, was to pursue these concerns *at the expense of everything else,* missing the whole point of the Law. In Jesus' vision, the sole purpose of the Law was to please God with one's heart and to share responsibility for the welfare of one's fellow man. "Why do you see the speck in your neighbor's eye, but do not notice the log in your own eye?" he thunders during one of his speeches.[21] "Shame on you, scribes and Pharisees," he rails elsewhere, speaking as one who has observed Pharisaic customs up close: "for you tithe mint, dill, and cumin, but you neglect the weightier matters of the law: *justice and mercy and faith.*"[22]

It was all very clear to him now. Neither the Essenes, the Pharisees, nor John had held the key to the solution of Israel's ills, though each, in their own way, had made a major contribution to Jesus' development as a religious reformer. The only solution, in his eyes, was to *go back* to the fundamental idea of Israel as a land of God—as a community that did not cleave to Roman dictates nor to the vainglorious pretensions of the Herodian dynasty, but to the principles of God's rule.

Once again, it was Jeremiah who showed the way. It was Jeremiah who had spoken of God's kingly reign shepherding the poor and downtrodden of Israel back to a newly unified home, centered on Mount Zion. "Hark, the cry of my poor people from far and wide in the land," Jeremiah had said. "Is the Lord not in Zion? Is her King not in her?"[23] Take heart, Jeremiah urged, for only God has the power to restore Israel as a faithful and compassionate community; "among all the wise ones of the nations and in all their kingdoms, there is no one like you."[24] No other prophet in Hebrew Scripture so clearly articulated the promise of those words, *The Kingdom of God*. "Behold," Jeremiah said, "if you truly amend your ways, if you truly act justly with one another, if you do not oppress the alien, the orphan, and the widow, or shed innocent blood," then God "would dwell in this land."[25] A more succinct summary of Jesus' Kingdom program can scarcely be found.

"He who scattered Israel will gather him, and will keep him as a shepherd a flock," Jeremiah continues elsewhere. Jesus would pay homage to that vision when he said that "the Kingdom is like a shepherd who had a hundred sheep. One of them, the largest, went astray. He left the ninety-nine and looked for that one until he found it."[26]

This idea, of God's promise to gather the poor into his loving embrace as a shepherd carrying a lost sheep of the flock, would become the guiding theme of Jesus' teachings. Only by rallying to the core values that had produced God's nation to begin with could Israel be restored, would Palestine once again be ruled by justice, and would a man live in harmony with his neighbor, each sharing in the bounty of the Lord.

✣ ✣ ✣

This is the message that Jesus brought to his core constituency, the poor of Galilee, and they cleaved to it with all their hearts. They only had one question: *when*? When would this great Kingdom of God come about? We are hungry *now*, they said; we are homeless *now*, we cannot wait much longer. Will a *mashiach* come to evict the hated Romans and the predatory Herodian dynasty? Or will God send a new Flood, or a series of plagues perhaps, to bend humankind to his will?

The answer to this difficult question is uniquely Jesus'. Regardless of the debt he owes to Jeremiah, or to John, or to the Pharisees, the practical vehicle for implementing the Kingdom of Jesus was his inspired idea, and his alone, for it is found nowhere else in the Old Testament. Perhaps its purest expression can be found in the Gospel of Thomas. Contrary to the eschatological vision of John the Baptist, the Pharisees, or the Essenes, Jesus says that "[the Kingdom of God] will not come by waiting for it. It will not be a matter of saying 'Here it is' or 'There it is.'"[27] In Luke, Jesus puts it even more strongly: "The kingdom of God is not coming with things *that can be observed.*"[28] Clearly, this confounded the apostles and the thousands who took his words to heart. What is this supposed to mean? If you can't even tell if or when it comes, how can you know that the Kingdom of God has arrived? Then Jesus delivers his last devastating line: "For in fact, *the kingdom of God is among you.*"

What Jesus is saying is this: there is no point in sitting around and waiting for some great cataclysm, some instrument of God's terrible wrath, to come about and do the work for you. We, the people, says Jesus, have the power to take destiny in our *own* hands, to join together to rid our villages and towns of the greed, the injustice, the disease that has plunged Palestine into despondency. "The Kingdom," says Jesus in the Gospel of Thomas, "*is inside of you.*"[29] One can *glimpse* the heavenly Kingdom, *experience* and *live* the Kingdom today—by acts of compassion toward one's fellow man and obedient love of God. We are, perhaps, reminded of the words of the Mahatma Gandhi, urging his followers to "be the change you want to see."

Jesus' manifesto was a call to all Jews to rise up and build the Kingdom of God now, today, irrespective of the Romans or the priesthood or anyone else responsible for the decay of Israel. Jesus, to put it bluntly, believed in people power. He believed that by sowing the seeds of a new sense of social solidarity, grounded in faith, between landowner and serf, toll collector and fisherman, he could restore the Kingdom of God just as it had been in the earliest days of the settlement in the Promised Land.

For Jesus, the Kingdom was not a political institution, but a state of grace, in anticipation of the great Kingdom of Heaven after death. As Martin Buber put it: "the Kingdom . . . is no other-worldly consolation, no vague heavenly bliss. It is the perfect life of man with man." It is, in short, a compact for living that extends the Covenant of Moses into a new and more intimate sphere of human relations.

To get this revolutionary idea across, Jesus used two strategies. For the victims of oppression, the vast proletariat of disenfranchised farmers and laborers, he used the vision of the imminent Kingdom of God as a fulcrum of hope and consolation. "Happy are the poor, for theirs is the kingdom of heaven," Jesus says in the oldest stratum of Q sayings, which would form the basis for the "Sermon on the Mount" in Luke and Matthew, and possibly in Thomas.[30] "Happy are the mourners, for they shall be comforted; happy are the hungry, for they shall be satisfied." With this soaring rhetoric, Jesus shows himself the pupil of John, using a favorite oratorical device known as *macarisms* or beatitudes. The Hebrew Scriptures, and particularly the Psalms, are full of such proverbs that promise the secret to finding true happiness. But Jesus turns this familiar device on its head by using another favorite formula in the ancient Near East, the paradox. *Happy are the hungry* is a typical phrase designed to jolt Jesus' audience. It is an oxymoron, for the misery of hunger cannot be a conduit to happiness. And yet that is precisely the case, says Jesus, because your suffering today will lead to your happiness in the Kingdom tomorrow.

Happy are the mourners. Jesus' audience must have been stunned. As he well knew, there was hardly a peasant family in Galilee that was not touched by malnutrition and disease, that had not experienced the despair of burying a child or a loved one. And yet, Jesus said, the deeper your sorrow and grief today, so much greater will your be joy in the grace to come.

To underscore the validity of this vision, Jesus used his healing ability to full effect. Not only did his natural talent for healing legitimize him as a man favored by God; each act of healing was also a tangible example of the restorative power of a community embracing solidarity and compassion—a vivid example of the Kingdom of God in action.

Jesus knew that his message was bound to resonate with the people among whom he had worked for so many years and whose plight he knew so well. He spoke their language; they were bound to respond to his words of hope and promise. The hard part, however, was to convince his other target group, namely the agents of corruption themselves: the soldiers, publicans, landowners, and other elites who continued to exploit the Galilean masses for their personal gain.

It is in his confrontation with these groups that we see Jesus deploy himself as the apocalyptic prophet in the image of John. Scholars often refer to this group of Jesus' sayings as the Eschatological Discourse, found in Mark's Chapter 13 and Matthew's Chapter 24. By threatening God's imminent judgment, Jesus pressures the offending parties to abandon their selfish accumulation of power and wealth, to share their bounty with the poor, and to embrace the justice of God's kingdom.

John had spoken of the urgent need to repent because the day of judgment was imminent. For this particular target audience, Jesus continued John's theme, emphasizing its urgency by intimating that the *Dies Irae* would catch them unprepared. "Keep alert, for you do not know when the time will come," Jesus threatens in Mark; "you do not know when the master of the house will come, in the evening, or at midnight, or at cockcrow, or at dawn, or else he may find you asleep when he comes suddenly."[31]

Whether the audience to whom Jesus directed himself responded to his message, or even grasped his meaning, is not immediately clear. In fact, the Gospels seem to intimate that Jesus' own followers, the apostles, had a hard time understanding what the New Kingdom program was all about. Repeatedly, they asked their Teacher to explain it. Every time, Jesus came back with that favorite device of a Near Eastern sage, a story, one more mysterious than the next. Often, these parables were inspired by Jesus' exposure as a young man to Galilee's agriculture. "The Kingdom of God," Jesus explained, "is like a mustard seed, the smallest of all the seeds on earth, that, when sown, becomes the greatest of all shrubs.[32] Or "the Kingdom of God is like a seed that sprouts while the farmer is asleep; it grows into a stalk, the head, and finally the grain, which the farmer cuts with his sickle."[33]

The apostles must have nodded, but it is doubtful that they grasped what Jesus was talking about. Even today we have trouble figuring out what Jesus meant. The obvious question is, why? Why is Jesus so ambiguous about his great vision? Surely in time he would have honed his pitch, his "stump speech," as he traveled from one village to the next? Why does he couch his program in terms that many of his contemporaries—certainly his illiterate and poorly educated fishermen—would have been hard pressed to understand?

The answer may be more obvious than we think. To see it, we must remember that Jesus was still a relatively young man, only recently set free from the shadow of a charismatic and domineering teacher. What's more, there was so little time. Most sages, philosophers and spiritual leaders we know from antiquity took *years* to formulate their doctrine. Jesus was operating in a span of mere months. He was literally developing his Kingdom manifesto as he went along.

My conclusion is that the "Kingdom" philosophy we see in the Gospels is not an arbitrary grouping of sometimes contradictory statements, but the *process* by which Jesus is slowly refining his teaching. We all know that the best way to grasp a complex idea is to try to explain it to others. That is what Jesus was doing; like a Socrates, he was weighing and formulating and honing that great vision that the Spirit had shown him and even now was helping him to put into practice.

For eighteen months, Jesus traveled tirelessly through the hills and fields of Galilee and the Lower Gaulanitis, carrying the message of the Kingdom of God to the villages and towns. Mark puts it most succinctly: "Jesus came into Galilee, preaching the Gospel of the kingdom of God, and saying, The time is fulfilled, and the kingdom of God is at hand."[34] At every turn, this campaign was fired by Jesus' anger over the misery he was witnessing among the Galilean poor. His guiding theme remained the words of Isaiah, which Luke has him read in the village assembly of Nazareth: "The Spirit of the Lord is upon me, for he has anointed me to bring good news to the poor. He has sent me to proclaim release to the captives and recovery of sight to the blind, to let the oppressed go free, to proclaim the year of the Lord's favor."[35] The "good news"(*euangelion* in Greek, translated in English as "goodspell" or "Gospel") was rooted in Jesus' firm belief that he would succeed—that the villages and towns in the wake of his visits would hearken to his words and embrace God's new society of faith, justice, and compassion.

As a visible demonstration of the Kingdom-of-God society in which all social barriers were removed, Jesus made a point of sharing a meal with anyone who cared to have him. Consequently, Jesus found himself eating with tax collectors and sinners, Pharisees and peasants, rich and poor. His Pharisaic teachers would have been horrified, for there was no telling whether the food was kosher or whether the cups and plates were ritually pure.[36] As John Crossan has argued, this "fellowship of the meal" may have its root in Qumranite customs. After an elaborate purification ceremony, as we have seen, the Essenes/Qumranites would share a meal in their refectory, sitting on mats, arranged in rows that ran parallel to the walls of the room. On the menu were bread, dates, date honey, dairy products, and sometimes meat. For the Qumranites, this custom of breaking bread together was a spiritual substitute for Temple sacrifice, just as their ritual immersion prior to the meal superseded the ritual cleansing in a *mikveh* before entering the Temple.

It is quite possible that the Qumranite idea of a shared meal as a spiritual act was communicated to Jesus by John. But in Jesus' hands, this table fellowship gained an entirely new meaning. Whereas the table of Qumran was shared only with the members of the cult, Jesus welcomed people from every walk of life, without any regard for the social barriers that had bifurcated Galilean society. For him, the Kingdom of God was explicitly egalitarian and inclusive.

Lest his followers miss the point, he expounded on it in several parables. During one dinner, Jesus criticized his host for inviting only his friends, relatives, and neighbors. "When you give a banquet," Jesus told him, "invite the poor, the crippled, the lame, and the blind"—the constituency that Jesus himself knew so well.[37] People had to understand that divisiveness would not be tolerated in a Kingdom-of-God society; favoritism or preferential treatment at the expense of another would no longer exist. Nor would the Kingdom be organized as a hierarchical power structure such as Rome's, where "rulers lord it over them, and their great ones are tyrants," as Jesus says in the Gospel of Mark. "But it will not be so among you; whoever wishes to become great must first be your servant."[38]

During another banquet, held at a wedding, Jesus watched as his companions jockeyed for the seats of honor. In Jewish tradition, guests were seated in order of seniority, starting from the left side of the table. Jesus corrected them, saying, "When you are invited, sit down at the lowest place, so that when your host comes, he may say to you, 'Friend, move up higher.' For all those who exalt themselves will be humbled, and those who humble themselves will be exalted."[39]

THE SON OF MAN

Did Jesus' Kingdom-of-God ideology change his understanding of himself? How did he see his own role in God's great plan? This question is, not surprisingly, a subject of intense debate between conservative and liberal exegetes. Christians will argue, as first postulated by Paul, that Jesus was the *only* son of God, sent to earth to assume mortal form and redeem mankind through his sacrifice on the cross. Today, the idea of Jesus's divinity is the very foundation of Christian doctrine.

Did the historical Jesus recognize himself as a divine being as well? At no point in the Gospels do we see him making an unequivocal statement to that effect. Rather, it is others—sometimes supernatural beings such as devils and demons, sometimes the evangelists themselves—who identify him as such. At the core of this debate, I believe, lies the question of whether the historical Jesus considered himself an observant Jew or a member of a new religion about to be formed. Many scholars of the historical Jesus, including best-selling author and Princeton professor Elaine Pagels, believe strongly that Jesus was not starting a new religion, but operating within the old. Jesus himself affirmed this when he said, "Think not that I came to destroy the Law, or the prophets; I did not come to destroy, but to fulfill."[40]

For an observant Jew of the first century C.E., then, God was an all-powerful, majestic being whose name no one even dared pronounce. In Judaism, as indicated earlier, the word "God" is not spoken or written but indicated by a code, the *tetragrammaton* YHWH (for *Yahweh*), or by the word *Adonai* (my Lord). Even today, Jews refer to God indirectly with the word *HaShem* ("the Name"). For a mortal being to believe that he was of the same divine substance as the Father ran counter to everything Jewish monotheism stood for. Indeed, the first of the Ten Commandments (in both the books of Exodus and Deuteronomy) read that *you shall have no other gods before me.*

By the same token, there is every indication that Jesus had developed a deeply intimate bond with YHWH that went well beyond the traditional relationship between a Jew and his God. As we have seen, this very close bond was probably nurtured by Jesus' experience as a *mamzer* and social outcast in his village; the death of his own father, Joseph, while Jesus was still young; and his years of solitary wandering through the villages of Galilee. In other words, though Jesus may have never considered himself the biological, consubstantial son of God, he certainly thought of God as his *Abba,* his spiritual father. Indeed, this intimate connection with God, amplified by his recognition of his extraordinary healing powers, remained the strongest motivating force throughout Jesus' career.

When seen in the context of the Hebrew Scriptures, however, this close relationship was neither new nor unique. The book of Exodus states: "Thus says the Lord: Israel is my firstborn son."[41] In the Book of Psalms, which Jesus often referred to, he may have read Psalm 68: "A father of the father-less, and a judge of the widows, is God in his holy habitation."[42] Psalm 89 reads: "You are my father, my God, and the rock of my salvation."[43]

Nor did Jesus consider this intimate relationship with God as a father to be exclusively his. On the contrary: in Matthew, Jesus explicitly refers to his followers as "children of your Father in heaven."[44] What's more, the prayer that Jesus taught his disciples, and that Christians recite to this day, opens with the words "*Our* Father, who art in heaven. . . ." Jesus strongly advo-cated the idea that YHWH was a merciful and forgiving Father to all of his Creation; a God, moreover, who took passionate interest in the well-being of those who turned to him. "Be merciful even as your Father is merciful," he tells his disciples in Q.[45] In one of the oldest strata of that document, Jesus marvels at the Father's generosity toward his children. "What father of yours, if the son asks for a loaf of bread, would give him a stone, or if he asks for a fish will give him a snake?" he asked rhetorically. "Therefore, if you . . . know how to give good gifts to your children, how much more will the Father Above give good things to those who ask him!"[46] And in the Gospel of Thomas, he explains the role of the merciful Father in the Gnostic concept of the Kingdom thus: "When you come to know your-selves, then you will become known, and you will realize that it is you who are the sons of the living Father."

How, then, did Jesus see himself? In the original strata of sayings con-tained in the canonical and extracanonical Gospels, Jesus refers to himself as "Son of Man."[47] In the four canonical Gospels alone, the words "Son of Man" appear eighty-one times. More significantly, the term is always used *by Jesus himself*—never by the apostles or the evangelists. This suggests that it is very likely an authentic appellation employed by Jesus.

But what does it mean, *Son of Man?* This question has produced reams of scholarly print, but experts are still divided. On the surface, the term seems to originate in the Book of Ezekiel. Here, the prophet is addressed by God as "son of man" (*ben adam*) more than ninety times. It is generally believed that the term means "mortal being" or "mere mortal" and dis-tances the prophet from the divine majesty of the God with whom he is speaking. It is possible that Jesus borrowed this expression to indicate his deep sense of humility before his divine Father. In that sense, we should translate the Gospel version of "Son of Man" as a self-deprecating form of speech, meaning "I, this mere mortal" or "I, a mere son of the people."

Son of Man is also used in one other place in Hebrew Scriptures: namely, in the Book of Daniel (where it appears in the Greek Septuagint version of the Hebrew Bible as *anthropou*). In Daniel, the term is probably used in a very different sense. It appears in Daniel's vision of the night, in which *"one like a son of man* came with the clouds of heaven. And he came to the Ancient One and was presented before him. To him was given dominion and glory and kingship, that all peoples, nations, and languages should serve him."[48] This, of course, is a very different image from what we see in Ezekiel. Daniel's Son of Man appears to be a herald of the coming eternal reign of God, after the wicked rulers and kingdoms have all been vanquished. Scholars are divided over the question of whether this Son of Man is an angel descending through the clouds or rather the symbol of Israel (akin to the allegory in Exodus we saw earlier) being raised up to God. What is clear is that this term is not a deprecating form of speech, as in Ezekiel, but an allusion to a specific being who is closely linked to an eschatological realization of the Kingdom of God.

That image may have resonated with Jesus, assuming he ever had the chance to read the book of Daniel. In its final form, the book probably was not completed until the middle of the second century B.C.E. Though it is an integral part of the Hebrew canon, in the third division of *Writings,* its distribution in the early first century C.E. is unclear.

JESUS AS THE MESSIAH

Did Jesus also see himself as the Messiah? This is another subject of intense debate.[49] Christian doctrine emphatically extends the interpretation of "Son of Man" into Messianic territory. It points, by way of evidence, to the extracanonical Book of Enoch (a book included in neither the Hebrew Bible nor the Old Testament), in which the term is almost synonymous with "the Messiah."[50] The evangelists, too, explicitly link the title to Daniel's vision of a messianic herald. Mark has Jesus declare to the high priest that "you will see the Son of Man seated at the right hand of the Power," and "coming with the clouds of heaven," invoking, if not actually quoting, Daniel's apocalyptic imagery. For the synoptic evangelists, the idea of Jesus as the Messiah sealed the role of Jesus as the one foretold in Hebrew

Scripture. "Now the birth of Jesus the Messiah took place in this way," says Matthew in the opening chapter of his Gospel.[51]

As we have seen, messianic expectation was certainly "in the air" in Jesus' time. Disillusionment with the Roman occupation and blatant exploitation by the Herodian regime fed the yearning for the "Anointed One"—the *mashiach* who would defeat Israel's enemies and restore the nation under God. While the Pharisees sought solace in priestly ritual in their homes, and Essenes created their own "virtual" kingdom in the desert, the people at large continued to pin their hopes on the ultimate redemptive power of an agent of God to save Israel. No wonder, then, that any dissident of renown was immediately looked upon as a possible Messiah. John the Baptist was questioned if he was the one.[52] Inevitably, so was Jesus. "Who do the people say that I am?" Jesus asks his apostles in the Gospel of Mark. The answers varied. "John the Baptist," some say; "Elijah," others believe; "one of the prophets," another group replies. Ah, says Jesus, "but who do *you* say I am?" Peter answers him, in all earnestness, "You are the Messiah." But then Jesus turns and *rebukes* him, ordering him not to convey such notions to anyone else.[53]

This suggests that Jesus knew very well that "Messiah" was a loaded term. In Hebrew Scripture, the Messiah is not a spiritual savior, as Christians would assume, but a warlike hero of Davidic lineage; a *commander* who meets Israel's enemies in open battle and defeats them by virtue of his superior military genius. The title of Messiah therefore implied a political agenda, that is, a confrontational posture toward the established elites of Palestine, all of whom were engaged in oppressing the Jewish masses. For example, Simon bar Kochba, the highly skilled guerrilla leader who would lead a revolt against the Roman occupation from 132 to 135 C.E., was hailed by some as the Messiah.

This may explain why even within the Gospels themselves—whose agenda is clearly to present Jesus as the Messiah—Jesus himself is ambivalent about the title. Some scholars go even further and maintain that this idea of Jesus being the Messiah does not appear in the oldest sayings strata at all (for example, in those sayings in Q that the noted scholar Burton Mack considers to belong to the oldest traditions about Jesus). They believe that references to "Christ" (the Greek translation of "Messiah") only begin to surface after 50 C.E., when Paul's letters started to circulate widely.

JESUS AS A PROPHET

With the question of whether Jesus considered himself a "prophet," however, we are on more solid ground. While he certainly accepted the apostles' honorific "Rabbi" or "Teacher," Jesus probably did see himself as a legitimate prophet sanctioned by God. John, as we have seen, was also considered both Teacher *and* Prophet. As countless sayings testify, Jesus certainly believed he spoke with the authority of one blessed with the Spirit. As such, he must have seen himself as a legitimate descendant of the great pre-exilic prophets, Amos, Micah, Hosea, and, above all, Jeremiah. The experience of these figures illustrates the great psychological burden that is typically borne by a prophet whose enlightenment has elevated him far above his peers and yet, paradoxically, has also charged him with a grave and sometimes impossible responsibility.

The Gospels give some hints that Jesus experienced this psychological burden as well, particularly in the way in which his generally calm and peaceful demeanor could sometimes be replaced by a sudden outburst of temper. Jesus was acutely aware that, like his great role models, his mission did not make him very popular among Palestine's elites.[54] This made him resolute and single-minded, if not impatient, as many of his more strident sayings and exhortations show. The evil in the nation was too great; not a moment should be wasted if the Kingdom was truly to come about. The message certainly resonated with his core constituency, the masses of displaced Galilean peasants. But they, naturally, were not the ultimate focus of Jesus' campaign.

On the contrary. If Jesus was truly to realize his blueprint for a compassionate society under God, he knew that the real work would have to be done in the towns and cities of Galilee, where the brokers, the tax collectors, the merchants, the landowners, and other elites would be found. And they, as he soon would find out, would prove to be a far greater obstacle to overcome.

TEN

THE ROAD TO JERUSALEM

The Gospels show us a Jesus who plots the strategy of his campaign with the diligence of a modern political candidate. Unlike John and most of the Old Testament prophets, Jesus did not remain in one place, but rather kept his band of followers on the go. His was a campaign on the move, from village to town, from town to city, in a never-ending quest to exhort as many of Galilee's more affluent citizens as possible to embrace the Kingdom Society.

One of his strategy sessions is clearly described in Luke. "The Lord," says the evangelist, "appointed seventy others and sent them on ahead of him in pairs to every town and place where he himself intended to go." By organizing and dispatching these advance parties, Jesus tried to ensure that the audience in these townships would be receptive and his time would not be wasted. "Do not move from house to house," Jesus counsels his *schaliachim,* his delegates, but where you receive a warm welcome, "stay in that house, eating and drinking whatever they provide." Lead by example: attend to the sick "and say to them, 'The Kingdom of God has come near to you.'" What's more, delegates should dress exactly like the poor and downtrodden they represent: "no purse, no bag, no sandals"—no material possessions whatsoever.[1]

Even so, Jesus was well aware of the challenge his followers faced in converting the hearts and minds of the well-to-do. "See," he adds apologetically, "I am sending you out like lambs in the midst of wolves."[2] And if a town seems a lost cause, he urges them to move on. "Shake the dust from your feet," says Jesus in Q, "and say, 'Nevertheless, be sure of this, the realm of God has come to you.'"[3]

Matthew, too, gives us a glimpse of Jesus' planning. "Go nowhere among the Gentiles," Jesus instructs his followers. That meant predominantly Gentile places like Tiberias or the cities of the Decapolis. Their efforts should be reserved for Jewish communities, "the lost sheep of the

225

house of Israel" only. "Enter no town of the Samaritans," he adds, referring to the region of Samaria, populated by Jews whose forefathers had
intermarried with Babylonian settlers and whom most other Jews considered untouchable.[4]

Thus equipped, Jesus and his followers set out to canvass the Galilee.
One minute they are hugging the northern shores of the Sea of Galilee; the
next sees them tramping through the Gaulanitis to Caesarea Philippi, while
soon thereafter they're tirelessly covering the land of the Gerasenes, just
north of the Gentile region of the Decapolis. During one of their crossings
over the Sea of Galilee, a violent gale catches them by surprise. Jesus, however, calms the waters and directs their ship to safety.[5] For those of us who
have traveled to Israel and seen the lake with their own eyes, it is difficult
to believe that anyone could be caught by a storm on so placid a body of
water. But the people who live on the lake can attest that looks can be
deceiving and that sudden gales are by no means a rare occurrence.
Scientists, including oceanographer Ayal Anis, now believe they have discovered the reason for this strange phenomenon. With the support of the
U.S.-Israel Binational Science Foundation, Anis demonstrated that the
unique topography of the Galilean hill country, aligned east to west, is to
blame. These hills essentially act as a funnel, pushing winds that collide with
the countercurrent of winds coming off the Golan Heights to the east.
Trapped in the basin, these winds can unleash a sudden swirl of fury.
During one such storm in March 1992, scientists measured waves ten feet
high crashing into downtown Tiberias, causing significant damage.

As Jesus moved from village to village, more followers joined his ranks. One
was a young woman named Mary, from the town of Magdala. Magdala, as
we have seen, was a major center of the Galilean fish-processing industry.
Mary may have been from an affluent family involved in this trade, for Luke
states that she belonged to a group of women who "provided for them out
of their own resources."[6] Mary's status as the daughter of a wealthy family
is also attested by the fact that she was free to go and join the Jesus movement. In Galilean society, this was virtually unheard of. Most women
remained in the homes of their fathers until they were married; if not, they
were expected to stay and care for their parents and siblings.

Mary, on the other hand, is a surprisingly independent spirit who is clearly attracted to this charismatic preacher from Nazareth. The evangelists are rather coy about her role in the movement, though the Gospels admit that she was a witness to the crucifixion and later led the group of women to Jesus' tomb to anoint his body with oil and myrrh. There, according to John, she was not only the first "apostle" to see the empty tomb, but also the first individual to whom Jesus appeared after the resurrection.[7] Seen in the context of ancient Judaism, Mary's prominent role is nothing short of amazing, for the word of a female eyewitness had little credibility in a Jewish court.

Mary wanted to embrace the resurrected Jesus, but he said, "Do not touch me." These clues hint at a very special relationship between Mary Magdalene and Jesus that, most recently, has become the fodder of sensationalist "revelations" in thrillers like *The Da Vinci Code*. The truth is that scholars have known about the close relationship between Jesus and Mary for a long time—specifically, from a number of "Gospel" documents that Church fathers chose not to include in the canon of the New Testament. These ancient texts, which date from the late first and second centuries C.E., express the views of certain dissident Christian movements that scholars refer to as "Gnostics." These movements were influenced by the ancient idea that a complete immersion in the Divine ultimately leads to a secret knowledge of the divinity within oneself. In the Gnostic interpretation, for example, Jesus speaks in parables because true knowledge of God is a precious and potentially dangerous secret that can only be shared with those who prove themselves worthy of that knowledge.

Many of these texts, such as those called the Gospel of Peter, Gospel of Mary, Acts of Philip, and Pistis Sophia, were known as early as the eighteenth or nineteenth century. But the true extent of this Gnostic movement only came to light with the discovery of the Dead Sea Scrolls, fifty-two ancient texts, near the Egyptian village of Nag Hammadi in 1945. Several of these texts describe a romantic attachment between Jesus and Mary. "The companion (*koinonos*) of the [Savior is] Mary Magdalen," says the Gospel of Philip. "But [Christ loved] her more than [all] the disciples and used to kiss her [often] on her [mouth]." The Gospel then continues to say that Jesus' relationship with Mary led to tension within the movement. "The rest of [the disciples were offended by it . . .]," the text continues.

"They said to him, 'why do you love her more than all of us?' The Savior answered and said to them, 'Why do I not love you as [I love] her?'"[8]

In the Gospel of Mary, this tension escalates into a direct confrontation between Mary and her principal opponents, Andrew and Simon Peter. The scene takes place after the death and resurrection of Jesus. "Sister," Peter begins, "we know that the Savior loved you more than the rest of woman. Tell us the words of the Savior which you remember which you know, but we do not, nor have we heard them."[9] Eager to share what she has learned from Jesus, Mary tells the apostles what has transpired between the two of them. She describes how she saw Jesus in a vision, and how he taught her about the spirit and the struggle of the soul with evil powers. When Mary ends her story, the room falls silent. Finally, Andrew stands up and says, "Say what you wish to say about what she has said. I at least do not believe that the Savior said this. For certainly these teachings are strange ideas." Peter is skeptical too. He gets up and says "Did He really speak privately with a woman and not openly to us? Are we to turn about and all listen to her? Did He prefer her to us?"

At this point, Mary bursts into tears. "My brother Peter," she cries, "what do you think? Do you think that I have thought this up myself in my heart, or that I am lying about the Savior?" The apostle Levi comes to her rescue. "Peter," he rebukes him, "you have always been hot-tempered." And he continues: "if the Savior made her worthy, who are you indeed to reject her? Surely the Savior knows her very well."[10] In the Gospel of Thomas, Simon Peter moves to oust Mary from the movement altogether. "Make Mary leave us," he pleads with Jesus, "for females don't deserve life."[11]

It is difficult to ascertain whether these texts are based on authentic traditions. As Elaine Pagels has argued, the conflict between Mary and Peter probably reflected the very real tensions between Gnostic groups and the "orthodox" movement, which ultimately became the Church, in the second century C.E. Part of this tension involved the role of women in early Christian communities. In many of the so-called dissident groups that did not subscribe to the theology of Paul, women often held prominent positions. They worked as teachers, healers, and even priests; some were revered as prophets. Most importantly, women were believed to be as capable of possessing knowledge and receiving divine revelation as men were.

In the nascent Church, by contrast, the role of women was increasingly marginalized. The impetus to this process came from Paul, or at least those who wrote epistles under his name. In the letter to the Colossians, probably written by the same author who wrote the epistle to the Ephesians, Paul is quoted as saying: "wives, be subject to your husbands, as is fitting in the Lord."[12] The letter to Timothy, probably written by an anonymous author after Paul's death, pushes the anti-feminist agenda even further: "I permit no woman to teach or to have authority over a man," Paul is quoted as saying; "she is to keep silent."[13]

The growing strain between traditional and dissident views of the role of women was bound to have an impact on the way Mary Magdalene was portrayed in traditional Church writings. Knowing full well the reverence that many Gnostic communities had for the Magdalene, Church fathers began to cast Mary in a deliberately negative light. She became the "penitent" Magdalene, guilty of transgression and perversions that are intimated but never detailed. By the third century, she was identified with the sinner who, in the Gospel of Luke, washed Jesus' feet with her hair. By the sixth century, Pope Gregory I went a step further and declared her, quite without foundation, to be a "fallen woman" and a prostitute—a connotation that has stubbornly clung to her, at least in Catholic dogma, for centuries, right through to Mel Gibson's unfortunate *Passion of the Christ*. That did not prevent her from becoming a saint, for she had "repented," after all; but for hundreds of years, the name of Mary Magdalene was inextricably bound up with the specter of sin.[14] Nevertheless, the treatment of poor Mary in the early Church suggests that for some she posed a clear threat—as tangible evidence, perhaps, that women could speak with as much apostolic authority as men.

From a strictly historical point of view, however, there is not much information that can help us reconstruct the relationship between Jesus and Mary. If the Gnostic texts are correct, she was his confidante, his loyal companion, and possibly his lover. Seen from a Jewish perspective, there was nothing wrong with that. Most prophets were either married or were known to have had relations with a woman. By exception, Jeremiah wasn't married, and, as far as we know, John wasn't either. In fact, the precedent of *gentile, not if she was*

Jeremiah may have held Jesus back from marrying the woman he loved. Then again, if Mary was truly from a prominent family in Magdala, her parents would certainly have objected to her union with a *mamzer* from Nazareth. Perhaps they could not stop her from traveling with him, but they certainly could refuse to grant permission for marriage, which would have been a formidable legal and moral obstacle. But this, of course, is mere speculation.

What is clear is that Mary played a very special role in Jesus' life as well as his death. By casting her as the first and principal witness to Jesus' resurrection, the single most important event in traditional Christian theology, the Gospels pay clear homage to her prominence—regardless of whether she was Jesus' girlfriend or not.

JESUS AT THE CROSSROADS

In the early months of what we assume was the year 30 C.E., the Jesus movement reached a crossroads. It was winter; provisions were scarce; and some followers may have returned to their villages to care for their families. What's more, the sense of safety, the freedom of movement, that they had enjoyed over the past eighteen months was once again in doubt. Herod Antipas, Tetrarch of Galilee, had gotten wind of the stir that Jesus created among the cities and villages of his territory. Mark reports that he questioned his advisers. "Some," Mark states, "were saying, 'John the baptizer has been raised from the dead; and for this reason these powers are at work in him.' But others said, 'It is Elijah.' And others said, 'It is a prophet, like one of the prophets of old.'" Herod seized on the first explanation. No, he says, it's "John, whom I beheaded."[15]

There is no reason to doubt that Antipas would have found out about Jesus, certainly given the "publicity" he was receiving as a result of his healings and the crowds that came to hear him speak. As we have seen, in ancient Palestine the boundaries between the religious, social, and political spheres were blurred. Religion, as Antipas well knew, was a powerful conduit for thoughts and ideas well beyond the realm of cultic practice. Mark, in fact, uses Antipas's suspicions to play into his conspiracy theory, according to which "Herodians" and "Pharisees" join forces to "entrap" Jesus with his words.[16] As we have seen, the point of this conspiracy is to "prove" the devious opposition of the Pharisaic community to everything that Jesus stood for.

This is almost certainly the creative imagination of the evangelist. The Pharisees may have benefited from economic opportunities offered by the Antipas administration, but there is no evidence anywhere that they were somehow "in cahoots" with a regime that, Vichy-like, was collaborating with the Roman occupation. What's more, Antipas didn't need to "entrap" Jesus in sophisticated Pharisaic debate. First, he wouldn't have understood half of it. Second, if he wanted to silence Jesus, he could simply do what he did with John: dispatch a platoon of loyal troops, most of whom were Gentile mercenaries, and have Jesus thrown in jail. Problem solved.

In fact, the opposite appears to be the case. Luke tells us that when Antipas became concerned over what was taking place right under his nose, it was a group of Pharisees who came to warn Jesus about the threat. "Get away from here," these Pharisees urged, "for Herod wants to kill you."[17] Luke then continues, in nearly the same breath, with Jesus sitting down for an amicable dinner with "a leader of the Pharisees" on the Sabbath.[18] Both references underscore what we noted earlier: that far from being Jesus' sworn enemies, many Pharisees would have found much in common with Jesus' teaching, even if they took issue with his liberal interpretation of the Law.

As it was, Jesus took the warning to heart. He called Herod "that fox"—a rather daring thing to do, for Antipas had informers everywhere—but he knew he could not afford to ignore what the Pharisees had said. He also knew that it could not have come at a worse time, and for a very simple reason: Jesus had come to the conclusion that his Galilean strategy had run its course.

The idea that Jesus believed his campaign had failed may come as a shock to some. But the Gospels, using one of the oldest strata of oral traditions, are unequivocal on the issue.[19] Jesus had tirelessly wandered from township to village, preaching and ministering to crowds both large and small. He had spoken and taught until his voice must have been hoarse and his throat raw. He had dined with tax collectors, Pharisees, and stewards; he had used his healing powers on all who had flocked to him, sometimes well into the night. He had tried so very hard to build a grass-roots movement, to reform Judaism *from within*. And yet, and yet: Galilean society had *not* heeded his call. They had *not* opened their doors to the poor; had *not* shared their table with the blind, the dumb, and the lame; had *not* opened their granaries to the hungry, nor returned their ill-gotten land to those who had owned and tilled it for generations. Only the paupers, that vast mass of humanity, had hearkened to his words. Only they had believed his promise that the Kingdom was at hand, which made his lack of success even more bitter. "Woe to you, Chorazim!" he cries in Q, later to be absorbed in the Gospels of Luke and Matthew. "Woe to you, Bethsaida!" he adds, pinning the blame on the very cities that had formed the geographic boundary of his principal activity. "If the forceful deeds performed among you had been done in Tyre and Sidon, they would have changed their ways long ago, sitting in sackcloth and ashes!" That was harsh judgment indeed. Tyre and Sidon were Gentile cities, located just west of Galilee on the Phoenician coast. If the "forceful deeds" Jesus had performed would have swayed even these godless pagans, then the hearts of the Galilean elites must truly be as hard as stone.

We can imagine the depth of Jesus' despair. So much time, so much effort wasted—it would have been better to try to convert the Gentiles! But the bitterest denunciation was reserved for Capernaum, the city of Simon Peter, where Jesus had started his campaign with such high hopes. "And you, Capernaum," he cries, "do you think you will be praised to high heaven? You will be told to *go to hell!*"[20]

What to do now? Jesus weighed his options. First, he decided to take the advice of the Pharisees. According to Luke, he withdrew to Bethsaida. This made sense. Bethsaida, as we will remember, was located just across the border in the territory of Tetrarch Philip. For the time being, Jesus was safe. From there, according to a reference in the Gospel of John, he moved farther into the Gaulanitis, farther away from Galilee, to a place named Bethany-across-the-Jordan.[21] It was familiar territory, for John the Baptist had operated there not too long before. What's more, early Church documents indicate that Jesus may have had relatives living in the nearby town of Kochaba.[22]

Jesus needed to think. He needed to pray to *Abba* and ask for guidance. And then the answer came to him. Once again, it was Jeremiah who showed him the way. Jeremiah, who had faced an equally heartless and indifferent audience. Jeremiah, who also had lost heart, but who had been summoned by God to "Stand up! Gird your loins, and tell them everything that I command you."[23] As Jesus knew, the key was Jerusalem, as it had been throughout Israel's history. Whoever took Jerusalem took the country. "Stand in the gate of the Lord's house!" God had told Jeremiah. "Go and say, 'Hear the word of the Lord, all you people of Judah, you that enter these gates to worship the Lord!'"[24] And Jeremiah had heeded God's word. It had been a daring gambit, to try to rally the nation in the heart of the Temple, but Jeremiah had pulled it off. And standing on a hillock outside of Kochaba, Jesus must have decided to do the same.

Fortunately, the timing was propitious. It was the beginning of the Jewish month of Nisan. In under two weeks' time, thousands of Jews from all over Palestine, and indeed from all over the Diaspora, would converge on Jerusalem for Passover. By going to Jerusalem at this time, Jesus would be able to proclaim the good news of the New Kingdom to all of Israel. Of course, there were dangers involved. Jesus would be operating right under the noses of the collaborationist priesthood, including the high priest, Yosef Bar Kayafa—Caiaphas—himself. No doubt security would be tight, with the Roman military ready to pounce at the slightest sign of unrest. But Jesus wasn't interested in inciting a political rebellion; he was only inter-ested in doing what Jeremiah had done: rallying the people behind his program of social and religious renewal.

He looked up, turned to his followers, and said, "Let us go to Judea again."[25] The apostles were stunned, and with good reason. They did not know what Jesus was planning, but they had an inkling that it might mean trouble. "They were on the road, going up to Jerusalem," Mark tells us, "and Jesus was walking ahead of them; they were amazed, and those who fol-lowed were afraid."[26]

Jesus now took the southern route through the Jordan Valley, essentially retracing his steps along the path on which he had fled north after John's arrest. From Kochaba they would have followed the course of the River Yarmuk, which cut a serpentine path through the rugged hills of the Transjordan plateau. After a day or so, they passed the sprawling gardens of Hammath Gader on their left. Known for its mineral springs, Hammath Gader was feverishly transforming itself into a resort for the growing expatriate community of Roman officials. From there, the Yarmuk led them to the Jordan just below the Gentile city of Scythopolis, formerly known as Beth She'an, always careful to remain on the eastern banks within the territory of Philip's tetrarchy. Here the landscape changed. The terraced hills and cliffs of Moab gave way to the dry landscape of the Jordan rift, dotted here and there with copses of date palms.

As they continued along the eastern shore of the river, all through the region of the Decapolis, their footpath began to descend. Even though it was only the month of Nisan, the sun grew warmer during the day, though at night they huddled close to ward off the cold of the desert. Just beyond Aenon, near Salim, where John had once baptized large crowds of people, they crossed the Jordan to avoid entering into Perea, the territory of Antipas, still under the cloud of war. A half day's walk from there, the group entered Judea and Roman territory. Now the path veered away from the Jordan and into the Judean hills, past the wine-producing center of Keruchim. Beyond lay the infinite wastes of the Judean desert, so that, after many hours of trudging in the heat, all were grateful to see the palm groves of Phasaelis, watered by springs that today are called Wadi Fasa'il.

Phasaelis had been founded by Herod the Great in memory of his brother Phasael. It was bequeathed to Herod's sister Salome, who in turn presented it upon her death to the empress Livia, wife of the emperor Augustus.[27] Since it was a largely Gentile city, Jesus would have been careful to steer clear of its walls and elect to camp outside, near one of the brooks flowing from the springs.

The next day, they rose early and pushed on, hoping to reach Jericho before the heat of midday. Shortly before entering the city, they met up with throngs of worshipers heading toward Jerusalem for Passover. According to Luke, Jesus singled out a tax (or "toll") collector named Zaccheus and told him he planned to stay at his house that very night.[28] Since Jericho was a strategic crossing point of several main roads leading to Jerusalem, toll collectors there were in a position to exact substantial sums. Indeed, Zaccheus "was the chief tax collector, and he was rich." But Jesus' stay at his house had its intended effect. Zaccheus promised that "half of my possessions, Lord, I will give to the poor; and if I have defrauded anyone of anything, I will pay back four times as much."[29]

Jesus was jubilant. Here, at last, was a sinner prepared to help build the Kingdom! His enthusiasm was infectious; the apostles sensed it as well. Jesus' natural charisma blossomed once again and lifted everyone in the group, like boats at high tide. Yes, they told one another, this is a sign, a good sign, and "they supposed that the kingdom of God was imminent."[30]

Full of ardor and energy, they got up and prepared to join a "large crowd" about to leave Jericho for Jerusalem. A blind beggar named Bartimaeus, son of Timaeus, was sitting by the roadside. When he heard that Jesus was among the crowd, he called out to him, "My teacher, let me see again." "Go," Jesus responds in Mark's Gospel, "your faith has made you well."[31]

And so they went, climbing the steep winding road from Jericho to Jerusalem. It was hot, they were thirsty, and their feet were sore, but all was forgotten when they saw the sun sparkle on the golden cornice of the Temple, rising like a chimera of snow-white marble from the haze of the desert. Jesus had planned to rest in Bethany, in the house of Mary and Martha, relatives of his mother's family, but his followers could not be contained.[32] On they went, dancing, laughing, and singing hymns, waving fronds from Jericho's date palms, inexorably drawn to that spectacular vision of the Temple on the horizon, now only a two-hour walk, less than two miles away. They crossed the fields and orchards of the Mount of Olives and slowly descended into the Kidron Valley, momentarily awed by the sheer splendor of Herod's complex, easily the most magnificent thing they or their fathers or grandfathers had ever seen. Then, as they approached the city gates, they resumed their singing and dancing, waving their palm fronds, happy to experience this glorious day and be welcomed into the embrace of God.

Upon entering the city gate, the Gospels tell us, Jesus was received with joy. He was riding on a donkey, and "the whole multitude of the disciples began to praise God joyfully." The Gospel description of this "Palm Sunday welcome" follows the prophecy of Zechariah to the letter: "Shout aloud, O Jerusalem—Lo, your king comes to you, triumphant and victorious, humble and riding on a donkey."[33] Many pilgrims must have looked and stared, trying to figure out who this man was, who so purposefully moved toward the Temple with a group of singing people in his wake. Some of the Pharisees in their midst urged Jesus to maintain a low profile, knowing full well that the Roman forces in the city were on full alert. "Rabbi," they said,

235

"order your disciples to stop." Jesus would have none of it. He too was touched by the surge of enthusiasm that had intoxicated his band of followers. Silence them? How? "I tell you," Jesus said, smiling no doubt, "if they were silent, the stones would shout out!"[34]

They pressed on, up the staircase through the Twin Gates, and onto the Temple platform. They lingered in the first court, the "Court of Women," so that Mary Magdalene and the other women in the group could pray. But "it was already late," says Mark.[35] The Nicanor Gate, which led into the second court and the sanctuary proper, was about to be closed. They caught a brief glimpse of the magnificent Temple itself, its marble painted saffron by the light of the dying sun. Just beyond, partly shaded, was the embroidered tapestry that shielded the inner sanctum from public view. Every time a priest emerged, the tapestry moved ever so slightly, revealing its intricate pattern of vines, symbolizing the twelve tribes of Israel. Hushed by this spectacle, the apostles stood and stared, overwhelmed by the splendor of the shrine. Then the Levites came and started to usher the pilgrims back into the forecourt.

Most of the followers, especially those who were poor, had never seen the Temple before. They were awe-struck. "Look, Rabbi," one of them gushed, "what large stones and what large buildings!"[36] But Jesus was not impressed. As we have seen, he had inherited a healthy skepticism of the Jerusalem priesthood and the machinery of ritual sacrifice—a skepticism that had only deepened with his reading of Amos, Micah, and Jeremiah. His aversion had been further nurtured in the dissident milieu of John's Qumranite ideology.

But that did not mean that Jesus did not have the highest reverence for the Temple sanctuary itself. He, like all other Jews in first-century Palestine, believed that the Temple was truly the sacred "throne of the Lord." It was this whole business of animal sacrifice and the vulgarity of Herod's Hellenistic "improvements" to the Temple that filled Jesus with distaste. When he looked at the gilded Corinthian capitals and the expanse of marble pavement stretching out across the esplanade, he saw only the sweat and blood of the peasant families at whose expense all this excess had been built. He may have remembered Jeremiah's rebuke, spoken right here in the Temple: "Thus says the Lord: . . . I did not speak to [your ancestors] or command them concerning burnt offerings and sacrifices. But this command I gave them: 'Obey my voice, and I will be your God!'" And he would have recalled Jeremiah's dire warning of what God would do if the people did not heed his call to repent: "I will do to the house that is called by my name what I did to Shiloh."[37]

That Jeremiah was on his mind is attested in the Gospel of Thomas, where Jesus quotes Jeremiah almost verbatim, using the same term "house" to denote the Temple: "I shall destroy [this] house, and no one will be able to build it."[38] Mark uses the same saying for his narrative, in which Jesus asks: "Do you see these great buildings? It will all be torn down, and not one stone will be left upon the other."[39] But Mark changes the intent of the saying. In his Gospel, Jesus' charge against the legitimacy of the sacrificial cult and the priesthood is turned into a prophecy of Jesus' own death and resurrection. Later, during the indictment by the chief priests, Mark introduces witnesses who quote Jesus as saying: "I will destroy this Temple that is made with human hands, and in three days I will build another, not made with hands."[40] Many years later, John conflated both into one cohesive prophecy: "Destroy this temple, and in three days I will raise it up."[41]

In the Gospel of Mark, however, the apostles did not yet sense the ominous meaning of Jesus' words. They probably stood and looked at him, momentarily taken aback by his sudden change of mood. Then they gathered themselves and followed him out of the forecourt. By nightfall they were back in Bethany, in the house of Mary and Martha.

It was a Wednesday, quite possibly the 13th of the Jewish month of Nisan in the year 3790—April 5 in the year 30 C.E., by our reckoning.

THE ARRIVAL OF PILATE

If Jesus and his followers had looked up toward the north, they undoubtedly would have seen a larger-than-usual contingent of Roman soldiers looking down from the parapets of the Antonia Fortress. This complex, as we saw earlier, had been built by Herod adjacent to the Temple for the specific purpose of maintaining law and order throughout the Temple precinct. Herod had anticipated that his vast esplanade would also make a convenient rallying point for demonstrations, or even a riot. In this, as in so many other cases, Herod was proven right. In 4 B.C.E., upon the king's death, this very forecourt had been the place where protestors had staged a demonstration against Archilaus and pelted a Roman cohort with stones, leading to reprisals that left three thousand worshipers dead. Significantly, this incident had taken place during the feast of Passover.

Ever since, Passover had been a time when the Roman forces went on high alert. Security was always tight during the three major festivals of Succoth, Weeks, and Passover, but Passover was especially sensitive. After all, this festival marked not only the agricultural feast of unleavened bread, but also the deliverance of Israel from an imperial tyrant, in this case the Pharaoh of Egypt. Consequently, it was Pilate's policy to beef up the Roman military presence whenever Passover was near.

Pilate, however, was painfully aware that his military resources were scarce. The principal force in Greater Syria, four legions strong, was bivouacked in Antioch-in-Syria, headquarters of the regional Roman Command. Given that, as a result of Tiberius's curious experiment with centralized management, Pilate's boss Aelius Lamia was based in Rome rather than Antioch, it was unlikely that Pilate would be able to call in any reinforcements on short notice.

Instead, he had only a small detachment of auxiliaries to maintain the peace. He knew the reason. Palestine was poor, so its tax yield did not justify the cost of maintaining a full Roman legion. Rome was sensitive to this issue: some time back, Cicero had made quite a stir by claiming that some of Rome's provinces could not justify the money it cost to defend them. Consequently, legions were usually stationed in big cities that could support a large garrison with taxes paid in coin, rather than in agricultural produce.[42] We're not sure how many troops Pilate had under his command, but it could not have numbered more than four or five cohorts of six hundred men each. Two of these cohorts were stationed at the Antonia Fortress. The other, more fortunate, ones were in permanent quarters in Caesarea on the Mediterranean coast. In addition, Pilate maintained a squadron of horse.

Pilate knew that two cohorts were wholly inadequate to police a city swelled by tens of thousands of pious worshipers. Since it was less than two years since the last Passover incident, the Temple massacre over the Aqueduct Affair, and tensions still ran high, the prefect had decided to travel to Jerusalem himself and inspire his troops and his subjects with his presence. He would leave a nominal presence in Caesarea and take all his remaining forces to Jerusalem.

It took him between two and three days to reach the city. First he followed the coastal road through the Plain of Sharon to Lydda. At this strategic intersection, he swung east toward Jerusalem, steadily ascending the winding road through the Judean foothills until he could see the west side of the Temple shimmering in the distance. Pilate himself probably rode on a horse, screened by his cavalry for protection, and preceded by the *aquilifer,* who carried the Roman standard. This standard-bearer, in turn, was followed by the *milites,* or foot soldiers, though they could hardly be called the cream of the Roman forces. With the expansion of the Roman Empire, Rome itself did not have enough soldiers to police its vast new territory, so it increased the number of its legions by recruiting soldiers in the provinces. By the time of Jesus, there were thirty legions serving in various parts of the Empire, plus large numbers of "auxiliary" forces.

The difference between a legionnaire and an auxiliary is significant. Legionnaires were selected from the most promising local recruits and given superior training and equipment. They were invariably both bright and tall. The Roman army placed a premium on height, with a minimum requirement of five feet eight inches. This would have disqualified most young men on the Italian mainland; based on excavations at Pompeii and Herculaneum, Roman men were between five feet four inches and five feet eight inches high, whereas women rarely exceeded five feet five inches. Foreign legionnaires automatically became Roman citizens upon their enlistment in the Roman army and were therefore a highly disciplined and motivated force.

Auxiliaries were a different sort altogether. Culled from second-class recruits, they were given inferior equipment and often wore an odd assortment of clothing and armor. Unlike a legionnaire, an auxiliary had to serve for twenty-five years, with an exemplary record, before being granted Roman citizenship. They received less pay, lower-quality food rations, and certainly less respect from the other ranks.

Judea ranked low in the hierarchy of Roman imperial possessions, so Pilate probably would have been given cohorts consisting of auxiliaries rather than legionnaires. Since no Jew would have served in the Roman army of occupation, most of these auxiliaries would have been recruited in Syria or in Phoenicia. As Gentiles, lacking the discipline of Roman legionnaires, they were looked upon by the Judeans with scorn.

The sentiment was mutual. During the Passover of 44 C.E., fourteen years after Jesus' arrest, a detachment of Roman auxiliaries would once again be ordered to provide a show of force to preempt any civil disturbance. On this occasion, a group of soldiers decided to take up position on the roof of the Temple portico. Naturally, the worshipers took immediate umbrage at Roman soldiers treading on the roof of their sacred Temple. Insults were tossed back and forth. On impulse, one of the soldiers turned, raised his robe, and "mooned" the worshipers, punctuating this gesture with bursts of flatulence. Outraged, the crowd began throwing stones, demanding that the offending soldier be punished. This took the serving prefect of Judea, Ventidius Cumanus, completely by surprise. Rather than placating the crowd by reprimanding the culprit, he sent in reinforcements from the Antonia instead. As the soldiers swarmed over the forecourt and into the Courts, panic ensued. Men, women, and children rushed the gates, where they were trampled by others desperate to flee the forecourt. In the melee, says Josephus, some 30,000 pilgrims were crushed to death.[43]

Such a force of auxiliaries, then, had now arrived in Jerusalem to maintain the peace during the most volatile time of the year. To do so, they had been issued the standard kit of a Roman soldier. This included a helmet of the traditional *Montefortino* type used throughout the late Republic period. Only elite forces had recently begun to receive the superior Gallic helmet with its trademark scalloped ear and neck guards. These are often—incorrectly—depicted in paintings of Jesus' Passion, since it is highly unlikely that auxiliaries would have been equipped with them. Next came a short sword known among the ranks as the *gladius hispaniensis,* in fond memory of the swords first used by the Spanish auxiliaries of Hannibal. It was a feared weapon, for with its twenty-inch length and razor-sharp edge it could be used to both parry and thrust, usually with lethal results. For protection, the soldiers were issued a shield that veterans still called the *scutum,* even though it had long since shed its oval shape. This shield was a short, rectangular design, less than three feet high, and made from strips of wood about two inches thick. But the most prized possession of an auxiliary soldier was the weapon that would figure prominently in Jesus' Passion, the six-foot javelin, or *pilum.* The Roman army knew various types of spears, either for close-in work or for use as long-range missiles, but the *pilum* was a happy combination of both. Its twenty-inch metal tip, sharpened to a point, was traditionally affixed to the wooden shaft with two iron rivets until the renowned general Marius changed this design by using one rivet of iron and one of wood. Now the *pilum* broke on impact with an enemy's body so that it could not be thrown back at the Romans. Handling the heavy *pilum* was difficult, however, and often reserved for specialists, known as *immunes.* Immunes were skilled soldiers who had been specifically trained for a range of tasks required of an occupying army. One of these was the art of prisoner crucifixion.

THE NIGHT OF UNLEAVENED BREAD

As Jesus and his followers began their walk back to Bethany and the gates of the Temple were closed, the Night of Unleavened Bread began. On this evening, the head of every Jewish household was expected to search his home and gather any remaining crumbs of *chametz*—leavened bread made from wheat, oats, or barley dough that had risen through contact with water. Such leaven was utterly eschewed during the Week of Unleavened Bread, which would officially begin the next day. During the next seven days, Jews all over Palestine and the Diaspora would consume the hard, cracker-like bread made from unleavened dough and remember the day when their forefathers hastily prepared to flee from Egypt, with no time to wait for the dough to rise.

All over Jerusalem, fathers and husbands lit an oil lamp and embarked on their quest. Not a single morsel of leaven should remain to despoil the house during the Passover feast.[44] To mark the point where the search began, every man placed a piece of bread in a prominent place, such as a windowsill overlooking the street.

Back in the Upper City, in one of the palatial mansions within view of the Temple, Caiaphas would have been doing the same. On that night, Caiaphas had been in office as the *Kohen Gadol,* high priest of the Jewish nation, for twelve years. They had been twelve difficult years, punctuated with unrest, mass demonstrations, and occasional violence, but through it all Caiaphas had rigorously maintained sacrificial operations at the Temple. One of the ways in which he had been able to accomplish this was by cultivating a close working relationship with Rome. One might not like the Romans, he must have thought, but they were here, and one had to make the best of the situation. He had worked hard to forge a businesslike understanding with Roman prefects, specifically the current one, Pontius Pilate. Caiaphas knew that as long as the peace was maintained, Pilate was willing to grant the high priest—and the Priestly Council he chaired, the Great Sanhedrin—considerable autonomy in domestic affairs. It was a *Realpolitik* that was wholeheartedly encouraged by his father-in-law, Annas, who ruled one of Jerusalem's principal families and had himself held the high office from 6 to 15 C.E. Indeed, by assiduously cultivating close ties with the Roman prefecture, Annas would ensure that four of his sons would be appointed high priest in the years to come—in addition to the husband of his daughter, Caiaphas himself. That this invariably put him at odds with the Judean population was inevitable. As we have seen, Annas was viewed as a collaborationist who worked for his own interests rather than the interests of his people. But that had been the way of his office ever since the second century C.E.

In due course, Caiaphas finished the search of his house and found himself back at the door where he had started. "Blessed be Thou," he intoned, "who hast commanded us to remove the leaven." He straightened up, and continued, "All leaven which by chance remains in this house and which has escaped our observation will be destroyed and be like the dust of the earth." A servant stepped forward and held up a small cloth. In this the high priest carefully deposited all the leaven that he had collected. Careful not to spill anything, the servant tied the cloth into a tiny sack and hung it from a hook on one of the crossbeams. For good measure, he placed an oil lamp just underneath, lest the mice try to get at it.

THURSDAY, THE 14TH OF NISAN (APRIL 6, 30 C.E.)

Jesus and his followers woke early. They washed, shared a breakfast of crisp *matzo* bread, and prepared to leave for the Temple. They knew that on this day, after sunset, the feast of Passover would begin. Passover, or *Pesach* in Hebrew, was the joyous celebration of Israel's release from slavery in Egypt, when the children of Israel were spared or "passed over" as the angel of God slew all the Egyptian first-born. To mark their homes as Jewish, the Israelites were instructed to sacrifice a lamb and paint the door lintel with its blood.[45] They were to roast the lamb and eat it with unleavened bread while waiting for the signal to leave Egypt forever. Moses later decreed that Jews should "observe this rite as a perpetual ordinance."[46]

To do so, thousands of Jews from all over Palestine and the Roman world had converged on the Temple on this day, the 14th of Nisan, to sacrifice a Passover lamb on the altar. After they arrived in the forecourt, all worshipers and their lambs were organized in *kittot* or groups of thirty people each, since no more than thirty people could be present in the Court of the Priests at one time. After a group of thirty went in, the doors were closed, and the ceremony could begin. First, the lambs were tied to upright stakes in a section known as the Slaughtering House. The animals smelled the blood of the altar and bleated with all their might, trembling with fear. Then, on the cue of the choirmaster, the Levite choir began to sing the *Hallel* ("Praise God," with excerpts from Psalms 113 through 118), giving the signal to the priests to proceed. Gripping their beautifully carved ornamental knives, the priests quickly cut the throats of the lambs with one stroke, but carefully, so that the blood was caught in special silver vessels held by assistants. Blood was holy; as the essence of life, it could never be consumed by man, but belonged to YHWH alone. The silver vessels were passed along a long line of priests from the stakes to the altar, where senior prelates used special whisks of silver and gold to sprinkle the blood on the flames.

Meanwhile, each lamb was butchered. Organs destined for sacrifice—such as the neck, the liver, and the stomach—were separated from the consumable meat. This meat was then divided into two shares: one for the priesthood, and the other for the owner to take back home, to be eaten during the Passover meal.

The paschal lamb had to be between eight days and one year old, and free of any blemish.[47] Priests were posted at the gates to inspect the lambs brought into the esplanade and to reject any specimen that was discovered to have an injury or a blemish, no matter how small. The Temple recognized, naturally, that during the long journey from all corners of the nation much could happen, and a perfectly healthy lamb could meet with an unfortunate accident. So each year thousands of lambs were brought into Jerusalem and offered for sale to pilgrims—at high-season prices.

Originally, the sale of these paschal lambs took place on the Mount of Olives, at a special market called *Chanut*. But as Bruce Chilton writes, it was Caiaphas who had ordered the vendors to move from the Mount of Olives into the great forecourt of the Temple.[48] From his perspective, this change of venue had numerous advantages. First, priests could ensure that the animals offered for sale did indeed meet the stringent criteria of unblemished purity. Second, it minimized the chaotic conditions at the city gates, where formerly pilgrims and their animals had struggled to get through, often leaving a great many piles of manure in their wake. Third, the lucrative commerce in paschal lambs and doves would now take place under the noses of Caiaphas' priests—making sure that the Temple received a proper commission on each and every sale.

It may have looked good on paper, but in practice it was a disaster. What Caiaphas did not foresee is that the chaotic conditions that usually prevailed at the Chanut market and the city gates were now transferred inside the Temple proper. Instead of being an assembly area for the orderly processing of pilgrims and their sacrificial animals, the forecourt became a melee of anxious worshipers, pushing and shoving to get to the stalls before the best lambs were sold, meaning their journey to the sanctuary would be for naught. Worse, in order to purchase these animals, worshipers had to convert their common currency—either Herodian coins, money issued by the Romans, or foreign currency—into the only denomination permitted inside the Temple walls, the *shekel*. This magnified the already-chaotic conditions tenfold. The moneychangers who normally plied their trade inside the colonnade of the promenade were overwhelmed by the sheer press of thousands of pushing, begging, and shouting pilgrims. All sense of order in the Temple was lost as pilgrims fought to secure a place in one line or another, desperate to get their lambs before it was too late.

This is when Jesus appeared in the forecourt, and we can imagine his reaction. This was supposed to be the great day, the moment when Jesus would make his dramatic appeal to the nation, exhorting all of Israel, gathered in the Temple, to join him in building the Kingdom of God. No doubt he had rehearsed his words carefully throughout the long trek from the hills of Batanaea to the walls of Jerusalem. In his mind he may have seen himself, standing on one of the blocks or tables in the forecourt, opening his speech with the traditional invocation of a Hebrew prophet: *Thus says the Lord of hosts, the God of Israel.*

"Thus says the Lord of hosts, the God of Israel.
Amend your ways and your doings,
And let me dwell with you in this place!"[49]

Now the moment had arrived, and there he found himself, standing on one of the tables near the stalls of the moneychangers, surrounded by the seething mass of shoving worshipers. He shouted at the top of his lungs, anxious for the multitudes to turn away from the frenzied commerce and hear him. Perhaps he spoke the words that Jeremiah himself had hurled at this crowd seven hundred years earlier. If so, they would certainly have been appropriate:

Do not trust in these deceptive words.
"This is the temple of the Lord,
the temple of the Lord, the temple of the Lord."
For if you truly amend your ways and your doings,
If you truly act justly one with another,
If you do not oppress the alien, the orphan, or the widow,
or shed innocent blood in this place . . .
then I will dwell with you in this place.[50]

Some paused, momentarily intrigued; others strained to understand his words above the din of the forecourt. But the audience was soon carried along by others fighting to keep their position in the line for the money changers. Jesus saw it. He felt this moment, this great opportunity slipping from his grasp. And a great anger welled up inside him.

We have no evidence that this is how the tragic events of that day took shape. What we do know is what happened next. For Jesus turned his wrath on those who were ostensibly responsible for denying him his moment: the money changers. There they sat, hulking behind their tables, haggling over rates of exchange or counting their piles of currency—on this, the most sacred of all days, when the destiny of Israel hung in the balance. "And he began to drive out those who were selling and those who were buying in the temple, and he overturned the tables of the moneychangers and the seats of those who sold doves," says Mark.[51] And in that moment, Jesus did quote from Jeremiah's Temple sermon: "Has this house, which is called by my name, become a den of robbers?"[52]

These words, *a den of robbers,* reverberated against the limestone finish of the colonnade and were carried aloft to the upper floor of the Royal Stoa. There his words *were* heard, and they sealed Jesus' fate.

Slowly, the gears of Temple security began to turn. A gaggle of Levitical Guards, who served as the Temple police, rushed to the scene. As they converged on the Temple forecourt, the Roman patrols stationed on the roof of the Antonia stood to and summoned their commander. Horns were blown and orders shouted, and now the pandemonium was total. Seeing the onrushing guards, the crowds pushed and shoved to get out of the way. Bleating animals broke free, got lost in the multitude, and were trampled. Mothers screamed for children. The Temple forecourt became a scene of chaos.

Jesus did not wait for the Guards to apprehend him. Screened by thousands of bewildered pilgrims, he and his followers slipped away, no doubt determined to try again during the seven-day festival.

The Gospels don't portray the events in this manner. As we saw before, the evangelists were not concerned with chronology but with arranging the story in a way that sustained their theological message. In the Gospel of Mark, for example, Jesus returns the next day for a quiet conversation with the "priests, the scribes, and the elders."[53] In Mark's view, Jesus was the victim of a carefully plotted conspiracy that unfolded over many weeks and months, involving all the religious elites of the land. But many scholars of the historical Jesus agree that it was his impetuous attack on the money changers that brought him to the attention of the authorities and instantly branded him as a wanted man. Until then, it is doubtful that a *hasid* from Galilee would have appeared on the priesthood's radar; they had other, more urgent matters to attend to, such as avoiding an outbreak of violence like that of less than two years earlier. Rather, by inciting a violent demonstration in what was already a tense situation, Jesus had provoked the entire security apparatus of the Temple and the Roman army.

His angry outburst, *you have made it a den of thieves*—quoted from Jeremiah—was undoubtedly reported to the senior priesthood. This would have given the warrant for Jesus' arrest even greater priority. Even though they did not accord the Book of the Prophets equal authority with the Book of Law, the Sadducees would have been quite familiar with Jeremiah, and they would have known all too well that Jesus' outburst (and Jeremiah's) was directed not at the money changers but at the priests and their sacrificial system. Jeremiah had accused the priests of robbery because of their ruthless tithing of the harvest, ignoring the socioeconomic conditions of the peasantry. Jesus undoubtedly felt the same way, but by calling the high priest a thief, he may also have rekindled the people's hatred for this illegitimate usurper who had "stolen" Israel's highest office. What's more, the recent Aqueduct Affair—with the high priest embroiled in controversy over the use of Treasury funds—would have added a painful sting to the accusation. Jesus, in sum, had hurled at the priesthood one of the worst insults imaginable, and it hit very close to home.

We can only imagine Caiaphas's reaction. The last thing the high priest needed was a repeat of last season's protests. He insisted that this desperado be tracked down and caught immediately, at all costs, before he could instigate another riot. It had to be done quickly, using units of his own Temple Guard, before the Romans decided to intervene and turn all of Jerusalem upside down, destroying the sanctity of the festival in the process. And so it came to pass.

ELEVEN

ARREST AND EXECUTION

The first thing Caiaphas would have done was to post guards at all the gates leading out of the city. Then, with Jerusalem sealed off, he would have dispatched roving patrols on the main roads leading away from the city, including the eastern road leading to Bethany and Jericho beyond. Jerusalem itself was packed to the hilt with thousands of peasants squeezed into every nook and cranny. His best chance of catching the fugitive would be *outside* the city, on the open roads.

We do not know if Jesus and his followers were aware of the manhunt that was now underway, but their actions suggest that, at the very least, they were aware of the threat. To attempt to escape the city in broad daylight would have been madness. Better to wait for nightfall, and then, under cover of night, slip out of the city and try to reach Bethany before the coming of dawn.

Until then, however, the group had to keep a low profile and find a place where they would be safe from patrols and could share a meal. Mark tells us that Jesus dispatched two followers to look for shelter, which, at the very least, suggests that the stay in Jerusalem had not been planned in advance. After all, sunset would bring the beginning of Passover, one of the holiest feasts in the liturgical year. The Passover meal itself required elaborate preparations, and under normal circumstances we would expect Jesus and his followers to be back in Bethany. There, no doubt, Mary and Martha had been cooking and preparing the Passover meal since dawn.

But now Jesus and the disciples find themselves trapped in the city, faced with the need to find a house and lay low before attempting their escape. No one knows of a family that can offer sanctuary at such short notice. Where should they look? How should they even approach anyone? Jesus sends two of his disciples to go on a reconnaissance mission. They are to look for a *servant,* for a servant would typically serve a master with a house big enough to accommodate him. How to find such a servant? At the nearest city well, of course; sooner or later, everyone needs to go out and fetch fresh water, certainly on a day as holy as Passover. The two disciples follow Jesus' instructions to the letter. They spot a servant carrying a large jar of water, follow him back to his master's house, and boldly approach the owner, saying, "The Rabbi asks, where is a guest room where I may eat the Passover with my disciples?"[1]

The Gospel does not tell us if this master is annoyed at having such a large group of uninvited guests at such short notice, though his wife may have been. Preparing the *Seder* or Passover meal was (and still is) an elaborate process. First, the lamb meat brought back from the Temple was unwrapped and roasted on skewers made of pomegranate wood, using an oven set up especially for Passover in the courtyard of the house. While on the grill, the lamb was spiced with garlic cloves and repeatedly basted with honeyed olive oil. Other servants, meanwhile, were busy baking cakes of unleavened bread. Back in the kitchen, maids would have been preparing the bitter herbs prescribed for the Seder, such as parsley, mallows, chicory, and radishes. The purpose of these bitter herbs was to remind the Jews of their bitter time in Egypt. During the meal, the herbs would be dipped in a kind of sop called *charoseth,* consisting of various fruits pounded into a paste and mixed with vinegar and salt water. All of these items were carefully arranged in different vessels, each cleaned for this use.[2]

The actual portion of lamb meat eaten by each person during the Seder was very small. Therefore, the women would also be busy cooking a rich stew of lentils and barley to help round out the meal. They first heated the onions, garlic, carrots, and celery in olive oil until the vegetables were soft. They then added barley and lentils, covered the pot, and allowed it to simmer.

Meanwhile, the table was set. Deep wooden plates with high rims, of the type found at Qumran, were placed on the table. So were clay drinking cups, for wine was an important component of the paschal supper. The Mishnah says that in order to share Israel's joy of release on Passover night, the poorest, too, should have "no fewer than four cups of wine, and even if [the funds] come from public charity."[3] The wine consumed by Jesus and his followers would have been the usual local red variety. Only the rich could afford the fine Cypriot wine favored by the Romans. This wine would be mixed, one part wine to two parts water.

At last, sunset arrived and night fell. Jesus and his disciples reclined at the table in their hideaway, the followers jostling to get at Jesus' left. Jesus, however, was pensive. He had to face the possibility that their escape would not be successful or that somewhere on the long journey home he would be apprehended. With this in mind, he told them that if for any reason he could no longer be with them, they should continue this ritual of breaking bread, so as to honor his name and remember his teachings. "I confer on you, just as my Father has conferred on me, a kingdom, so that you may eat and drink at my table in my kingdom," says Jesus in Luke.[4] The "last supper" had become the first Eucharist (from the Greek word *eucharistia,* meaning "thanksgiving"), a rite celebrated by Christians as an integral element of the Mass. The words spoken during the Eucharist—"Blessed are you, Lord God of all creation, through your goodness we have this wine to offer, fruit of the vine and work of human hands"—are rooted in the traditional Jewish blessing of *Kiddush:* "Blessed are you, O Lord our God, King of the universe, who creates the fruit of the vine...." Jesus, however, brought an entirely new dimension to the *Kiddush* by adding that "This bread and this wine is my body and my blood that will be given up for you," thus sealing a new "covenant" between God and man.[5] The Last Supper with Jesus' disciples had become a spiritual substitute for the ritual *sacrifice* at the Temple—an idea that, as we have seen, was also current among the Essenes.

In the centuries to come, the "Last Supper" would become one of the most popular motifs in Christian art, from Leonardo da Vinci's fresco in the Convent of Santa Maria delle Grazie in Milan to the famous version by the Spanish surrealist Salvador Dalí. In virtually all of these portrayals—including the scene in Mel Gibson's *The Passion of the Christ*—Jesus is depicted with a big loaf of bread. None of the artists (nor, it seems, the filmmakers) realized that this was the first day of the Week of Unleavened Bread. Even touching such a loaf during this holy time would have been unthinkable. The bread that Jesus broke during the first Eucharist was not a loaf of bread at all, but the crispy, wafer-like bread known as *matzo.*

After the meal was finished, Mark reports, the followers sang hymns, as was customary on Passover. Eventually, they fell silent, and now their eyes would have turned to Jesus. The events of the day were slowly beginning to sink in, and they were looking to him for guidance. And Jesus, in turn, would have been hard pressed to hide his disillusionment. His great oration to all of Israel had come to naught. The city had turned its back on him in the hour of its greatest need. Not surprisingly, Jesus was "distressed and agitated."[6] *O Jerusalem,*

Jerusalem! he exclaimed; "How often would I have gathered your children together as a hen gathers her brood under her wings, and you refused."[7]

ARREST AND TRIAL

Sometime later that night, the followers deemed it safe to try to leave the city. They slipped past the walls unseen and, once in the Valley of Kidron, were swallowed up in the pitch-black night. The Gospels tell us that Jesus headed for the Mount of Olives. This made sense, for as we have seen, the road to Bethany and on to Jericho ran straight up the gentle slopes of this hill. But the followers were tired; the excitement of the day and the effects of a heavy meal must have made them sleepy. Midway on the Mount of Olives was a cave used for pressing oil, known as *gat-shemanim,* the origin of the name "Gethsemane." In the winter months, the cave would have been empty and well suited for a place of refuge. Believing themselves to be out of danger, the followers grate-fully collapsed on the floor of the cave and fell promptly asleep.

These and all events that followed are known to us from one source only, and that is Mark. Neither the Gospel of Thomas nor Q contain any reference to the Passion of Jesus, and the information in Matthew, Luke, and John is clearly derived from Mark, though with various embellishments. This has led scholars to conclude that the Passion material in Mark was based on an older document, now lost, putatively referred to as the "Cross Gospel." Fragments of this Cross Gospel may also have survived in another Christian text, the so-called Gospel of Peter, which was discovered in Egypt in 1886. Though church fathers from the third to the sixth century did not deem this document sufficiently authoritative for inclusion in the final canon of the New Testament, there is some indication that the Gospel of Peter enjoyed wide popularity in the century following the death of Jesus. Unlike "sayings documents" like Thomas and Q, the Gospel of Peter pro-vides a concise narrative of the Passion events, with details that deviate significantly from the version portrayed in the New Testament. Interestingly, the Gospel makes no attempt to link the events of the Passion with prophecy in the Hebrew Scriptures, though this, as we have seem, is a leading theme in Mark's Gospel.

In recent years another document has come to light that has stimulated as much excitement as the Gospel of Peter did in the late nineteenth cen-tury. This is the now-famous Gospel of Judas, which was published in 2006 in an initial translation by the National Geographic Society. This document, however, originated much later than the canonical Gospels, Q, or Thomas, and possibly later than the Gospel of Peter. As we have seen, there were many Christian sects and movements in the second and third centuries C.E. that broke away from the orthodox doctrine originally formulated by Paul. These movements sought to bolster their authority by writing "Gospels" ascribed (pseudonymously) to notable figures in Jesus' immediate circle, just as the "orthodox" group had done with the canonical Gospels. The sect that produced the Gospel of Judas, for reasons not fully understood, specifically sought to exculpate Judas—the disciple who "betrayed" Jesus.

Mark is explicit about Judas' purported guilt. "Judas Iscariot, who was one of the twelve," Mark tells us, "went to the chief priests in order to betray him." The chief priests were both surprised and delighted, "and promised to give him money." We can imagine why. The high priest would have known that the chances of catching Jesus in a city teeming with thousands of strangers—including many other Galileans—would have been almost impossible. The offer of one of Jesus' followers to lead the Guard to Jesus' hideout must have been heaven-sent. With this information, the priests could recall their roving patrols and concentrate their forces on the area where Jesus was believed to be later that night. Judas knew that later in the evening, the group was going to attempt a breakout toward the east, across the Mount of Olives.

Many scholars are inclined to accept the story of Judas, based on the so-called criterion of embarrassment. There is no way to cast the betrayal by one of Jesus' closest companions in a favorable light. It must have been one of those historical events that were too well known for the evangelists to ignore. Moreover, the theme of the apostles failing Jesus is a keynote of Mark's Gospel. Mark's disciples are dim-witted; they don't understand what Jesus is talking about; they fret and complain, or fight amongst themselves about who is the best and the brightest. In this, they are not unlike the Israelites in the desert, who try Moses' patience with their tireless whining and their weak faith in the Lord.

✤ ✤ ✤

So if we assume that Judas's betrayal was a historical fact, the question is: why? What could have motivated Judas to undertake such a despicable act?

What grievance did he have against Jesus? Mark doesn't tell us. The Gospel of Judas does. It argues that Judas acted according to Jesus' own specific instructions. According to this Gospel, Jesus knew that he had to suffer and die in order to fulfill what was foretold in the Scriptures. He merely relied on Judas to expedite his arrest and execution. Far from being a traitor, then, Judas was a deeply loyal and obedient follower who executed Jesus' order to the letter, notwithstanding his deep sorrow. The Gospel text may, in fact, reveal the hand of a Gnostic author for whom Jesus was a divine being through and through. Seen from this perspective, the "betrayal" was an act of mercy that released Jesus from his corporeal bonds and restored him as a divine being.

Scholarship has taken a different approach. It has, first and foremost, sought to analyze the provenance of Judas's name. The term *Iskariot* has often been linked to the name *sicarius,* Latin for "daggerman," an epithet sometimes associated with the Jewish party of the Zealots. These, as we will remember, were a group of tax evaders who in the decades to come would begin to form a militia. By attacking Roman and Jewish collaborationist interests, they are believed to have instigated the Jewish War of 66 C.E. Many Judeo-Christians felt that this rebellion was a catastrophe and that the Zealots were terrorists rather than resistance fighters. Judas probably fit that picture nicely.

But there may be another, more plausible explanation for Judas's name. *Iskariot* may simply indicate that Judas was a man (*Ish*) from *Kerioth*, a town in southern Judea. This is significant, for that would have made Judas the only non-Galilean in Jesus' inner circle. Given what we know about the Judean prejudice against Galileans, Judas may have felt that as a native Judean, he was best qualified to find a way out of the impasse—by entering into direct, face-to-face negotiations with the Temple authorities.

After all, there was no telling to what extent the priests were prepared to go to punish the group for its violent demonstration in the Temple fore-court. The Gospels certainly indicate that the apostles were fearful. They believed that their own lives, and not just Jesus', were in danger. By striking a deal by which Jesus, and *only* Jesus, would be taken into custody and the rest would be allowed to go free, Judas may have thought that he had made the best of an otherwise hopeless situation. For the last eighteen months, Jesus had repeatedly demonstrated his skill in parrying with learned scribes and Pharisees, and besting them in debate. By giving him an honest opportunity to make his case, in front of the full college of the Sanhedrin, Judas may have thought he was, indeed, acting in Jesus' best interests. After all, that was the reason Jesus had traveled to Jerusalem to begin with: to address the religious leaders and citizens of Jerusalem. It was a great deal preferable to the idea of running around like a fugitive, at risk of being cut down at any moment by an eager Guardsman.

That Judas had the full confidence of Jesus, and therefore enjoyed a close relationship with him, is suggested by John's claim that Judas was entrusted with the group's "money-box."[8] If he selected Judas as the movement's treasurer, Jesus must have trusted the man as an honest and reliable companion.

This leads us to the next question: namely, what was going through the mind of Jesus himself? Naturally, he would have been deeply concerned about the men and women in his care. Though Mark doesn't indicate this, it would have been wholly out of character for Jesus not to think about the safety of those who had faithfully followed him for these last few months and years. They were his "Kingdom," the tangible expression of the society he was trying to build, no matter how much they sometimes disappointed him. I believe Jesus would have agreed with Judas that it was his first priority to see the women and the men safely into Bethany. The evangelist John seems to agree; in his version of Mark's Passion, the Temple guards ask Jesus if he is the one they're looking for. "I am he," is the response; "so, if you seek me, let these men go."[9]

Likewise, the prospect of facing the Great Sanhedrin and arguing his Kingdom ideology may not have fazed Jesus in the least. Indeed, he might have welcomed it; his calm demeanor during the actual arrest and subsequent indictment certainly seems to indicate as much. Lastly, the fact that none of the Gospels place Judas at the actual indictment proceedings and subsequent "trial" is a major point in his favor. As one who had known Jesus throughout the Galilean campaign, Judas would have been a highly credible witness whose testimony of the Temple disturbance could have been quite damaging. No doubt the chief priests would have pressed him to appear, perhaps by offering him more money (since the thirty shekels of silver was, by any measure, a paltry sum). But Judas must have declined to do so, for clearly that was never his intention. He had secured the release of the followers and given Jesus his day in court; he would not be party to anything that could incriminate his teacher and leader.

And what is the worst that could have happened? Let's look at the precedents. The "worst case," obviously, is what happened to John, who was beheaded. But that took place in Perea, under the jurisdiction of a Herodian, the tetrarch Antipas, and under the threat of war. Jesus was not in Perea, nor in Galilee, for that matter: he was in Judea. That placed him under the jurisdiction of the Sanhedrin and, by extension, the Romans. Jesus had never done or said anything to upset the Romans. On the contrary; when asked about paying the Roman tribute, clearly a major factor in the oppression of the Galilean peasantry, Jesus had said that one should "Give Caesar what belongs to Caesar, [and] give God what belongs to God." This quote appears in all the synoptic Gospels as well as Thomas, which argues strongly for its authenticity.[10] Unlike the later Zealots, Jesus did not believe resistance to the Roman occupation was the solution to Israel's ills. The Hebrew Scriptures were full of stories of what happened when Israel went against a far more powerful enemy. Jesus had no great love for the Romans and certainly despised their pagan influence; but his family had observed, firsthand, the devastation wrought by Roman reprisals in his own native Galilee. He had no intention of bringing such a calamity on his people again. Jesus' sole focus was to reform Judaism from within, to purge it and restore it as a reflection of the Kingdom of God that was to come. So from that quarter, Jesus must have believed he had nothing to fear.

That left the priestly authorities. Here again, the precedent of his great model, the prophet Jeremiah, may have been foremost in his mind. As it happened, Jeremiah had also run afoul of the Temple authorities after his great sermon in the Temple forecourt. Jeremiah's repeated calls for repentance to avoid God's wrath had provoked the ire of the priest Pashhur, the chief officer in charge of the Temple Guard, "who heard Jeremiah prophesying these things."[11] Pashhur arrested Jeremiah, ordered him to be beaten, and threw him in the stockade located in the Temple proper. He assumed that a night in jail would bring Jeremiah to his senses. But the next day Jeremiah repeated his sermon with even greater ferocity, crying, "I must shout, 'Violence and destruction!'" His oratory won the day. Jeremiah was released, though forbidden to enter the Temple area. So the prophet simply began dictating his sermons to a devoted follower, Baruch, who went to the Temple and preached on his master's behalf.

Closer to home, in Jesus' own century, there were other examples of dissidents who attacked the priesthood and got away with it. One such individual was a man whose story bears a remarkable similarity to that of Jesus. He too was a peasant; he too decided to go to the Temple during a major festival and urged the crowds to take heed. Remarkably, his name was Jesus also—Jesus, son of Ananias, to be exact. The festival was Pentecost in the year 62 C.E., during the prefecture of Albinus. This Jesus walked into the Temple forecourt and began to cry, "A voice from the east, a voice from the west, a voice from the four winds, a voice against Jerusalem and the holy house, and a voice against this whole people!" This he continued to do, day and night, until he was arrested and scourged for his trouble. Jesus *bar* Ananias absorbed his punishment with equanimity, was released, and promptly resumed his rounds, screaming his dire predictions at the top of his lungs.[12]

In fact, the only dissident who had been accused of denouncing the Temple and punished as a blasphemer with death was the disciple Stephen. Stephen had been dragged in front of the Sanhedrin, says Luke, the author of Acts, by members of a local synagogue of "Freedmen," who then presented "false witnesses" about some of Stephen's statements to the court.[13] Scholars caution that the circumstances of his death as described in Acts are remarkably similar to those of Jesus. What's more, the Sanhedrin is never seen to rule for or against Stephen; he is simply "dragged out of the city" by a mob and stoned to death.[14]

Prophets had always run the gauntlet in Israel, walking a fine line between communicating the will of the Lord and securing the confidence of the ruling power. It was not an occupation for the squeamish—a reason, perhaps, why so many prophets in Israel's history embraced their calling only with reluctance. But there is absolutely no reason why Jesus should have thought that a death sentence was inevitable. A prison sentence, yes; a thorough beating, almost certainly; but this would have been an acceptable price to pay if, by doing so, he secured a hearing in front of the religious leadership of the nation.

I am well aware that this reconstruction contradicts Mark's Gospel, in which Jesus repeatedly voices a premonition of his coming death *by crucifixion*. That foreshadowing, however, can only be the product of Mark's desire to cast key events as the fulfillment of prophecy, either by the Scriptures or by Jesus himself.[15] Such fulfillment, as we have seen, was meant to corroborate Mark's case that Jesus was the Messiah foretold in the Old Testament. But nowhere do the Hebrew Scriptures state that the Messiah *must die* in order to redeem his people. On the contrary; a dead commander would not be much use in the liberation of his people.

In fact, historical precedent argues against the premonition of death. Jesus had every reason to think that if apprehended, he would face the Council of the Sanhedrin and suffer corporal punishment. And while a death sentence was always a possibility *in extremis,* it was certainly not inevitable; and if, for any reason, Jesus had been condemned to die, he would have been executed by stoning (as in the case of Stephen) or beheading (as in the case of John the Baptist and James, brother of Jesus, who was condemned on orders of king Herod Agrippa I). Josephus also reports the execution of James, but states that he was thrown off the Temple parapet and stoned to death.[16]

The *Tractate Sanhedrin* in the Mishnah lists four methods of execution used by the Sanhedrin: stoning, burning, decapitation, and strangulation.[17] Jewish authorities did not use crucifixion; that was a Roman form of execution, and Jesus had no reason to think that the Romans would take an interest in his case. His crime, such as it was, was disturbing the peace in the Temple forecourt, provoking the priesthood, and prophesying, like Jeremiah, that the Temple would be destroyed. All these were matters of a religious nature, which therefore fell under the jurisdiction of the Great Council of the Sanhedrin.

This is extremely important, because the *full* Sanhedrin consisted of some seventy-one members, many of whom were not Sadducees, but Pharisees.[18] As I have sought to argue in the foregoing, the Pharisees had ample reason to take issue with some of Jesus' teachings, but no motive whatsoever for seeing him removed from the scene. On the contrary; if there was one foe with whom the Pharisees were in almost daily conflict, it was the Sadducees, not a poor *hasid* from the provinces. A *hasid,* moreover, who taught an interpretation of the Law that had much in common with that great Pharisaic sage, Rabbi Hillel, albeit in a rather unorthodox manner. Far from being a threat, Jesus would have been perceived as an ally against the Sadducee hegemony.

Jesus had, therefore, every reason to believe that if and when he had his day in court—in front of a true quorum of the Sanhedrin—he could rely on a sympathetic hearing from the Court's quite powerful Pharisaic wing. The Gospels admit as much by confirming that it was Joseph of Arimathea, "a respected member of the Council" and thus very likely a Pharisee, who later appealed to Pilate for the release of Jesus' body.[19]

THE ARREST ON THE MOUNT OF OLIVES

It was now late on the evening of Passover, and the Temple Guards were closing in on Jesus' hideaway on the Mount of Olives. Already they had posted sentinels at all footpaths leading to the Bethany road. With the hill thus secured, they could proceed to tighten the noose around Jesus.

Popular paintings and films always picture this moment as a serene, moonlit scene, with Jesus praying to God in quiet solitude while the apostles sleep. The reality was nothing like this. On Passover night, the Mount of Olives would have been covered with hundreds of pilgrims, camping out under the stars, unable to afford the high-season rates for inns and private rooms in the city. The usually tranquil hill would be teeming with families hunkered around campfires, celebrating Passover with whatever they had been able to get their hands on. Few of them would have been able to afford a paschal lamb; instead, they would have scraped together enough pennies to buy a dove, and they would now be filling their bellies with vegetable stew, scooped out of the communal pot with a piece of hardtack *matzo*.

The Temple Guards knew this, of course, which is exactly why they insisted that Judas tag along. For only Judas could work his way through the multitude of standing, eating, and sleeping peasants, look each man in the eye, and identify Jesus to the Guards. This takes time—enough time for the followers to doze off and for Jesus to reflect on what lies ahead of him. But then the Guards are upon him. Judas steps forward and makes the agreed signal: he kisses Jesus, as disciples often did. Jesus looks around: his loyal followers, his apostles, have all deserted him and fled into the night. He is alone. Resistance is futile. He gives himself up; he is bound and led away, back toward Jerusalem.

But then Jesus senses that something is terribly wrong. He is not led to the Temple stockade, as Jeremiah was. He is taken straight to the magnificent home of Joseph son of Caiaphas, the high priest himself. Mark's description of this setting corresponds to the "Priestly House" excavated by Israeli archaeologist Nahman Avigad to a remarkable degree. Here, in this lavish home, was a large courtyard similar to the place where Peter warms his hands by the fire and is recognized by one of the servant girls.[20] Here, too, was an assembly hall for private gatherings, adorned with painted panels. It was in exactly such a room that Jesus is now destined to be arraigned.

"Now the chief priests and the whole council," Mark continues, "were looking for testimony against Jesus to put him to death."[21] This is Mark's imagination. It would have been impossible to squeeze all seventy-one members of the Sanhedrin into Caiaphas's salon; that is why full sessions of the Sanhedrin usually took place in the *Lishkat La-Gazit,* the Chamber of Hewn Stones in the Temple. The third-century Mishnah, which, as always, we must treat with some circumspection, states that "a tribe, a false prophet, or a high priest can only be tried by a court of seventy-one judges."[22] Naturally, one could question whether Jesus would have qualified as a "false prophet"; the principal reason for his arrest was his disturbance in the Temple. Even so, the Tractate Sanhedrin decrees that a minimum of twenty-three members was needed in order to constitute a quorum for any cases involving witnesses.[23] It would have been well-nigh impossible to summon even twenty-three members to Caiaphas's house on such short notice, certainly on Passover night. Sessions of the Sanhedrin invariably took place by day, not by night. Lastly, according to the Mishnah, the antebellum Sanhedrin was known for the *middath r'hzamim,* "quality of mercy."[24] It tended to err in favor of the defendant and, unless a particularly egregious crime was involved, went out of its way to try to find extenuating circumstances. Josephus furthermore attests that Pharisaic members of the Sanhedrin were less rigid in the execution of justice than the Sadducees.[25]

Caiaphas, of course, was a Sadducee, and Sadducees believed in rigorous application of the law on the principle "an eye for an eye."[26] Therefore, we may conclude that the men who gathered that night to decide on the fate of Jesus were not a representative quorum of the Sanhedrin but a group of

Caiaphas's cronies, the chief priests, Sadducees like himself, who were still smarting from the insult hurled at them in the Temple. In fact, by ordering Jesus to be brought to his home, under cloak of darkness, Caiaphas planned to circumvent the Sanhedrin and bring the *hasid* from Galilee to speedy judgment before his Pharisaic opponents could get wind of it. For Caiaphas knew that if Jesus were to be heard by the full Sanhedrin, a good many members of the Council would sympathize with his cause, and Jesus might get off with a mere beating.

The point of the whole exercise in the high priest's mansion, of course, was to condemn the insolent preacher to death. Caiaphas could not have it any other way. An example had to be set: blasphemy against the Temple and invective against the priesthood would not be tolerated. Outside, in the Lower City and beyond, there were at that moment thousands of peasants living in the most abject poverty, many of whom held the priesthood partly responsible for their condition. If he let this dissident go, who knew what could happen? How much support did this peasant enjoy among the pilgrims now crowding the city? Like Antipas before him, Caiaphas could not take the risk, no matter how slight, that this Jesus was the spearhead of a movement that, once unleashed, would be impossible to stop. And so, like Antipas, he resolved to nip the danger in the bud.

There he stands, this rake-thin *hasid* with his unkempt beard and matted hair, dumbfounded and wholly unprepared for the trap that Caiaphas has set for him. The chief priests confer. What can they accuse him of? After all, all the legalities must be observed. Despite the secrecy and irregularity of this hearing, the fact is that this had been a very public arrest, coming on the heels of a very public disturbance during one of the most public festivals in the year. What witnesses do we have? What did the man say?

The witnesses come forward, no doubt prepped by the priestly scribes. "We heard him say," says one, "I will destroy this temple that is made with hands, and in three days I will build another, not made with hands." A very unwelcome prophecy, to be sure, but not a capital crime. After all, many prophets had foretold the very same thing. The interrogation of the "eyewitnesses" continues. Word by word, Jesus' sermon in the Temple is parsed and analyzed. "He spoke about a kingdom," one may have said. In the

Gospel of Mark, Caiaphas then turns to Jesus and asks, "Are you the Messiah, the Son of the Blessed One?" Matthew puts it this way: "Tell us if you are the Messiah, the Son of God."[27] The phrasing of both questions is so Christian in tone and intent that it is almost certainly dialog written much later by the evangelists. Nothing in Hebrew Scripture suggests that the Messiah was also *the* Son of God.

But it may very well be that, somewhere along the way, the interrogation by the chief priests veered toward Jesus' messianic ambitions. John the Baptist was asked if he was the Messiah; it is quite plausible that Jesus would have been questioned along those lines as well. This is when Mark quotes Jesus as saying, "You will see the Son of Man seated at the right hand of the Power, and coming with the clouds of heaven." Whether Jesus really spoke this elaborate formula, paraphrasing both Psalm 110 and the Book of Daniel, is not clear.[28] But he may very well have identified himself as the Son of Man, just as he did throughout his campaign.

Up to this point, Caiaphas would have observed the proceedings with growing alarm. While the high priest very much wanted to see Jesus dead, he was unsure of how he should go about it. Scholars have debated this issue and remain sharply divided over the question of whether Caiaphas did, in fact, have the power to condemn a man to death. The Gospels seem to indicate that he did not, which is why Jesus was eventually handed over to the Romans.

The answer is actually quite simple. The Sanhedrin certainly had the power to sentence a man to death, as is attested in great detail in the Mishnah. We have seen how the Temple precinct was cordoned off by a low fence called the *soreg*. According to Josephus, marble tablets were posted at intervals of a hundred paces, warning any Gentile trespasser that if he was found beyond this boundary, he would be stoned to death. This precedent implicitly granted the Sanhedrin the authority to condemn those who violated the sanctity of the Temple. Paul discovered this, to his discomfort, when he was accused of taking Gentiles past the *soreg* and only escaped execution by appealing to his right, as a Roman citizen, to a proper trial under Roman law.[29] This account fits with a discovery in 1935, when archaeologists uncovered the very tablet described by Josephus in the Herodian wall located close to the Lion's Gate. The inscription, written in Greek, includes the word *thanathos*—Greek for "death."

My point, however, is that while the *Sanhedrin* may have had the power over life and death, the *high priest* and his immediate circle, by themselves, certainly did not—not while acting on their own initiative, without the sanction of the Priestly Council. And that put Caiaphas in a Catch-22 situation. Without the Sanhedrin, he could not condemn Jesus to death. But by involving the Sanhedrin, he ran the risk of Jesus' being exonerated by his opponents, the Pharisees.

Caiaphas then came up with the perfect solution: to turn the entire matter over to the man with whom he was on such excellent terms, namely Pontius Pilate. If asked, Pilate could order a man to death with a flick of the wrist. What's more, the prefect had the military resources to contain an uprising, should the execution of Jesus actually provoke such a thing.

At any other time, the idea of a Jewish high priest handing over a peasant rabbi to the hated Roman army would have been inconceivable. But Caiaphas was no ordinary high priest. Like his father-in-law Annas before him, he had cultivated a special relationship with the Roman prefect. This impression is reinforced by the way Pilate was able to get his hands on the Temple treasury without so much as a word of protest from the priesthood, as well as by the exceptional length of Caiaphas's term in office: eleven years. Usually, high priests—who in this period served at the pleasure of the Roman prefect—remained in office for no more than four years. Pilate must have been satisfied indeed with this very pliable high priest. Their close collaboration is also attested by the fact that when Pilate was dismissed from his office by his immediate superior—the new governor of Syria, Vitellius—Caiaphas was ousted as well.

Moreover, in the eyes of his Sadducee judges, Jesus was "not one of us." He was not a Judean, but a Galilean, a tribe whose religious integrity had always been suspect. Nor did Jesus belong to any of the power structures that may have rallied to his defense. Jesus was, in the truest sense of the word, a religious dissident. He was a social activist without a constituency among the elites. He stood alone. Therefore he was expendable.

All that remained for Caiaphas to do, therefore, was to find a suitable charge that would get the Romans involved. This was the whole objective of the mock indictment of Jesus in Caiaphas's residence, for the high priest knew all too well that without the participation of the Sanhedrin, these proceedings had no legal foundation whatsoever. And in this respect, the topic of Jesus' teachings must have had Caiaphas's keen interest. Jesus, some said, had talked about a *new kingdom*. A kingdom of God, to be sure, a theme that could be found throughout the Scriptures, but Caiaphas was confident that the Romans neither knew nor cared about the finer points of Jewish theology. It was a matter of record that Jesus had spread word of the coming of a new kingdom in Palestine of which, one could argue, he would be the herald, or even the Anointed One. That would please the Romans. They knew how to handle characters who went around preaching the overthrow of Roman law and order.

Caiaphas stood up and for appearance's sake tore his clothes, to demonstrate his outrage at this case of "blasphemy."[30] He could see the bewilderment on the face of the peasant rabbi in front of him. Still smarting from the humiliation in the Temple, the high priest must have savored the moment.

The realization that he would face a *Roman* tribunal must have come as a rude shock to Jesus. By rights, he should have been heard by a quorum of the Sanhedrin, where there was always the possibility that some on the Council would stand up for him. But in a Roman hearing, Jesus knew he wouldn't stand a chance. The Romans had little patience for the strange aspirations of this native religion. All they cared about was maintaining the peace and crushing those who threatened to upset it.

It is difficult to ascertain when and where the "trial," the next act in the drama, actually took place. The evangelists, and particularly Mark, often liked to telescope events into a short span of days. The idea of Jesus' arrest, trial, execution, and resurrection all taking place in seventy-two hours also appealed to early Christianity, as the custom arose to celebrate these events in a "Holy Week."

And so the Gospels tell us that while the Passover festival was still going on, Pilate sat in judgment of Jesus. This would imply that it was Friday, Passover day; in some eight hours, the Sabbath would begin. No doubt there was a large group of Jewish petitioners, advisers, and others eager to see Pilate and conclude their business before sundown. But Mark's account insists that "as soon as it was morning . . . they bound Jesus, led him away, and handed him over to Pilate," who thereupon initiated a hearing.[31] If our reckoning is correct, it must have been "the first hour" of the 15th of Nisan.[32]

FRIDAY, THE 15TH OF NISAN, ABOUT 7:00 A.M.

As the hearing opens, Mark tells us, Pilate reveals himself to be a most concerned and compassionate judge. Pilate is surprised that Jesus has little to say to his accusers. "Have you no answer?" he asks Jesus, perhaps wondering if the prisoner needs more time to study the prosecution's case. "See how many charges they bring against you!"[33]

In the Gospel of John, the portrayal of Pilate as a deeply reluctant judge, vexed by the obvious innocence of Jesus, is developed even further. Pilate, in fact, seems to engage in what could best be described as a Socratic debate.

"Are you the King of the Jews?" the prefect wants to know.

"Is this your question, or did others tell you about me?" Jesus fires back.

"I'm not a Jew, now, am I?" Pilate replies, somewhat defensively. "Your own nation and the chief priests have handed you over to me. What have you done?"

"My kingdom is not of this world."

Pilate ponders these words. "So," he says at last, "are you a king?"

"You say that I am a king," Jesus answers with the panache of a philosopher. "I came into this world to testify to the truth."

"Ah," says Pilate, "but what is truth?"

The Roman prefect nods sagely. He turns back to his audience, raises his hand, and declares that "I cannot find fault in this man."[34]

Howls arise from the crowd who have come to attend the trial. Undaunted, Pilate repeats this statement two more times, but the mob is ready to tear the place to pieces. Pilate walks back to Jesus and pleads with him: "Why do you refuse to speak to me? Do you not know that I have the power to release you or to crucify you?"

The chief priests, sensing that the momentum of the case is turning against them, unleash their last and most devastating volley. Pilate is hit with the oldest trick in the book: the charge of sedition against Rome. "If you release this man," they cry out, "you are no friend of the emperor. Everyone who claims to be a king sets himself against the emperor."[35]

This is an accusation that even Pilate cannot ignore. Deeply perturbed, he has no choice but to accede to the people's wishes. A formal charge is brought and recorded on a scroll. It reads: JESUS OF NAZARETH THE KING OF THE JEWS. But Pilate has the last word. When the chief priests object to the language, arguing that it should say "*I am* the King of the Jews," the Roman prefect resolutely refuses to do it. "What I have written, I have written," he says. And so, his dignity intact, Pilate makes his exit and the executioners take over.[36]

Few serious scholars contest the assertion that this dialog, filled with allusions to Scripture, is the work of John rather than the historical record. John, like Matthew and Luke, had only the sparse account of Mark to go on, so he filled in the blanks with theological material as best he could. We know, for example, that the Pilate depicted in the Gospels bears little resemblance to the historical Pilate. The latter, as we have seen, was a man who from the beginning of his term deliberately provoked Jewish sensitivities and wasted no time in crushing anyone whom he deemed a political liability. "Pilate," says the Jewish historian Philo, writing around 41 C.E., "[used] briberies, insults, robberies, outrages, wanton injuries, [and] constantly repeated executions without trial." A man, in short, of "ceaseless and supremely grievous cruelty."[37]

Why, then, would the evangelist Mark, on whose account the other evangelists rely, want to cast Pilate in such a favorable light? The reason is simple: Jewish Christianity, at the time of Mark's writing, was struggling mightily to win the respect of the Roman empire—and to carefully distance itself from the Jewish Revolt in Palestine (66–70 C.E.) that had caused the Empire so much trouble. It would not do for Mark to put the blame for the death of his hero on the very Romans—and other Hellenistic subjects of Rome—whom he was trying to convert. So who could take the blame for Jesus' condemnation instead? Why, the Pharisees, of course—the immediate precursors of the rabbis who, after the destruction of the Temple, took over the religious leadership of the nation. As the evangelists saw it, the Jews of *their* time, in the last quarter of the first century, had rejected the Messiah—the very man who had come to redeem them.

Jewish Christians were ostracized, banned from synagogues, in some quarters even persecuted. Since the Jewish rabbinical hierarchy had declared war on Christianity, it stood to reason that they were the ones who had condemned Jesus to begin with. "His blood be on us, and on our children!" the priests cry lustily in Matthew's account.[38] Some twenty-five years after Mark, when John wrote *his* Gospel, the relations between Jews and Christian Jews in Palestine had deteriorated to such a degree that John no longer bothered to make a distinction between "priests and Pharisees." In John's view, *all* the Jews were to blame.[39]

One cannot fault the evangelists for conveying the fear of a nascent Church in mortal danger. Their rejection by rabbinic Jewry stung, for Jesus had been a Jewish rabbi himself. What's more, it left early Christianity without a mooring, adrift in a pagan world that was only gradually warming up to the concept of Judeo–Christian monotheism. What the evangelists did not anticipate, however, is that by shifting the blame on Jesus' murder from the Romans to the *Sippenhaft,* the collective guilt of Judaism as a whole, they were laying the moral justification for centuries of anti-Semitic persecution to come.

When we look at the "trial" from a strictly historical perspective, the story is markedly different. After the indictment in the house of Caiaphas, Jesus would have been transferred into the custody of Pilate; all this is historically plausible. The Gospels refer to Pilate's "headquarters" (*praetorium,* literally the seat of the *praetor* or "commander"). We know of two locations that would have qualified: One was the old palace of Herod, a sprawling complex in the southwestern part of the city that was equipped with its own barracks and defensive towers. The other was the Antonia Fortress, the Herodian citadel adjacent to the Temple complex, where the main garrison of Jerusalem was based. Herod's palace would have been more comfortable, but it is more likely that Pilate chose to stay in the Antonia so that he could immediately order a sortie of his troops if the Passover crowd in the Temple showed an inclination toward insurrection.

Whether Pilate did supervise a "trial" is highly debatable. Next to architecture, Roman law was Rome's highest achievement; indeed, it was the reason that territories in the empire could look upon the *Pax Romana* as a blessing. But the type of jurisdiction made famous by the likes of Cicero, the *Ius Civile,* applied to Roman citizens only. As far as "territorials" were concerned, a far more ill-defined code applied, known as the *Ius Gentium—* the "law of nations." Praetors who dispensed law under this jurisdiction were given wide latitude, basically improvising as they went along. As we saw earlier, this is why Paul, a native of Tarsus and a Roman citizen, insisted on a trial in Rome rather than being at the mercy of a colonial kangaroo court in Caesarea or Jerusalem.

In fact, Mark's description of Jesus' trial follows the proceedings of a hearing under the *Ius Civile* to a T. If one or more citizen-accusers (*delatores* in Latin) leveled a charge at a defendant, and if this accusation was corroborated by at least two witnesses, then it was up to the defense to explain to the court why the defendant was innocent. In the Gospels, the role of Jesus' *delatores* is played by the "chief priests." The part of the "witnesses" is provided by the Jewish spectators—under the direction of the priests, of course. And the defense is provided by no one but Jesus himself. This is why, as the Gospels tell us, Pilate is "roundly amazed" that Jesus does not respond to the charges against him. Under the *Ius Civile,* in the absence of a proper defense, the verdict could be judged invalid and an appeal invited. That certainly would have been the case in Rome, where Mark may have witnessed many such trials in preparation for his story.

But this was Jerusalem, not Rome, and Jesus was a colonial, not a Roman citizen. The elaborate mechanism of the "trial" outlined here did not apply, for Jesus had been apprehended following a terrorist act (the disturbance in the Temple) and denounced by the highest Jewish authority in the land—the high priest. Under the *Ius Gentium,* under these conditions, there was no need for a trial. A mere declaration of the charge would have sufficed, followed by a nod of the praetor's head confirming the inevitable punishment. Sedition was automatically punishable by death, and Pilate had never shied away from punishing those who opposed him with the most severe measures at his disposal. So Philo is probably quite correct when he states that Pilate constantly ordered "executions without trial."

Jesus must have been in shock. All his life, from the earliest days of his childhood, he had witnessed the consequences of revolt against the might of Rome. He had always been careful to avoid a confrontation with the Roman occupation authority. Now here he stood, accused of plotting a rebellion against the Roman state. And Roman law required that such an act be punished with the most horrific instrument in its arsenal of horrors: crucifixion.

With the verdict read, Jesus was led away. Caiaphas's henchmen returned to their master, eager to give him the good news. Pilate turned to other matters, or perhaps to another meeting with petitioners and clients. Within the hour, the two men solely responsible for the death of Jesus—Caiaphas and Pilate—had already forgotten the rabbi from Galilee. He was as good as dead.

THE SCOURGING

Was Jesus executed forthwith? The Gospel of Mark tells us he was.[40] Some historians have charged that Pilate would not have risked offending Jewish sensibilities by executing Jesus during the Passover festival. But this is probably incorrect; the Covenant Law specifically decreed that executions (and many other undertakings) could proceed during religious festivals, provided that they never took place on the Sabbath.[41] Pilate may indeed have ordered Jesus put to death immediately, lest his imprisonment become a rallying cry for his (presumed) followers in the densely packed city. The way Pilate may have figured it, by the time the city had gone about its Passover rituals, the death of Jesus would be a fait accompli. Any chance of a spontaneous uprising on Jesus' behalf would have been nipped in the bud.

That meant that the Roman execution detail had to proceed at once with the scourging of the condemned.

The purpose of a thorough scourging is simple: to cause enough blood loss to weaken the victim prior to crucifixion. In 71 B.C.E., the Roman consul Crassus ordered Spartacus and his slave rebel army crucified along the Via Appia as a public warning. Six thousand slaves were crucified along Rome's busiest road at ten-yard intervals; many of these men, hardened by years of battle, survived for two days or more. But Jewish law demanded that a "hanged man" be taken down "from the tree" before sundown.[42] It was therefore important to bring the condemned man a few steps closer to death before he actually wound up at the stake.

In the courtyard of the Antonia, Jesus was flogged with a special whip, called a *flagrum*. Then the Roman soldiers threw knucklebones in a terrifying game called *Basilinda*, which, roughly translated, means "kingmaker." Such Roman dice from the time of Jesus have been recovered from the excavation of Sepphoris (the very city where Jesus worked as a youth). A Basilinda "game board" is still visible today on the pavement of the *Lithostrothon,* preserved in the monastery of the Sisters of Zion. Whoever won the game could choose a prisoner for special treatment. This unfortunate victim was first mock-worshiped as a king, then beaten senseless.

After the flogging was done, Jesus and other prisoners were lined up for their last journey to the execution grounds. Crucifixion was a time-consuming and labor-intensive affair, so the Gospels are probably correct when they state that Jesus was executed with other condemned men. Perhaps a crucifixion had already been planned to coincide with the Passover festival (which would have been entirely in character for Pilate).

The Gospels offer a dramatic scene of Jesus' last appearance, with Pilate telling the crowd "Ecce homo"—behold the man. But it is far more likely that there was no public showing. The last thing Pilate needed was a public display of a Jewish rebel in the city proper while the man was still alive, with the risk of provoking a rebellion. Indeed, in John's scenario, the sole purpose of the "crowds" howling for the death of Jesus is to shift the collective complicity of Jesus' murder onto the Jews.

Nor was there a dramatic choice between Jesus and a thief called Barrabas after the scourging. There is no evidence of any amnesty during Jewish holidays in Palestine—not in Roman records, nor in the Talmudic literature, nor in the works of Josephus (who might have seized on such a show of mercy to underscore the fundamentally benign character of Roman rule). The Romans did not practice democracy in the colonies, and they were not about to give the rabble a say in how they maintained law and order. The very thought of releasing a career criminal like Barrabas on the eve of the most volatile day in the year would have struck Pilate as absurd.

THE CRUCIFIXION

Jesus was hauled to his feet and ordered to carry the instrument of his own death. Dressed in his rough tunic, which was now encrusted with dried blood, he was led out of the gates of the Antonia Fortress to the place of execution.

Pilgrims refer to the route of Jesus' Passion as the Via Dolorosa, Latin for "Road of Sorrow." According to local tradition, it begins some three hundred steps from St. Stephen's Gate near the Madrasa al-Dawadarrya, and continues through the warren of narrow streets to the Church of the Holy Sepulchre. Along the way are plaques commemorating the fourteen stations of the Cross, each marking the spot where the Gospels place a certain event in the Passion story.

The Madrasa, an Islamic school, is the site where archaeologists have tentatively identified the remains of the Roman Antonia fortress. Nearby is a lovely Franciscan monastery that contains the presumed site of the Flagellation. Farther down the cobblestone pavement is a fragment of a Roman arch, long associated with the scene in the Gospels when Jesus, bleeding from his scourging, is shown to the people by Pilate. The arch can also be glimpsed in the nearby convent of the Sisters of Zion; part of this Roman structure runs right behind the altar of its chapel. However, archaeologists now believe that the arch dates from the time of Hadrian, around 135 C.E.—over a hundred years after the crucifixion of Jesus.

Is the Via Dolorosa truly the road Jesus walked from the Antonia Fortress to the execution hill? Unfortunately, the answer is no. The Jerusalem that Jesus knew was thoroughly destroyed—literally obliterated—by a vengeful Roman army after the second major Jewish rebellion, led by Bar Kochba in 135 C.E. Much of what we see in the Old City today was, in fact, built during the Mamluk period (1248–1516 C.E.), when Jerusalem was one of the foremost cities of the Turkish Empire.

The image of Jesus carrying his cross along the Via Dolorosa has indelibly impressed itself on generations of Christians. But this image is not accurate either. Wood was extremely sparse in Jerusalem, so the Romans had to compromise. They had erected a number of permanent upright stakes in the designated kill zone, a hill known as Skull (*Calvaria* in Latin; *Golgotha* in Aramaic). Jesus, like other condemned criminals, carried only a crossbeam, known as a *patibulum*. What's more, carrying the entire cross would have been beyond the strength of any ordinary man, whether scourged or not. But the crossbeam was heavy enough—at least seventy-five pounds, by some scholars' reckoning.

There is no way to establish for certain where Golgotha was located. Tradition holds that the place is marked by the Church of the Holy Sepulchre in the Christian Quarter of Jerusalem's Old City. As early as the second century, we are told, Christian pilgrims came to pray at the spot, even though it was then covered by a pagan temple dedicated to Venus. In the fourth century, Queen Helena, mother of the emperor Constantine, ordered the pagan shrine torn down and began to excavate. In due course, workers located a pit into which a number of "used" crosses had been flung. This was sufficient proof for the Queen Mother, who unerringly identified one particular cross as the one used for the crucifixion of Jesus.

There is only one problem. Some archaeological studies, since contested, indicate that the Temple of Venus was located *inside* the original walls that encircled Jerusalem in Jesus' time. And as both Biblical and Roman sources attest, an execution hill like Golgotha was always located *outside* the city walls.

Another site with a claim to be Calvary is the Garden Tomb in East Jerusalem, just outside Nablus Road. It is well outside the original city; what's more, the place prides itself on a hill (called *el-Edhemieh*) that to this day bears an uncanny resemblance to a human skull. It also has a nearly intact Jewish tomb, complete with a ridge to hold a rolling stone; and as we shall see shortly, the tomb where Jesus was ultimately laid to rest was reported to be close to the execution site. Unfortunately, the Garden Tomb itself has recently been proven to date from the second century B.C.E. Some scholars now surmise that several Jewish tombs could be hidden under the soil of the *eastern* side of the hill, today the site of a Muslim cemetery.[43]

Regardless of where Jesus was taken, it could not have been a very great distance from the Antonia Fortress; such a decision would defy military logic. By choosing an execution ground within sight of the Antonia, the garrison commander could keep a close eye on things as executions got under way.

Slowly, Jesus makes his way through the city and out the gates, stumbling under the weight of the crossbeam. The sun is up, but the air is still cold. There are only a few people in the street, since most Jews are preparing to go to the Temple, which lies in the opposite direction. The few passersby are mostly women and servants, carrying pitchers; they have been tasked to get water from public cisterns for the rites of purification at home. These people stop and stare, overwhelmed by pity for this man in tattered clothes and horrified by the cruelty of the Romans. But all stay well away. Contact with this man, whose wounds are bleeding profusely under the chafing weight of the wood, would contaminate them and render the water they are carrying impure.

Halfway to the hill, Jesus can't take it any longer. Once, as a *tektoon*, Jesus had been strong and muscular; but the years in the field, subsisting on a diet of handouts, have left him thin and gangly. He falls. The Roman officer in charge of the execution detail curses in Aramaic—like most soldiers of the garrison, he is a Syrian recruit, not a native of the Italian peninsula. He kicks the prostrate man under the beam repeatedly, but Jesus lacks the strength to get up.

With his sweaty brow pressed in the dirt of the Holy City, Jesus no doubt wants to die right there and then. But the officer of the detail is a resourceful man. He looks around for a big, strong bystander—and sees Simon of Cyrene.[44] We don't know who this man is; the Gospels do not give any further details. But Simon complies. He knows that contact with Jesus' blood will make him instantly impure, but he doubts that he can make the Roman officer understand. And so he stretches out his hands, takes the rough wooden beam, and hefts it on his shoulder. Jesus is dragged to his feet. The procession continues.

Shortly thereafter, Jesus arrives, exhausted, at the place of execution. He is stripped. The Romans take perverse delight in inflicting this last insult on the condemned, for they know that modesty is a prized virtue among Jews. Naked, Jesus is forced down onto the crossbeam. His arms are stretched out and bound to it. Now, with their victim immobilized, the Romans can proceed at leisure with the actual crucifixion. Out comes a handful of metal nails, which they dangle before Jesus' eyes. The Roman nails were quite large—some six inches in length—and immensely strong. The biggest man in the cohort, a soldier with the muscled arms of a wrestler, pulls a mallet from his knapsack and takes one of the nails. Slowly, giving Jesus ample time to observe his movements, he places the nail above Jesus' left forearm, near the radius. A tiny prick—just enough to draw blood. Then he raises the mallet and brings it down on the nail with all his strength. The nail drives through the arm, producing a gush of blood—though not as much as we might think. Jesus has been slowly bleeding to death for quite some time now, and his blood pressure is well below normal.

But the pain is overwhelming, excruciating, impossible to bear. The nail has hit the median nerve, causing causalgia—one of the most intense pains imaginable. Jesus screams. The Romans laugh. The executioner gets up, brushes the dirt off his knees, and in the same leisurely manner makes his way to the other side to repeat the procedure with the right forearm. Then two or three soldiers raise the crossbar, with Jesus attached to it, and place it in a notch on top of the stake. Jesus is now suspended from a cross in the shape of a capital T, the form of cross known as *tau*. The *patibulum* is fastened to the stake with a rope, and perhaps with a nail for good measure.

Christian paintings invariably depict Jesus nailed to a cross through his hands, towering high above the people. This popular image is wrong on three counts: First, the soft tissue of the human hand is not strong enough to hold the weight of a human body. Second, Jesus was crucified on a T rather than a true cross. And third, he was raised just a foot or so above the ground, within easy reach of his executioners. This made it easier to get the victims on and off the cross, as well as to taunt and spit on them. It also simplified the last procedure, which was to affix the feet of Jesus to the upright stake.

Christian art typically shows a nail going through the *fronts* of both feet before entering the cross. But in that posture, the feet cannot support the body. In reality, the Romans squeezed the ankles of Jesus sideways into a small wooden block, shaped in the form of a U; this block was then affixed to the upright stake, with the nail cutting through both the heel or ankle bones and the block. The action also pressed the legs together and bent them, so that Jesus seemed to be kneeling sideways.

The details of this gruesome procedure only came to light in 1986, when the skeleton of another Jewish victim from the first century was excavated in the vicinity of Jerusalem. The anklebones of the condemned man, known as Yehohanan, were still affixed to a Roman nail, which had been bent. Fragments of wood were visible on both sides of the ankles. What's more, Yehohanan's radii had been chafed, indicating that he had hung from nails driven into his forearms.[45]

The Roman soldiers step back. Jesus is suspended from the T-bar, shivering from shock and loss of blood. In this posture, it becomes increasingly difficult to breathe. This is the exquisite cruelty of the punishment: in order to breathe, he must lift himself up; by lifting himself up, he puts more strain on his nailed limbs, bringing fresh pain.[46]

As is customary, the Romans nail a sign to the cross that describes the crime of the accused. After all, the ultimate purpose of a public crucifixion is to act as a deterrence. In Jesus' case, the notice reads, mockingly, *King of the Jews.*

It is the fourth hour: Friday, the 15th of Nisan, around 10:00 A.M.[47]

✛ ✛ ✛

For five long hours, Jesus struggles on the cross. Each breath he takes sears his body with pain, and yet the will to breathe is too strong: it forces him to lift himself on his arms and his feet again and again. Before his eyes, Jerusalem wakes up and goes about its business. It is Passover Day. All around the city, people head for the Temple in their best garments, preparing to thank God for the deliverance from Egypt.

The soldiers and a few bystanders are sitting down. Now that the initial excitement of the crucifixion is over, they are bored. They throw dice for the clothes of Jesus and the other accused, which was by custom the prerogative of the execution detail. Foreign auxiliaries in the employ of Rome made the paltry salary of 225 *denarii* per year, less deductions for food and arms, so any opportunity for additional income was greatly prized.

Jesus is now terribly thirsty; the loss of blood and the rising heat of the day have dehydrated him. He calls repeatedly for water. At last, a soldier takes pity on him. With his spear, he jabs a sponge and dunks it in the bucket of wine mixed with water that the soldiers have brought along for refreshment.[48] His comrades loudly protest, but the soldier lifts the dripping sponge and holds it out for Jesus to suck from. Jesus drinks greedily, but the succor is short-lived. The soldier pulls the sponge away, grins, and squeezes the rest of the liquid onto the soil.

The sun slowly tracks across the killing field. The cicadas in the olive trees nearby begin their afternoon song, providing a welcome relief from the unending moans coming from the broken bodies on the stakes. Most sightseers have gone home. Suddenly Jesus cries out with all his might, *"Eloi, Eloi, lama sabachthani?"*

Here, as in other places, the Gospel of Mark may be using the original Aramaic of the Cross Gospel, the Passion tradition underlying his story. We can certainly imagine Jesus, at this supreme moment of agony, feeling utterly abandoned by his *Abba.* On the other hand, the cry *Lord, Lord, why have you forsaken me?* is a verbatim quote from Psalm 22 and may have been interpolated by the evangelist to underscore the idea that Scriptural prophecy has been fulfilled.

Exhausted, Jesus sags against the ropes and nails that hold him. He no longer has the strength to force air into his lungs. The young dissident from Nazareth dies of asphyxiation, compounded by shock and blood loss, shortly after the ninth hour, at approximately 3:10 P.M.

AFTERMATH

The Roman soldiers decide to call it a day. Already the sun has bathed the city walls with the golden light that heralds the dusk. They cannot leave the victims on the crosses, as they would anywhere else in the Roman Empire. In Jerusalem, in deference to the Mosaic Laws, a "hanged man" must be taken down before sundown.[49] And so they take the mallet and move from cross to cross, smashing the legs of each condemned man. The purpose is simple: once his legs are broken, the victim can no longer raise himself to breathe. One by one, the condemned men struggle, gulp for air, and suffocate in agony.[50] Within a few minutes, all the victims are dead. One of the soldiers raises his mallet to break the legs of Jesus too; but then he wonders whether Jesus is already dead. The soldier takes his *pilum* and pierces Jesus' side.[51] There is no reaction. Jesus has been dead for more than an hour.

The ropes are untied and the nails are driven out—carefully, so as not to break them. The soldiers fight over who gets what. They know that people in Palestine and Syria attribute magical powers to nails used in a crucifixion. Each nail can command a hefty price, if the negotiation is done right. One by one, the corpses are dumped in a pit nearby, to be carrion for birds and wild dogs. It is the last humiliation of crucifixion—denying a man a proper burial in his family plot or tomb. In later years, the *Mishnah* and the *Talmud* will confirm that condemned men may not be buried in their family plots, only in designated graveyards.[52]

Suddenly, a man rushes up to the centurion in charge of the cohort, breathlessly holding out a written order from Pilate. The order states that if the officer can confirm that Jesus is dead, he is to release the corpse to the bearer. The centurion is surprised, but not unduly so. The man in front of him is well dressed and has several servants in tow. No doubt, the man has paid Pilate a princely bribe to save Jesus' body from disgrace. Matthew concurs: the man from Arimathea was a *rich* man.[53]

Why did Joseph of Arimathea, a member of the Great Sanhedrin, bother to claim the body of Jesus? The reason is what we have known all along:

there were several Pharisees on the Council who were sympathetic to Jesus' cause. Joseph may have genuinely felt that Jesus was a holy man and deserved a decent burial. To arrange for a burial plot on such short notice would have been out of the question. If the Mishnah is correct, it would also have been against Pharisaic custom. The solution, then, was to have the body of Jesus rushed to Joseph's *own* tomb—even if it was just a temporary measure. Here, Jesus could be cleansed, wrapped, and perfumed in secrecy, away from prying eyes.

But there was another problem. Covenant Law—to which Joseph, as a Pharisee, adhered to the letter—insisted on a prompt burial, before the beginning of the Sabbath, even if it necessitated the use of a temporary resting place. So Joseph was racing against the clock. He had to move the body of Jesus in secrecy to his tomb and complete the most basic burial rites before sundown, when the Sabbath began.

Who helps him to accomplish all this? All of the apostles have fled. Indeed, we don't even hear of Peter until Mary Magdalene tracks him down in his place of hiding. But, more than likely, Joseph has anticipated this and brought along two or three sturdy servants with a litter to carry the body.

The burial party arrives at the tomb sometime between the tenth or eleventh hour. Mary Magdalene and two other women follow, carrying pitchers of water, a sponge and washing cloth, and burial linen to wrap the body. Very little time remains before sundown. But the body must be wrapped in fragrant spices, so as to cover the odors of decomposition. This is customary because, during the first three days after death, the bereaved are expected to visit a tomb to ascertain that its occupant is truly dead, not just in a deep coma. A passage in the Semahot notes two occasions on which a man was found alive and lived to old age. The Midrash states that "for three days [after death] the soul hovers over the body, intending to re-enter it, but as soon as it sees its appearance change, it departs, as it is written."[54]

Myrrh and frankincense are the two most popular perfuming agents, but these are far beyond the means of Jesus' traveling band of followers. The Gospel of John claims that another wealthy individual, a man called Nicodemus, comes to the rescue. His servants bring jars of myrrh and aloes "about a hundred pounds in weight," which is John's way of saying that there was ointment aplenty.[55]

Joseph's servants carry Jesus' body through the narrow opening of Joseph's tomb and place it on one of the three stone benches that line the small burial chamber.[56] Mary immediately goes to work. First she takes the stone jar, pours water into the bowl, and proceeds to wash the body. Joseph of Arimathea looks anxiously outside. The burial proceedings *must* be terminated at sundown, when the Sabbath begins.

With only a few minutes left before the sun sets, Joseph intervenes. There is no time to apply the perfuming agent of myrrh. In fact, myrrh was an adhesive agent—Mary can only apply this ointment in the final step of burial preparation. It is decided that Jesus will be loosely wrapped in linen, and that Mary and her female companions must come back on the third day, after the Sabbath, to finish anointing him. The burial linen consists of separate strips of cotton that can be easily wrapped around a lifeless corpse—no fewer than three, and no more than seven. Starting at the feet, Mary and the other women wrap the legs, the torso, and finally the neck. The head is wrapped in a separate piece—the *sudarium*.

It is time. The sun has set. Joseph leads the women and the servants out of the tomb. Outside, the sky is turning dark. The servants roll a stone in front of the entrance and mark it with whitewash—a sign to all who pass that there is a fresh body inside. Mary casts one final look back. In a few days, she knows, she will return.

Three days go by, during which Jews believe that "the soul hovers over the body." According to the reckoning of the Jewish calendar, the "first day" would have begun at sundown on Passover Day—the day of execution. Sabbath is the second day. And so it is on Sunday, the third day, that Mary, Salome, and Mary the mother of James rise just before sunup.[57] They would have delegated the task of grinding flour and baking bread to other women in the group. They dress quickly, then hoist the vessels of myrrh on their shoulders. There is no one to help them. Even now, the men are still in hiding, afraid to show themselves lest one of Pilate's roving patrols catch them in the city.

But in fact, the execution of the Galilean rabbi is long forgotten. The Passover celebrations have gone off without any further public disturbance. Back in Herod's old palace, Pilate is already up. With most of the pilgrims now flooding out of the gates, he can order his *Tribunus laticlavius* to prepare for the journey home. If they move quickly, they can be on the road by the fourth hour and reach Caesarea by sundown.

Mary and her companions make their way to Joseph's tomb. All during the journey, Mary is wondering how three women can move the heavy stone from the entrance to the grave. She hopes there will be a friendly farmer or a servant boy along the way who can lend them a hand. And indeed, as she approaches the tomb, she sees a man sitting nearby. Perhaps it is the gardener. Mary knows that wealthy individuals like Joseph are meticulous about the grounds around their family tombs. This man looks like a young and healthy fellow for whom rolling a stone will be an easy task. But then she looks past him to the tomb and stops in her tracks. The vessel with the precious myrrh falls to the ground. Her hand flies to her mouth. The stone has already been rolled away.

This is where the Gospel of Mark and the story of the historical Jesus come to an end. And this is where the story of Jesus, the Christ, begins.

EPILOGUE

The death of its leader devastated the Jesus movement. The apostles were stunned—and deathly afraid. Some fled to Galilee. Others hid in the far corners of the city. To truly grasp the state of these followers, imagine yourself as a disciple of Gandhi or the Dalai Lama. For nearly two years, you go wherever the great leader goes. You are in awe of him. You cherish everything he says and seal it in your heart. You love the man. He is more than your spiritual teacher; he *is* who you want to be.

And then one day, the police are at the door. The great man is put in handcuffs, in front of popping flashbulbs, and shoved into a police car. He has been accused of a horrible crime. You can't believe it, but there he is, in a courtroom, in shackles. With every word from the prosecutor's lips, your world is slowly falling to pieces.

This is how the apostles must have felt—as well as all the other followers, male and female, who had traveled with Jesus. Why was his young life so violently extinguished just as his message was beginning to make an impact? Why was he not allowed to complete his mission? The Gospels suggest that the apostles had still not grasped the full scope of Jesus' program—the Kingdom of God, the reign of social justice and divine peace. And even if they did, what was the purpose of preaching the coming of a spiritual Messiah when the Messiah himself was dead? "We trusted that it was he who would have redeemed Israel," one follower notes mournfully on the way to Emmaus. How could they possibly continue the movement without Jesus' charismatic leadership—or without suffering the same fate that had befallen their leader?

How they yearned to see his face, hear his gentle voice, and feel the warm glow of his presence. And so, they *did* see him. They *did* feel his presence, though they knew he was no longer of this world. Or was he?

The Resurrection of Jesus falls outside the scope of this book, for it cannot be corroborated by any archaeological or historical evidence. There are numerous Gospel accounts of Jesus appearing to his disciples after his death, but the reports are not always consistent. At times, Jesus appears as a man of flesh and blood. He breaks bread with his companions[1] and invites the disbelieving Thomas to touch his wounds.[2] At other moments, Jesus appears as a transcendent being who is capable of moving in and out of rooms without passing through a door, and must warn Mary Magdalene *noli me tangere*—"do not touch me," because "I have not yet ascended to the Father." As elsewhere in the Gospel narratives, we may see different oral traditions at work.

From a strictly historical point of view, what matters is that the followers of Jesus *did* believe that Jesus had risen. And therefore—whether physically or spiritually—Jesus *had* risen. The divine spirit that had touched and inspired him was now spreading among the apostles themselves.

And so it was that in those harrowing weeks following the trauma of Jesus' crucifixion, his group of followers found the resolve and the will to continue. Jesus was no longer of the living, but neither was he dead; they distinctly felt his presence, and they cleaved to the words his spirit whispered in their hearts during their sessions of intense prayer.

It was clear, however, that the group was in need of guidance. Should they remain in Jerusalem, or return to Galilee where Jesus had worked and preached for most of his life? Or should they cast their net wider, into cities and communities farther up north, places where Jesus himself had never been?

James, the brother of Jesus, argued for a base in Jerusalem itself. Clearly, Jesus' message was destined for Jews, James said; it therefore behooved the movement to stay at the center of Judaism and continue to promote Jesus' reforms from within. James spoke with authority, despite the fact that he was a recent "convert" to the cause. Many agreed with him and continued to do what they and Jesus had done all their lives: observe the Law, worship in the Temple, and preach the good news.

This was the moment when a man appeared on the scene who, after Jesus, would exert the greatest influence on the development of Christianity. His name was Paul. Paul (originally named Saul) was born in Tarsus, the capital of Cilicia. In 64 B.C.E., the city had been conquered by Rome, but its citizens accepted its fate with equanimity. In fact, the community of Tarsus was so fastidious in its tribute and allegiance to Rome (which included supplying mercenary soldiers) that Augustus granted the capital the exceptional status of a free Roman city.

Philosophers of every ilk flocked to Tarsus in the hope of finding patronage. Though Paul was born to a Jewish family, his sharp intellect drank in the Greek oratory of the street. "The inhabitants of Tarsus have become so enthusiastic for philosophy and the area of education," wrote the first-century Roman geographer Strabo, "that they have surpassed Athens, Alexandria, and any other place." Even after Paul was educated in Jerusalem, he remained fond of the philosophical dialectic that was the bread and butter of his home town. It was a world far removed from the illiterate peasant culture of Lower Galilee. Paul understood this and, with the supreme self-confidence of an educated Pharisee, saw that he alone was equipped to turn this freewheeling cult into a proper religious movement.

In recent years, it has become fashionable to blame Paul for adapting the life and teachings of Jesus, the Jew, into the exalted theology of Jesus, the Christ. Paul, perhaps the first intellectual to come in touch with the Jesus movement, must have grasped that without the charismatic presence of Jesus himself, the New Kingdom movement would have fizzled and gone the way of other would-be reformers—notably, John the Baptist. Jesus' social agenda may simply have been too radical, and his attitude to the Law too liberal, to sustain any long-term support among the Jewish intelligentsia or the people without the impetus of the man himself.

But Paul was genuinely attracted to Jesus' inclusive approach to Jewish monotheism. Jesus' call to universal social compassion had struck a chord. Paul may have remembered from his years in Cilicia that many Gentiles in Asia Minor were intrigued by the simplicity and nobility of a religion that recognized but one God. A God, moreover, who was merciful and just, unlike the hedonistic gods of Rome, who were more concerned with pleasure than with the well-being of mankind. But he also recognized that the more onerous precepts of Judaism—circumcision, the dietary laws, the strict limitations of the Sabbath—were a deterrent for many of these "God-fearing" people. He therefore must have sensed that Jesus' brand of a "liberal" and more human Judaism would appeal not just to the Jewish poor but to *all* the downtrodden within the Roman empire. And in this, as we know, he was not mistaken.

That in the process the man from Nazareth became divine was perhaps inevitable. Rome was a world in which prominent men (such as Julius Caesar) could plausibly claim that they were legitimate sons of a god, and virtually every emperor after Augustus was posthumously worshiped as a deity. It would have been very difficult for Paul to convince his Greco–Roman audience that a peasant from Galilee, crucified as a terrorist, could somehow be a herald of God's kingdom.

Hebrew Scriptures also called their kings "sons of God," but that appellation meant something very different to Romans than to Jews, as Paul well knew. Romans were Europeans, and Europeans were not comfortable with the ephemeral mysteries of the Near East. They wanted something tangible. Jews eschewed the representation of living beings and were horrified by the very thought of depicting YHWH. The Romans reveled in it; for them, as for the Greeks, gods were anthropomorphic beings whose physical perfection was proof positive of their divine status. This is why Greek and Roman gods are invariably depicted as young and beautiful men and women in the nude. Thus, for Paul's Gentile audience, Jesus became the tangible expression of a new monotheism: a physical manifestation of an unseen God.

The urgent question that had vexed Jesus' followers was why, if Jesus had truly been infused with the Spirit of YHWH, God had allowed him to be killed in so shameful and gruesome a manner. And using his superior skill in logic, Paul had grasped the answer: Jesus died on the cross because this was precisely what God had intended all along. Why? Because his crucifixion served, in a way, as the ultimate Passover sacrifice—a sacrifice that wiped clean the sinful slate of mankind and allowed everyone who believed in him to find salvation. Now everything fell into place. By offering himself up as the true paschal lamb, Jesus had made Temple sacrifice redundant and its corrupt priesthood irrelevant. And to prove it, God had raised Jesus from the dead.

The Resurrection was the divine imprimatur on the sacrifice of Jesus. It also marked an all-new covenant between God and Man—one that superseded the old covenant of Moses. Paul was a Pharisee—he had been educated by Gamaliel, a pupil and grandson of the great Rabbi Hillel— and, as we have seen, Pharisees believed that the souls of the righteous would find eternal life. The idea that Jesus was resurrected by God not only underscored the divine importance of his mission, but also gave living proof that the apocalyptic changes he foretold had finally begun.

The Jerusalem church led by James, however, was deeply concerned by Paul's campaign among Gentiles who neither practiced circumcision nor observed the laws of purity. Paul was summoned to Jerusalem to explain himself. Depending on which source we read—Luke's Acts of the Apostles or Paul's Letter to the Galatians—this momentous conference took place sometime after 51 C.E., some twenty years after the crucifixion.

Paul knew that in contrast to his own missionary work in Asia Minor and beyond, the Palestinian church of James was floundering. Jewish Christians were on the defensive throughout Judea. So to disqualify Paul's theology and policies among the Gentiles was to condemn the movement to a slow death; to endorse Paul's campaign was to drive an indelible wedge between Jewish and non-Jewish followers of Jesus. A vexing dilemma.

Paul brought it down to one simple question: could a Gentile who was not familiar with Jewish scripture, who was not circumcised and did not observe the Law or the Sabbath, be allowed to join the congregation if his faith in Jesus the Christ was honest and true? Paul's answer was yes. He insisted that the cleansing spirit of the Holy Spirit was, in essence, the Gentile equivalent of circumcision. And so the Jerusalem Conference ended in a stalemate. The two factions, in effect, agreed to disagree. Paul could go and minister to the Gentiles and Jews of Asia Minor, if he so chose; but James and Peter would continue to work among circumcised Jews only.

Acts, like most of the New Testament, was written after the Pauline faction had triumphed and Paul's theology had become the principal doctrine of most (though not all) early Christian communities. By that time, the sentiments of James, leader of the Jerusalem church, had become irrelevant, for James himself was dead and his Palestinian church was in disarray. But James left a footnote of his opposition to the Pauline *kerygma* (or teachings), which, surprisingly, is contained in Paul's own letter to the Galatians. There, Paul confirms that "[James and Peter] asked only one thing, that we remember the poor, which was actually what I was eager to do."[3] James could not stop the momentum of Paul's theological mission among the Gentiles, but he would not permit anyone to lose sight of what, as we have seen, was the quintessential element of Jesus' teaching: his devotion to social justice. To minister to the poor was to minister to God. "Can faith alone save you?" James asks in the short but eloquent Letter of James, which somehow hung on to its tenuous place at the end of the New Testament.

"If a brother or sister is naked and lacks daily food, and one of you says 'I wish you well; make sure you stay warm and eat plenty,' without actually giving them these bare necessities of life, then what good is that?"[4]

One argument of this book has been to show that the historical Jesus was a Jew through and through. When asked by some Pharisees what commandment in the law was the greatest, he quoted the *Shema* that pious Jews recited twice a day: "You shall love the Lord your God with all your heart, and with all your soul, and with all your mind. This is the greatest and first commandment." But he hastened to add that love of God meant nothing if it was not expressed in tangible actions of compassion. That's why he immediately added the second commandment quoted in Leviticus: "You shall love your neighbor as yourself," adding, "on these two commandments hang all the Law and the Prophets."[5] For Jesus, these two tenets were indistinguishable, as they had been for another Jewish sage, Rabbi Hillel. Hillel, too, had once been asked to summarize the Law. His response was almost identical: "What is hateful to you, do not do to your neighbor: this is the whole Law; the rest is the explanation; go and learn."[6]

These were the two pillars of Jesus' Kingdom program: trust and faith in a merciful God; love and mercy for one's fellow man.[7] James, his brother, had recognized the essential moral foundation of Jesus' teachings. "Faith is this," James wrote in his letter: "if it is not backed up by good works, it is quite dead."[8]

Was Jesus' New Kingdom a revolutionary vision? I believe Jesus would have argued that it was not. It was his outrage over the shocking injustice perpetrated against Galilean peasants that drove his campaign for a radical realignment of contemporary society. This was not a revolution but a *restoration* of the fundamental values of covenantal Judaism—a return, in many ways, to the communal cohesiveness of post-conquest settlement in the Promised Land. Back then, as the Books of the Prophets suggest, there had been solidarity among the Jewish farmers and tribes as they faced down their common foes, the Canaanites and Philistines. Back then, Jews had lived in daily communion with God, observing his law and making sure that no one was left behind. Those early years in the Promised Land were perhaps as close as the nation had ever come to the Kingdom of God.

For Jesus, in other words, love of God and of one's neighbor was nothing new; it had lain at the core of Israel's raison d'être from the very beginning.

As time went on and Paul's Christian communities grew, other sects sprang up that had come to a different conclusion about who Jesus was and what his life meant for mankind. Some of these sects (including the one responsible for the Gospel of Thomas) hardly referred to the Crucifixion at all. Rather, they continued to debate the meaning of the Kingdom of God, believing these teachings to be the key to understanding the secret of the Divine. Other movements embraced the idea that Jesus had not really died on the cross; that a man who *looked* like Jesus had been crucified, a *Doppelgänger,* while Jesus hovered above and smiled. This same belief would later find currency in Islam, which continues to revere *Isa* or Jesus as a major prophet.[9]

In the end, the movement that advocated the Pauline kerygma trumped all. This may have come about because of its superior organization and hierarchical discipline, or because Paul's Christian theology was essentially populist and egalitarian. For Paul's teachings offered redemption to everyone, regardless of tribal affiliation, language, social class or race, as long as they believed in Christ.

In time, those Christian sects that did not follow Paul were branded as heretics. After Christianity gained power as a *religio licita* of the Roman Empire, it was Paul's theology that became the established dogma of the Church. Christian sects that did not subscribe to the Nicene creed—that Jesus was one in substance with the Father, both man and divine—were excommunicated and ostracized. Later, their members would be burned at the stake. The historical Jesus, the village teacher, the charismatic prophet and the healer, had truly become one with *Abba,* his father.

We may chastise Paul for "Hellenizing" Jesus, for molding him to conform to the European ideal of what the founder of a new religion should look like. Nevertheless, if it weren't for Paul, we would have never known about Jesus and the message he brought to mankind. Though he was no longer the man his apostles would have recognized, as the Christ Jesus entered a new realm of human devotion that made his teachings resonate around the world. Paul's kerygma gave Jesus an ethical relevance and moral authority far beyond what a village rabbi from Nazareth could have ever hoped to achieve. Though Jesus himself had always confined his teachings to the "lost sheep of Israel," avoiding Gentile territory whenever possible, it was, ironically, this Gentile world that embraced him just when his homeland turned its back to him.

✢ ✢ ✢

Many Christians sometimes wonder if probing into the life of the historical Jesus will affect their faith in Christ. Are "Jesus the Jew" and "Christ the Lord" not two different figures? they ask. And if so, where does that leave them as believers? The question has been pondered by many scholars. As early as 1964, the German theologian Ernst Käsemann argued that understanding the "Man of Nazareth" was inseparable from the theology of the "exalted Lord." Bruce Chilton has written that the search for the historical Jesus can often illuminate some fundamental mysteries about Jesus that the Gospels failed to explain. John Dominic Crossan has said that Christian faith is simply to see the historical Jesus as the manifestation of God.

I would agree. From my own experience as a believer, I have found that reconstructing the historical Jesus can only deepen our understanding of the motives and aspirations that drove Jesus to become the astonishing figure that he was. As I argued in the beginning of this book, the historical Jesus does not replace Jesus the Christ, for the essential purpose of Christian doctrine is to make the message of a Jewish reformer relevant for the urgent needs of the world at large. What's more, unlike the Jews of ancient Palestine, Christians need to have a tangible focal point for our vision of God, and that is what the image of the risen Christ has given us.

But whether we think of Jesus as a *hasid* from Galilee's rural culture or as the exalted Son of God, the core message is the same: Jesus offered a new and deeply intimate conduit for communicating with the Divine, unencumbered by ritual, class, or ideology. He fervently hoped and believed that this new intimacy with God would deepen our sense of self, and hence our responsibility for our fellow man. Perhaps the Gospel of John, that crucial intersection of history and creed, says it best: "I am the way, and the truth, and the life.... If you know me, you will know my father also."[10]

If there is anything that in this age of polarizing faiths and ideologies we can agree on, it must be those very words.

NOTES

INTRODUCTION

1.   For example, within the book of Genesis and the other four books of the Pentateuch, scholars have been able to isolate no fewer than four distinct strands of oral history. The oldest strain is named "J," since it refers to God as *Yahweh* (or *Jahweh* in German). This "Yahwist" author is our source for the story of the Garden of Eden, among others, and is particularly fond of wordplay and double entendres that we will encounter throughout this book. Some believe that *J* originated in the tenth century Kingdom of Judah, during or after the reign of either David or Solomon.

A second strain is identified by scholars as "E," based on this tradition's reference to God as *Elohim* or "the Lord." *E* probably originated during the period of the divided monarchy in the Northern Kingdom. This author or authors focused on Moses and the power of the Covenant as the quintessential element of Judaism.

The "D" author or authors worked primarily on the early version of the book of Deuteronomy, the focal point of the Covenant Law. It is possible that their book is the ancient source discovered by the priest Hilkiah in the archives of the Temple around 622 B.C.E. Deuteronomy focuses on the rites of worship to be conducted at the "central shrine" of the Temple in Jerusalem. It is therefore likely that this book originated in Judah, quite possibly among a group concerned with codifying and formalizing a national form of worship.

The Pentateuch was later expanded during or after the Babylonian Exile with another tradition, described by scholars as "P," or Priestly Source, which emphasizes the priestly role in the communication between the people and God. See Isbouts, Jean-Pierre, *The Biblical World*, p. 243.

2.   For a recent review of diverse opinions on the question whether the Bible is objective and true, see Padgett, Alan G., and Patrick R. Keifert (eds.), *But Is It All True? The Bible and the Question of Truth*, 2006.

3.   For a recent study of the use of Old Testament motifs in the gospels, see Porter, Stanley (ed.), *Hearing the Old Testament in the New Testament*, 2006.

4.   Acts 4:13.

5.   Colossians 4:10.

6.   1 Peter 5:13.

7.   Colossians 4:14.

8.   Mark 2:14; Matthew 9:9.

9.   John 19:26, 35.

10.   John 21:24.

11.   Several recent scholars have taken issue with the inclination of many postwar scholars to doubt the historicity of John's Gospel. For one of the most recent and most ably argued summaries of the case for John, see Moloney, Francis J., *The Gospel of John: Text and Context,* 2005.

30. This is illustrated by a large black obelisk, discovered in 1846 by Henry Layard near the ancient city of Nimrud, in which Shalmaneser receives tribute from a prostrated king. The inscription reads: "The tribute of Jehu son of Omri" (*ia-ú-a mar hu-um-ri-i*).

31. The Book of Kings states that Tiglath-pileser moved on the Northern Kingdom of Israel, conquering "Kedesh, Hazor, Gilead, and Galilee, [and] all the land of Naphtali, and he carried the people captive to Assyria" (2 Kings 15:29).

32. See Gal, Zvi, "Israel in Exile: Deserted Galilee Testifies to Assyrian Conquest of the Northern Kingdom," in *Biblical Archaeology Review* 24(3), May/June 1998.

33. Isaiah 9:1.

34. The extent to which king Josiah was able to exert control over the former Assyrian province of Megiddo is a subject of intense debate. The most important city of Assyrian Galilee, as the name implies, was the fortress town of Megiddo, where the Assyrians built an orthogonal city with planned streets and palaces (stratum III). However, the successive layer of habitation, presumably built after the Assyrians evacuated the area, contained no Judahite objects or ostraca of any kind. Israel Finkelstein and Neil A. Silberman, among others, have suggested that the fortress was taken over by Egyptian forces instead after the death of Josiah, and that the annexation of Galilee by Josiah is legendary, written by scribes eager to highlight Josiah's restoration attempts. See Finkelstein, Israel, and Neil Silberman, *The Bible Unearthed*, New York: Touchstone, 2001, pp. 347–353.

35. Josiah's scribes also set to work to document the history of the twelve tribes of Israel, so as to corroborate their monarch's historic claim over these lands. This, scholars believe, is what prompted the creation of the so-called "Deuteronomistic History," an oeuvre based on oral tradition and various royal and temple records, which ultimately produced the books of Deuteronomy, Joshua, Samuel, and Kings (1 and 2).

36. Jeremiah 17:10–11.

37. Ezra 10:11.

38. The first action of Antiochus III was to grant the Jewish populace special privileges and a reduction of the tax burden (Josephus, *Antiquities* XII:138–144). These tax concessions were mostly directed at the governing elites of Jerusalem, including Temple officials, so it is unclear to what extent Galilean farmers benefited from this cozy arrangement. But Antiochus also affirmed the Covenant Laws as the official jurisdiction for all Jews in Palestine.

39. "Galilee of the Gentiles" and similar designations appear in Isaiah 9:1 (LXX Isaiah 8:23); LXX Joel 4:4; 1 Maccabees 5:15; and Matthew 4:15.

40. On the Maccabean putative rescue of beleaguered Jewish communities in Galilee, see 1 Maccabees 5:9–23.

41. When the Seleucid general Bacchides initiated a new campaign against the Maccabees, he made a point of camping on the Sea of Galilee so as to conduct a number of punitive campaigns against Jewish villages, ostensibly to punish those who had expressed their support for the revolt down south. Indeed, Josephus confirms that when the leadership of the revolt passed to another brother named Jonathan, this commander "would not allow the Galileans, who were his own people, to be attacked by his enemy" (Josephus, *Antiquities* XIII.154).

42. Josephus, *Antiquities* XIII.318.

43. Eric Gruen has emphasized the Hellenistic tendencies of the Hasmonean dynasty,

pointing out that they "engaged regularly in diplomatic dealings with Greek kings, adopted Greek names, donned garb and paraded emblems redolent with Hellenic significance, erected monuments, displayed stelai and minted coinage inspired by Greek models." Many of its kings and princes were given Greek names, including Aristobulus, Antigonus, and Alexander.

44. Matthew 4:15; John 1:46.

45. See Chancey, Mark A., *Greco-Roman Culture and the Galilee of Jesus,* Cambridge: Cambridge University Press, 2005.

46. A dunam is a measure used throughout the Middle East to this day. In Palestine it equals some one thousand square meters, though elsewhere in the Middle East exact sizes may vary.

CHAPTER 1: THE BETROTHAL OF JOSEPH AND MARY

1. Mark 6:3.
2. Genesis 11:10–26.
3. Matthew 1:1–16.
4. Matthew 1:17.
5. Luke 1:26–27.
6. Luke 3:23–38.
7. John 1:45.
8. Luke 1:26.
9. Micah 5:2.
10. Matthew 2:6.
11. Matthew 2:1.
12. Mishnah Ketubot, 5:1.
13. Luke 10:35.
14. Luke 15:8.
15. Exodus 21:10.
16. Mishnah Ketubot 5:8–9.
17. Genesis 24:1–9.
18. Genesis 27:46.
19. Mark 6:3.
20. Luke 13:19.
21. Luke 6:44, 13:8–9.
22. Tosefta Ketubot 7:6.
23. Matthew 1:18.
24. Deuteronomy 22:20–21.
25. Matthew 1:19.
26. Genesis 17:16–19.
27. Matthew 1:23.
28. Isaiah 7:14.
29. Matthew 1:24–25.
30. Genesis 16:11–12.
31. Genesis 18:9–14.
32. Luke 1:11–19.
33. 1 Samuel 1:11.

34. In the words of Joseph Fitzmyer, "The infancy narrative was in a large part freely composed by Luke on the basis of information obtained from earlier models and in imitation of some OT motifs." Fitzmyer, Joseph A., S.J., *The Gospel According to Luke I–IX,* 1981.

35. Luke 1:26–37.

36. These attacks often provoked defensive arguments, known as *apologia,* by Christian thinkers such as Quadratus (writing around 125 C.E.), Justin of Samaria (100–165 C.E.), and Tertullian (ca. 155–230 C.E.), each trying to soften the Roman attitude toward Christianity with reason.

37. Mark 6:3; Matthew 13:55.

38. Romans 1:3.

39. 2 Timothy 2:8.

40. Hebrews 7:14.

41. 2 Samuel 7:12–14, my italics.

42. 1 Kings 18:12.

43. John Dominic Crossan has argued that the Lucan Nativity narrative is in fact a rebuttal to the cult of Augustus as a god. He points out that Luke mentions Augustus at the very beginning of the pericope, and believes that the point of the story is to stress that the "true" God is not to be found in the palaces of the Palatine but in the humble stable of a peasant. See, for example, Crossan, John Dominic, "The Infancy and Youth of the Messiah" in *Biblical Archaeology Review,* 1994.

CHAPTER 2: HEROD AND THE BIRTH OF JESUS

1. Josephus, *Antiquities* XIV.158; *Jewish War* I.199–200.
2. Josephus, *Antiquities* XIV.274; *Jewish War* I.221.
3. Josephus, *Jewish War* I.303, 307.
4. Herod, says Josephus, "slew so many men without his giving him any command to do it, either by word of mouth, or by his letter, and this in contradiction to the law of the Jews." *Jewish War* I.10 §6.
5. Deuteronomy 17:15.
6. Josephus, *Antiquities* XV.365–369.
7. Josephus, *Antiquities* XIII.14 §2.
8. Josephus, *Jewish War* II.163.
9. Josephus, *Antiquities* XV.
10. Matthew 2:1, Luke 1:5.
11. Luke 2:2.
12. Attempts by conservative scholars to place Quirinius in Syria at an earlier date (based on an inscription found in Antioch, which credits one of his military victories) are not convincing.
13. Micah 5:2.
14. For the putative origin of Jesus in the Gospel of John, see Meeks, Wayne A., "Galilee and Judea in the Fourth Gospel," in *Journal of Biblical Literature,* 85(2) (June 1996), pp. 159–169.
15. Matthew 2:2.
16. Chilton, Bruce, *Rabbi Jesus,* pp. 8–9.

17. Christison, A., "On the natural history, action and uses of Indian hemp," *Monthly Journal of Medical Science*, London and Edinburgh, 1851, pp. 26–45.

18. Matthew 2:1–8.

19. Josephus, *Antiquities* XVII.811.

20. Josephus, *Antiquities* XVII.6.5.

21. Matthew 2:22.

CHAPTER 3: GROWING UP IN GALILEE

1. Mishnah Yebamot 4:13.

2. Safrai, Ze'ev, *The Economy of Roman Palestine*, p. 46.

3. Mishnah Baba Mesia 8:6.

4. Matthew 13:33.

5. Safrai, Ze'ev, *The Economy of Roman Palestine*, p. 105.

6. Babylonian Talmud Baba Mesia 59b.

7. Finley, *The Ancient Economy*, p. 105. The Romans called the amount of land a man could plow in a day a jugum, the unit by which they measured the size of a man's holdings.

8. Quoted from a 1997 UN survey, in Hudson-Rodd et al., 2001, 2004.

9. Q 9.

10. Leviticus 19:9; Deuteronomy 24:19.

11. Luke 3:17.

12. Leviticus 26:5.

13. Q 65; Mark 12:1–9; Luke 13:6–9; Luke 20:9–16; Matthew 20:1–16.

14. Genesis 14:20.

15. Numbers 18:21–26.

16. Leviticus 25:2–7; Exodus 23:10–11.

17. Jospehus, *Antiquities* IV.71; Numbers 18:15–16; Exodus 13:13, 22:29, 34:20.

18. Josephus, *Antiquities* XVI.163.

19. Matthew 17:24–27; Josephus, *Antiquities* VIII.19.

20. Oakman, Douglas E., *Jesus and the Economic Questions of His Day*, 1986.

21. Engels, Donald, *Roman Corinth: An Alternative Model for the Classical City*, 1990.

22. Josephus, *Antiquities* XII.138-144.

23. Josephus, *Against Apion*, 1.60.

24. Sanders, E. P., *The Historical Figure of Jesus,* pp. 146–169.

25. Josephus, *Antiquities* XV.109, 365.

26. Josephus, *Antiquities* XVII.810.

27. Josephus, *Antiquities*, XVII.6 §2.

28. Josephus, *Antiquities*, XVII.6 §4.

29. Josephus, *Antiquities*, XVII.9 §3.

CHAPTER 4: REVOLT AND REPRISALS

1. Nicolaus of Damascus, a Syrian by birth, was a scholar who had been retained as a tutor at the court of Antony and Cleopatra; after their deaths he successfully petitioned Herod the Great for a position. Josephus's description of Herod reportedly drew heavily from Nicolaus's works.

2.   Josephus, *Antiquities*, XVII.9 §6.
3.   Josephus, *Antiquities*, XVII.10 §2–3.
4.   Josephus, *Antiquities*, XVII.10 §5.
5.   Josephus, *Antiquities*, XVII.10 §6.
6.   Josephus, *Antiquities*, XVII.10 §7.
7.   Luke 24:13.
8.   Josephus, *Jewish War*, II.499–502. It was one of the duties of a vassal king of Rome to contribute forces in time of crisis. Indeed, the situation of 4 B.C.E. would be repeated seventy years later, at the outbreak of the Jewish War, when Cestius Gallus, legate of Syria, not only dispatched his four legions and Roman auxiliary forces, but also secured several thousand soldiers sent by vassal kings in the region, notably Agrippa II, Antiochus of Commagene, and Sohaemus of Emesa, in addition to other forces provided by local Gentile communities.
9.   Mark 12:17; also Thomas 100.
10.   Luke 7:1–10; also Matthew 8:5–10.
11.   Mark Chancey has made a convincing argument that the centurion, or *ekatóntarchos* in Luke's parlance, must have been a commander of the Herodian auxiliary forces originally organized by King Herod and inherited by his son Antipas. There is no evidence that Roman forces were stationed in Galilee before 120 C.E.—certainly not during the reign of Antipas, who was considered a loyal vassal of Rome.
12.   See Hekster, Olivier, and John Rich, "Octavian and the Thunderbolt: The Temple of Apollo Palatinus and Roman traditions of temple building," *The Classical Quarterly* (2006), 56:149–168.
13.   Propertius, Elegies, II.31.11.
14.   Josephus, *Antiquities*, XVII.11 §2.
15.   One could take a sister-in-law in marriage only if she had been childless, according to the so-called Levirate Marriage described in Deuteronomy 25:5–6. Otherwise, the prohibition of Leviticus applied: "you shall not uncover the nakedness of your brother's wife; it is your brother's nakedness"; Leviticus 18:16.
16.   Josephus, *Antiquities*, XVII.13 §2.
17.   Josephus, *Antiquities*, XVII.1 §1.
18.   Tacitus, *Annales*, 2.42.
19.   Josephus, *Jewish War*, II.433. Several scholars have concluded that the Judas movement was actually a radical offshoot of the Pharisee party. Significantly, one of the prominent Jews who joined Judas and became a major head of the movement was "Saddok the Pharisee," a man not mentioned anywhere else. It is possible that this movement switched from passive to active resistance by mid-century, but by then Judas would have been a mere memory.

CHAPTER 5: JESUS AND JOSEPH IN SEPPHORIS
1.   Joshua 1:2f; Deuteronomy 9:24–29; Book of the Jubilees 13:3; Sirach 46.
2.   Josephus, *Antiquities* XV.5–6; X.214.
3.   The grain-tax on private land in Roman Egypt ranged anywhere from 1/2 to 2 artabae per arura. Wallace, Sherman LeRoy, *Taxation in Egypt from Augustus to Diocletian*, p. 31.

4.   Midrash Rabbath on Lamentations 2.5, quoted in David A. Fiensy, *The Social History of Palestine in the Herodian Period*, p. 54.

5.   Exodus 21:2; Deuteronomy 15:1–8; Leviticus 25:35–42.

6.   The Mishnah said: "A loan secured by prozbul is not cancelled by the seventh year. This is one of the things that Hillel the elder ordained." Mishnah Shebiit 10:3.

7.   In the event that the farmer did lose his land to creditors, the Law also provided for a so-called Jubilee Year, when the original family inheritance, if lost through debenture, should be returned. Both Philo and Josephus refer to the Jubilee Year, and Josephus confirms that "at that season debtors are absolved from their debts and slaves are set at liberty, that is to say those [who were enslaved by Law]." It is however, highly questionable whether this provision was actually honored, at least during the Herodian period.

8.   Wallace, Sherman LeRoy, *Taxation in Egypt from Augustus to Diocletian*, p. 12.

9.   In the early years of the Roman occupation, the Romans charged an *annual* harbor tax for Joppa, Palestine's only native harbor at the time, of only 20,665 *modia,* the equivalent of some 135 tons of wheat. This shows that Palestinian grain exports at this time were a trifle, compared to wheat exports from other nearby regions, particularly Egypt. Josephus, *Antiquities*, XIV.206; see also Safrai, Ze'ev, *The Economy of Roman Palestine*, p. 223.

10.   Thomas 63.

11.   Mark 10:25; Luke 18:25; Matthew 19:24. Those who heard Jesus say these words replied, "Then who can be saved?"

12.   Josephus, *Jewish War*, I.326; *Antiquities*, XIV.450, XVII.217; Horsley, p. 216.

13.   Josephus, *Jewish War*, II.17 §6.

14.   Grumiau, S., *Growing Up Under the Burmese Dictatorship: The Situation Facing Children after 41 Years of Military Rule in Burma.*

15.   For example, if one acre (0.4 hectare) of a paddy field can produce between thirty and forty baskets of rice (a basket of rice weighs around 23 kg) per harvest, the SPDC insists on being sold ten or twelve baskets, at a price five to ten times lower than the market price.

16.   "Lease" rates ranged from 3,000 to 6,000 kyat. Hudson-Rodd, N., and M. Nyunt, *Control of Land and Life in Burma.* p. 23.

17.   Stang, D. *Amazon nun's brother speaks about her murder.* See: http://news.mongabay.com/2007/0607-david_stang.html

18.   UNICEF 2002 data as cited in the Burma report.

19.   Luke 16:1–13; also see Luke 12:42; Matthew 20:8–12.

20.   Luke 20:10–12.

21.   Matthew 20:1–3.

22.   Q 39.

23.   Specifically, the phrase in Mark, "ουχ ουτοζ εοτιν ο τεκτων" was translated in the King James Bible as "Is this not the carpenter . . . ?" Mark 6:3.

24.   Josephus, *Antiquities*, XIII.324.

25.   Josephus, Antiquities, XIV.414, *Jewish War* I.304.

26.   Mark 6:3.

27.   Pliny, *Epistles* 10.31–32.

28.   In Urso, the term a citizen could be forced to work was limited, but other such constraints may not have been applicable in other, less developed societies such as Antipas's

Galilee. Duncan-Jones, Richard, *Structure and Scale in the Roman Economy*, p. 174.

29. Weiss, Zeev, The 2006 Sepphoris Expedition Sponsored by the Hebrew University (et al.), July 2–14/August 15–29, 2006.

30. Weiss, Zeev, *Archeological Report of the 2006 Sepphoris Expedition*, pp. 6–7.

31. For this reason, the excavators of Sepphoris, including Shirley Jackson Case of the University of Chicago, have speculated that Joseph and Jesus may have worked on building the theater, since it was clearly the most ambitious and labor-intensive project in the city. But it is doubtful that we will ever know for sure.

32. Duncan-Jones, Richard, *Structure and Scale in the Roman Economy*, p. 178.

33. Luke 7:22; John 7:15.

34. For example, in *Reader's Digest's Jesus and His Times,* 1990, pp. 147–155.

35. Josephus, *Vita,* 54.

36. See, for example, Chancey, Mark A., *The Myth of a Gentile Galilee.*

37. Significantly, Sepphoris refused to come to the aid of the Temple when the Romans drew near. Josephus, *Vita,* 348.

38. Josephus, *Vita,* 38.

39. Matthew 5:17.

40. Luke 2:41-47. Luke claims that it was the custom of Jesus' parents to travel to Jerusalem "every year" to celebrate the Passover feast. In the time of Antipas, however, when Judea was Roman territory, Galilean villagers seldom traveled to Jerusalem to attend the annual festivals. If anything, villagers selected a small group of people from their midst to make the annual pilgrimage. Hence, Luke's suggestion that Joseph and Mary would have had the time and resources to make the five-day journey to Jerusalem on an annual basis is highly suspect. We must remember that Luke did not write in Palestine proper, but in a city in the Diaspora, possibly Damascus, and heavily relied on local Jewish customs to "flesh out" his story.

41. Josephus, *Vita,* 67.

42. Luke 24:44.

43. Josephus, *Antiquities,* XVIII.2 §3.

CHAPTER 6: THE ITINERANT WORKER AND HEALER

1. The possibility that Jesus spoke Greek has intrigued scholars, for the Gospels were written in the *koinè* Greek of the first century C.E. Several authors have pointed to the presence of Greek inscriptions on many potsherds or *ostraca* in Lower Galilee, arguing that Jesus should have had at least a passing knowledge of the language. Joseph Fitzmyer, however, claims that most of these inscriptions date from the second century C.E., when the presence of a permanent Roman garrison invariably led to an increase of Greek use throughout the region. Fitzmyer, Joseph A., "Did Jesus Speak Greek?" *Biblical Archaeology Review* 18(5).

2. Matthew 26:73.

3. One Church tradition maintains that Joseph was a widower, and that James, and perhaps Jesus' other siblings as well, were the offspring of Joseph's first marriage. The primary purpose of this belief was to keep Mary's virginity intact, an idea cherished by later Church tradition, despite the obvious reference in Mark's Gospel to Joseph's other

children. The tradition has no historical attestation, however, and so for the purpose of this story we will assume that Joseph and Mary were a healthy, loving couple who consummated their marriage and were blessed with many children, as was common in Palestine.

4.   Q 19, which, according to Burton Mack, belongs to some of the oldest sayings traditions about Jesus. Mack, Burton L., *The Lost Gospel: The Book of Q and Christian Origins.*

5.   This outburst is heavily attested, which strongly argues for its authenticity: Q 52; Luke 14:26–27; Thomas 55.

6.   Matthew 12:46–49.

7.   Burnett and Peel, 2001; Davies and Webb, 2000, as cited in Thomas and Lau, 2002, "Psychological well-being of child and adolescent refugee and asylum seekers," p. 2.

8.   Harvey, Mary, and P. Tummala-Narra (eds.). *Sources and expressions of resiliency in trauma survivors: Ecological theory, multicultural practice*, p. 15.

9.   Tedeschi, Richard G., Crystal L. Oark, and Lawrence G. Cahoun, *Posttraumatic Growth: Positive Changes in the Aftermath of Crisis,* 1998; p. 53.

10. Pargament, Kenneth, *The Psychology of Religion and Coping: Theory, Research, Practice*, p. 110.

11. Mishnah Maaserot 2:3.

12. Mark 6:8.

13. Source: Mayo Clinic, Rochester, Minnesota.

14. Garnsey, Peter, *Cities, Peasants, and Food in Classical Antiquity*, p. 240.

15. Fernandez, Isabel D., John H. Himes, and Mercedes de Onis, "Prevalence of nutritional wasting in populations," pp. 282–292.

16. Cahill, Jane, K. Reinhard, D. Tarler, and P. Warnock, "It had to happen: Archaeologists examine remains of ancient bathroom," *Biblical Archaeology Review* 17(3): 64–69.

17. Mora, Jose O., Miguel Gueri, and Olga Mora, "Vitamin A deficiency in Latin America and the Caribbean: An overview," pp. 179–186.

18. Garnsey, Peter, *Cities, Peasants, and Food in Classical Antiquity,* Chapter 14.

19. Fornaciari, G., E. Menacagli-Trevisani, and B. Ceccanti, *Indagini paleonutrizionali e determinazione del piombo osseo mediante spettroscopia ad assorbimento atomico sui resti scheletrici di epoca tardo-romana della 'Villa dei Gordiani,'* 1984; pp. 172-177.

20. Brentlinger, P. E., M. A. Hernán, S. Hernández-Díaz, L. S. Azaroff, and M. McCall, "Childhood malnutrition and postwar reconstruction in rural El Salvador: A community-based survey," pp. 184–190.

21. Of course, the ancient world had no concept of what we would call everyday hygiene. The potential for contamination in rural societies was rampant, not in the least because, as analysis of fecal sediments from Judea has shown, farmers often used raw sewage to irrigate their fields. In many ways, the Mosaic Laws shielded observant Jewish families from the most egregious lapses in hygiene, both because of its dietary regimen and its emphasis on consuming vegetable food and fruits, on which there were no cultic restrictions on consumption whatsoever. According to the Mosaic Laws, for example, it was forbidden to use the milk of animals which visibly suffered from some sort of malady. Similarly, an animal that had died a natural death (or in any way met its end other than through ritual slaughter) was considered *nebelah* and unfit for consumption. Thus, many observant Jewish families escaped the risk of disease by not eating contaminated meat.

22. Zias, Joe, "Health and Healing in the Land of Israel: A Paleopathological Perspective," *Mikhmanim*, Spring 1999.
23. Matthew 9:36.
24. Josephus, *Antiquities*, XVIII:3 §63–64.
25. 1 Kings 17:8-24.
26. 2 Kings 4:34, 4:42–44.
27. Isaiah 26:19; 29:19.
28. Matthew 11:5.
29. Josephus, *Antiquities* XIV.2.1. §22.
30. Mishnah Taanit 3:8.
31. Josephus, *Antiquities*, VIII.2 §5.
32. Meier, John P., *A Marginal Jew: Rethinking the Historical Jesus*, Vol. 2, Chapter 18.
33. Bultmann, Rudolph, *The Gospel of John*. Louisville, Ky.: Westminster John Knox Press, 1971.
34. Mark 1:23–28; also Luke 4:33–37.
35. Mark 2:5.
36. Exodus 20:5 and 34:7; also Psalm 109:13–14.
37. Psalm 103:3.
38. John 9:1–2.
39. John 9:3.
40. Mark 2:5.
41. Mark 2:6–7.
42. 2 Samuel 12:13.
43. Jeremiah 3:22.
44. Mark 2:10–12.
45. For example, Mark 5:34; also Luke 7:50.
46. See Eberhart, Inger, "Quantum Field Theory and Healing."
47. Rife was subsequently put on trial for having invented a "phony" medical cure. In 1958, the State of California Public Health Department conducted a hearing that ordered the testing of Rife's Frequency Instrument. The Palo Alto Detection Lab, the Kalbfeld Lab, the UCLA Medical Lab, and the San Diego Testing Lab all participated in the evaluation procedure. All of the labs reported that it was safe to use. However, the American Medical Association declared it unsafe and banned it from the market. See Valone, Thomas, *Bioelectromagnetic Healing: A Rationale for Its Use*. Integrity Research Institute, Washington, D.C., 2003, p. 13.
48. CranioSacral Therapy, for instance, monitors the rhythm created by the continual filling and intermittent draining of cerebrospinal fluid within the meningeal membranes. Mechano-electric measurements of palpatory sensations and corresponding electrical activity via electrocardiograph, electromyography, and distinct strain gauge found electrical patterns corresponding with each palpatory sensation. See Upledger, John E., and Jon D. Vredevoogd, *Craniosacral Therapy*.
49. Mark 5:25–30; also Matthew 9:18–26; Luke 8:40–56.
50. Q 16; subsequently Luke 7:24–28 and Matthew 11:2–5.

7. IN THE FOOTSTEPS OF JEREMIAH

1. Tedeschi, Richard G., et al., *Posttraumatic Growth: Positive Changes in the Aftermath of Crisis,* 1998.

2. Jeppson and Hjern, Traumatic stress in context, 2005.

3. See Annan, J., C. Blattman, and R. Horton, "The state of youth and youth protection in Northern Uganda: Findings from the Survey for War Affected Youth." At www.sway-uganda.org, 2006, p. 11.

4. McFarlane, A., and van der Kolk, B., "Trauma and its challenge to society" (1996), p. 33.

5. See, for example, Thabet, A., Abed, Y., and Vostanis P., "Emotional problems in Palestinian children living in a war zone: a cross-sectional study," *Lancet* 2002(359), pp. 1801–4.

6. Exodus 19:3–6.

7. Isaiah 61:1.

8. Luke 4:18.

9. 2 Samuel 7:14.

10. Psalm 42:1.

11. Mishnah Abot 3:5.

12. In the Book of Enoch we read, "And the spirits of you who have died in righteousness will live, and your spirits will rejoice and be glad, and the memory of them will remain in front of the Great One for all the generations of eternity." As for sinners, "Know that their souls will be made to go down into Sheol, they will be wretched, and their distress will be great." The Book of Enoch 103:4, 7.

13. Wisdom of Solomon 3:15.

14. Micah 1:1.

15. Jeremiah 1:9–10.

16. Jeremiah 17:10–11.

17. *Après nous, le deluge:* "After us comes the flood"; a desire to splurge before a looming catastrophe strikes.

18. Tosefa Shabbat 13.2.

19. Mark 15:34; Psalms 22:1.

20. Berakhot 8a–b.

21. Jeremiah 7:22–23.

22. Jeremiah 17:10.

23. Micah 6:7–8.

24. Birmingham, George A., *Jeremiah the Prophet,* New York: Harper & Brothers, 1939, p. 31.

25. Jeremiah 2:2.

26. Jeremiah 8:7.

27. Jeremiah 20:14–15.

28. John 7:2–10.

29. John 7:1.

30. John 4:5, 7.

31. Jeremiah 26:1–6.

32. Though it is likely that Jeremiah's Temple sermon was written much later, during or after the Exile, Jesus must have assumed from the book's preamble that it was written right after the death of King Josiah in the battle of Megiddo in 609 B.C.E., when the future of Josiah's reform program and, indeed, the fate of the nation was much in doubt.

33. Mark 13:1.

34. Matthew 12:6–7.

35. Strabo, *Geography,* 17:3:25, 17:840.

36. Tacitus, *Annals,* 1:80, 6:27, 32. Also Suetonius, *Tiberius,* 63.

CHAPTER 8: A DISSIDENT NAMED JOHN

1. Josephus, *Antiquities*, XVIII.5 §2.

2. Psalms of Solomon XVII:31–32.

3. Psalms of Solomon XVIII:6–8.

4. Daniel 9:11.

5. Luke 3:1.

6. Josephus, *Antiquities*, XVIII.5 §2.

7. Mark 1:5; Matthew 3:5.

8. Luke 3:3.

9. John 1:28.

10. John 3:23.

11. Josephus, *Jewish War*, II.8 §3.

12. Josephus, *Antiquities*, XVIII.1 §5.

13. Josephus, *Jewish War*, II.8 §2.

14. Josephus, *Jewish War*, II.8 §4.

15. Philo, *Hyp.* 11.1.

16. Pliny the Elder, *Natural History*, Book 5.73.

17. Josephus, *Jewish War*, II.8 §13.

18. Luke 3:17.

19. Josephus, *Jewish War*, II.8 §3.

20. 1QS 6.18–23.

21. Isaiah 40:3.

22. Mark 1:2–3; Matthew 3:3.

23. Josephus, *Jewish War*, II.8 §2.

24. Luke 1:80.

25. Luke 3:10–14.

26. Luke 3:7; also Q 4.

27. Mark 1:6, 2 Kings 1:8.

28. Luke 7:26, 28.

29. Habakkuk Pesher 7:4.

30. The documents refer to the appearance of a "wicked priest" in Jerusalem, who, we assume, was Jonathan, the high priest appointed by Alexander Balas. The Teacher had besieged Jonathan to implement numerous reforms in the interpretation of the Law, but Jonathan had spurned him; in fact, he had even tried to have the Teacher killed. "The evil doer is the Wicked Priest," we read, "and the upright man is the Teacher of Righteousness."

31. The "wicked," scholars theorize, were probably the Pharisees, whom the Qumran community considered too lenient and "smooth" in their application of the Law. The Qumranite designation for the Pharisees, "seekers after smooth things" (*dorshe halaqot*), is a word pun on dorshe halakot, "seekers of laws," as the Pharisees may have called themselves. 15[7].12.

32. Luke 3:12 and John 3:26.

33. Mark 1:10–11.

34. 2 Samuel 7:12–14.

35. Mark 6:29.

36. Acts 19:1–3.

37. See Gibson, Shimon, and James Tabor, "John the Baptist's cave: The case in favor," *Biblical Archaeology Review* 31(3), May/June 2005. Also Shanks, Hershel, "John the Baptist's cave??? The evidence is thin," *Biblical Archaeology Review* 30(6), Nov/Dec 2004. The finding was originally published in Gibson, Shimon, *The Cave of John the Baptist*.

38. Q 5; also Luke 4:1–13.

39. Matthew 3:14.

40. John 1:30.

41. John 4:1.

42. Scholarship is divided over the question whether this Philip was Antipas's brother Philip, tetrarch of the Gaulanities, or Herod Philip I.

43. Leviticus 18:16.

44. Mark 6:20.

45. Mark 6:17–28.

46. 874–853 B.C.E.

47. Matthew 14:5.

48. Josephus, *Antiquities*, XVIII.5 §2.

49. Hanson, K. C., and Douglas E. Oakman, *Palestine in the time of Jesus*; pp. 32–34.

50. For example, two were set aside for collecting the half-shekel "Temple tax." Another received anonymous contributions for burnt offerings and sin offerings (in the form of turtledoves). Others collected donations for wood and incense to be burned in the Temple, for pigeon offerings, or for any voluntary gifts.

51. Luke 21:1–4.

52. Cicero, *Pro Flacco*, §28.

53. Josephus, *War*, II.50; *Antiquities*, XVII:264.

54. Mishnah Sheqalim, 4.

55. P. T. Sheqalim IV, 48a; T. B. Ketuboth 105a–106a. See also S. Safrai et al., *The Jewish People in the First Century*, Vol. 2, p. 879.

56. Josephus, *Antiquities*, XVIII.3 §2.

57. Josephus, *Antiquities*, XVIII.3 §2.

58. Hirsen, James, *Roman Law and Jesus*, doctoral research essay. Santa Barbara: Fielding Graduate University, 2007.

59. Mishnah Sanhedrin 1:5.

60. Mark 1:14.

CHAPTER 9: IN THE KINGDOM OF GOD

1.   Josephus, *Antiquities*, XVIII.2 §1.

2.   Mark 1:21–22, my italics.

3.   Both Hollenbach and Sanders have tried to link accounts of demonic possession to the incidence of mental illness in Roman-occupied Palestine. Hollenbach states that "the colonial situation of domination and revolution nourishes mental illness in extraordinary numbers of the population," and suggests that demonic possession was actually a "socially acceptable form of oblique protest against, or escape from, oppressions." Hollenbach, P. W., "Jesus, demoniacs, and public authorities: A socio-historical study," p. 575. Sanders, furthermore, has argued that Jesus' exorcisms challenged the ruling political and religious authorities for his apparent ability to control demonic powers and attract huge crowds in the process. Sanders, E. P., *Jesus and Judaism,* p. 173.

4.   See Strange, James F., and Hershel Shanks, "Synagogue where Jesus Preached Found at Capernaum," *Biblical Archaeological Review* 9(6), Nov/Dec 1983.

5.   Mark 2:3–4.

6.   Strange, James F. and Hershel Shanks, "Has the House Where Jesus Stayed in Capernaum Been Found?" *Biblical Archaeological Review* 8(6), Nov/Dec 1982.

7.   Mark 1:19–20.

8.   Luke 5:4–7.

9.   Mark 8:7.

10.   T. B. Sabbath 199a.

11.   According to scientists of the Yigal Allon Kinneret Limnological Laboratory, the St. Peter's fish feeds on seaweed. As such it is essential to the ecosystem of the lake, for it controls growth that otherwise would upset the sea's chemical balance.

12.   Matthew 8:23.

13.   Wachsmann, Shelley, "The Galilee Boat—2,000 year-old hull recovered intact," *Biblical Archeological Review* 14(5), Sept/Oct 1988.

14.   Carmi, Israel, "How old is the Galilee Boat?" *Biblical Archeological Review* 14(5), Sept/Oct 1988.

15.   Mishnah Kelim 10:5; Mishnah Nedarim 6:4.

16.   Partners or "κοινωνοι" Luke 5:10.

17.   Wüllner 1967:23–24, as quoted in K. C. Hanson et al, *Palestine in the Time of Jesus.*

18.   Nehemiah 5:1–13.

19.   The segment reads: "Woe is me because of the house of Boethus, woe is me because of their staves!/Woe is me because of the house of Hanin, woe is me because of their whisperings!/Woe is me because of the house of Kathros, woe is me because of their pens!/Woe is me because of the house of Ishmail the son of Phabi, woe is me because of their fists!/For they are high priests and their sons are (Temple) treasurers and their sons-in-law are trustees and their servants beat the people with staves," in B. Pesach 57a. See also Fiensy, David A., *The Social History of Palestine in the Herodian Period,* pp. 51–52.

20.   Josephus, *Jewish War*, II.17 §6.

21.   Thomas 26; Matthew 7:3.

22.   Q 34; Luke 11:39–52; Matthew 23:23.

23.   Jeremiah 8:19.

24. Jeremiah 10:7.
25. Jeremiah 7:1–7.
26. Thomas 107.
27. Thomas 113.
28. Luke 17:20.
29. Thomas 3.
30. Q 8; also Luke 6:20–23, Thomas 54.
31. Mark 13:33, 35.
32. Matthew 13:31.
33. Mark 4: 26–29.
34. Mark 1: 14–15.
35. Luke 4:18.
36. The fact that Jesus dines with sinners, says Patrick Mullen in a recent study, "challenges the [Pharisees] to inclusivity and humble honesty, and to recognition of their own need for forgiveness." Mullen, J. Patrick, *Dining with Pharisees,* p. 125.
37. Luke 14:12–13.
38. Mark 10:42–43.
39. Luke 14:7–11. The saying is sometimes considered a paraphrase of Proverbs 25:6–7: "Do not put yourself forward in the king's presence or stand in the place of the great, for it is better to be told 'Come up here' than to be put lower in the presence of a noble."
40. Matthew 5:17.
41. Exodus 4:22.
42. Psalm 68:5, my italics.
43. Psalm 89:26, my italics.
44. Matthew 5:45.
45. Q 10; Luke 6:36.
46. Q 27; Luke 11:11–13.
47. For example, Q 19: "Foxes have dens, and birds of the sky have nests, but the son of man has nowhere to lay his head."
48. Daniel 7:13.
49. See, for example, Case, Shirley Jackson, "The alleged messianic consciousness of Jesus," *Journal of Biblical Literature* 46(1/2) (1927), pp. 1–19.
50. "This is the Son of Man who has righteousness and with whom righteousness dwells. He will reveal all the treasures of that which is secret, for the Lord of Spirits has chosen him, and through uprightness his lot has surpassed all others, in front of the Lord of Spirits, forever. And this Son of Man, who you have seen, will rouse the kings and the powerful from their resting places, and the strong from their thrones, and will loose the reins of the strong, and will break the teeth of the sinners. And he will cast down the kings from their thrones, and from their kingdoms, for they do not exalt him, and do not praise him, and do not humbly acknowledge from where their kingdom was given to them." The Book of Enoch 46:3–5.
51. Matthew 1:18.
52. Luke 3:15.
53. Mark 8:27–30.
54. Note, for example, the following saying in Q (34): ". . . God said, 'I will send them

prophets and wise men, some of whom they will kill and prosecute,' in order to hold this generation accountable for the blood of all the prophets shed from the foundation of the world, from the blood of Abel to the blood of Zechariah who perished between the altar and the sanctuary. Truly, I tell you, this generation will be held accountable."

CHAPTER 10: THE ROAD TO JERUSALEM

1. Luke 10:4–9.
2. Luke 4:3.
3. Q 20.
4. Matthew 10:5.
5. Mark 4:35; Matthew 8:23; Luke 8:22.
6. Luke 8:2–3.
7. John 20:15–17.
8. Gospel of Philip, 63:32–64:5, as translated in J. M. Robinson, *The Nag Hammadi Library.*
9. Gospel of Mary 5:5–6.
10. Gospel of Mary 9:2–8.
11. Gospel of Thomas 114.
12. Colossians 3:18.
13. Timothy 2:12. See also Pagels, Elaine, *The Gnostic Gospels,* 1979.
14. Pious tradition has it that Mary Magdalene, for reasons unknown, fled to France, where she was entombed after her death in Vézelay.
15. Mark 6:14–16.
16. Mark 12:13.
17. Luke 13:31.
18. Luke 14:1.
19. Specifically, Q 22.
20. Matthew 11:21; Luke 10:13–15; my italics.
21. John 10:40.
22. Eusebius, *Historia Ecclesiastica,* 1.7.14.
23. Jeremiah 1:17.
24. Jeremiah 7:2.
25. John 11:7.
26. Mark 10:32.
27. Josephus, *Antiquities,* XVIII.2 §2.
28. Luke 19:1–9.
29. Luke 19:8.
30. Luke 19:11.
31. Mark 10:46–52.
32. Mark 11:11; Luke 10:38; Matthew 21:17; John 11.
33. Zechariah 9:9.
34. Luke 19:39–40.
35. Mark 11:11.
36. Mark 13:1.

37. Jeremiah 7:14.
38. Thomas 71.
39. Mark 13:2.
40. Mark 14:58.
41. John 2:19.
42. See Duncan-Jones, Richard, *Structure and Scale in the Roman Economy*, pp. 30, 44.
43. Josephus, *Jewish War*, II:10–13.
44. Mishnah Pesachim 1.
45. Exodus 12:6–7.
46. Exodus 12:24.
47. Exodus 7:3–11.
48. Chilton, Bruce, *Rabbi Jesus*, p. 220.
49. Jeremiah 7:3.
50. Jeremiah 7:4–7.
51. Mark 11:15.
52. Jeremiah 7:11.
53. Mark 11:27.

CHAPTER 11: ARREST AND EXECUTION

1. Mark 14:14.
2. I am indebted to several books and articles by Miriam Feinberg Vamosh in which she has described the Pesach meal as it would have been cooked and served in first-century Palestine.
3. Mishnah Pesachim, 10.1.
4. Luke 22:29–30.
5. Mark 14:22–24; Matthew 26:26–28; Luke 22:17–20.
6. Mark 14:33.
7. Q 49; also Luke 13:34–35.
8. John 12:6.
9. John 18:8.
10. Mark 12:14–17; Matthew 22:17–21; Luke 20:22–25; Thomas 100.
11. Jeremiah 20:1.
12. Josephus, *Jewish War*, VI.300–309.
13. Acts 6:8–8:1. Stephen's accusers told the Sanhedrin that "this man never stops saying things against this holy place and the law; for we have heard him say that this Jesus of Nazareth will destroy this place and will change the customs that Moses handed on to us" (Acts 6:13–14). The synagogue appeared to have been frequented by Diaspora Jews, particularly freed slaves from Northern Africa and Asia Minor.
14. In his retort, Stephen argues that "it was Solomon who built a house for [God]. Yet the Most High does not dwell in houses made with human hands," quoting 1 Kings 8:27–30 (Acts 7:47–48). Exactly why Stephen was arrested, or why he should be condemned of blasphemy, is not made clear. Other than the above excerpt from the Book of Kings, which would have been well known to his audience, Stephen never appeared to have done or said anything against the sanctity of the Temple and the priesthood.
15. Mark 14:49.

16. Josephus, *Antiquities,* XX.9 §1.

17. Mishnah Sanhedrin 7:1.

18. "The great Sanhedrin," says the Mishnah, "was [made up of] seventy-one members, and the small one was [made up of] twenty three." The number of seventy-one was reportedly derived from the Book of Numbers, in which it was said, "Gather for me seventy of the elders of Israel" (Numbers 11:16). The number was increased by one in order to avoid a hung jury in the case of voting (Sanhedrin 1:6).

19. Mark 15:43.

20. Mark 14:66–68.

21. Mark 14:55.

22. Mishnah Sanhedrin 1:5.

23. "Cases involving the death penalty are judged before twenty-three [judges]." Mishnah Sanhedrin 1:4.

24. Danby, Herbert, *Tractate Sanhedrin*, pp. 11–14.

25. Josephus, *Antiquities*, XIII.10 §6.

26. So strict was the Sadducee interpretation of the penal code that when, during the reign of Salome Alexandra, the Pharisees took control of the Sanhedrin and abolished it, a national festival was held. Megillat Taanit §4.

27. Mark 14:61; Matthew 26:63.

28. Psalm 110:1; Daniel 7:13–14.

29. Acts 21:26–30.

30. Mark 14:63. Tearing one's clothes was visible proof of righteous rage or despair, just as Reuben had done upon finding that the pit that once held his brother Joseph was empty (Genesis 37:29). In the Book of Acts, Paul and Barnabas tear their clothes as a sign of distress after being mistaken for gods (Acts 14.14).

31. Mark 15:1.

32. By Roman reckoning, a daylight hour in late winter was approximately fifty minutes. The first hour was the hour at sunrise; the twelfth hour was the hour just before sunset. The sixth hour in the daytime would have corresponded with noon.

33. Mark 15:4.

34. John 18:33–38.

35. John 19:10–12.

36. John 19:19–22.

37. Philo, *Embassy to Gaius,* 302; my italics.

38. Matthew 27:25.

39. "[Pilate] said to the Jews, "Here is your King!" They cried out, "Away with him! Away with him! Crucify him!" John 19:14–15.

40. Mark 19:16.

41. Numbers 28:16; Deuteronomy 16:23.

42. Deuteronomy 21:22–23.

43. For the full story of the Garden Tomb, see Barkay, Gabriel "The garden tomb: was Jesus buried here?" *Biblical Archaeology Review* 12(2), March/April 1986.

44. Mark 15:21.

45. For a detailed description of Roman crucifixion in Palestine and the available forensic evidence, see Vassilios Tzaferis, "Crucifixion—The archaeological evidence," *Biblical Archaeology Review* 11(1), Jan/Feb 1985.

46. Dr. Frederick Zugibe, formerly chief medical examiner of Rockland County, New York, conducted bizarre experiments with volunteers to reach the alternate conclusion that crucifixion does not lead to asphyxiation but to death by shock. See Zugibe, Frederick T., "Two questions about crucifixion," *Biblical Archaeology Review* 5(2), April 1989.

47. Mark 15:25.

48. Mark 15:36.

49. The Book of Deuteronomy states that "When someone is convicted of a crime punishable by death and is executed, and you hang him on a tree, his corpse must not remain all night upon the tree; you shall bury him that same day, for anyone hung on a tree is under God's curse. You must not defile the land that the Lord God gave you for possession." Deuteronomy 21:22–23. This was affirmed in the Mishnah (Mishnah Sanhedrin 6:4).

50. John 19:32.

51. John 19:34.

52. Mishnah Sanhedrin 6:5.

53. Mark 15:42–45; Matthew 27:57–58; John 19:38.

54. Midrash Job 14:22.

55. As a fragrance, myrrh had a long history in ancient Judaism. Exodus refers to myrrh as one of the three compounds of "sacred anointing oil" to be used in the sanctuary (Exodus 30:23). The Psalms refer to myrrh as a perfuming agent for clothes (Psalm 45:8).

56. For an up-to-date description of excavated Jewish tombs from this period, see Magness, Jodi, "What did Jesus' tomb look like?" *Biblical Archaeology Review* 32(1), Jan/Feb 2006.

57. Mark 16:1–2.

EPILOGUE

1. Luke 24:30.

2. John 20:27.

3. Galatians 2:10.

4. James 2:14–16.

5. Mark 12:28–31.

6. Babylonian Talmud Shabbat 31a.

7. Matthew 22:36–40.

8. James 2:17.

9. For Muslims, it was inconceivable that a holy man like Jesus would be permitted by God to die such a shameful death as crucifixion; therefore, it is written that "they neither killed nor crucified him; it only appeared to be that way to them" (Q 4.157). In fact, the Qur'an maintains, "God took him up to Himself" (Q 4.158).

10. John 14:6.

BIBLIOGRAPHICAL SOURCES

HISTORY OF ISRAEL

Cline, Eric. *From Eden to Exile: Unraveling Mysteries of the Bible*. Washington, D.C.: National Geographic Society, 2006.

Coogan, Michael D. (ed.). *The Oxford History of the Biblical World*. New York: Oxford University Press, 2001.

Coote, R. B., and K. W. Whitelam. *The Emergence of Early Israel in Historical Perspective*. Sheffield, England: Almond Press, 1987.

Davies, W. D., et al. *The Cambridge History of Judaism*. Vols. I–III. Cambridge: Cambridge University Press, 1999.

Eynikel, Erik. *The Reform of King Josiah and the Composition of the Deuteronomistic History*. Leiden, Holland: E. J. Brill, 1996.

Finkelstein, Israel, et al. (eds.). *From Nomadism to Monarchy: Archaeological and Historical Aspects of Early Israel*. Jerusalem: Israel Exploration Society, 1994.

Finkelstein, Israel, and Neil Asher Silberman. *The Bible Unearthed: Archaeology's New Vision of Ancient Israel and the Origin of Its Sacred Texts*. New York: The Free Press, 2001.

Hallo, William W., and William K. Simpson. *The Ancient Near East: A History*. Fort Worth: Harcourt Brace, 1998.

Harrington, Daniel. *The Maccabean Revolt: Anatomy of a Biblical Revolution*. A Michael Glazier Book. Collegeville, Minn.: Liturgical Press, 1991.

Isbouts, Jean-Pierre. *The Biblical World: An Illustrated Atlas*. Washington, D.C.: National Geographic Society, 2007.

Levy, T. E. (ed.). *The Archaeology of Society in the Holy Land*. London: Leicester University, 1995.

Silberman, Neil Asher, et al. *The Archaeology of Israel: Constructing the Past, Interpreting the Present*. Sheffield, England: Sheffield Academic Press, 1997.

GALILEE

Chancey, Mark A. *The Myth of a Gentile Galilee*. Cambridge: Cambridge University Press, 2002.

———. *Greco–Roman Culture and the Galilee of Jesus*. Cambridge: Cambridge University Press, 2005.

Freyne, Séan. *Galilee from Alexander the Great to Hadrian, 323 B.C.E. to 135 C.E.: A Study of Second Temple Judaism*. Wilmington, Del.: Michael Glazier, 1980.

Goodman, Martin. *State and Society in Roman Galilee, A.D. 132–212*. Totowa, N.J.: Rowman & Allanheld, 1983.

Hezser, Catherine. *Jewish Literacy in Roman Palestine.* Tübingen, Germany: Mohr Siebeck, 2001.

Horsley, Richard A. *Bandits, Prophets and Messiahs: Popular Movements in the Time of Jesus.* Harrisburg, Pa.: Trinity Press, 1999.

————. *Galilee: History, Politics, People.* Harrisburg, Pa.: Trinity Press, 1995.

————. *Jesus and the Spiral of Violence: Popular Jewish Resistance in Roman Palestine.* Minneapolis: First Fortress Press, 1993.

HISTORICAL JESUS, BIOGRAPHIES

Borg, Marcus J. *Jesus: Uncovering the Life, Teachings and Relevance of a Religious Revolutionary.* San Francisco: HarperSanFrancisco, 2006.

Charlesworth, James H. (ed.). *Jesus' Jewishness: Exploring the Place of Jesus in Early Judaism.* New York: Crossroad, 1991.

Chilton, Bruce. *Rabbi Jesus.* New York: Doubleday, 2000.

Crossan, John Dominic, *Jesus: A Revolutionary Biography.* New York: HarperCollins Publishers, 1994.

————. *Who Killed Jesus? Exposing the Roots of Anti-Semitism in the Gospel Story of the Death of Jesus.* New York: HarperCollins, 1995.

Crossan, John Dominic, and Jonathan L. Reed. *Excavating Jesus: Beneath the Stones, Behind the Texts.* New York: HarperCollins, 2001.

Ehrman, Bart. *Jesus: Apocalyptic Prophet of the New Millennium.* New York: Oxford University Press, 1999.

Fredriksen, Paula. *Jesus of Nazareth, King of the Jews.* New York: Alfred A. Knopf, 1999.

Horsley, Richard A. *Jesus and Empire: The Kingdom of God and the New World Disorder.* Minneapolis: Fortress Press, 2003.

McCane, Byron R. *Roll Back the Stone: Death and Burial in the World of Jesus.* Harrisburg, Pa.: Trinity Press International, 2003.

Meier, John P. *A Marginal Jew: Rethinking the Historical Jesus.* Vols. 1, 2, and 3. New York: Doubleday, 1994.

Porter, J. R. *Jesus Christ: The Jesus of History, the Christ of Faith.* New York: Barnes & Noble, 1999.

Sanders, E. P. *Jesus and Judaism.* Philadelphia: Fortress, 1985.

————. *The Historical Figure of Jesus.* London: Penguin, 1992.

Stemberger, Günter. *Jewish Contemporaries of Jesus: Pharisees, Sadducees, Essenes.* Minneapolis: Fortress, 1995.

Van Aarde, Andries. *Fatherless in Galilee: Jesus as a Child of God.* Harrisburg, Pa.: Trinity Press International, 2001.

Wilson, Ian. *Jesus: The Evidence.* London: Phoenix Illustrated, 1998.

NEW TESTAMENT TEXTS, NON-CANONICAL
SOURCES, AND THE MISHNAH

Danby, Herbert. *Tractate Sanhedrin, Mishnah and Tosefta, with commentary*. New York: Macmillan, 1919.

Ehrman, Bart D. *Lost Christianities: The Battles for Scripture and the Faiths We Never Knew*. Oxford: Oxford University Press, 2003.

Fitzmyer, Joseph A., S.J. *The Gospel According to Luke I–IX*. Garden City, N.Y.: Doubleday, 1981.

Herzog, William R. *Parables as Subversive Speech: Jesus as Pedagogue of the Oppressed*. Louisville: Westminster/John Knox Press, 1994.

Humphrey, Hugh M. *From Q to "Secret" Mark: A Composition History of the Earliest Narrative Theology*. London: T & T Clark, 2006.

Kasser, Rodolphe, Marvin Meyer, and Gregor Wurst. *The Gospel of Judas*. Washington, D.C.: National Geographic Society, 2006.

Kee, Howard Clark. *The Beginnings of Christianity: An Introduction to the New Testament*. London: T & T Clark, 2005.

Kloppenborg, John S. *Excavating Q: The History and Setting of the Sayings Gospel*. London: T & T Clark, 2000.

Mack, Burton L. *The Lost Gospel: The Book of Q and Christian Origins*. San Francisco: HarperSanFrancisco, 1993.

Moloney, Francis J. *The Gospel of John: Text and Context*. Leiden, Holland: Brill, 2005.

Mullen, J. Patrick. *Dining with Pharisees*. Collegeville, Minn.: Liturgical Press, 2004.

Neusner, Jacob. *Introduction to Rabbinic Literature*. New York: Doubleday, 1999.

———. *Judaism When Christianity Began: A Survey of Belief and Practice*. Louisville: John Knox Press, 2002.

———. *The Mishnah: A New Translation*. New Haven: Yale University Press, 1988.

Padgett, Alan G., and Patrick R. Keifert (eds.). *But Is It All True? The Bible and the Question of Truth*. Grand Rapids, Mich.: Eerdmans, 2006.

Pagels, Elaine. *Beyond Belief: The Secret Gospel of Thomas*. New York: Random House, 2003.

———. *The Gnostic Gospels*. New York: Random House, 1979.

Porter, Stanley (ed.). *Hearing the Old Testament in the New Testament*. Grand Rapids, Mich.: Eerdmans, 2006.

——— (ed.). *Paul and his Theology*. Pauline Studies, Vol. 3. Leiden, Holland: Brill, 2006.

Resseguie, James L. *Narrative Criticism of the New Testament: An Introduction*. Grand Rapids, Mich.: Baker, 2005.

Robinson, J. M. (gen. ed.). *The Nag Hammadi Library*. New York: HarperCollins, 1990.

Sanders, E. P. *Jewish Law from Jesus to the Mishnah: Five Studies*. Philadelphia: Trinity Press International, 1990.

Schiffman, Lawrence H. *Reclaiming the Dead Sea Scrolls: The History of Judaism, the Background of Christianity, the Lost Library of Qumran.* New York: Doubleday, 1995.

Valantasis, Richard. *The New Q: A Fresh Translation with Commentary.* London: T & T Clark, 2005.

Whiston, William. *The Complete Works of Josephus.* Grand Rapids, Mich.: Kregel, 1981.

DIET, HEALTH, AND DISEASE

Brentlinger, P. E., M. A. Hernán, S. Hernández-Díaz, L. S. Azaroff, and M. McCall. "Childhood malnutrition and postwar reconstruction in rural El Salvador: A community-based survey." *Journal of the American Medical Association* 281 (January 1999), 184–190.

Eberhart, Inger. "Quantum Field Theory and Healing," doctoral paper. Santa Barbara: Fielding Graduate University, 2006.

Fernandez, Isabel D., John H. Himes, and Mercedes de Onis. "Prevalence of nutritional wasting in populations: Building explanatory models using secondary data." *Bulletin of the World Health Organization* 80(4) (2002), 282–291.

Fornaciari, G., E. Menacagli-Trevisani, and B. Ceccanti. "Indagini paleonutrizionali e determinazione del piombo osseo mediante spettroscopia ad assorbimento atomico sui resti scheletrici di epoca tardo-romana della 'Villa dei Gordiani' (Roma)." *Archivio per l'antropologia e l'etnologia* 114 (1984).

Garnsey, Peter. *Food and Society in Classical Antiquity.* Cambridge: Cambridge University Press, 2000.

Hollenbach, P. W. "Jesus, demoniacs, and public authorities: A socio-historical study." *Journal of the American Academy of Religion* 49(4) (1981).

Mora, Jose O., Miguel Gueri, and Olga Mora. "Vitamin A deficiency in Latin America and the Caribbean: An overview." *Revisa Panamericana de Salud Pública* 4(3) (September 1998), 178–186.

NCCAM. "Energy Medicine: An Overview." nccam.nih.gov, 2006.

Nelson, Lonnie A., and Gary E. Schwartz. "Human biofield and intention detection: Individual differences." *Journal of Alternative and Complementary Medicine* 11(1) (2005), 93–101.

Oschman, J. *Energy Medicine: The Scientific Basis of Bioenergy Therapies.* Philadelphia: Churchill Livingstone, 2000.

Rein, Glen. "Biological Effects of Quantum Fields and Their Role in the Natural Healing Process." *Frontier Perspectives* 7 (1998), 16–23.

Temenski, Lynn. "Putative Biofield Energy Healing Methods: Potentials for Veritable Integrity." Doctoral paper. Santa Barbara: Fielding Graduate University, 2006.

Upledger, John E., and Jon D. Vredevoogd. *Craniosacral Therapy.* Seattle: Eastland Press, 1983.

Vallbona, C., and T. Richards. "Evolution of magnetic therapy from alternative to traditional medicine." *Physical Medicine and Rehabilitation Clinics of North America* 10(3) (1999), 729–754.

Valone, Thomas. *Bioelectromagnetic Healing: A Rationale for Its Use.* Washington, D.C.: Integrity Research Institute, 2003.

SOCIOECONOMIC HISTORY

Duncan-Jones, Richard. *Money and Government in the Roman Empire.* Cambridge: Cambridge University Press, 1994.

———. *Structure and Scale in the Roman Economy.* Cambridge: Cambridge University Press, 1990.

Engels, Donald. *Roman Corinth: An Alternative Model for the Classical City.* Chicago: University of Chicago Press, 1990.

Evans, Jane DeRose. *The Coins and the Hellenistic, Roman, and Byzantine Economy of Palestine.* Boston: American Schools of Oriental Research, 2006.

Fager, Jeffrey A. *Land Tenure and the Biblical Jubilee: Uncovering Hebrew Ethics through the Sociology of Knowledge.* Sheffield, England: Sheffield Academic Press, 1993.

Fiensy, David A. *The Social History of Palestine in the Herodian Period: The Land Is Mine.* Lewiston, N.Y.: Edwin Mellen Press, 1991.

Finley, M. I. *The Ancient Economy.* London: Hogarth Press, 1985.

Garnsey, Peter. *Cities, Peasants, and Food in Classical Antiquity.* Cambridge: Cambridge University Press, 1998.

———. *Social Status and Legal Privilege in the Roman Empire.* Oxford: Clarendon Press, 1970.

Hamel, Gildas. *Poverty and Charity in Roman Palestine, First Three Centuries C.E.* Berkeley: University of California Press, 1990.

Oakman, Douglas E. *Jesus and the Economic Questions of His Day.* Queenstown, Ontario: Edwin Mellen Press, 1986.

Pastor, Jack. *Land and Economy in Ancient Palestine.* New York: Routledge, 1997.

Safrai, Ze'ev. *The Economy of Roman Palestine.* London: Routledge, 1994.

Wallace, Sherman LeRoy. *Taxation in Egypt from Augustus to Diocletian.* New York: Greenwood Press, 1969.

JUDEA AND ROME DURING THE EARLY IMPERIAL PERIOD

Archer, Léonie J. *Her Price Is Beyond Rubies: The Jewish Woman in Graeco–Roman Palestine.* Sheffield, England: JSOT Press, 1990.

Berlin, Andrea, and Andrew Overman. *The First Jewish Revolt: Archaeology, History, and Ideology.* New York: Routledge, 2004.

Daniel-Rops, Henri. *Daily Life in Palestine at the Time of Christ.* London: Weidenfeld and Nicolson, 1962.

Edwards, D. *Religion and Society in Roman Palestine: Old Questions, New Answers.* New York: Routledge, 2004.

Elsner, Jas. *Imperial Rome and Christian Triumph.* New York: Oxford University Press, 1998.

Frevel, Christian (ed.). *Medien im antiken Palästina: Materielle Kommunikation und Medialität als Thema der Palästinaarchäologie.* Tübingen, Germany: Mohr Siebeck, 2005.

Gibson, Shimon. *The Cave of John the Baptist.* New York: Doubleday, 2004.

Grant, Robert M. *Augustus to Constantine: The Emergence of Christianity in the Roman World.* New York: Barnes & Noble, 1996.

Ilan, Tal. *Jewish Women in Greco–Roman Palestine.* Peabody, Mass.: Hendrickson, 1996.

Jeffers, James S. *The Greco–Roman World of the New Testament Era: Exploring the Background of Early Christianity.* Downers Grove, Ill.: InterVarsity Press, 1999.

Mommsen, Theodor. *A History of Rome under the Emperors.* New York: Routledge, 1996.

Richardson, Peter. *Herod: King of the Jews and Friend of the Romans.* Columbia: University of South Carolina Press, 1996.

Roller, Duane W. *The Building Program of Herod the Great.* Berkeley: University of California Press, 1998.

Safrai, S., et al. (eds.). *The Jewish People in the First Century.* Vol. 2. Philadelphia: Fortress, 1976.

Sperber, Daniel. *The City in Roman Palestine.* Oxford: Oxford University Press, 1998.

Udoh, Fabian E. *To Caesar What Is Caesar's: Tribute, Taxes, and Imperial Administration in Early Roman Palestine (63 B.C.E.–70 C.E.).* Providence: Brown Judaic Studies, 2005.

Wroe, Ann. *Pilate: The Biography of an Invented Man.* London: Vintage, 1999.

PSYCHOLOGICAL ANALYSIS OF INTERNAL DISPLACEMENT AND POST-TRAUMATIC STRESS

Ajdukovic, M., and D. Ajdukovic. "Impact of displacement on the psychological well-being of refugee children." *International Review of Psychiatry* 10(3) (August 1998), 186–195.

Anagnostopoulos, D., M. Vlassopoulos, and H. Lazaratou. "Forced migration, adolescence, and identity formation." *American Journal of Psychoanalysis* 66(3) (September 2006), 225–237.

Boothby, N. "Displaced children: Psychological theory and practice from the field." *Journal of Refugee Studies* 5 (1992), 106–122.

De Merode, Janet. "Resilience and coping in displaced children and adolescents: Learnings from the recent literature on Burma." Doctoral paper. Santa Barbara: Fielding Graduate University, 2007.

Eisenbruch, M. "From post-traumatic stress disorder to cultural bereavement: Diagnosis of Southeast Asian refugees." *Social Science and Medicine* 33(6) (1991), 673–680.

Friedman, M., J. Jaranson, A. J. Marsella, T. Bornemann, S. Ekblad, and J. Orley. "The applicability of the posttraumatic stress disorder concept to refugees." In Anthony J. Marsella, Thomas Bornemann, Solvig Ekblad, and John Orley (eds.), *Amidst Peril and Pain: The Mental Health and Well-being of the World's Refugees.* Washington, D.C.: American Psychological Association, 1994.

Fuchs, Tracy L. "Latin America Indigenous Land Tenure: Social Group Dynamics Drive Child Trauma." Doctoral paper. Santa Barbara: Fielding Graduate University, 2007.

Ghazaleh, Ivone. "Trauma and Resilience of Children and Adolescents in the West Bank and Gaza Strip." Doctoral paper. Santa Barbara: Fielding Graduate University, 2007.

Grumiau, S. *Growing Up Under the Burmese Dictatorship: The Situation Facing Children After 41 Years of Military Rule in Burma.* Brussels: International Confederation of Free Trade Unions, August 2003.

Harvey, M., and P. Tummala-Narra (eds.). *Sources and Expressions of Resiliency in Trauma Survivors: Ecological Theory, Multicultural Practice.* Binghamton, N.Y.: Haworth Maltreatment & Trauma Press, 2007.

Hudson-Rodd, N., and M. Nyunt. *Control of Land and Life in Burma.* Tenure Brief No. 3. Madison, Wis.: Land Tenure Center, University of Wisconsin-Madison, 2001.

Hudson-Rodd, N., M. Nyunt, S. T. Tun, and S. Htay. *State Induced Violence and Poverty in Burma.* Geneva: International Labor Organization, June 2004.

Jeppsson, O., and A. Hjern. "Traumatic stress in context: A study of unaccompanied minors from Southern Sudan." In David Ingleby (ed.), *Forced Migration and Mental Health: Rethinking the Care of Refugees and Displaced Persons.* New York: Springer, 2005.

McFarlane, A., and B. van der Kolk. "Trauma and its challenge to society." In B. van der Kolk, A. McFarlane, and L. Weisaeth (eds.), *Traumatic Stress: The Overwhelming Experience on Mind, Body, and Society.* New York: Guilford, 1996.

Osuna, Brenda L. "Consequences of internal displacement in East Africa, with a focus on Sudan, Uganda and Ethiopia." Doctoral paper. Santa Barbara: Fielding Graduate University, 2007.

Pynoos, R., A. Steinberg, and A. Goenjian. "Traumatic stress in childhood and adolescence: Recent developments and current controversies." In B. van der Kolk, A. McFarlane, and L. Weisaeth (eds.), *Traumatic Stress: The Overwhelming Experience on Mind, Body, and Society.* New York: Guilford, 1996.

Schnapper, L. (ed.). *Teenage Refugees from Ethiopia Speak Out.* New York: Rosen Publishing Group, 1997.

Tedeschi, Richard G., Crystal L. Oark, and Lawrence G. Cahoun. *Posttraumatic Growth: Positive Changes in the Aftermath of Crisis.* Mahwah, N.J.: Lawrence Erlbaum, 1998.

Thomas, T., and W. Lau. "Psychological well-being of child and adolescent refugee and asylum seekers: Overview of major research findings of the past ten years." National Inquiry into Children in Immigrant Detention. Australian Human Rights and Equal Opportunity Commission, 2002.

INDEX

316